INTEGRAL PSYCHOLOGY
THE PSYCHOLOGICAL SYSTEM OF SRI AUROBINDO

Integral Psychology

THE PSYCHOLOGICAL SYSTEM OF SRI AUROBINDO

(In Original Words & In Elaborations)

INDRA SEN

SRI AUROBINDO INTERNATIONAL CENTRE OF EDUCATION
PONDICHERRY

First Edition 1986
Second Edition 1998

© Sri Aurobindo Ashram Trust 1986
Published by Sri Aurobindo International Centre of Education, Pondicherry
Printed at Sri Aurobindo Ashram Press, Pondicherry - 605 002
PRINTED IN INDIA

J534/27.10.95/1000

TO SRI AUROBINDO AND THE MOTHER

The insights presented here have been obtained through study and Sadhana under Sri Aurobindo and the Mother.

To Them, they are offered with joy and in gratitude.

The same are presented to all seekers and enquirers of the truths of human nature, for their joy and deep satisfaction.

ABOUT THE AUTHOR

Dr. Indra Sen was born on May 13, 1903, in the Jhelum district in Punjab, now in Pakistan. He had his schooling in Delhi, pursued his higher studies in the University of Delhi, from where he did M.A. in Philosophy. He was appointed professor of Philosophy and Psychology in the same University in 1928.

A memorable event, during the early years at the University of Delhi, was his meeting with C.G. Jung, who was visiting India for his own research work. Jung suggested that he should go to Germany for doctoral studies.

In 1931, he went to the University of Freiburg, where he did a thesis in Psychology for the Ph.D. degree. He also attended lectures given by Martin Heidegger and taught Indian Philosophy and Sanskrit at the University of Köenigsburg, the birthplace of Kant. The deepest impressions on him, at the time, were made by the psychology of Jung and the philosophy of Hegel.

On his return home in 1933, he resumed his teaching work at the University of Delhi and began a rich and many-sided intellectual life.

Two events marked this phase:

For the first time in academic circles, he investigated a case of reincarnation, which came to be known as the "Shanti Devi" case and stands even today as a significant scientific document.

He was President of the Psychology Section of the Indian Science Congress, at which he presented a paper entitled, "The Urge for Wholeness", which won wide acclaim.

But the spiritual aspirant in him was not fulfilled. For him, the study of philosophy was not enough without a corresponding spiritual realisation.

In 1939, he came into contact with Sri Aurobindo and the Mother. From 1940 onwards, he devoted himself to the study and sadhana of Integral Yoga under Sri Aurobindo and the Mother and came to regard the psychological principles involved in Integral Yoga as wonderful insights in human nature.

In 1945, he left his work at the University of Delhi and came to live in the Ashram. However, he continued to participate in the National Congresses of Philosophy, Psychology, Education and Yoga – presenting the perspectives of Sri Aurobindo's works in these fields. He also taught a course in Integral Psychology at the International Centre of Education at the Ashram.

He passed away in Pondicherry on March 16, 1994.

THE AUTHOR

INTRODUCTION

Sri Aurobindo's writings span a wide spectrum. These include the highest type of metaphysical writings, at the apex of which I would place *The Life Divine*. In the field of literature with a philosophical message, *Savitri* stands alone. Dante's *Divine Comedy* perhaps compares with *Savitri* in its philosophical depth, but the *Divine Comedy* does not have the philosophical sophistication or literary intricacies that one finds in *Savitri*. Apart from these two monumental works, for a practising Yogi and a psychologist, the importance of the volumes under the title *The Synthesis of Yoga* wherein Sri Aurobindo expounds the theory and practice of Integral Yoga can hardly be surpassed. I am not mentioning his other writings as the list would be too long and too varied.

Dr. Indra Sen has undertaken a major task in expounding the important psychological principles in Sri Aurobindo's writings for the benefit of students of psychology. He has accomplished this task by means of lengthy extracts of significant passages from the writings of Sri Aurobindo as well as through his own expositions of his principles. Dr. Indra Sen is eminently qualified to do so. He has been a Professor of philosophy and psychology at the University of Delhi (Hindu College) but gave up his assignment to go to the Ashram at Pondicherry to study and practise Integral Yoga at the feet of the Master and the Mother. The present work, actually a collection of his writings on Integral Yoga over several years, is the product of nearly half a century of study and practice. He has been the President of the Psychology Section of the Indian Science Congress, recipient of the Eastern-Western Psychology Lecture Award of the Swami Pranavananda Psychology Trust, and a regular contributor to professional journals of psychology and philosophy. I, therefore, feel privileged and honoured to write this Introduction to Dr. Indra Sen's book.

The book is divided in three parts. Part One is a collection of extracts from the writings of Sri Aurobindo. The attempt here is to place before the reader the principles of psychology that are inherent in Integral Yoga. The focus is on consciousness and on personality. Perhaps the central point in Sri Aurobindo's theory of personality is the concept of quality of consciousness in the human and its different levels. Sri Aurobindo speaks of four levels of human consciousness: (i) The subconscient and the submental level comprising the material basis of our life and body and which appear to us as inconscient. (ii) The subliminal level which comprises the inner life, inner mind and the inner physical and with the soul or psychic entity supporting these. (iii) The normal waking consciousness which the subconscient and subliminal "throw up on the surface, a wave of their secret urge". (iv) And most importantly, the superconscience, overarching and enveloping our submental, subliminal and waking consciousness. This superconscience is an extension of the earlier levels of consciousness as are accepted in contemporary psychology. This concept of the superconscient, often used interchangeably with the term superconscience, or rather the experiences at the superconscient level, "humanity speaks of vaguely as Spirit, God, the Oversoul".

Sri Aurobindo's significant contribution to human psychology is, in my opinion, this extension of human consciousness upwards. If Sigmund Freud drew attention to the lower levels of consciousness, Sri Aurobindo did the same for the higher level. The superconscience is above and beyond our present level of awareness and in which are included the higher planes of mental being as well as the heights of supramental and pure spiritual being. The normal waking human consciousness is hedged between, it seems to me, the twin forces of the Freudian Id and the Aurobindian Superconscient. If Freud's contribution to psychology has been to bring the primitive, instinctual urges within the boundaries of the Psychological Man, Sri Aurobindo's contribution has been to bring the concept of the Transcendent, the Divine and its pull within the boundaries of the same Psychological Man. Like Freud again, Sri Aurobindo has depended heavily on clinical experiences for evidence. Freud's case histories have been the neurotic personalities visiting his Vienna clinic and Sri Aurobindo's has been the yogic aspirants residing in his Ashram. Personal clinical experiences have been important for both.

I cannot avoid drawing the attention of the reader to the fact that although personal clinical evidence abounds for the existence of the unconscious and for that of the superconscience or the transcendent, laboratory testing of the implications and consequences of these have not been conspicuously successful. 'Can I bring God in the laboratory' is a question that excites and haunts me.

Dr. Indra Sen's inclusion of a section on Practical Guidance from the Integral Psychology point of view is an important contribution. Dr. Sen writes: "The human ego is most touchy and sensitive and gets easily hurt. Sensitiveness is an extremely common problem." And Sri Aurobindo writes under the caption 'True Remedy for Sensitiveness': "One has not to cure oneself of one's sensitiveness, but only acquire the power to rise to a higher consciousness taking such disenchantments as a sort of jumping board. One way is not to expect even square dealings from others, no matter who the others are. And besides, it is good to have such experiences of the real nature of some people to which a generous nature is often blind; for that helps the growth of one's consciousness." After this, can anyone say that mystics are impractical? Many of us who have undergone such hurts shall find the words of this sage a solace and a pointer to a new road for further growth.

In discussing the crisis of life in contemporary society, Dr. Indra Sen rightly says: "The contemporary crisis is virtually a crisis of personality, the surface personality being cultivated too exclusively, being taken as the whole man and full satisfaction sought from it which it cannot give." Apropos of this I quote a beautiful sentence of Dr. Indra Sen: "The inner or really the inmost consciousness is a complete new world of thought, feeling and will, possessed of self-existence, independence, creativity, mastery of body, life and mind and the environment. It opens up a life of intrinsic values, a life of positive pursuit and enjoyment of these values and thus gives to the life of external values a perspective altogether new and different." At the individual level, meditation and at the group level, education are obviously the means for developing this type of new personality. Having studied persons practising meditation as well as on the basis of personal experience of this, I am constrained to insert a dissenting note at this stage. Meditation, both in its personal growth as well as in its symptom relief function, is not a simple solution. As in psychotherapies including psychoanalysis, in the initial stages, meditation can increase the psychic turbulence and not bring in instant harmony, peace and balance. For teenagers and young adults, perhaps football and hockey are to be preferred to meditation and intensive introspection. I say this because the craze for meditation and its alleged benefits are too much bruited about and for which there is little empirical support. We have in our studies established that much of the supposed gains from meditation are not due to meditation per se but to the meditation subculture in which the lay meditator stays for a while. However, meditation practised seriously may lead to an enhanced capacity and range of functioning of the human brain and development of paranormal powers.

Dr. Indra Sen has made a strong and convincing plea for serious study of psychological principles embedded in ancient Indian texts and in case histories of Yogis. In this he finds full support from an outstanding Indian psychologist, Professor G. Bose of Calcutta University, who has also written a commentary on Patanjali's Yoga Sutra from the psychoanalytic viewpoint. Dr. Sen's present book will give substance and support to this legitimate hope. In fact a desire to explore psychological principles and concepts indigenous to India is already noticeable amongst some Indian psychologists. It is to be hoped that we will transit fast from description of these concepts to experimental verification and modification of these.

Many Indian minds have a fascination for the writings of Carl Jung. Dr. Indra Sen is no exception. He has devoted quite some space to a discussion of Jung's views mostly, I believe, to authenticate Indian concepts including those of Sri Aurobindo. This is one approach from which I respectfully differ from Dr. Indra Sen. Quoting authority or *Sabda Pramana*, even if of a person like Jung, is no substitute for hard experimental verification of the Indian concepts. Let these concepts be operationalised, tested and those which do not satisfy the acid test of the laboratory be rejected, howsoever ancient and holy these may be. The only condition for these tests should be an absence of experimenter bias.

From the psychological point of view, a fascinating concept is that of the Silent Mind. I first read of it in Satprem's *Adventure of Consciousness* at Pondicherry in the summer of 1982. As I was meeting Dr. Indra Sen daily and discussing various aspects of Sri Aurobindo's psychic experiences, I requested Dr. Indra Sen for discussion of this topic. Dr. Indra Sen very kindly agreed and the write-up of this discussion has been published in the *Indian Journal of Psychology* and reprinted in this book. Dr. Indra Sen said: "As silence grows, commitment to images and words and their successive movements perhaps becomes less and seeing things as a whole becomes more." I believe the phrase *citta vritti nirodha*, the Patanjal definition for yoga, literally means the silencing of the mind, though there are deeper and more subtle philosophical nuances to this definition. Irrespective of all this, silencing of the mind has immense implications both for mental health and for spiritual growth. As the Mother has said, there are some persons whose minds are constantly 'running'. She advises: "You must tranquilise it (the mind), pacify it, make it silent.... If it makes too much noise, you must tell it: 'Be still! Now silence, keep quiet!' Dr. Indra Sen has referred to Sri Aurobindo's the *Sakshi* (Witness) or the 'standing back' principle for silencing the mind and which may lead to the realisation of one's inner Self or Purusha. Sri Aurobindo himself learnt the silencing technique from Lele, the Maharashtrian yogi, following a slightly different technique. I also know of some Western psychologists experimenting with thought control through negative reinforcements. This concept of the Silent Mind appears to me to be the most important single concept in Indian Yogic thought and is also amenable to experimental treatment. Studies on the stream of consciousness or flow of ideas are already underway in the West and this persuades me to hope that experiments on the Silent Mind would not be far off. I quote a sentence on this from the *Adventure of Consciousness* by Satprem: "All kinds of discoveries are made... when the mental machinery stops, and the first is that if the power to think is a remarkable gift, the *power not to think* is even more so; let the seeker try it for just five minutes and he will see what stuff he is made of!"

Dr. Indra Sen's book is the first serious and systematic attempt by an Indian psychologist to expound the thoughts of Sri Aurobindo in the language of psychology. Many of us are beholden to him for this.

December 31, 1986

H. C. Ganguli
Professor of Psychology
University of Delhi
Delhi 110 007, India

PREFACE

'Man' is the key to life and Existence. It is man that seeks to know himself and his world. Our world has a quality and a character that correspond to the quality and character of our personality. A true and full knowledge of ourselves is, therefore, of prime importance. Through a knowledge of our more competent parts, we are able to solve the problems of the superficial parts and of the world that they create. It is the higher values of life that can truly and more satisfactorily harmonise and replace the lower ones.

It may also be stated that a truer and fuller exploration of man's personality is a matter of yogic research. Our ordinary scientific research remains limited to the superficial parts, the phenomena, the psycho-physical behaviour. However, some attempts are being made in the present times to go beyond and explain what man really is.

The present book represents Sri Aurobindo's work in this field and it tries to do so comprehensively. Part One represents his conception of man in his own words, with editorial explanations, where necessary, to show its comparative position in relation to modern scientific psychology.

Part Two gives elaborative and comparative studies in Integral Psychology. Therein Freud, Jung and academic psychology find their due places. It, however, needs to be remembered that these studies were made at different times and under different circumstances. But they all bear upon the same subject and represent the same standpoint.

Part Three deals with 'Integral Personality and Life', where the main issue is: how does Integral Personality hold the possibilities of meeting our problems in philosophy, in religion, culture and the practical affairs of life? In the end, under the title, 'Integral Personality and the Future', an attempt is made to show how the integral personality can give us an insight into the future course of human evolution.

However, Sri Aurobindo's main purpose was, in fact, to show how these possibilities could be realised in life. That is to say, he evolved an Integral Yoga for an integral transformation of life. This evidently involved the conception of Integral Personality and of an Integral Psychology, which form the subject-matter of this book.

Sri Aurobindo International Centre of Education is the educational project of Sri Aurobindo Ashram, Pondicherry, which seeks to represent to the world Sri Aurobindo's vision of the future in both thought and life. Sri Aurobindo's Integral Psychology stands as the foundation of his philosophy of life and existence, of his social and political thought and of creativity in art, literature and life.

The teaching of psychology in India poses a problem. Some teachers do feel that they are imparting to the younger generation a view of man, which is not supported by Indian life and knowledge. The students are told that man has no soul or spirit in him, that he is just a psycho-physical organism with a few externalist urges. But they find themselves helpless as we do not have textbooks embodying the best of both the Western and the Indian sum of knowledge on the subject. Could this book be, in any way, a supplement to the available books for a fuller knowledge of man and his personality?

Life always involves collaboration. The Ashram journal, *Mother India*, welcomed the theme of Integral Psychology for a serial publication and so the work could be undertaken and pursued. Sri Amal Kiran (K. D. Sethna), the editor, has, therefore, a hand in the matter – more than he might be aware of.

Then, while preparing the manuscript for the Press, Aster played a significant role. And she was helped in this by Violette and Geeta. All joy to them.

At the end, Aster prepared a beautiful Index. She had also looked to the proofs all along.

The Press has kept its reputation in book production and in particular made special efforts to print the diagrams and pictures.

All who have collaborated are entitled to the joy of the work.

Prof. Ganguli's 'Introduction' is a delicate piece of work, which he has done wonderfully. His problem is how to bring God (or Spirit) into the laboratory? But is God not already emerging in the laboratory under a new name, e.g., of 'wholeness'?

The collaboration of the Unseen Hand is immeasurable – what acknowledgement can one make of it!

INDRA SEN

CONTENTS

(Detailed contents are given at the commencement of each part)

PART ONE

INTEGRAL PSYCHOLOGY IN SRI AUROBINDO'S WORDS
(Page: 1)

Definition and Scope – Yoga and Psychology
Personality, its Harmonisation and Transformation
Branches of Psychology and other Psychological Systems
Varied Normal Activities
Practical Problems and Yogic Guidance

PART TWO

ELABORATIVE AND COMPARATIVE STUDIES
(Page: 81)

Contemporary Psychology and its Crisis
Integral Personality
Contemporary Psychologists and Personality
The Pursuit of Psychology: A Plea for a Larger Orientation
The Search for a Theory of Personality in Contemporary Psychology
A Study in Jung and Jungian Analysis
Freud and Personal Integration
Levels of Experience in Normal Personality
The Structure and Dynamics of Personality in Integral Yoga
Progress of Freudian Thought: A Study in Freudian Revisionists

PART THREE

INTEGRAL PERSONALITY AND LIFE
(Page: 255)

Integral Personality and its Great Possibilities for Man and His Culture
Integral Personality and the Pursuit of Philosophy, of Social and Political Life, Culture, Religion, Science and Technology
Integral Personality and Bodily Health and Excellence
Integral Personality and Mental Health and Excellence
Integral Personality and Education
Integral Personality and Creative Activity
Integral Personality and the Future

APPENDICES
(Page: 337)

A few charts, graphic representations showing different parts of personality, the worlds that they create and the process of Integral Yoga, glossary, etc.

BIBLIOGRAPHY, REFERENCES, INDEX
(Pages: 369, 374, 375)

PART ONE

INTEGRAL PSYCHOLOGY

INHERENT IN INTEGRAL YOGA

IN
SRI AUROBINDO'S WORDS

WITH
'INTRODUCTIONS' AND 'RECAPITULATIONS' BY THE EDITOR

PART ONE

CONTENTS

Introduction ... 5
   Definition and the Integral Scope of Psychology ... 6
   The Nature of Consciousness ... 7
   Yoga and Psychology ... 10

Recapitulation ... 13
   Our Ordinary Make-up ... 14
   Our Fuller Personality ... 15
   Principal Domains of Consciousness ... 16
   Integration and Harmonisation of Personality ... 22
   The Transformation of Nature ... 25

Recapitulation ... 27
   The Chakras – The Yogic Subtle Centres of
   Consciousness and the Integral Personality ... 30

Recapitulation and Introduction ... 34
   Branches of Psychology: ... 35
      The Psychology of Social Development ... 35
      Child Psychology and Educational Psychology ... 37
      Psychology of the Animals and the Plants ... 37
   The Science and Art of Healing ... 39
   The Psychical Phenomena ... 41
   Spiritism ... 44

Introduction ... 46
   Integral Psychology and other Psychological Systems ... 46
   The Old Indian System ... 48
   Psycho-analysis of Freud and the Way of Indulgence ... 49
   Psycho-analysis and Spiritual Experience ... 52

Introduction ... 53
   Varied Activities and Normal Personality ... 53
   Mind and the Sense-organs ... 55
   The Sense-mind ... 55

Abnormal States	... 56
Ordinary Perception and Action	... 57
Emotional Reactions	... 58
Memory, Judgment and Imagination	... 60
Desire as the Will Clutching at Results	... 61
The Ego or the Separative 'I-ness'	... 63
Our Mind and its Control of the Physical Life	... 64
Towards an Ideal Soul and Mind	... 65
The Spiritual Energy or Yoga-Force	... 66
Spiritual Experience	... 68

Introduction ... 69
- Practical Guidance ... 69
- Difficulties and Perplexities ... 69
- Circumstances and Difficulties ... 69
- Difficulties of Character ... 70
- The Practical Way ... 70
- The Imperturbable Calm ... 71
- True Remedy for Sensitiveness ... 71
- Evil Persona ... 72
- The Cultivation of Integral Personality ... 72

Final Recapitulation ... 76
- Integral Psychology as a System ... 76

INTRODUCTION

Psychology is a most dynamic science. Though yet so young it has created a vast body of knowledge covering a wide field of life, individual and social, normal and abnormal, educational and cultural, industrial and vocational. Above all, it has given an approach, the psychological approach, to entire human living, because man is essentially a psychological fact.

But the modern science of psychology is yet very unsure of itself and its vast body of knowledge tells us an enormous lot about the reactions of personality to the environment but not of what personality itself is. Gardner Murphy, an eminent contemporary psychologist says, "Nobody knows anything much about the nature of man. We are in a position to raise a great many questions, to raise questions perhaps so grave and so fundamental that we begin to wonder if we even have a method for approaching an ultimate solution".

Jung was a bold Western Psychologist. He persistently inquired into the meanings of Yogic and Religious experiences, and came to the conclusion that there is surely a 'Centre' or 'Self' in personality besides the ego behind the various 'polarities' or dualities of life.

If psychology is to rise equal to its numerous tasks and explain life effectively it must become sure of what man is. But then it must inquire into the nature of man in an unhampered way (without assumptions) to know the entire truth of the matter.

Sri Aurobindo's *The Synthesis of Yoga* and his *Letters on Yoga* (3 vols.) are works on yoga, not directly on psychology. The aim here is understanding life with a view to achieving its perfection. This normative attitude of self-education and self-perfection provides the very test of verification which is so much insisted upon by science. And yoga aims at going to the heart of the matter, it does not limit itself to the phenomenon of mind only or its reactions to the environment.

The psychologist will have to adjust himself to this approach of yoga and not insist on his own terminology. If he is able to do so, he might find in the following excerpts from Sri Aurobindo's *Synthesis* and *Letters* an account of human personality which might give him a clarity and a certitude which he much needs and seeks. A general reader, if he gets a sound foundation as to what man is, would be able to pursue self-education and self-perfection more confidently.

(Editor)

Definition and the Integral Scope of Psychology

Psychology is the science of consciousness and its states and operations in Nature and, if these can be glimpsed or experienced, its states and operations beyond what we know as Nature.

It is not enough to observe and know the movements of our surface Nature and the superficial nature of other living creatures just as it is not enough for science to observe and know as electricity only the movements of lightning in the clouds or for the astronomer to observe and know only those movements and properties of the stars that are visible to the unaided eye. Here as there a whole world of occult phenomena has to be laid bare and brought under control before the Psychologist can hope to be master of his province.

Our observable consciousness, that which we call ourselves, is only the little visible part of our being. It is a small field below which are depths and farther depths and widths and ever wider widths which support and supply it but to which it has no visible access. All that is our self, our being; what we see at the top is only our ego and its visible nature.

Even the movements of this little surface nature cannot be understood nor its true law discovered until we know all that is below or behind and supplies it – and know too all that is around it and above.

For below this conscient nature is the vast inconscient out of which we come. The Inconscient is greater, deeper, more original, more potent to shape and govern what we are and do than our little derivative conscient in nature. Inconscient to us, to our surface view, but not inconscient in itself or to itself, it is a sovereign guide, worker, determinant, creator. Not to know it is not to know our nether origins and the origin of the most part of what we are and do. And the Inconscient is not all.

For behind our little frontal ego and nature is a whole subliminal kingdom of inner consciousness with many planes and provinces. There are in that kingdom many powers, movements, personalities which are part of ourselves and help to form our little surface personality and its powers and movements. This inner self, these inner persons we do not know, but they know us and observe and dictate our speech, our thoughts, feelings, doings even more directly than the Inconscient below us.

Around us too is a circumconscient Universal of which we are a portion. This circumconscient is pouring its forces, suggestions, stimuli, compulsions into us at every moment of our existence.

Around us is a universal Mind of which our mind is a formation and our thoughts, feelings, will, impulses are continually little more than a personally modified reception and transcription of its thoughtwaves, its force-currents, its foam of emotion and sensation, its billows of impulse.

Around is a permanent universal Life of which our petty flow of life-formation that begins and ceases is only a small dynamic wave.[1]

*

We become aware, in a certain experience, of a range of being superconscient to all these, aware too of something, a supreme highest Reality, sustaining and exceeding them all, which humanity speaks of vaguely as Spirit, God, the Oversoul: from these superconscient ranges we have visitations, and in our highest being we tend towards them and to that supreme Spirit. There is then in our total range of existence a superconscience as well as a subconscience, overarching and perhaps enveloping our subliminal and our waking selves, but unknown to us, seemingly unattainable and incommunicable.[2]

The Nature of Consciousness

Consciousness is not, to my experience, a phenomenon dependent on the reactions of personality to the force of Nature and amounting to no more than a seeing or interpretation of these reactions. If that were so, then when the personality becomes silent and immobile and gives no reactions, as there would be no seeing or interpretative actions, there would therefore be no consciousness. That contradicts some of the fundamental experiences of Yoga, e.g., a silent and immobile consciousness infinitely spread out, not seeing and interpreting contacts but motionlessly self-aware, not dependent on the reactions, but persistent in itself even when no reactions take place. The subjective personality itself is only a formation of consciousness which is a power inherent, not in the activity of the temporary manifested personality, but in the being, the Self or Purusha.

Consciousness is a reality inherent in existence. It is there even when it is not active on the surface, but silent and immobile; it is there even when it is invisible on the surface, not reacting on outward things or sensible to them, but withdrawn and either active or inactive within; it is there even when it seems to us to be quite absent and being to our view unconscious, and inanimate.

Consciousness is not only power of awareness of self and things, it is or has also a dynamic and creative energy. It can determine its own reactions or abstain from reactions; it can not only answer to forces, but create or put out from itself forces. Consciousness is Chit but also Chit Shakti.

Consciousness is usually identified with mind, but mental consciousness is only the human range which no more exhausts all the possible ranges of consciousness than human sight exhausts all the gradations of colour or human hearing all the gradations of sound – for there is much above or below that is to man invisible and inaudible. So there are ranges of consciousness above and below the human ranges with which the normal human has no contact and they seem to it unconscious, – supramental or overmental and submental ranges.[3]

*

The gradations of consciousness are universal states not dependent on the outlook of the subjective personality; rather the outlook of the subjective personality is determined by the grade of consciousness in which it is organised according to its typal nature or its evolutionary stage.

It will be evident that by consciousness is meant something which is essentially the same throughout but variable in status, condition and operation, in which in some grades or conditions the activities we call consciousness can exist either in a suppressed or an unorganised or a differently organised state; while in other states some other activities may manifest which in us are suppressed, unorganised or latent or else are less perfectly manifested, less intensive, extended and powerful than in those higher grades above our highest mental limit.⁴

*

Consciousness has no need of a clear individual "I" to dispose variously the centralising stress, – wherever the stress is put the "I" attaches itself to that, so that one thinks of oneself as a mental being or physical being or whatever it may be. The consciousness in me can dispose its stress in this way or the other way – it may go down into the physical and work there in the physical nature keeping all the rest behind or above for the time or it may go up into the overhead level and stand above mind, life and body seeing them as instrumental lower forms of itself or not seeing them at all and merged in the free undifferentiated self or it may throw itself into an active dynamic cosmic consciousness and identify with that or do any number of other things without resorting to the help of this much overrated and meddlesome fly on the wheel which you call the clear individual "I". The real "I" – if you want to use that word – is not "clear" individual "I", that is, clear-cut limited separative ego, it is as wide as the universe and wider and can contain the universe in itself....⁵

*

As the consciousness in us, by its external concentration of stress, has to put all these things behind – behind a wall or veil, it has to break down the wall or veil and get back in its stress into these inner parts of existence – that is what we call living within; then our external being seems to us something small and superficial, we are or can become aware of the large and rich and inexhaustible kingdom within. So also consciousness in us has drawn a lid or covering or whatever one likes to call it between the lower planes of mind, life, body supported by the psychic and the higher planes which contain the spiritual kingdom where the self is always free and limitless, and it can break or open the lid or covering and ascend there and become the self free and wide and luminous or else bring down the influence, reflection, finally even the presence and power of the higher consciousness into the lower nature.⁶

Yoga and Psychology

Yogic methods have something of the same relation to the customary psychological workings of man as has the scientific handling of the natural force of electricity. And they, too, are formed upon a knowledge developed and confirmed by regular experiment, practical analysis and constant result. All Rajayoga, for instance, depends on this perception and experience that our inner elements, combinations, functions, forces, can be separated or dissolved, can be new-combined and set to novel and formerly impossible workings or can be transformed and resolved into a new general synthesis by fixed internal processes. Hathayoga similarly depends on this perception and experience that the vital forces and functions to which our life is normally subjected and whose ordinary operations seem set and indispensable, can be mastered and the operations changed or suspended with results that would otherwise be impossible and that seem miraculous to those who have not seized the rationale of their process. And if in some other of its forms this character of Yoga is less apparent, because they are more intuitive and less mechanical, nearer, like the Yoga of Devotion, to a supernal ecstasy or, like the Yoga of Knowledge, to a supernal infinity of consciousness and being, yet they too start from the use of some principal faculty in us by ways and for ends not contemplated in its everyday spontaneous workings. All methods grouped under the common name of Yoga are special psychological processes founded on a fixed truth of Nature and developing, out of normal functions, powers and results which were always latent but which her ordinary movements do not easily or do not often manifest.[7]

*

We see, then, what from the psychological point of view and Yoga is nothing but practical psychology, – is the conception of Nature from which we have to start. It is the self-fulfilment of the Purusha through his Energy. But the movement of Nature is twofold, higher and lower, or, as we may choose to term it, divine and undivine. The distinction exists indeed for practical purposes only; for there is nothing that is not divine, and in a larger view it is as meaningless, verbally, as the distinction between natural and supernatural, for all things that are are natural. All things are in Nature and all things are in God. But, for practical purposes, there is a real distinction. The lower Nature, that which we know and are and must remain so long as the faith in us is not changed, acts through limitation and division, is of the nature of Ignorance and culminates in the life of the ego; but the higher Nature, that to which we aspire, acts by unification and transcendence of limitation, is of the nature of Knowledge and culminates in the life divine. The passage from the lower to the higher is the aim of Yoga; and this passage may effect itself by the rejection of the lower and escape into the higher, – the ordinary viewpoint, – or by the transformation of the lower and its elevation to the higher Nature. It is this, rather, that must be the aim of an integral Yoga.[8]

*

All Yoga proceeds in its method by three principles of practice; first, purification, that is to say, the removal of all aberrations, disorders, obstructions brought about by the mixed and irregular action of the energy of being in our physical, moral and mental system; secondly, concentration, that is to say, the bringing to its full intensity and the mastered and self-directed employment of that energy of being in us for a definite end; thirdly, liberation, that is to say, the release of our being from the narrow and painful knots of the individualised energy in a false and limited play, which at present are the law of our nature. The enjoyment of our liberated being which brings us into unity or union with the Supreme, is the consummation; it is that for which Yoga is done.[9]

*

...the whole method of Yoga is psychological; it might almost be termed the consummate practice of a perfect psychological knowledge.[10]

*

...an ordinary psychology which only takes mind and its phenomena at their surface values, will be of no help to us; it will not give us the least guidance in this line of self-exploration and self-conversion. Still less can we find the clue in a scientific psychology with a materialistic basis which assumes that the body and the biological and physiological factors of our nature are not the starting-point but the whole real foundation and regards human mind as only a subtle development from the life and the body. That may be the actual truth of the animal side of human nature and of the human mind insofar as it is limited and conditioned by the physical part of our being. But the whole difference between man and the animal is that the animal mind, as we know it, cannot get for one moment away from its origins, cannot break out from the covering, the close chrysalis which the bodily life has spun round the soul, and become something greater than its present self, a more free, magnificent and noble being, but in man mind reveals itself as a greater energy escaping from the restrictions of the vital and physical formula of being. But even this is not all that man is or can be: he has in him the power to evolve and release a still greater ideal energy which in its turn escapes out of the restrictions of the mental formula of his nature and discloses the supramental form, the ideal power of a spiritual being. In Yoga we have to travel beyond the physical nature and the superficial man and to discover the workings of the whole nature of the real man.[11]

RECAPITULATION

Psychology continues to be divided into many schools, there is no agreement even regarding its subject matter and its method. But is it really necessary? Human personality, as conscious, unconscious, superconscious and as behaviour are also of interest to us. Consciousness is obviously the central fact and then introspection must be the central method. And we cannot limit ourselves to the empirical only. Physics itself is going beyond the empirical. With the advance of knowledge all sciences are bound to go beyond the empirical to be able to explain the world more satisfactorily. Phenomenon and Reality are, after all, one piece and cannot be arbitrarily separated. In the West, at one time it was found necessary and science chose to limit itself. In India, the unity of all knowledge has always been stressed.

The definition here propounded explicitly covers consciousness, its states and operations in nature as also its relations with facts beyond nature. The scope marks out very many domains and spheres of consciousness not distinctly known to psychology, but recognised and repeatedly verified by Yoga.

Again, consciousness cannot be an epiphenomenon as 19th century materialism took it to be in Europe.

Consciousness or awareness is a primary, most vivid, decisive fact of human living, felt and known directly like all primary qualities of experience. It is in fact more primary than the primary qualities of colour, taste, smell, etc., as these depend on it. It is not a matter of inferential knowledge. It is also not identical with its reactions as is ordinarily believed, since it can be quite immobile too. Such immobile consciousness is, however, a matter of a special effort of self-dissociation from the superficial involvements of life and of seeking a poise of depth. This effort is difficult, but it is highly rewarding as then a consciousness immobile and self-existent becomes a surprising vivid fact. And, what is more important, consciousness strikes one as real, as ultimate.

The passages from Sri Aurobindo on consciousness are an elaborate exposition of what consciousness essentially is in man and in the universe and how it stands interrelated in them. Obviously psychology and metaphysics get intermixed and we need to be careful, recognise the relatively separate field of psychology and also its deeper and wider relations with the total reality.

In this instalment we venture upon an elaborate mapping out of Integral personality. (Editor)

Our Ordinary Make-up

To the ordinary man who lives upon his own waking surface, ignorant of the self's depths and vastnesses behind the veil, his psychological existence is fairly simple. A small but clamorous company of desires, some imperative intellectual and aesthetic cravings, some tastes, a few ruling or prominent ideas amid a great current of unconnected or ill-connected and mostly trivial thoughts, a number of more or less imperative vital needs, alternations of physical health and disease, a scattered and inconsequent succession of joys and griefs, frequent minor disturbances and vicissitudes and rarer strong searchings and upheavals of mind or body, and through it all Nature, partly with the aid of his thought and will, partly without or in spite of it, arranging these things in some rough practical fashion, some tolerable disorderly order, – this is the material of his existence. The average human being even now is in his inward existence as crude and undeveloped as was the bygone primitive man in his outward life. But as soon as we go deep within ourselves, – and Yoga means a plunge into all the multiple profundities of the soul, – we find ourselves subjectively, as man in his growth has found himself objectively, surrounded by a whole complex world which we have to know and to conquer.

The most disconcerting discovery is to find that every part of us – intellect, will, sense-mind, nervous or desire self, the heart, the body – has each, as it were, its own complex individuality and natural formation independent of the rest; it neither agrees with itself nor with the others nor with the representative ego which is the shadow cast by some central and centralising self on our superficial ignorance. We find that we are composed not of one but many personalities and each has its own demands and differing nature. Our being is a roughly constituted chaos into which we have to introduce the principle of a divine order. Moreover, we find that inwardly too, no less than outwardly, we are not alone in the world; the sharp separateness of our ego was no more than a strong imposition and delusion; we do not exist in ourselves, we do not really live apart in an inner privacy or solitude. Our mind is a receiving, developing and modifying machine into which there is being constantly passed from moment to moment a ceaseless foreign flux, a streaming mass of disparate materials from above, from below, from outside. Much more than half our thoughts and feelings are not our own in the sense that they take form out of ourselves; of hardly anything can it be said that it is truly original to our nature. A large part comes to us from others or from the environment, whether as raw material or as manufactured imports; but still more largely they come from universal Nature here or from other worlds and planes and their beings and powers and influences; for we are overtopped and environed by other planes of consciousness, mind planes, life planes, subtle matter planes, from which our life and action here are fed, or fed on, pressed, dominated, made use of for the manifestation of their forms and forces.[12]

Our Fuller Personality

Our visible life and the actions of that life are no more than a series of significant expressions, but that which it tries to express is not on the surface; our existence is something much larger than this apparent frontal being which we suppose ourselves to be and which we offer to the world around us. This frontal and external being is a confused amalgam of mind-formations, life-movements, physical functionings of which even an exhaustive analysis into its component parts and machinery fails to reveal the whole secret. It is only when we go behind, below, above into the hidden stretches of our being that we can know it; the most thorough and acute surface scrutiny and manipulation cannot give us the true understanding or the completely effective control of our life, its purposes, its activities: that inability indeed is the cause of the failure of reason, morality and every other surface action to control and deliver and perfect the life of the human race. For below even our most obscure physical consciousness is a subconscious being in which as in a covering and supporting soil are all manner of hidden seeds that sprout up, unaccountably to us, on our surface and into which we are constantly throwing fresh seeds that prolong our past and will influence our future, – a subconscious being, obscure, small in its motions, capriciously and almost fantastically subrational, but of immense potency for the earth-life. Again behind our mind, our life, our conscious physical there is a large subliminal consciousness, – there are inner mental, inner vital, inner more subtle physical reaches supported by an inmost psychic existence which is the connecting soul of all the rest; and in these hidden reaches too lie a mass of numerous pre-existent personalities which supply the material, the motive-forces, the impulsions of our developing surface existence. For in each one of us here there may be one central person, but also a multitude of subordinate personalities created by the past history of its manifestation or by expressions of it on these inner planes which support its present play in this external material cosmos. And while on our surface we are cut off from all around us except through an exterior mind and sense-contact which delivers but little of us to our world or of our world to us, in these inner reaches the barrier between us and the rest of existence is thin and easily broken; there we can feel at once – not merely infer from their results, but feel directly – the action of the secret world-forces, mind-forces, life-forces, subtle physical forces that constitute universal and individual existence; we shall even be able, if we will but train ourselves to it, to lay our hands on these world-forces that throw themselves on us or around us and more and more to control or at least strongly modify their action on us and others, their formations, their very movements. Yet again above our human mind are still greater reaches superconscient to it and from there secretly descend influences, powers, touches which are the original determinants of things here and, if they were called down in their fullness, could altogether alter the whole make and economy of life in the material universe.[13]

Principal Domains of Consciousness

A superficial observation of our waking consciousness shows us that of a great part of our individual being and becoming we are quite ignorant; it is to us the Inconscient, just as much as the life of the plant, the metal, the earth, the elements. But if we carry our knowledge farther, pushing psychological experiment and observation beyond their normal bounds, we find how vast is the sphere of this supposed Inconscient or this subconscious in our total existence, – the subconscient, so seeming and so called by us because it is a concealed consciousness, – what a small and fragmentary portion of our being is covered by our waking self-awareness. We arrive at the knowledge that our waking mind and ego are only a superimposition upon a submerged, a subliminal self, – for so that self appears to us, – or, more accurately, an inner being, with a much vaster capacity of experience; our mind and ego are like the crown and dome of a temple jutting out from the waves while the great body of the building is submerged under the surface of the waters.

This concealed self and consciousness is our real or whole being, of which the outer is a part and a phenomenon, a selective formation for a surface use. We perceive only a small number of the contacts of things which impinge upon us; the inner being perceives all that enters or touches us and our environment. We perceive only a part of the workings of our life and being; the inner being perceives so much that we might almost suppose that nothing escapes its view. We remember only a small selection from our perception, and of these even we keep a great part in a store-room where we cannot always lay our hand upon what we need; the inner being retains everything that it has ever received and has it always ready to hand. We can form into co-ordinated understanding and knowledge only so much of our perceptions and memories as our trained intelligence and mental capacity can grasp in their sense and appreciate in their relations; the intelligence of the inner being needs no training, but preserves the accurate form and relations of all its perceptions and memories and, though this is a proposition which may be considered doubtful or difficult to concede in its fullness, – can grasp immediately, when it does not possess already, their significance. And its perceptions are not confined, as are ordinarily those of the waking mind, to the scanty gleanings of the physical senses, but extend far beyond and use, as telepathic phenomena of many kinds bear witness, a subtle sense the limits of which are too wide to be easily fixed. The relations between the surface will or impulsion and the subliminal urge, mistakenly described as unconscious or sub-conscious, have not been properly studied except in regard to unusual and unorganised manifestations and to certain morbidly abnormal phenomena of the diseased human mind; but if we pursue our observation far enough, we shall find that the cognition and will or impulsive force of the inner being really stand behind the whole conscious becoming; the latter represents only that part of its secret endeavour and achievement which rises successfully to the surface of our life. To know our inner being is the first step towards a real self-knowledge.

If we undertake this self-discovery and enlarge our knowledge of the subliminal self, so conceiving it as to include in it our lower subconscient and upper superconscient ends, we shall discover that it is really this which provides the whole material of our apparent being and that our perceptions, our memories, our effectuations of will and intelligence are only a selection from its perceptions, memories, activities and relations of will and intelligence; our very ego is only a minor and superficial formulation of its self-consciousness and self-experience. It is, as it were, the urgent sea out of which the waves of our conscious becoming arise. But what are its limits? How far does it extend? What is its fundamental nature? Ordinarily we speak of a subconscious existence and include in this term all that is not on the waking surface. But the whole or the greater part of the inner or subliminal self can hardly be characterised by that epithet; for when we say subconscious, we think readily of an obscure unconsciousness or half-consciousness or else a submerged consciousness below and in a way inferior to and less than our organised waking awareness or, at least, less in possession of itself. But we find, when we go within, that somewhere in our subliminal part, – though not co-extensive with it since it has also obscure and ignorant regions, – there is a consciousness much wider, more luminous, more in possession of itself and things than that which wakes upon our surface and is the percipient of our daily hours; that is our inner being, and it is this which we must regard as our subliminal self and set apart the subconscient as an inferior, a lowest occult province of our nature. In the same way there is a superconscient part of our total existence in which there is what we discover to be our highest self, and this too we can set apart as a higher occult province of our nature.

But what then is the subconscient and where does it begin and how is it related to our surface being or to the subliminal of which it would seem more properly to be a province? We are aware of our body and know that we have a physical existence, even very largely identify ourselves with it, and yet most of its operations are really subconscious to our mental being; not only does the mind take no part in them but, as we suppose, our most physical being has no awareness of its own hidden operations or, by itself, of its own existence: it knows or rather feels only so much of itself as is enlightened by mind-sense and observable by intelligence. We are aware of a vitality working in this bodily form and structure as in the plant or lower animal, a vital existence which is also for the most part subconscious to us, for we only observe some of its movements and reactions. We are partly aware of its operations, but not by any means of all or most of them, and rather of those which are abnormal than those which are normal; its wants impress themselves more forcibly upon us than its satisfactions, its diseases and disorders than its health and its regular rhythm, its death is more poignant to us than its life is vivid: we know as much of it as we can consciously observe and use or as much as forces itself upon us by pain and pleasure and other sensations or as a cause of nervous or physical reaction and disturbance, but no more. Accordingly, we suppose that this vital-physical part of us also is not conscious of its own operations or has only a suppressed consciousness or no consciousness like the plant or an inchoate consciousness like the incipient animal; it becomes conscious only so far as it is enlightened by mind and observable by intelligence.

This is an exaggeration and a confusion due to our identification of consciousness with mentality and mental awareness. Mind identifies itself to a certain extent with the movements proper to physical life and body and annexes them to its mentality, so that all consciousness seems to us to be mental. But if we draw back, if we separate the mind as witness from these parts of us, we can discover that life and body, – even the most physical parts of life, – have a consciousness of their own, a consciousness proper to an obscurer vital and to a bodily being, even such an elemental awareness as primitive animal forms may have, but in us partly taken up by the mind and to that extent mentalised. Yet it has not, in its independent motion, the mental awareness which we enjoy; if there is mind in it, it is mind involved and implicit in the body and in the physical life: there is no organised self-consciousness, but only a sense of action and reaction, movement, impulse and desire, need, necessary activities imposed by Nature, hunger, instinct, pain, insensibility and pleasure. Although thus inferior, it has this awareness obscure, limited and automatic; but since it is less in possession of itself, void of what to us is the stamp of mentality, we may justly call it the submental, but not so justly the subconscious part of our being. For when we stand back from it, when we can separate our mind from its sensations, we perceive that this is a nervous and sensational and automatically dynamic mode of consciousness, a gradation of awareness different from the mind: it has its own separate reactions to contacts and is sensitive to them in its own power of feeling; it does not depend for that on the mind's perception and response. The true subconscious is other than this vital or physical substratum; it is the Inconscient vibrating on the borders of consciousness, sending up its motions to be changed into conscious stuff, swallowing into its depths impressions of past experience as seeds of unconscious habit and returning them constantly but often chaotically to the surface consciousness, missioning upwards much futile or perilous stuff of which the origin is obscure to us, in dream, in mechanical repetitions of all kinds, in untraceable impulsions and motives, in mental, vital, physical perturbations and upheavals, in dumb automatic necessities of our obscurest parts of nature.

But the subliminal self has not at all this subconscious character: it is in full possession of a mind, a life-force, a clear subtle-physical sense of things. It has the same capacities as our waking being, a subtle sense and perception, a comprehensive extended memory and an intensive selecting intelligence, will, self-consciousness; but even though the same in kind, they are wider, more developed, more sovereign. And it has other capacities which exceed those of our mortal mind because of a power of direct awareness of the being, whether acting in itself or turned upon its object, which arrives more swiftly at knowledge, more swiftly at effectivity of will, more deeply at understanding and satisfaction of impulse. Our surface mind is hardly a true mentality, so involved, bound, hampered, conditioned is it by the body and bodily life and the limitations of the nerve-system and the physical organs. But the subliminal self has a true mentality superior to these limitations; it exceeds the physical mind and physical organs although it is aware of them and their works and is, indeed, in a large degree their cause or creator. It is only subconscious in the sense of not bringing all or most of itself to the surface, it works always behind the veil: it is rather a secret intraconscient and circumconscient than a subconscient; for it envelops quite as much as it supports the outer nature. This description is no doubt truest of the deeper parts of the subliminal; in other layers of it nearer to our surface there is a more ignorant action and those who, penetrating within, pause in the zones of lesser coherence or in the No-man's-land between the subliminal and the surface, may fall into much delusion and confusion: but that too, though ignorant, is not of the nature of the subconscious; the confusion of these intermediate zones has no kinship to the Inconscience.

We might say then that there are three elements in the totality of our being: there is the submental and the subconscient which appears to us as if it were inconscient, comprising the material basis and a good part of our life and body; there is the subliminal, which comprises the inner being, taken in its entirety of inner mind, inner life, inner physical with the soul or psychic entity supporting them; there is this waking consciousness which the subliminal and the subconscient throw up on the surface, a wave of their secret surge. But even this is not an adequate account of what we are; for there is not only something deep within behind our normal self-awareness, but something also high above it: that too is ourselves, other than our surface mental personality, but not outside our true self; that too is a country of our spirit. For the subliminal proper is no more than the inner being on the level of the Knowledge-Ignorance, luminous, powerful and extended indeed beyond the poor conception of our waking mind, but still not the supreme or the whole sense of our being, not its ultimate mystery. We become aware, in a certain experience, of a range of being superconscient to all these three, aware too of something, a supreme highest Reality sustaining and exceeding them all, which humanity speaks of vaguely as Spirit, God, the Oversoul: from these superconscient ranges we have visitations and in our highest being we tend towards them and to that supreme Spirit. There is then in our total range of existence a superconscience as well as subconscience and inconscience, overarching and perhaps enveloping our subliminal and our waking selves, but unknown to us, seemingly unattainable and incommunicable.

But with the extension of our knowledge we discover what this spirit or oversoul is: it is ultimately our own highest deepest vastest Self, it is apparent on its summits or by reflection in ourselves as Sachchidananda creating us and the world by the power of His divine Knowledge-Will, spiritual, supramental, truth-conscious, infinite. That is the real Being, Lord and Creator, who, as the Cosmic Self veiled in Mind and Life and Matter, has descended into that which we call the Inconscient and constitutes and directs its subconscient existence by His supramental Will and knowledge, has ascended out of the Inconscient and dwells in the inner being constituting and directing its subliminal existence by the same will and knowledge, has cast up out of the subliminal our surface existence and dwells secretly in it overseeing with the same supreme light and mastery its stumbling and groping movements. If the subliminal and subconscient may be compared to a sea which throws up the waves of our surface mental existence, the superconscience may be compared to an ether which constitutes, contains, overroofs, inhabits and determines the movements of the sea and its waves. It is there in this higher ether that we are inherently and intrinsically conscious of our self and spirit, not as here below by a reflection in silent mind or by acquisition of the knowledge of a hidden Being within us; it is through it, through that ether of superconscience, that we can pass to a supreme status, knowledge, experience. Of this superconscient existence through which we can arrive at the highest status of our real, our supreme Self, we are normally even more ignorant than of the rest of our being; yet is it into the knowledge of it that our being, emerging out of the involution in Inconscience is struggling to evolve.[14]

Integration and Harmonisation of Personality

In some human beings it is the physical Purusha, the being of body, who dominates the mind, will and action; there is then created the physical man mainly occupied with his corporeal life and habitual needs, impulses, life-habits, mind-habits, body-habits, looking very little or not at all beyond that, subordinating and restricting all his other tendencies and possibilities to that narrow formation. But even in the physical man there are other elements and he cannot live altogether as the human animal concerned with birth and death and procreation and the satisfaction of common impulses and desires and the maintenance of the life and the body: this is his normal type of personality, but it is crossed, however feebly, with influences by which he can proceed, if they are developed, to a higher human evolution. If the inner subtle-physical Purusha insists, he can arrive at the idea of a finer, more beautiful and perfect physical life and hope or attempt to realise it in his own or in the collective or group existence. In others it is the vital self, the being of life, who dominates and rules the mind, the will, the action; then is created the vital man, concerned with self-affirmation, self-aggrandisement, life-enlargement, satisfaction of ambition and passion and impulse and desire, the claims of his ego, domination, power, excitement, battle and struggle, inner and outer adventure: all else is incidental or subordinated to this movement and building and expression of the vital ego. But still in the vital man too there are or can be other elements of a growing mental or spiritual character, even if these happen to be less developed than his life-personality and life-power. The nature of the vital man is more active, stronger and more mobile, more turbulent and chaotic, often to the point of being quite unregulated, than that of the physical man who holds on to the soil and has a certain material poise and balance, but it is more kinetic and creative: for the element of the vital being is not earth but air; it has more movement, less status. A vigorous vital mind and will can grasp and govern the kinetic vital energies, but it is more by a forceful compulsion and constraint than by a harmonisation of the being. If, however, a strong vital personality, mind and will can get the reasoning intelligence to give it a firm support and be its minister, then a certain kind of forceful formation can be made, more or less balanced but always powerful, successful and effective, which can impose itself on the nature and environment and arrive at a strong self-affirmation in life and action. This is the second step of harmonised formulation possible in the ascent of the nature.

At a higher stage of the evolution of personality the being of mind may rule; there is then created the mental man who lives predominantly in the mind as the others live in the vital or the physical nature. The mental man tends to subordinate to his mental self-expression, mental aims, mental interests or to a mental idea or ideal the rest of his being: because of the difficulty of this subordination and its potent effect when achieved, it is at once more difficult for him and easier to arrive at a harmony of his nature. It is easier because the mental will once in control can convince by the power of the reasoning intelligence and at the same time dominate, compress or suppress the life and the body and their demands, arrange and harmonise them, force them to be its instruments, even reduce them to a minimum so that they shall not disturb the mental life or pull it down from its ideative or idealising movement. It is more difficult because life and body are the first powers and, if they are in the least strong, can impose themselves with an almost irresistible insistence on the mental ruler. Man is a mental being and the mind is the leader of his life and body; but this is a leader who is much led by his followers and has sometimes no other will than what they impose on him. Mind in spite of its power is often impotent before the inconscient and subconscient which obscure its clarity and carry it away on the tide of instinct or impulse; in spite of its clarity it is fooled by vital and emotional suggestions into giving sanction to ignorance and error, to wrong thought and to wrong action, or it is obliged to look on while the nature follows what it knows to be wrong, dangerous or evil. Even when it is strong and clear and dominant, Mind, though it imposes a certain, a considerable mentalised harmony, cannot integrate the whole being and nature. These harmonisations by an inferior control are, besides, inconclusive, because it is one part of the nature which dominates and fulfils itself while the others are coerced and denied their fullness. They can be steps on the way, but not final; therefore in most men there is no such sole dominance and effected partial harmony, but only a predominance and for the rest an unstable equilibrium of a personality half formed, half in formation, sometimes a disequilibrium or unbalance due to the lack of a central government or the disturbance of a formerly achieved partial poise. All must be transitional until a first, though not final, true harmonisation is achieved by finding our real centre. For the true central being is the soul, but this being stands back and in most human natures is only the secret witness or, one might say, a constitutional ruler who allows his ministers to rule for him, delegates to them his empire, silently assents to their decisions and only now and then puts in a word which they can at any moment override and act otherwise. But this is so long as the soul personality put forward by the psychic entity is not yet sufficiently developed; when this is strong enough for the inner entity to impose itself through it, then the soul can come forward and control the nature. It is by the coming forward of this true monarch and his taking up of the reins of government that there can take place a real harmonisation of our being and our life.[15]

The Transformation of Nature

...When these different parts are all under the control of the Psychic and turned by it towards the reception of the higher consciousness, then there begins the harmonisation of all the parts and their progressive recasting into moulds of the higher consciousness growing in peace, light, force, love, knowledge, Ananda which is what we call the transformation.[16]

*

The soul, the psychic entity, then manifests itself as the central being which upholds mind and life and body and supports all the other powers and functions of the Spirit; it takes up its greater function as the guide and ruler of the nature. A guidance, a governance begins from within which exposes every movement to the light of Truth, repels what is false, obscure, opposed to the divine realisation: every region of the being, every nook and corner of it, every movement, formation, direction, inclination of thought, will, emotion, sensation, action, reaction, motive, disposition, propensity, desire, habit of the conscious or subconscious physical, even the most concealed, camouflaged, mute, recondite, is lighted up with the unerring psychic light, their confusions dissipated, their tangles disentangled, their obscurities, deceptions, self-deceptions precisely indicated and removed; all is purified, set right, the whole nature harmonised, modulated in the psychic key, put in spiritual order. This process may be rapid or tardy according to the amount of obscurity and resistance still left in the nature, but it goes on unfalteringly so long as it is not complete. As a final result the whole conscious being is made perfectly apt for spiritual truth of thought, feeling, sense, action, tuned to the right response, delivered from the darkness and stubbornness of the tamasic inertia, the turbidities and turbulences and impurities of the rajasic passion and restless unharmonised kinetism, the enlightened rigidities and sattwic limitations or poised balancements of constructed equilibrium which are the character of the Ignorance.[17]

*

A psychic or, more widely speaking, a psycho-spiritual transformation of this kind would be already a vast change of our mental human nature.[18]

*

Purification of the nature by the "influence" of the Spirit is not what I mean by transformation; purification is only part of a psychic change or a psycho-spiritual change – the word besides has many senses and is very often given a moral or ethical meaning which is foreign to my purpose. What I mean by the spiritual transformation is something dynamic. It is a putting on of the spiritual consciousness, dynamic as well as static, in every part of the being down to the subconscient. That cannot be done by the influence of the Self leaving the consciousness fundamentally as it is with only purification, enlightenment of the mind and heart and quiescence of the vital. It means a bringing down of the divine Consciousness static and dynamic into all these parts and the entire replacement of the present consciousness by that.[19]

RECAPITULATION

We have mapped out human personality elaborately enough. We have given a picture of our fuller personality and then a large account of our Integral Personality under "Principal Domains of Consciousness". The concept of Integral Personality is a most valuable contribution from India which opens up new fields of investigation for the science of psychology. The entire tradition of Yoga bears testimony to the various fields of experience of Integral Personality and contemporary Yogic experience confirms it. The factual reality of these fields cannot be doubted, but they need to be explored and substantiated in terms of scientific psychology. This is, in fact, the exclusive or at least the primary responsibility and privilege of the Indian Psychologist.

Let us briefly restate what Integral Personality is.

Our ordinary personality is an organisation of interactions with the environment. It is a surface formation dealing with the surface or the phenomena of nature. It is intensely self-centred or marked off from the not-self of the rest of nature. It is also deeply a part of the same nature. This is the domain of consciousness or personality which we ordinarily take as the whole personality or the primary subject-matter of the science of psychology.

But by a persistent practice of yogic introspection, if we withdraw from it, dissociate ourselves from it, we land in a field of wider mind, life and body, a universality of them. In relation to this, our ordinary personality becomes clearly a separated particularity of personality. This experience is really wonderful. There universal forces of nature become a direct perception, they do not remain inferences as ordinarily they are. Telepathy then becomes an exercisable function. A yet further inward withdrawal lands us in a luminous and blissful core-consciousness, which renders our wider personality (called by Sri Aurobindo the subliminal) an external fact. This is felt as self-existent and independent of circumstances. The discovery of this domain of consciousness holds the key to many problems of scientific psychology. There, we feel, sex is not final to life, reaction to environment is not essential and normality is not merely social conformity. This is very illuminating to a student of human personality.

Introspection is a profound discipline for yoga. The foregoing discoveries it makes by following an in-look in its action of observation. Our ordinary posture of consciousness is one of outlook. But it also pursues an up-look in its investigation and then it discovers a large field of consciousness of increasing luminosity and universality. It seems to command all existence. It is also unitary in nature. This Sri Aurobindo calls Superconsciousness or the Superconscient. And then there is a reverse movement of down-look, which lands us in the subconscious and the unconscious or the Inconscient. This is a field of obscurity and lack of organisation and order.

Such then is the wide field of Integral Personality and all directly observable by a due cultivation of introspection.

Is this prospect not a thing of great challenge? Our excerpts need to be read over and again in order to be duly appreciated. The subject of integration of all the foregoing diverse fields of personality has just come up. This integration involves transformation. Both integration and transformation are capital issues of life, education and psychology.

Education and culture bring about modifications in the natural endowment of man. These modifications are the essence of civilization and of progress in the quality of human living. Now, the question is: Is a real and effective change in the quality of life possible? Freud's answer is that it is not possible. What is possible is a recanalisation of the original energy along new lines, into new fields of life and experience. Sex-energy remains sex-energy but it might take on art or religion as its expression. At the root and in essential character it will remain a sex-craving. A sublimation is all that is possible, but no transformation. Man is born with instincts and he lives by instincts, whatever their external expression may be. Even spiritual experiences of utter selflessness are, to Freud, sublimations or veiled expressions of the self-seeking sex-instinct.

'The integration of personality', which is the high aim of education to-day, can at best be, according to him, an economic balance among the three factors of personality, the Ego, the Id and the Superego. Such economic balance is really an adjustment, a working arrangement, not a transcendence of the conflict inherent in the make-up of the personality. An Integration or Harmonisation is, therefore, not possible.

Even General Psychology – apart from Freud's Psychoanalysis – which accepts integration of personality as a possibility aims at a summation of the varied functions. But Integration really implies an integrating principle. In the West, it was C. G. Jung alone who felt the need of 'a centre' in personality behind the dualities or polarities of the ego. This 'centre' is endowed with an integrative function. But he did not investigate how to activise the centre and achieve integration of personality.

The position of Indian Psychology on this entire subject is very different. Man has an animal inheritance and as such he is much divided and suffers from much inner conflict, but he has also a soul, which is all-conscious, blissful and unitary. Man can, through yogic discipline, dissociate himself from the divided animal nature and identify himself with the holistic divine principle in him, his soul, and live a life of spontaneous joy, unitary will and clarity of perception. Thus integrated living is a complete possibility. And this has been demonstrated again and again in the lives of saints and yogis in varying forms and degrees.

However, Sri Aurobindo's Integral Yoga and Integral Psychology affirm that it is possible to attempt and achieve, under the influence and action of the soul or, as called by him, the Psychic Being, a real change in our ordinary nature, from its animal quality to the divine quality, from a divided to a holistic state, from a state of partial consciousness to that of integral consciousness. This means change to a spiritual quality, for the Spirit is qualitatively different from the Mind. Mind is environment-dependent; Spirit is self-existent. Mind is largely, in Freud's words, "nine-tenths" unconscious, Spirit is entirely conscious. The change contemplated in the nature of man is really a spiritualisation of human nature. This, Sri Aurobindo calls Transformation. This is for human nature and progress *the issue*. And this was essentially *the issue* of Sri Aurobindo's quest in life.

Sri Aurobindo worked out in detail the processes of integration and harmonisation and transformation. He also demonstrated them through the practice of his Integral Yoga.

The preceding excerpts give a broad idea of the subject. The excerpts that follow are on the Chakras or the subtle centres of consciousness affirmed by Yoga and the various branches of psychology handled by Sri Aurobindo. Still later will come those on Psychoanalysis and other subjects. (Editor)

The Chakras – The Yogic Subtle Centres of Consciousness and the Integral Personality

We can easily see how largely man, even though in his being an embodied soul, is in his earthly nature the physical and vital being and how, at first sight at least, his mental activities seem to depend almost entirely on his body and his nervous system. Modern Science and psychology have even held, for a time, this dependence to be in fact an identity; they have tried to establish that there is no such separate entity as mind or soul and that all mental operations are in reality physical functionings. Even otherwise, apart from this untenable hypothesis the dependence is so exaggerated that it has been supposed to be an altogether binding condition, and any such thing as the control of the vital and bodily functionings by the mind or its power to detach itself from them has long been treated as an error, a morbid state of the mind or a hallucination. Therefore the dependence has remained absolute, and Science neither finds nor seeks for the real key of the dependence and therefore can discover for us no secret of release and mastery.

The psycho-physical science of Yoga does not make this mistake. It seeks for the key, finds it and is able to effect the release; for it takes account of the psychical or mental body behind of which the physical is a sort of reproduction in gross form, and is able to discover thereby secrets of the physical body which do not appear to a purely physical enquiry. This mental or psychical body, which the soul keeps even after death, has also a subtle pranic force in it corresponding to its own subtle nature and substance, – for wherever there is life of any kind, there must be the pranic energy and a substance in which it can work, – and this force is directed through a system of numerous channels, called *nāḍī*, – the subtle nervous organisation of the psychic body, – which are gathered up into six (or really seven) centres called technically lotuses or circles, *cakra*, and which rise in an ascending scale to the summit where there is the thousand-petalled lotus from which all the mental and vital energy flows. Each of these lotuses is the centre and the storing-house of its own particular system of psychological powers, energies and operations, each system corresponding to a plane of our psychological existence, – and these flow out and return in the stream of the pranic energies as they course through the *nāḍī*s.

This arrangement of the psychic body is reproduced in the physical with the spinal column as a rod and the ganglionic centres as the Chakras which rise up from the bottom of the column, where the lowest is attached, to the brain and find their summit in the *brahma-randhra* at the top of the skull. These Chakras or lotuses, however, are in physical man closed or only partly open, with the consequence that only such powers and only so much of them are active in him as are sufficient for his ordinary physical life, and so much mind and soul only is at play as will accord with its needs. This is the real reason, looked at from the mechanical point of view, why the embodied soul seems so dependent on the bodily and nervous life, – though the dependence is neither so complete nor so real as it seems. The whole energy of the soul is not at play in the physical body and life, the secret powers of mind are not awake in it, the bodily and nervous energies predominate. But all the while the supreme energy is there, asleep; it is said to be coiled up and slumbering like a snake, – therefore it is called the *kuṇḍalinī* shakti, – in the lowest of the Chakras, in the *mūlādhāra*. When by *prāṇāyāma* the division between the upper and lower *prāṇa* currents in the body is dissolved, this Kundalini is struck and awakened, it uncoils itself and begins to rise upward like a fiery serpent breaking open each lotus as it ascends until the Shakti meets the Purusha in the *brahma-randhra* in a deep Samadhi of union.

Put less symbolically, in more philosophical though perhaps less profound language, this means that the real energy of our being is lying asleep and inconscient in the depths of our vital system, and is awakened by the practice of Pranayama. In its expansion it opens up all the centres of our psychological being in which reside the powers and the consciousness of what would now be called perhaps our subliminal self; therefore as each centre of power and consciousness is opened up, we get access to successive psychological planes and are able to put ourselves in communication with the worlds or cosmic states of being which correspond to them; all the psychic powers abnormal to physical man, but natural to the soul develop in us. Finally, at the summit of the ascension, this arising and expanding energy meets with the superconscient self which sits concealed behind and above our physical and mental existence; this meeting leads to a profound Samadhi of union in which our waking consciousness loses itself in the superconscient. Thus by the thorough and unremitting practice of Pranayama the Hathayogin attains in his own way the psychic and spiritual results which are pursued through more directly psychical and spiritual methods in other Yogas. The one mental aid which he conjoins with it, is the use of the Mantra, sacred syllable, name or mystic formula which is of so much importance in the Indian systems of Yoga and common to them all. This secret of the power of the Mantra, the six Chakras and the Kundalini Shakti is one of the central truths of all that complex psycho-physical science and practice of which the Tantric philosophy claims to give us a rationale and the most complete compendium of methods. All religions and disciplines in India which use largely the psycho-physical method, depend more or less upon it for their practices.[20]

*

On the whole, for an integral Yoga the special methods of Rajayoga and Hathayoga may be useful at times in certain stages of the progress, but are not indispensable. It is true that their principal aims must be included in the integrality of the Yoga; but they can be brought about by other means. For the methods of the integral Yoga must be mainly spiritual, and dependence on physical methods or fixed psychic or psycho-physical processes on a large scale would be the substitution of a lower for a higher action.[21]

*

All these centres are in the middle of the body; they are supposed to be attached to the spinal cord; but in fact all these things are in the subtle body, *sūkṣma deha*, though one has the feeling of their activities as if in the physical body when the consciousness is awake.[22]

*

In the process of our yoga the centres have each a fixed psychological use and general function which base all their special powers and functionings. The *mūlādhāra* governs the physical down to the subconscient; the abdominal centre – *svādhiṣṭhāna* – governs the lower vital; the navel centre – *nābhipadma* or *maṇipūra* – governs the larger vital; the heart centre – *hṛdpadma* or *anāhata* – governs the emotional being; the throat centre – *viśuddha* – governs the expressive and externalising mind; the centre between the eye-brows – *ājñācakra* – governs the dynamic mind, will, vision, mental formation; the thousand-petalled lotus – *sahasradala* – above commands the higher thinking mind, houses the still higher illumined mind and at the highest opens to the intuition through which or else by an overflooding directness the overmind can have with the rest communication or an immediate contact.[22]

*

In the outer surface nature mind, psychic, vital, physical are jumbled together and it needs a strong power of introspection, self-analysis, close observation and disentanglement of the threads of thought, feeling and impulse to find out the composition of our nature and the relation and interaction of these parts upon each other. But when we go inside, we find the sources of all this surface action and there the parts of our being are quite clearly distinct from each other; it is as if we were a group-being, each member of the group with its separate place and function, and all directed by a central being who is sometimes in front above the others, sometimes behind the scenes.[24]

RECAPITULATION AND INTRODUCTION

Integral Psychology means the psychology of the Integral Personality, and Integral Personality means a personality with its conscious, subconscious and superconscious domains integrated into a powerful personality, a personality of wide and large capacities of Knowing, Feeling and Willing. But our ordinary personality is a thing of reactions to environmental stimuli.

When we withdraw from our commitment to these superficial reactions, to this 'me' and to this 'situation', we get behind the finite appearances into a wider background of 'Self' and of 'Environment', a more generalised form of both of them. With that an awareness of the subtler centres of consciousness or the *chakras* tends to emerge and these command the varied functions and capacities of the Integral Personality. And a concentration on the various centres leads to the development of the same progressively. The writer, in his pursuit of Yoga, has since May, '83 in particular wanted to improve the quality of his sleep as also of his dreams. To this end, he wanted to get at the centre at the soles of the feet, which commands specifically the subconscious. This is particularly an identification of Integral Yoga. It took some time to get at the sole-centre in a conscious way. That more or less achieved, concentration there became enjoyable. And the modifications noticed in sleep and the content of the dreams has been all a matter of joy and surprise. And this gives a greater zest to the pursuit for the future. The modifications noticed have been these: A feeling of awareness and some control regarding the night, reposefulness of sleep, less disorderliness in the dream activity and a sense of continuity between the day and the night, waking and sleeping. Previously the nights were gaps, interruptions in the waking life. Dreams showed much disorderliness, pleasure-gratification, less quietude and peacefulness. (July, '84)

These Chakras are common knowledge for Hathayoga, Rajayoga, Tantra and most other forms of Sadhana. The Integral Yoga of Sri Aurobindo and the Mother confirms their existence and functions though it does not insist on the necessity of activating them directly. As integration proceeds by the processes of Integral Yoga, they get into prominence of themselves.

The modern science of psychology cannot afford to limit itself to reactions alone. It has to explore ways and means of discovering these centres of larger functions of personality.

Sri Aurobindo's Integral Yoga involves Integral Psychology of human personality. That is quite comprehensive. On Social Psychology too Sri Aurobindo wrote comprehensively. On education briefly, but the central idea is clear and strong. On illness, physical as well as mental, we have a clear standpoint. The psychology of animals presents new insights. The psychology of plants is a new branch. All these reflect the standpoint of Integral Psychology and admit of investigation and elaboration. (Editor)

Branches of Psychology

The Psychology of Social Development

The primal law and purpose of the individual life is to seek its own self-development. Consciously or half-consciously or with an obscure unconscious groping it strives always and rightly strives at self-formulation, – to find self, to discover within itself the law and power of its own being and to fulfil it. This aim in it is fundamental, right, inevitable because, even after all qualifications have been made and caveats entered, the individual is not merely the ephemeral physical creature, a form of mind and body that aggregates and dissolves, but a being, a living power of the eternal Truth, a self-manifesting spirit. In the same way the primal law and purpose of a society, community or nation is to seek its own self-fulfilment; it strives rightly to find itself, to become aware within itself of the law and power of its own being and to fulfil it as perfectly as possible, to realise all its potentialities, to live its own self-revealing life. The reason is the same; for this too is a being, a living power of the eternal Truth, a self-manifestation of the cosmic Spirit, and it is there to express and fulfil in its own way and to the degree of its capacities the special truth and power and meaning of the cosmic Spirit that is within it. The nation or society, like the individual, has a body, an organic life, a moral and aesthetic temperament, a developing mind and a soul behind all these signs and powers for the sake of which they exist. One may see even that, like the individual, it essentially is a soul rather than has one; it is a group-soul that, once having attained to a separate distinctness, must become more and more self-conscious and find itself more and more fully as it develops its corporate action and mentality and its organic self-expressive life.[25]

*

A change of this kind, the change from the mental and vital to the spiritual order of life, must necessarily be accomplished in the individual and in a great number of individuals before it can lay an effective hold upon the community. The Spirit in humanity discovers, develops, builds into form in the individual man; it is through the progressive and formative individual that it offers the discovery and the chance of new self-creation to the mind of the race. For the communal mind holds things subconsciently at first or, if consciously, then in a confused chaotic manner: it is only through the individual mind that the mass can arrive at a clear knowledge and creation of the thing it held in its subconscient self. Thinkers, historians, sociologists who belittle the individual and would like to lose him in the mass or think of him chiefly as a cell, an atom, have got hold only of the obscurer side of the truth of Nature's workings in humanity. It is because man is not like the material formations of Nature or like the animal, because she intends in him a more and more conscious evolution, that individuality is so much developed in him and so absolutely important and indispensable. No doubt what comes out in the individual and afterwards moves the mass, must have been there already in the universal Mind and the individual is only an instrument for its manifestation, discovery, development; but he is an indispensable instrument and an instrument not merely of subconscient Nature, not merely of an instinctive urge that moves the mass, but more directly of the Spirit of whom that Nature is itself the instrument and the matrix of his creations. All great changes therefore find their first clear and effective power and their direct shaping force in the mind and spirit of an individual or of a limited number of individuals. The mass follows, but unfortunately in a very imperfect and confused fashion which often or even usually ends in the failure or distortion of the thing created. If it were not so, mankind could have advanced on its way with a victorious rapidity instead of with the lumbering hesitations and soon exhausted rushes that seem to be all of which it has yet been capable.[26]

Child Psychology and Educational Psychology

The discovery that education must be a bringing out of the child's own intellectual and moral capacities to their highest possible value and must be based on the psychology of the child-nature was a step forward towards a more healthy because a more subjective system; but it still fell short because it regarded the child as an object to be handled and moulded by the teacher, to be educated. But at least there was a glimmering of the realisation that each human being is a self-developing soul and that the business of both parent and teacher is to enable and to help the child to educate himself, to develop his own intellectual, moral, aesthetic and practical capacities and to grow freely as an organic being, not to be kneaded and pressured into form like an inert plastic material. It is not yet realised what this soul is or that the true secret, whether with child or man, is to help him to find his deeper self, the real psychic entity within. That, if we ever give it a chance to come forward, and still more if we call it into the foreground as "the leader of the march set in our front," will itself take up most of the business of education out of our hands and develop the capacity of the psychological being towards a realisation of its potentialities of which our present mechanical view of life and man and external routine methods of dealing with them prevents us from having any experience or forming any conception. These new educational methods are on the straight way to this truer dealing. The closer touch attempted with the psychical entity behind the vital and physical mentality and an increasing reliance on its possibilities must lead to the ultimate discovery that man is inwardly a soul and a conscious power of the Divine and that the evocation of this real man within is the right object of education and indeed of all human life if it would find and live according to the hidden Truth and deepest law of its own being.[27]

Psychology of the Animals and the Plants

... Animals are predominantly the vital creation on earth – the mind in them also is a vital mind – they act according to the push of the forces and have a vital but not a mental will.

*

Even the animal is more in touch with a certain harmony in

things than man. Man's only superiority is a more complex consciousness and capacity (but terribly perverted and twisted by misuse of Mind) and the ability (not much used as yet) of reaching towards higher things.

*

Human life and mind are neither in tune with Nature like the animals nor with Spirit – it is disturbed, incoherent, conflicting with itself, without harmony and balance. We can then regard it as diseased, if not itself a disease.

*

The plants are very psychic, but they can express it only by silence and beauty.

*

It is true that the plant world – even the animals if one takes them the right way – can be much better than human beings. It is the mental distortion that makes men worse.

*

... it is a more simple and honest consciousness – that of the animal. Of course it expects something, but even if it does not get, the affection remains. Many animals, even if ill-treated, do not lose their love which means remarkable psychic development in the vital.

*

The emotional being of animals is often much more psychic than that of men who can be very insensitive. There were recently pictures of the tame tigress kept by a family and afterwards given by them to a Zoo. The look of sorrow on the face of the tigress in her cage at once gentle and tragically poignant is so intense as to be heart-breaking.

*

Most animals do not usually attack unless they are menaced or frightened or somehow made angry – and they can feel the atmosphere of people.

*

...to watch the animals with the right perception of their consciousness helps to get out of the human mental limitations and see the Cosmic Consciousness on earth individualising itself in all forms – plant, animal, man and growing towards what is beyond man.[28]

The Science and Art of Healing

The human body has always been in the habit of answering to whatever forces chose to lay hands on it and illness is the price it pays for its inertia and ignorance. It has to learn to answer to the one Force alone, but that is not easy for it to learn....

All illnesses pass through the nervous or vital-physical sheath of the subtle consciousness and subtle body before they enter the physical. If one is conscious of the subtle body or with the subtle consciousness, one can stop an illness on its way and prevent it from entering the physical body. But it may have come without one's noticing, or when one is asleep or through the subconscient, or in a sudden rush when one is off one's guard; then there is nothing to do but to fight it out from a hold already gained on the body. Self-defence by these inner means may become so strong that the body becomes practically immune as many yogis are. Still this "practically" does not mean "absolutely". The absolute immunity can only come with the supramental change. For below the supramental it is the result of an action of a Force among many forces and can be disturbed by a disruption of the equilibrium established – in the supramental it is a law of the nature; in a supramentalised body immunity from illness would be automatic, inherent in its new nature.[29]

*

...illnesses try to come from one person to another – they attack, by a suggestion... the nervous being and try to come in.

Even if the illness is not contagious, this often happens, but it comes more easily in contagious illnesses. The suggestion or touch has to be thrown off at once.

There is a sort of protection round the body which we call the nervous envelope – if this remains strong and refuses entrance to the illness force, then one can remain well even in the midst of plague or other epidemics – if the envelope is pierced or weak, then the illness can come in.[30]

*

Your theory of illness is rather a perilous creed – for illness is a thing to be eliminated, not accepted or enjoyed. There is something in the being that enjoys illness, it is possible even to turn the pains of illness like any other pain into a form of pleasure; for pain and pleasure are both of them degradations of an original Ananda and can be reduced into the terms of each other or else sublimated into their original principle of Ananda. It is true also that one must be able to bear illness with calm, equanimity, endurance, even recognition of it, since it has come, as something that had to be passed through in the course of experience. But to accept and enjoy it means to help it to last and that will not do; for illness is a deformation of the physical nature just as lust, anger, jealousy, etc., are deformations of the vital nature and error and prejudice and indulgence of falsehood are deformation of the mental nature. All these things have to be eliminated and rejection is the first condition of their disappearance while acceptance has a contrary effect altogether.[31]

*

Illness marks some imperfection or weakness or else opening to adverse touches in the physical nature and is often connected also with some obscurity or disharmony in the lower vital or the physical mind or elsewhere.[32]

*

It is very good if one can get rid of illness entirely by faith and yoga-power or the influx of the Divine Force. But very often this is not altogether possible, because the whole nature is not open or able to respond to the Force. The mind may have faith and respond, but the lower vital and the body may not follow. Or, if the mind and vital are ready, the body may not respond, or may respond only partially, because it has the habit of replying to the forces which produce a particular illness, and habit is a very obstinate force in the material part of the nature. In such cases the use of the physical means can be resorted to, – not as the main means, but as a help or material support to the action of the Force. Not strong and violent remedies, but those that are beneficial without disturbing the body.[33]

*

The way in which the pains went shows you how to deal with the whole nature, – for it is the same with the mental and vital as with the physical causes of ill-ease and disturbance. To remain quiet within, to hold on to the faith and experience that to be quiet and open and let the Force work is the one way. Naturally, to be wholly conscious is not possible yet, but to feel it, to open, to let it work, to observe its result, that is the first thing. It is the beginning of consciousness and the way to complete consciousness.[34]

The Psychical Phenomena

The phenomena of this vital consciousness and sense, this direct sensation and perception of and response to the play of subtler forces than the physical, are often included without distinction under the head of psychical phenomena.[35]

*

...There are, however, two different kinds of action of these inner ranges of the consciousness. The first is a more outer and confused activity of the awakening subliminal mind and life which is clogged with and subject to the grosser desires and illusions of the mind and vital being and vitiated in spite of its wider range of experience and power and capacities by an enormous mass of error and deformations of the will and knowledge, full of false suggestions and images, false and distorted intuitions and inspirations and impulses, the latter often even depraved and perverse, and vitiated too by the interference of the physical mind and its obscurities. This is an inferior activity to which clairvoyants, psychists, spiritists, occultists, seekers of powers and siddhis are very liable and to which all the warnings against the dangers and errors of this kind of seeking are more especially applicable.[36]

*

The range of the psychic consciousness and its experiences is almost illimitable and the variety and complexity of its phenomena almost infinite. Only some of the broad lines and main features can be noted here. The first and most prominent is the activity of the psychic senses of which the sight is the most developed ordinarily and the first to manifest itself with any largeness when the veil of the absorption in the surface consciousness which prevents the inner vision is broken. But all the physical senses have their corresponding powers in the psychical being, there is a psychical hearing, touch, smell, taste: indeed the physical senses are themselves in reality only a projection of the inner sense into a limited and externalised operation in and through and upon the phenomena of gross matter. The psychical sight receives characteristically the images that are formed in the subtle matter of the mental or psychical ether, *cidākāśa*. These may be transcriptions there or impresses of physical things, persons, scenes, happenings, whatever is, was or will be or may be in the physical universe. These images are very variously seen and under all kinds of conditions; in Samadhi or in the waking state, and in the latter with the bodily eyes closed or open, projected on or into a physical object or medium or seen as if materialised in the physical atmosphere or only in a psychical ether revealing itself through this grosser physical atmosphere; seen through the physical eyes themselves as a secondary instrument and as if under the conditions of the physical vision or by the psychical vision alone and independently of the relations of our ordinary sight to space. The real agent is always the psychical sight and the power indicates that the consciousness is more or less awake, intermittently or normally and more or less perfectly, in the psychical body. It is possible to see in this way the transcriptions or impressions of things at any distance beyond the range of the physical vision or the images of the past or the future.

Besides these transcriptions or impresses the psychical vision receives thought images and other forms created by constant activity of consciousness in ourselves or in other human beings, and these may be according to the character of the activity images of truth or falsehood or else mixed things, partly true, partly false, and may be too either mere shells and representations or images inspired with a temporary life and consciousness and, it may be, carrying in them in one way or another some kind of beneficent or maleficent action or some willed or unwilled effectiveness on our mind or vital being or through them even on the body. These transcriptions, impresses, thought images, life images, projections of the consciousness may also be representations or creations not of the physical world, but of vital, psychic or mental worlds beyond us, seen in our own minds or projected from other than human beings. And as there is this psychical vision of which some of the more external and ordinary manifestations are well enough known by the name of clairvoyance, so there is a psychical hearing and psychical touch, taste, smell, – clairaudience, clairsentience are the more external manifestations, – with precisely the same range each in its own kind, the same fields and manner and conditions and varieties of their phenomena.[37]

*

The awakening of the psychical consciousness liberates in us the direct use of the mind as a sixth sense, and this power may be made constant and normal. The physical consciousness can only communicate with the minds of others or know the happenings of the world around us through external means and signs and indications, and it has beyond this limited action only a vague and haphazard use of the mind's more direct capacities, a poor range of occasional presentiments, intuitions and messages. Our minds are indeed constantly acting and acted upon by the minds of others through hidden currents of which we are not aware, but we have no knowledge or control of these agencies. The psychical consciousness, as it develops, makes us aware of the great mass of thoughts, feelings, suggestions, wills, impacts, influences of all kinds that we are receiving from others or sending to others or imbibing from and throwing into the general mind atmosphere around us. As it evolves in power, precision and clearness, we are able to trace these to their source or feel immediately their origin and transit to us and direct consciously and with an intelligent will our own messages. It becomes possible to be aware, more or less accurately and discerningly, of the activities of mind, whether near to us physically or at a distance, to understand, feel or identify ourselves with their temperament, character, thoughts, feelings, reactions, whether by a psychic sense or a direct mental perception or by a very sensible and often intensely concrete reception of them into our mind or on its recording surface. At the same time we can consciously make at least the inner selves and, if they are sufficiently sensitive, the surface minds of others aware of our own inner mental or psychic self and plastic to its thoughts, suggestions, influences or even cast it or its active image in influence into their subjective, even into their vital and physical being to work there as a helping or moulding or dominating power and presence.[38]

Spiritism

It is quite possible for the dead or rather the departed – for they are not dead – who are still in regions near the earth to have communication with the living; sometimes it happens automatically, sometimes by an effort at communication on one side of the curtain or the other. There is no impossibility of such communication by the means used by the spiritists; usually, however, genuine communications or a contact can only be with those who are yet in a world which is a sort of idealised replica of the earth-consciousness and in which the same personality, ideas, memories persist that the person had here. But all that pretends to be communications with departed souls is not genuine, especially when it is done through a paid professional medium. There is there an enormous amount of mixture of a very undesirable kind – for apart from the great mass of unconscious suggestions from the sitters or the contributions of the medium's subliminal consciousness, one gets into contact with a world of beings which is of a very deceptive or self-deceptive illusory nature. Many of these come and claim to be the departed souls of relatives, acquaintances, well-known men, famous personalities, etc. There are also beings who pick up the discarded feelings and memories of the dead and masquerade with them. There are a great number of beings who come to such séances only to play with the consciousness of men or exercise their powers through this contact with the earth and who dope the mediums and sitters with their falsehoods, tricks and illusions. (I am supposing, of course, the case of mediums who are not themselves tricksters.) A contact with such a plane of spirits can be harmful (most mediums become nervously or morally unbalanced) and spiritually dangerous. Of course, all pretended communications with the famous dead of long past times are in their very nature deceptive and most of those with the recent ones also – that is evident from the character of these communications. Through conscientious mediums one may get sound results (in the matter of the dead), but even these are very ignorant of the nature of the forces they are handling and have no discrimination which can guard them against trickery from the other side of the veil. Very little genuine knowledge of the nature of the after-life can be gathered from the séances; a true knowledge is more often gained by the experience of individuals who make serious contact or are able in one way or another to cross the border.[39]

INTRODUCTION

Integral Psychology and other Psychological Systems

'*Manaḥ*' (Manas), '*Buddhi*', '*Citta*', '*Ahaṅkāra*' are the normal basic functions of the outer personality according to the traditional Indian Psychology. Manas represents perceptual activity, Buddhi intellectual, Chitta the general quality of consciousness and Ahankara the egoistic quality of the ordinary outer personality.

This is one *Tattva-vibhāga* or classification of primary facts.

The Upanishads affirmed five constituent '*Koṣas*' or Sheaths of the personality, the '*Annamaya*', the '*Prāṇamaya*', the '*Manomaya*', the '*Vijñānamaya*' and the '*Ānandamaya*', that is, the physical or material sheath, the vital or biological, the mental (the perceptual and intellectual in its analytic-discursive form) the superior mental or gnostic (its synthetic-intuitive form) and the *zone* or *plane* of bliss and delight. These Koshas cover the integral personality. The outer personality is represented here by the first three Koshas, the planes of physical, vital and mental life.

Sri Aurobindo's Integral Psychology affirms yet other parts and planes of Integral personality. They are the Body, the Life, the Mind, the Psychic Being and the Supermind. Alternatively, it also talks of the outer personality (which consists of Body, Life and Mind), the subliminal personality (which consists of Body, Life and Mind in their general form, while the outer personality represents them in their individual particular form), then the inmost personality or the Psychic Being (which is the true evolving spiritual principle in man) and, lastly, the supramental personality (which covers the *ranges* of consciousness above the Mind). In yet another form, Integral Personality is said to consist of the conscious, the subliminal, the subconscious and the superconscious.

It must, however, be remembered that the Integral Personality, as a whole, is a dynamic fact and its so-called parts are interpenetrating and they give rise to many intermediate qualities like the colours of the rainbow, the main prominent ones and the indefinite intermediate ones. Further, in each part there are internal distinctions. In the physical, e.g., the bones are more physical and less vital, whereas nerves are less physical and more vital. In the field of the vital again, sex, as the basic animal propensity, is the lower vital, whereas ambition as a characteristically human urge would be the higher vital.

The integral human personality is a highly complex fact, a microcosm, a true miniature picture of the macrocosm, the universe. We have to be prepared to recognise and appreciate all the distinctions of parts if we are to understand it well enough. Man is truly the key to the understanding of all that he has created, his sciences, his arts and crafts, his civilisations and cultures. But we must understand him in his wholeness, integrally, then alone can we appreciate and evaluate his varied creations and do so duly, rightly.

Now let us apply this standard to Psycho-analysis. Freud's field of work and investigation was the neurotic patient, one suffering from a mental disorder. Through long investigation and experience of such cases, he came to the conclusion that a repression of a sex-desire was almost always involved in them. From that he generalised that all human life and its varied activities are workings of sex. He extended the meaning of sex so as to include the thumb-sucking of the child and much other behaviour as infantile sexuality. He also stressed the avoidance of repression and suppression, as that leads to mental upsetting.

Sex, repression and subconsciousness then become the key-terms of Psycho-analysis. Now to what part of the Integral Personality do these really belong? Is it not to the vital or the life-principle in us? And there too the lower vital, the basic animal part is involved. In a social milieu where the values of this part are popular and dominant, no doubt this part will tend to prevail over the rest of the personality. But surely it is not the whole of the personality and when mind and reason are strongly cultivated, the picture would change and Freud himself admitted this as a possibility. And, in yoga, when the inmost psychic personality is cultivated, an effective liberation from sex becomes a vivid experience.

What we need to discover and recognise is the precise sphere and the conditions under which Psycho-analysis has a validity. That is what our excerpts broadly indicate.

Behaviourism is another school in contemporary psychology which stresses the body part of the Integral Personality more or less exclusively. Sometimes it is said that all is behaviour and that consciousness does not exist. Thinking, it is said, is sub-vocal speaking.

Gestaltism is yet another school with a capital idea of wholeness. But the precise sphere of validity is really the issue.

The Integral Personality, if duly appreciated with a large and free openness of mind, can offer a reconciliation of the foregoing and other conflicting schools of contemporary psychology and create possibilities of a fuller understanding of man. (Editor)

The Old Indian System

We have first, a body supported by the physical life-force, the physical *prāṇa* which courses through the whole nervous system and gives its stamp to our corporeal action, so that all is of the character of the action of a living and not an inert mechanical body. Prana and physicality together make the gross body, *sthūla śarīra*. This is only the outer instrument, the nervous force of life acting in the form of body with its gross physical organs. Then there is the inner instrument, *antaḥkaraṇa*, the conscious mentality. This inner instrument is divided by the old system into four powers: *citta* or basic mental consciousness; *manas*, the sense mind; *buddhi*, the intelligence; *ahaṅkāra*, the ego-idea. The classification may serve as a starting-point, though for a greater practicality we have to make certain farther distinctions. This mentality is pervaded by the life-force, which becomes here an instrument for psychic consciousness of life and psychic action on life. Every fibre of the sense mind and basic consciousness is shot through with the action of this psychic Prana, it is a nervous or vital and physical mentality. Even the Buddhi and ego are overpowered by it, although they have the capacity of raising the mind beyond subjection to this vital, nervous and physical psychology. This combination creates in us the sensational desire-soul which is the chief obstacle to a higher human as well as to the still greater divine perfection. Finally, above our present conscious mentality is a secret supermind which is the proper means and native seat of that perfection.[40]

*

The Chitta and the psychic part are not in the least the same. Chitta is a term in a quite different category in which are coordinated and put into their place the main functionings of our external consciousness, and to know if we need not go behind our surface or external nature.

'Category' means here another class of psychological factors, *tattva vibhāga*. The psychic belongs to one class – supermind, mind, life, psychic, physical – and covers both the inner and the outer nature. Chitta belongs to quite another class or category – buddhi, manas, chitta, prana, etc. – which is the classification made by ordinary Indian psychology; it covers only the psychology of the external being. In this category it is the main functions of our external consciousness only that are co-ordinated and put in their place by the Indian thinkers; chitta is one of these main functions of the external consciousness and, therefore, to know it we need not go behind the external nature.[41]

Psycho-analysis of Freud and the Way of Indulgence

The psycho-analysis of Freud is the last thing that one should associate with yoga. It takes up a certain part, the darkest, the most perilous, the unhealthiest part of the nature, the lower vital subconscious layer, isolates some of its most morbid phenomena and attributes to it and them an action out of all proportion to its true role in the nature. Modern psychology is an infant science, at once rash, fumbling and crude. As in all infant sciences, the universal habit of the human mind – to take a partial or local truth, generalise it unduly and try to explain a whole field of Nature in its narrow terms – runs riot here. Moreover, the exaggeration of the importance of suppressed sexual complexes is a dangerous falsehood and it can have a nasty influence and tend to make the mind and vital more and not less fundamentally impure than before.

It is true that the subliminal in man is the largest part of his nature and has in it the secret of the unseen dynamisms which explains his surface activities. But the lower vital subconscious, which is all that this psycho-analysis of Freud seems to know, – and even of that it knows only a few ill-lit corners, – is no more than a restricted and very inferior portion of the subliminal whole. The subliminal self stands behind and supports the whole superficial man; it has in it a larger and more efficient mind behind the surface mind, a larger and more powerful vital behind the surface vital, a subtler and freer physical consciousness behind the surface bodily existence. And above them it opens to higher superconscient as well as below them to lower subconscient ranges. If one wishes to purify and transform the nature, it is the power of these higher ranges to which one must open and raise to them and change by them both the subliminal and the surface being. Even this should be done with care, not prematurely or rashly, following a higher guidance, keeping always the right attitude; for otherwise the force that is drawn down may be too strong for an obscure and weak frame of nature. But to begin by opening up the lower subconscious, risking to raise up all that is foul or obscure in it, is to go out of one's way to invite trouble. First, one should make the higher mind and vital strong and firm and full of light and peace from above; afterwards one can open up or even dive into the subconscious with more safety and some chance of a rapid and successful change.[42]

*

The system of getting rid of things by *anubhava* can also be a dangerous one; for in this way one can easily become more entangled instead of arriving at freedom. This method has behind it two well-known psychological motives. One, the motive of purposeful exhaustion, is valid only in some cases, especially when some natural tendency has too strong a hold or too strong a drive in it to be got rid of by *vicāra* or by the process of rejection and the substitution of the true movement in its place; when that happens in excess, the sadhak has sometimes even to go back to the ordinary action of the ordinary life, get the true experience of it with a new mind and will behind and then return to the spiritual life with the obstacle eliminated or else ready for elimination. But this method of purposive indulgence is always dangerous, though sometimes inevitable. It succeeds only when there is a very strong will in the being towards realisation; for then indulgence brings a strong dissatisfaction and reaction, *vairāgya*, and the will towards perfection can be carried down into the recalcitrant part of the nature.

The other motive for *anubhava* is of a more general applicability; for in order to reject anything from the being one has first to become conscious of it, to have the clear inner experience of its action and to discover its actual place in the workings of the nature. One can then work upon it to eliminate it, if it is an entirely wrong movement, or to transform it if it is only the degradation of a higher and true movement. It is this or something like it that is attempted crudely and improperly with a rudimentary and insufficient knowledge in the system of psycho-analysis. The process of raising up the lower movements into the full light of consciousness in order to know and deal with them is inevitable; for there can be no complete change without it. But it can truly succeed only when a higher light and force are sufficiently at work to overcome, sooner or later, the force of the tendency that is held up for change. Many, under the pretext of *anubhava*, not only raise up the adverse movement, but support it with their consent instead of rejecting it, find justifications for continuing or repeating it and so go on playing with it, indulging its return, eternising it; afterwards when they want to get rid of it, it has got such a hold that they find themselves helpless in its clutch and only a terrible struggle or an intervention of divine grace can liberate them. Some do this out of a vital twist or perversity, others out of sheer ignorance; but in yoga as in life, ignorance is not accepted by Nature as a justifying excuse. This danger is there in all improper dealings with the ignorant parts of the nature; but none is more ignorant, more perilous, more unreasoning and obstinate in recurrence than the lower vital subconscious and its movements. To raise it up prematurely or improperly for *anubhava* is to risk suffusing the conscious parts also with its dark and dirty stuff and thus poisoning the whole vital and even the mental nature. Always therefore one should begin by a positive, not a negative experience, by bringing down something of the divine nature, calm, light, equanimity, purity, divine strength into the parts of the conscious being that have to be changed; only when that has been sufficiently done and there is a firm positive basis, is it safe to raise up the concealed subconscious adverse elements in order to destroy and eliminate them by the strength of the divine calm, light, force and knowledge. Even so, there will be enough of the lower stuff rising up of itself to give you as much of the *anubhava* as you will need for getting rid of the obstacles; but then they can be dealt with with much less danger and under a higher internal guidance.[43]

Psycho-analysis and Spiritual Experience

I find it difficult to take these psycho-analysts at all seriously when they try to scrutinise spiritual experience by the flicker of their torch-lights, – yet perhaps one ought to, for half-knowledge is a powerful thing and can be a great obstacle to the coming in front of the true Truth. This new psychology looks to me very much like children learning some summary and not very adequate alphabet, exulting in putting their a-b-c-d of the subconscient and the mysterious underground super-ego together and imagining that their first book of obscure beginnings (c-a-t cat, t-r-e-e tree) is the very heart of the real knowledge. They look from down up and explain the higher lights by the lower obscurities; but the foundation of these things is above and not below, *upari budhna eṣām*. The superconscient, not the subconscient, is the true foundation of things. The significance of the lotus is not to be found by analysing the secrets of the mud from which it grows here, its secret is to be found in the heavenly archetype of the lotus that blooms for ever in the Light above. The self-chosen field of these psychologists is besides poor, dark and limited; you must know the whole before you can know the part and the highest before you can truly understand the lowest. That is the promise of the greater psychology awaiting its hour before which these poor gropings will disappear and come to nothing.[44]

INTRODUCTION

Varied Activities of Normal Personality

What are the varied activities or processes of normal human personality in its dealings with the environment and with itself? They are sensation, perception, action, emotion, instinct, habit, memory, thinking, imagination, sentiment, voluntary action, self, character, temperament, etc.

The natural science of psychology has studied all these empirically in an extensive way and collected a large amount of data, which it has carefully classified. But the empirical approach often gets lost in the superficial multiplicity and detail and later has difficulty in finding the coherence and unity of things. This is a recurring experience in psychology at this time. About the reactions of personality we know a good deal but of personality itself next to nothing. This is due to not knowing the essential unity of the subject.

For yoga and yogic psychology, the first interest is the unity in personality and the essential truth of each activity in the right perspective. Here we do not have a plethora of empirical detail but a clear grip over the whole and a confidence to deal with personality and its problems. As an example we might mention the familiar idea of the three modes of nature and of personality, *viz.*, Tamas, Rajas, Sattwa, the principles of inertia, activity and balance or harmony. If one learns to recognise, appreciate and manipulate these, one more easily gets to control and direct one's life in all its innumerable reactions. The empirical data, because of its vast heap of facts, fails to give convenient keys to handle things. Further, the yogic psychology has a constant eye on potential capacity, the greater possibilities of activity. And that helps in the due appreciation of present functioning.

The yogic psychology and the scientific psychology are evidently mutually useful, either supplies to the other what the other needs.

Here we have brief excerpts representing the varied activities of the normal personality. Their essential strength consists in giving a deeper unifying truth of the matter in each case and all together give a fine grip over personality as a whole. We mentioned above the conventional terms of Indian psychology. The terms here are fewer but these cover the entire phenomena. If one tries to act on these terms and gain some experience of the working of personality, one would very likely get a clear idea of what personality is and how it should be managed.

Let us now illustrate the above. The first three excerpts bear upon mind and sensation. The truth they affirm is that mind in its own right is the sensing instrument. Its constant dependence on the sense-organs creates in it a serious limitation. If it could withdraw from this dependence it could see, hear, etc. by itself and more widely. This would mean a new relationship between body and mind and a rational basis for telepathy, clairaudience and other paranormal powers. We may recall McDougall, a distinguished recent psychologist, who observed that if telepathy came to be proved, psychology would have to be re-written. Evidently a re-written psychology will get much nearer to yogic psychology.

Another illustration. We have here two excerpts on emotions. Emotion is said to depend upon a pre-existing conation, *i.e.*, it has a parasitical character. Our excerpts too affirm that a desire is involved in the emotional reactions. But they affirm a deeper emotion of joy and love too, which is the feeling of the Psychic Being, not the superficial mental nature, and which is self-existent and non-parasitical. This is new to our psychology of emotion and opens up a possibility of emotional life beyond the ordinary divided and opposed sets of emotions.

Affection and conation are closely allied and they constitute the dynamic fact of personality. We have here two excerpts on Desire. Desire represents our entire conative side as emotion does the affective. Now Desires are many and they go on multiplying themselves. They arise out of a sense of want. But there is also a deeper will calm and steady, qualitatively different from Desire. This again is a new fact of immense value to personality and its greater possibilities.

We have also here an excerpt on the Ego or Separative I-ness. The science of psychology regards this as final to human self-hood. Here it is stated that it is transitional, a phase in the growth and evolution of personality. Is it not a challenging statement of the deepest interest for psychological inquiry and investigation?

Memory too is taken in its conscious form as we ordinarily know it, but also in its subconscious form in the individual as also in the race. Memory thus becomes a most important base for all functions of consciousness. Judgement and logical reason organise the material accumulated by memory into knowledge. Imagination aids by opening up new possibility. But the ordinary working of reasoning is slow and laborious and lacks directness. These faculties must lead on to intuition and its dependable certitudes. This subject is already actively under investigation in some scientific quarters.

The last four excerpts show the limitations of mind and the expression of the Spirit in consciousness. They greatly enlarge the scope of psychology. The issues raised by the excerpts of this section as a whole demand much reflection. (Editor)

Mind and the Sense-organs

Mind is capable of a sight that is independent of the physical eye, a hearing that is independent of the physical ear, and so with the action of all the other senses. It is capable too of an awareness, operating by what appears to us as mental impressions, of things not conveyed or even suggested by the agency of the physical organs, – and opening to relations, happenings, forms even and the action of forces to which the physical organs could not have borne evidence. Then, becoming aware of these rarer powers, we speak of the mind as a sixth sense; but in fact it is the only true sense organ and the rest are no more than its outer conveniences and secondary instruments, although by its dependence on them they have become its limitations and its too imperative and exclusive conveyors.[45]

The Sense-mind

Manas, the sense mind, depends in our ordinary consciousness on the physical organs of receptive sense for knowledge and on the organs of the body for action directed towards the objects of sense. The superficial and outward action of the senses is physical and nervous in its character, and they may easily be thought to be merely results of nerve-action; they are sometimes called in the old books pranas, nervous or life activities. But still the essential thing in them is not the nervous excitation, but the consciousness, the action of the chitta, which makes use of the organ and of the nervous impact of which it is the channel. Manas, sense-mind, is the activity, emerging from the basic consciousness, which makes up the whole essentiality of what we call sense. Sight, hearing, taste, smell, touch are really properties of the mind, not of the body; but the physical mind which we ordinarily use, limits itself to a translation into sense of so much of the outer impacts as it receives through the nervous system and the physical organs. But the inner Manas has also a subtle sight, hearing, power of contact of its own which is not dependent on the physical organs. And it has, moreover, a power not only of direct communication of mind with object, – leading even at a high pitch of action to a sense of the contents of an object within or beyond the physical range, – but direct communication also of mind with mind. Mind is able too to alter, modify, inhibit the incidence, values, intensities of sense impacts. These powers of the mind we do not ordinarily use or develop; they remain subliminal and emerge sometimes in an irregular and fitful action, more readily in some minds than in others, or come to the surface in abnormal states of the being. They are the basis of clairvoyance, clairaudience, transference of thought and impulse, telepathy, most of the more ordinary kinds of occult powers, – so called, though these are better described less mystically as powers of the now subliminal action of the Manas. The phenomena of hypnotism and many others depend upon the action of this subliminal sense-mind; not that it alone constitutes all the elements of the phenomena, but it is the first supporting means of intercourse, communication and response, though much of the actual operation belongs to an inner Buddhi. Mind physical, mind supraphysical, – we have and can use this double sense mentality.[46]

Abnormal States

The embodied mind in us is ordinarily aware only through the physical organs and only of their objects and of subjective experiences which seem to start from the physical experience and to take them alone, however remotely, for their foundation and mould of construction. All the rest, all that is not consistent with or part of or verified by the physical data, seems to it rather imagination than reality and it is only in abnormal states that it opens to other kinds of conscious experience. But in fact there are immense ranges behind of which we could be aware if we opened the doors of our inner being. These ranges are there already in action and known to a subliminal self in us, and much of our surface consciousness is directly projected from them and without our knowing it influences our subjective experience of things. There is a range of independent vital or *prāṇic* experiences behind, subliminal to and other than the surface action of the vitalised physical consciousness. And when this opens itself or acts in any way, there are made manifest to the waking mind the phenomena of a vital consciousness, a vital intuition, a vital sense not dependent on the body and its instruments, although it may use them as a secondary medium and a recorder. It is possible to open completely this range and, when we do so, we find that its operation is that of the conscious life force individualised in us contacting the universal life force and its operations in things, happenings and persons. The mind becomes aware of the life consciousness in all things, responds to it through our life consciousness with an immediate directness not limited by the ordinary communication through the body and its organs, records its intuitions, becomes capable of experiencing existence as a translation of the universal Life or Prana. The field of which the vital consciousness and the vital sense are primarily aware is not that of forms but, directly, that of forces: its world is a world of the play of energies, and form and event are sensed only secondarily as a result and embodiment of the energies. The mind working through the physical senses can only construct a view and knowledge of this nature as an idea in the intelligence, but it cannot go beyond the physical translation of the energies, and it has therefore no real or direct experience of the true nature of life, no actual realisation of the life force and the life spirit. It is by opening this other level or depth of experience within and by admission to the vital consciousness and vital sense that the mind can get the true and direct experience. Still, even then, so long as it is on the mental level, the experience is limited by the vital terms and their mental renderings and there is an obscurity even in this greatened sense and knowledge.[47]

Ordinary Perception and Action

Chitta, the basic consciousness, is largely subconscient; it has, open and hidden, two kinds of action, one passive or receptive, the other active or reactive and formative. As a passive power it receives all impacts, even those of which the mind is unaware or to which it is inattentive, and it stores them in an immense reserve or passive subconscient memory on which the mind as an active memory can draw. But ordinarily the mind draws only what it had observed and understood at the time, – more easily what it had observed well and understood carefully, less easily what it had observed carelessly or ill understood; at the same time there is a power in consciousness to send up to the active mind for use what that mind had not at all observed or attended to or even consciously experienced. This power only acts observably in abnormal conditions, when some part of the subconscious Chitta comes as it were to the surface or when the subliminal being in us appears on the threshold and for a time plays some part in the outer chamber of mentality where the direct intercourse and commerce with the external world takes place and our inner dealings with ourselves develop on the surface. This action of memory is so fundamental to the entire mental action that it is sometimes said, memory is the man. Even in the submental action of the body and life, which is full of this subconscient Chitta, though not under the control of the conscious mind, there is a vital and physical memory. The vital and physical habits are largely formed by this submental memory. For this reason they can be changed to an indefinite extent by a more powerful action of conscious mind and will, when that can be developed and can find means to communicate to the subconscient Chitta the will of the spirit for a new law of vital and physical action. Even, the whole constitution of our life and body may be described as a bundle of habits formed by the past evolution in Nature and held together by the persistent memory of this secret consciousness. For Chitta, the primary stuff of consciousness, is like Prana and body universal in Nature, but is subconscient and mechanical in nature of Matter.[48]

Emotional Reactions

But in fact all action of the mind or inner instrument arises out of this chitta or basic consciousness, partly conscient, partly subconscient or subliminal to our active mentality. When it is struck by the world's impacts from outside or urged by the reflective powers of the subjective inner being, it throws up certain habitual activities, the mould of which has been determined by our evolution. One of these forms of activity is the emotional mind, – the heart, as we may call it for the sake of a convenient brevity. Our emotions are the waves of reaction and response which rise up from the basic consciousness, *cittavṛtti*. Their action too is largely regulated by habit and an emotive memory. They are not imperative, not laws of Necessity; there is no really binding law of our emotional being to which we must submit without remedy; we are not obliged to give responses of grief to certain impacts upon the mind, responses of anger to others, to yet others responses of hatred or dislike, to others responses of liking or love. All these things are only habits of our affective mentality; they can be changed by the conscious will of the spirit; they can be inhibited; we may even rise entirely above all subjection to grief, anger, hatred, the duality of liking and disliking. We are subject to these things only so long as we persist in subjection to the mechanical action of the chitta in the emotive mentality, a thing difficult to get rid of because of the power of past habit and especially the importunate insistence of the vital part of the mentality, the nervous life-mind or psychic prana. This nature of the emotive mind as a reaction of chitta with a certain close dependence upon the nervous life-sensations and responses of the psychic prana is so characteristic that in some languages it is called chitta and prana, the heart, the life soul; it is indeed the most directly agitating and powerfully insistent action of the desire-soul which the immixture of vital desire and responsive consciousness has created in us. And yet the true emotive soul, the real psyche in us, is not a desire-soul but a soul of pure love and delight; but that, like the rest of our true being, can only emerge when the deformation created by the life of desire is removed from the surface and is no longer the characteristic action of our being. To get that done is a necessary part of our purification, liberation, perfection.[49]

*

All the complexity of our emotions and their tyranny over the soul arise from the habitual responses of the soul of desire in the emotions and sensations to these attractions and repulsions. Love and hatred, hope and fear, grief and joy all have their founts in this one source. We like, love, welcome, hope for, joy in whatever our nature, the first habit of our being, or else a formed (often perverse) habit, the second nature of our being, presents to the mind as pleasant, *priyam*; we hate, dislike, fear, have repulsion from or grief of whatever it presents to us as unpleasant, *apriyam*. This habit of the emotional nature gets into the way of the intelligent will and makes it often a helpless slave of this emotional being or at least prevents it from exercising a free judgment and government of the nature. This deformation has to be corrected. By getting rid of desire in the psychic prana and its intermiscence in the emotional mind, we facilitate the correction. For then attachment which is the strong bond of the heart, falls away from the heart-strings; the involuntary habit of *rāga-dveṣa* remains, but, not being made obstinate by attachment, it can be dealt with more easily by the will and the intelligence. The restless heart can be conquered and get rid of the habit of attraction and repulsion....

Attraction and repulsion, liking and disliking are a necessary mechanism for the normal man, they form a first principle of natural instinctive selection among the thousand flattering and formidable, helpful and dangerous impacts of the world around him. The buddhi starts with this material to work on and tries to correct the natural and instinctive by a wiser reasoned and willed selection; for obviously the pleasant is not always the right thing, the object to be preferred and selected, nor the unpleasant the wrong thing, the object to be shunned and rejected; pleasant and the good, *preyas* and *śreyas*, have to be distinguished, and right reason has to choose and not the caprice of emotion. But this it can do much better when the emotional suggestion is withdrawn and the heart rests in a luminous passivity. Then too the right activity of the heart can be brought to the surface; for we find then that behind this emotion-ridden soul of desire there was waiting all the while a soul of love and lucid joy and delight, a pure psyche....

But the purified heart is rid of anger, rid of fear, rid of hatred, rid of every shrinking and repulsion: it has a universal love, it can receive with an untroubled sweetness and clarity the various delight which God gives it in the world.[50] ●

Memory, Judgment and Imagination

Memory is the indispensable aid of the mind to preserve its past observations, the memory of the individual but also of the race, whether in the artificial form of accumulated records of the general race memory preserving its gains with a sort of constant repetition and renewal and, an element not sufficiently appreciated, a latent memory that can under the pressure of various kind of stimulation repeat under new conditions past movements of knowledge for judgment by the increased information and intelligence. The developed logical mind puts into order the action and resources of the human memory and trains it to make the utmost use of its materials. The human judgment naturally works on these materials in two ways, by a more or less rapid and summary combination of observation, inference, creative or critical conclusion, insight, immediate idea, – this is largely an attempt of the mind to work in a spontaneous manner with the directness that can only be securely achieved by the higher faculty of the intuition, for in the mind it produces much false confidence and unreliable certitude, – and a slower but in the end intellectually surer seeking, considering and testing judgment that develops into the careful logical action.

The memory and judgment are both aided by the imagination which, as a function of knowledge, suggests possibilities not actually presented or justified by the other powers and opens the doors to fresh vistas. The developed logical intelligence uses the imagination for suggesting new discovery and hypothesis, but is careful to test its suggestions fully by observation and a sceptical or scrupulous judgment. It insists too on testing, as far as may be, all the action of the judgment, rejects hasty inference in favour of an ordered system of education and induction and makes sure of all its steps and of the justice, continuity, compatibility, cohesion of its conclusions. A too formalised logical mind discourages, but a free use of the whole action of the logical intelligence may rather heighten a certain action of immediate insight, the mind's nearest approach to the higher intuition, but it does not place on it an unqualified reliance. The endeavour of the logical reason is always by a detached, disinterested and carefully founded method to get rid of error, of prejudgment, of the mind's false confidence and arrive at reliable certitudes.[51]

Desire as the Will Clutching at Results

The root of desire is the vital craving to seize upon that which we feel we have not, it is the limited life's instinct for possession and satisfaction. It creates the sense of want, – first the simpler vital craving of hunger, thirst, lust, then these psychical hungers, thirsts, lusts of the mind which are a much greater and more instant and pervading affliction of our being, the hunger which is infinite because it is the hunger of an infinite being, the thirst which is only temporarily lulled by satisfaction, but is in its nature insatiable. The psychic prana invades the sensational mind and brings into it the unquiet thirst of sensations, invades the dynamic mind with the lust of control, having, domination, success, fulfilment of every impulse, fills the emotional mind with the desire for the satisfaction of liking and disliking, for the wreaking of love and hate, brings the shrinkings and panics of fear and the strainings and disappointments of hope, imposes the tortures of grief and the brief fevers and excitements of joy, makes the intelligence and intelligent will the accomplices of all these things and turns them in their own kind into deformed and lame instruments, the will into a will of craving and the intelligence into a partial, a stumbling and an eager pursuer of limited, impatient, militant prejudgment and opinion. Desire is the root of all sorrow, disappointment, affliction, for though it has a feverish joy of pursuit and satisfaction, yet because it is always a straining of the being, it carries into its pursuit and its getting a labour, hunger, struggle, a rapid subjection to fatigue, and a sense of limitation, dissatisfaction and early disappointment with all its gains, a ceaseless morbid stimulation, trouble, disquiet, *aśānti*.[52]

*

The essential turn of the soul to possession and enjoyment of the world consists in a will to delight, and the enjoyment of the satisfaction of craving is only a vital and physical degradation of the will to delight. It is essential that we should distinguish between pure will and desire, between the inner will to delight and the outer lust and craving of the mind and body....

To tread down altogether the prana, the vital being, is to kill the force of life by which the large action of the embodied soul in the human being must be supported; to indulge the gross will to live is to remain satisfied with imperfection; to compromise between them is to stop half way and possess neither earth nor heaven. But if we can get at the pure will undeformed by desire, – which we shall find to be a much more free, tranquil, steady and effective force than the leaping, smoke-stifled, soon fatigued and baffled flame of desire, – and at the calm inner will of delight not afflicted or limited by any trouble of craving, we can then transform the prana from a tyrant, enemy, assailant of the mind into an obedient instrument.[53]

The Ego or the Separative 'I-ness'

This ego or "I" is not a lasting truth, much less our essential part; it is only a formation of Nature, a mental form of thought-centralisation in the perceiving and discriminating mind, a vital form of the centralisation of feeling and sensation in our parts of life, a form of physical conscious reception centralising substance and function of substance in our bodies. All that we internally are is not ego, but consciousness, soul or spirit. All that we externally and superficially are and do is not ego but Nature. An executive cosmic force shapes us and dictates through our temperament and environment and mentality so shaped, through our individualised formulation of the cosmic energies, our actions and their results. Truly, we do not think, will or act but thought occurs in us, will occurs in us, impulse and act occur in us; our ego-sense gathers around itself, refers to itself all this flow of natural activities. It is cosmic Force, it is Nature that forms the thought, imposes the will, imparts the impulse. Our body, mind and ego are a wave of that sea of force in action and do not govern it, but by it are governed and directed....[54]

*

If this is the truth of works, the first thing the sadhaka has to do is to recoil from the egoistic forms of activity and get rid of the sense of an "I" that acts He has to see and feel that everything happens in him by the plastic conscious or subconscious or sometimes superconscious automatism of his mental and bodily instruments moved by the forces of spiritual, mental, vital and physical Nature. There is a personality on his surface that chooses and wills, submits and struggles, tries to make good in Nature or prevail over Nature, but this personality is itself a construction of

Nature and so dominated, driven, determined by her that it cannot be free....⁵⁵

*

Thus calm, detached, a student of himself and a witness of his nature, he realises that he is the individual soul who observes the works of Nature, accepts tranquilly her results and sanctions or withholds his sanction from the impulse to her acts...⁵⁶

*

Thus he learns in place of mental control or egoistic will an inner spiritual control which makes him master of the Nature-forces that work in him and not their unconscious instrument or mechanic slave....⁵⁷

*

A vast universality of soul, an intense unity with all, is the base and fixed condition of the supramental consciousness and spiritual life. In that universality and unity alone can we find the supreme law of the divine manifestation in the life of the embodied spirit; in that alone can we discover the supreme motion and right play of our individual nature. In that alone can all these lower discords resolve themselves into a victorious harmony of the true relations between manifested beings who are portions of the one Godhead and children of one universal Mother....⁵⁸

Our Mind and its Control of the Physical Life

Our mind instead of being a thing powerful in its own strength, a clear instrument of conscious spirit, free and able to control, use and perfect the life and body, appears in the result a mixed construction; it is a predominantly physical mentality limited by its physical organs and subject to the demands and to the obstructions of the life in the body. This can only be got rid of by a sort of practical, inward psychological operation of analysis by which we become aware of the mentality as a separate power, isolate it for a free working, distinguish too the psychical and the physical prana and make them no longer a link for dependence, but a transmitting channel for the Idea and Will in the buddhi, obedient to its suggestions and commands; the prana then becomes a passive means of effectuation for the mind's direct control of the physical life. This control, however abnormal to our habitual poise of action, is not only possible, – it appears to some extent in the phenomena of hypnosis, though these are unhealthily abnormal, because there it is a foreign will which suggests and commands, – but must become the normal action when the higher Self within takes up the direct command of the whole being....[59]

Towards an Ideal Soul and Mind

The impressions of the sense-mind are used by a thought which exceeds them and which arrives at truths they do not give, ideative truths of thought, truths of philosophy and science; a thinking, discovering, philosophic mind overcomes, rectifies and dominates the first mind of sense impressions. The impulsive reactive sensational mentality, the life-cravings and the mind of emotional desire are taken up by the intelligent will and are overcome, are rectified and dominated by a greater ethical mind which discovers and sets over them a law of right impulse, right desire, right emotion and right action. The receptive, crudely enjoying sensational mentality, the emotional mind and life mind are taken up by the intelligence and are overcome, rectified and dominated by a deeper, happier aesthetic mind which discovers and sets above them a law of true delight and beauty. All these new formations are used by a general Power of the intellectual, thinking and willing man in a soul of governing intellect, imagination, judgment, memory, volition, discovering reason and ideal feeling which uses them for knowledge, self-development, experience, discovery, creation, effectuation, aspires, strives, inwardly attains, endeavours to make a higher thing of the life of the soul in Nature. The primitive desire-soul no longer governs the being. It is still a desire-soul, but it is repressed and governed by a higher power, something which has manifested in itself the godheads of Truth, Will, Good, Beauty and tries to subject life to them. The crude desire-soul and mind is trying to convert itself into an ideal soul and mind, and the proportion in which some effect and harmony of this greater conscious being has been found and enthroned, is the measure of our increasing humanity.... But this is still a very incomplete movement....[60]

The ethical mind becomes perfect in proportion as it detaches itself from desire, sense suggestion, impulse, customary dictated action and discovers a self of Right, Love, Strength, and Purity in which it can live accomplished and make it the foundation of all its actions. The aesthetic mind is perfected in proportion as it detaches itself from all its cruder pleasures and from outward conventional canons of the aesthetic reason and discovers a self-existent self and spirit of pure and infinite Beauty and Delight which gives its own light and joy to the material of the aesthesis. The mind of knowledge is perfected when it gets away from impression and dogma and opinion and discovers a light of self-knowledge and intuition which illumines all the workings of the sense and reason, all self-experience and world-experience.[61]

The Spiritual Energy or Yoga-Force

In the world so far as man is concerned we are aware only of mind-energy, life-energy, energy in Matter; but it is supposed that there is a spiritual energy or force also behind them from which they originate....[62]

If there is no such thing as spiritual consciousness, there can be no reality of Yoga, and if there is no Yoga-force, spiritual force, Yoga Shakti, then also there can be no effectivity in Yoga. A Yoga-consciousness or spiritual consciousness which has no power or force in it, may not be dead or unreal but it is evidently something inert and without effect or consequence. Equally, a man who sets out to be a Yogi or Guru and has no spiritual consciousness or no power in his spiritual consciousness – a Yoga-force or spiritual force – is making a false claim and is either a charlatan or a self-deluded imbecile; still more is he so if having no spiritual force he claims to have made a path others can follow. If Yoga is a reality, if spirituality is anything better than a delusion, there must be such a thing as Yoga-force or spiritual force.

It is evident that if spiritual force exists, it must be able to produce spiritual results – therefore there is no irrationality in the claim of those sadhakas who say that they feel the force of the Guru or the force of the Divine working in them leading towards spiritual fulfilment and experience. Whether it is so or not in a particular case is a personal question, but the statement cannot be denounced as *per se* incredible and manifestly false, because such things cannot be. Further, if it be true that spiritual force is the original one and the others are derivative from it, then there is no irrationality in supposing that spiritual force can produce mental results, vital results, physical results....[63]

*

The conditions and limits under which Yoga or sadhana has to be worked out are not arbitrary or capricious; they arise from the nature of things. These including the will, receptivity, assent, self-opening and surrender of the sadhaka have to be respected by the Yoga-force....

Still the Yoga-force is always tangible and concrete in the way I have described and has tangible results. But it is invisible – not like a blow given or the rush of a motor car knocking somebody down which the physical senses can at once perceive. How is the mere physical mind to know that it is there and working? By its results? But how can it know that the results were that of the Yogic force and not of something else? One of two things it must be. Either it must allow the consciousness to go inside, to become aware of inner things, to believe in the experience of the invisible and the supraphysical, and then by experience, by the opening of new capacities, it becomes conscious of these forces and can see, follow and use their workings, just as the Scientist uses the unseen forces of Nature. Or one must have faith to see how things happen, it will notice that when the Force was called in, there began after a time to be a result, then repetitions, more repetitions, more clear and tangible results, increasing frequency, increasing consistency of results, a feeling and awareness of the Force at work – until the experience becomes daily, regular, normal, complete. These are the two main methods, one internal, working from in outward, the other external, working from outside and calling the inner force out till it penetrates and is visible in the exterior consciousness. But neither can be done if one insists always on the extrovert attitude, the external concrete only and refuses to join to it the internal concrete – or if the physical mind at every step raises a dance of doubts which refuses to allow the nascent experience to develop. Even the Scientist carrying on a new experiment would never succeed if he allowed his mind to behave in that way.[64]

Spiritual Experience

...The decisive experiences cannot be brought, the permanence of a new state of consciousness in which they will be normal cannot be secured if the mind is always interposing its own reservations, prejudgments, ignorant formulas or if it insists on arriving at the divine certitude as it would at the quite relative truth of a mental conclusion, by reasoning, doubt, enquiry and all the other paraphernalia of Ignorance feeling and fumbling around after Knowledge; these greater things can only be brought by the progressive opening of a consciousness quieted and turned steadily towards spiritual experience....[65]

*

Mind by itself is incapable of ultimate certitude; whatever it believes, it can doubt; whatever it can affirm, it can deny; whatever it gets hold of, it can and does let go. That, if you like, is its freedom, noble right, privilege; it may be all you can say in its praise, but by these methods of mind you cannot hope (outside the reach of physical phenomena and hardly even there) to arrive at anything you can call an ultimate certitude.[66]

INTRODUCTION

Practical Guidance

Integral Yoga is practical psychology and Integral Psychology inherent in it, it is, therefore, essentially educational, *i.e.*, intending and promoting progressive integration in personality. Here is an entire section of excerpts affording precise direct guidance on the most concrete issues of life: brooding and difficulties, circumstances and difficulties, difficulties of character. We have then an excerpt on 'The Practical Way' to deal with our problems of anxiety, grief, etc., and on how to learn to look straight at ourselves and to trace the difficulty to its source. This discovery of truth itself has a marvellous healing power. But what helps most is the persistent cultivation of a general attitude of wideness, of universalisation, of non-insistence on self-will as against the self-will of others, of appreciation of the authority of truth over all and search for the same. In brief, it is the attitude of the ego's self-surrender to the Supreme and thus of cultivating in life a wideness, an all-comprehensiveness and a commanding height.

The human ego is most touchy and sensitive and gets easily hurt. Sensitiveness is an extremely common problem. One excerpt is on this subject.

In the end, there is a larger piece on 'The Cultivation of Integral Personality'. It sets out how one can go about building up a wholesome and harmonious personality for oneself. (Editor)

Difficulties and Perplexities

Difficulties and perplexities can never be got rid of by the mind brooding on them and trying in that way to get out of them; this habit of the mind only makes them recur without a solution and keeps up by brooding the persistent tangle. It is from something above and outside the perplexities that the solution must come.

It is this change of stress, a change in the poise and attitude of the mind that will be the more helpful process.[67]

Circumstances and Difficulties

That is the inconvenience of going away from a difficulty, – it runs after one, – or rather one carries it with oneself, for the difficulty is truly inside, not outside. Outside circumstances only give it the occasion to manifest itself and so long as the inner difficulty is not conquered, the circumstances will always crop up one way or another.[68]

Difficulties of Character

The difficulties of the character persist so long as one yields to them in action when they rise. One has to make a strict rule not to act according to the impulses of anger, ego or whatever the weakness may be that one wants to get rid of, or if one does act in the heat of the moment, not to justify or persist in the action. If one does that, after a time the difficulty abates or is confined purely to a subjective movement which one can observe, detach oneself from and combat.[69]

The Practical Way

If these things (trouble, anxiety, grief, revolt, disturbance in the mind) come, he must at once detect their source, the defect which they indicate, the fault of egoistic claim, vital desire, emotion or idea from which they start and this he must discourage by his will, his spiritualised intelligence, his soul unity with the Master of his being. On no account must he admit an excuse for them, however natural, righteous in seeming or plausible, or any inner or outer justification. If it is the Prana which is troubled and clamorous, he must separate himself from the troubled Prana, keep seated his higher nature in the Buddhi and by the Buddhi school and reject the claim of the desire soul in him; and so too if it is the heart of emotion that makes the clamour and disturbance. If, on the other hand, it is the will and intelligence itself that is at fault, then the trouble is more difficult to command, because then his chief aid and instrument becomes an accomplice of the revolt against the divine Will and the old sins of the lower members take advantage of this sanction to raise their diminished heads. Therefore there must be a constant insistence on one main idea, the self surrender to the Master of our being, God within us and in the world, the supreme Self, the universal Spirit....

When the trouble is too strong to be kept out, it must be allowed

to pass and its return discouraged by a greater vigilance and
insistence of the spiritualised Buddhi. Thus, persisting, it will be
found that these things lose their force more and more, become
more and more external and brief in their recurrence, until finally
calm becomes the law of the being.[70]

The Imperturbable Calm

The calm established in the whole being must remain the same
whatever happens, in health and disease, in pleasure and in pain,
even in the strongest physical pain, in good fortune and misfortune, our own or that of those we love, in success and failure,
honour and insult, praise and blame, justice done to us or
injustice, everything that ordinarily affects the mind.[71]

True Remedy for Sensitiveness

One has not to cure oneself of one's sensitiveness, but only
acquire the power to rise to a higher consciousness taking such
disenchantments as a sort of jumping-board. One way is not to
expect even square dealings from others, no matter who the others
are. And besides, it is good to have such experiences of the real
nature of some people to which a generous nature is often blind;
for that helps the growth of one's consciousness. The blow you
wince at seems to you so hard because it is a blow the world of
your mental formation has sustained. Such a world often becomes
a part of our being. The result is that a blow dealt to it gives almost
physical pain. The great compensation is that it makes you live
more and more in the real world in contradiction to the world of
your imagination which is what you would like the real world to
be. But the real world is not all that could be desired, you know,
and that is why it has to be acted upon and transformed by the
Divine Consciousness.... The thing is to learn to detach oneself
from any such experience and learn to look at such perversions of
others from a higher altitude from where one can regard these
manifestations in the proper perspective – the impersonal one.
Then our difficulties really and literally become opportunities. For
knowledge, when it goes to the root of our troubles, has in itself a
marvellous healing-power as it were. As soon as you touch the
quick of the trouble, as soon as you, diving down and down, get at

what really ails you, the pain disappears as though by a miracle. Unflinching courage to reach true Knowledge is therefore of the very essence of Yoga.[72]

Evil Persona

What you say about the "Evil Persona" interests me greatly as it answers to my consistent experience that a person greatly endowed for the work has, always or almost always, – perhaps one ought not to make a too rigid universal rule about these things, – a being attached to him, sometimes appearing like a part of him, which is just the contradiction of the thing he centrally represents in the work to be done. Or, if it is not there at first, not bound to his personality, a force of this kind enters into his environment as soon as he begins his movement to realise. Its business seems to be to oppose, to create stumblings and wrong conditions, in a word, to set before him the whole problem of the work he has started to do. It would seem as if the problem could not, in the occult economy of things, be solved otherwise than by the predestined instrument making the difficulty his own. That would explain many things that seem very disconcerting on the surface.[73]

The Cultivation of Integral Personality

If one stands back from the mind and its activities so that they fall silent at will or go on as a surface movement of which one is the detached and disinterested witness, it becomes possible eventually to realise oneself as the inner Self of mind, the true and pure mental being, the Purusha; by similarly standing back from the life activities, it is possible to realise oneself as the inner Self of life, the true and pure vital being, the Purusha; there is even a Self of body of which, by standing back from the body and its demands and activities and entering into a silence of the physical consciousness watching the action of its energy, it is possible to become aware of a true and pure physical being, the Purusha. So too, by standing back from all these activities of nature successively or together, it becomes possible to realise one's inner being as the silent impersonal Self, the witness Purusha.[74]

*

...The Purusha has to become not only the witness but the knower and source, the master of all the thought and action, and this can only be partially done so long as one remains on the mental level or has still to use the ordinary instrumentation of mind, life and body. A certain mastery can indeed be achieved, but mastery is not transformation; the change made by it cannot be sufficient to be integral: for that it is essential to get back, beyond mind-being, life-being, body-being, still more deeply inward to the psychic entity inmost and profoundest within us – or else to open to the superconscient highest domains. For this penetration into the luminous crypt of the soul one has to get through all the intervening vital stuff to the psychic centre within us, however long, tedious or difficult may be the process. The method of detachment from the insistence of all mental and vital and physical claims and calls and impulsions, a concentration in the heart, austerity, self-purification and rejection of the old mind movements and life movements, rejection of the ego of desire, rejection of false needs and false habits, are all useful aids to this difficult passage: but the strongest, most central way is to found all such or other methods on a self-offering and surrender of ourselves and of our parts of nature to the Divine Being, the Ishwara. A strict obedience to the wise and intuitive leading of a Guide is also normal and necessary for all but a few specially gifted seekers.[75]

*

As the crust of the outer nature cracks, as the walls of inner separation break down, the inner light gets through, the inner fire burns in the heart, the substance of the nature and the stuff of consciousness refine to a greater subtlety and purity, and the deeper psychic experiences, those which are not solely of an inner mental or inner vital character, become possible in this subtler, purer, finer substance; the soul begins to unveil itself, the psychic personality reaches its full stature. The soul, the psychic entity, then manifests itself as the central being which upholds mind and life and body and supports all the other powers and functions of the Spirit; it takes up its greater function as the guide and ruler of the nature. A guidance, a governance begins from within which exposes every movement to the light of Truth, repels what is false, obscure, opposed to the divine realisation: every region of the being, every nook and corner of it, every movement, formation, direction, inclination of thought, will, emotion, sensation, action, reaction, motive, disposition, propensity, desire, habit of the conscious or subconscious physical, even the most concealed, camouflaged, mute, recondite, is lighted up with the unerring psychic light, their confusions dissipated, their tangles disentangled, their obscurities, deceptions, self-deceptions precisely indicated and removed; all is purified, set right, the whole nature harmonised, modulated in the psychic key, put in spiritual order. This process may be rapid or tardy according to the amount of obscurity and resistance still left in the nature, but it goes on unfalteringly so long as it is not complete. As a final result the whole conscious being is made perfectly apt for spiritual experience of every kind, turned towards spiritual truth of thought, feeling, sense, action, tuned to the right responses, delivered from the darkness and stubbornness of the tamasic inertia, the turbidities and turbulences and impurities of the rajasic passion and restless unharmonised kinetism, the enlightened rigidities and sattwic limitations or poised balancements of constructed equilibrium which are the character of the Ignorance.

This is the first result, but the second is a free inflow of all kinds of spiritual experience, experience of the Self, experience of the Ishwara and the Divine Shakti, experience of cosmic consciousness, a direct touch with cosmic forces and with the occult movements of universal Nature, a psychic sympathy and unity and inner communication and interchanges of all kinds with other beings and with Nature, illuminations of the mind by knowledge, illuminations of the heart by love and devotion and spiritual joy and ecstasy, illuminations of the sense and the body by higher experience, illuminations of dynamic action in the truth and largeness of a purified mind and heart and soul, the certitudes of the divine light and guidance, the joy and power of the divine force working in the will and the conduct. These experiences are the result of an opening outward of the inner and inmost being and nature; for then there comes into play the soul's power of unerring inherent consciousness, its vision, its touch on things which is superior to any mental cognition; there is then, native to the psychic consciousness in its pure working, an immediate sense of the world and its beings, a direct inner contact with them and a direct contact with the Self and with the Divine, – a direct knowledge, a direct sight of Truth and of all truths, a direct penetrating spiritual emotion and feeling, a direct intuition of right will and right action, a power to rule and to create an order of the being not by the gropings of the superficial self, but from within, from the inner truth of self and things and the occult realities of Nature.[76]

*

A highest spiritual transformation must intervene on the psychic or psycho-spiritual change; the psychic movement inward to the inner being, the Self or Divinity within us, must be completed by an opening upward to a supreme spiritual status or a higher existence.[77]

*

As the psychic change has to call in the spiritual to complete it, so the first spiritual change has to call in the supramental transformation to complete it. For all these steps forward are, like those before them, transitional; the whole radical change in the evolution from a basis of Ignorance to a basis of Knowledge can only come by the intervention of the supramental Power and its direct action in earth-existence.[78]

FINAL RECAPITULATION

Integral Psychology as a System

We have now come to the close of the compilation from Sri Aurobindo's Integral Yoga to represent the Integral Psychology inherent in it. The compilation has been a brief one. The parts of Integral Psychology represented could have been more elaborately done and certain other topics, *e.g.*, Sleep and Dream and Types of Personality could have been added.

Now let us ask ourselves: Does it make out a Psychological System, a coherent individual view of human personality? If so, let us summarise it.

Psychology is the science of *consciousness* as embodied in the human individual, growing up in interaction with the environment, much dependent on the body and the unconscious, but tending to assert itself more and more as a purposive self-existent fact. Consciousness is for it a primary fact as 'matter' is for physics, and it seeks to investigate consciousness in the fullest measure without any self-imposed limitations.

The scope of psychology is as wide as consciousness itself in its various degrees of luminosity (lower and higher) and extensions as related to the phenomenal human manifestation of it. This includes the subconscious and the unconscious, individual, racial and cosmic and the superconscious, individual and cosmic, in various forms and degrees. And also the subliminal, which is generalised, but is not lower or higher than the normal human consciousness. So also other forms of consciousness that may be found in the course of investigations are parts of the scope of psychology.

It is also a part of this scope that we recognise human consciousness as a fact of cosmic evolution consisting of the three steps of Matter, Life and Mind so far covered, stretching out into further possibilities of higher integrations, the ranges yet superconscious. The evolutional adjustments achieved with the environment, the instincts, the habits, and other automatic actions and reactions constitute the unconscious of the individual, the race and cosmic existence. The new integrations called for show the trends of future growth.

Consciousness being the primary fact and field of investigation for psychology, its method will naturally be the one that can directly observe it, *i.e.*, introspection. But it is more difficult to make it dispassionate than the external observation employed by physics. But that has to be done, introspection is irreplaceable for psychology. However, consciousness being deeply embedded in the body, having grown in it evolutionally and being dependent on it for its expression, observation of bodily behaviour can be a study of consciousness. And introspection and observation of bodily reactions are both responsive to experimental handling. And all these – introspection, external observation and experiment – admit of indefinite variations.

The pursuit of Integral Psychology does involve, it may be stated, a motive to grow personally in the integration of life, as without this an appreciation of the higher integrations will be difficult. The knower has to be fairly adequate to the known, otherwise he cannot do justice to the object of knowledge. Thus Integral Psychology, covering as it does in its scope of study the superconscious, sets to itself a distinctive aim: that of personal growth enabling the researcher to appreciate more positively the higher integrations.

Thus we have here a system of psychology with a distinctive aim, distinctive subject-matter and scope, a distinctive method and a distinctive emphasis on evolution, cosmic and individual.

The varied activities of normal personality, all, more or less, derive their orientation from the above approach itself, sense-organs and sensations being evolutional adaptation or adjustments. They are limitations on the sensing mind, which, at the human level through self-consciousness, can rise above them and command greater capacities.

Instincts and emotions too are evolutional habits and can be exceeded. Superficially man is a sort of organisation of individual reactions to different environmental situations, but the deeper consciousness is a unitary super-consciousness, which is intrinsically joyous and integral in action. That gives another perspective to all the activities of the normal personality.

Thinking is the highest function of the phenomenal human personality. But to the deeper integral superconsciousness direct intuitive knowing is normal. In view of this, laborious discursive knowing of mind would acquire a new orientation. Its being always in a state of flux would also undergo modification, as silence is seen as natural to consciousness at the higher level. The problem of freedom too assumes a new form. At the level of the mind, our freedom consists of an ability to choose between given alternatives and we are not free from inner compulsions. But at the deeper superconscious level, the level of the experience of the Psychic Being, we have, along with intuitive seeing, spontaneous action with no compulsiveness whatsoever. It is the plane of unity of being, whole seeing and whole action.

Thus we arrive at a different view of personality as a whole, truly a system of psychology of original value, at the minimum a challenge to the contemporary science of psychology.

In the end, we might mention more pointedly a few important contributions it can make to general psychology. One: the mind is not essentially in a state of flux. Under the influence of the Psychic Consciousness, it can become quiet and even silent and then its capacity to think and to know becomes greater. We then cease to be helpless, more or less, in our thinking activity.

Two: levels of experience, following the steps of evolution, Matter, Life and Mind, should be three, physical, vital and mental. This appreciation enables us to identify activities as being primarily of one level or another and deal with them according to their basic characteristics and thus more effectively.

Three: all emotions are not parasitical in character. There is a joy that depends on the fulfilment of a desire, a pre-existing conation. But there is also a deeper joy, the joy of the Psychic Being which is self-existent and does not presuppose a conation.

Four: mental health is not just a matter of economic balance among the Id, the Ego and the Superego. The peace, the unity, the joy of the deeper Psychic Consciousness presents the true norm of mental health and the best integrative force in personality.

Five: 'transformation', *i.e.*, a real change in the quality of the animal impulses is possible through the deep and persistent working of the integral superconscious on them. This is different from their modification or sublimation.

Six: 'perception of Wholes' as a direct fact is a most happy contribution of the Gestalt School of Psychology. Now, in the scheme of Integral Psychology, it is to the Psychic Consciousness that the perception of wholes becomes spontaneous; 'wholes' become the primary interest and parts, the secondary.

The problems of the contemporary science of psychology are possibly due to the limitations of its perspective. It wants to be a science like other sciences and limit itself rigidly to the phenomenal mental activities. But the mental processes are not impersonal facts like those of physics. A mental process is somebody's. This is a unique feature of the subject-matter of psychology, and the science of psychology has to proceed on its own distinctive basis. Further, psychology can less easily ignore facts of ultimate reality than physics can. Psychology then becomes a matter of reactions and it lacks unity and then personality becomes un-understandable.

Psychology has evidently to discover its own true standpoint. A handicap here becomes a pervasive handicap.

Integral Psychology is free and wide in its approach, and bases itself on the larger experience of yoga and is able to present a fuller view of personality, which can offer solutions to the problems of scientific psychology. Actually the two seem to be complementary in character and entirely reconcilable. In fact the divergent schools of contemporary psychology can all find due legitimations in the wide scheme of Integral Psychology. (Editor) sciences like other sciences and limit itself rigidly to the phenomena of mental existence. But the general progress are not imperceptible like modern physics. A mental process is wholetaxy . This is the unique texture of the subject-matter of psychology, and the science is compelled by it to proceed on its own distinctive basis. Either growth of psychology can less easily fulfill them of an input entity than physics can. Psychology then becomes a matter of relationship until more unity and their per-entity becomes understood.

Psychology this evidently to discover its over-the studying the humble in how Abelone is a perspective modestly.

Unit of Psychology of free and wide that it appears in and hence much in the large experience of ease and it interrelations can take, view of personality which can often resolution to fly on from this science psychology. Certainly the two seem to be complete that it in contrast unfortunately redistillable. It has the first, then these if circumstance, psychology out of find due regulations in the real scheme of mental Psychology (Falled).

PART TWO

ELABORATIVE AND COMPARATIVE STUDIES

CONTENTS

Contemporary Psychology and its Crisis	85
The Yoga as the Pursuit of Integral Personality	92
The Integral Personality (in the language of poetry)	100
The Verification of the Truths of Integral Personality	107
Contemporary Psychologists and Personality	110
The Pursuit of Psychology	116
The Search for a Theory of Personality in Contemporary Psychology	125
Personality, Its Development and 'The Inner Voice': A Study in Jung	132
Progress of Jungian Thought: A Study in Jungian Analysis	144
Freud and Personal Integration or Development	152
Cultural Science Psychology and Integral Personality	164
The Urge for Wholeness	171
The Psychological System of Sri Aurobindo	175
The Silent Mind – A Discussion with Dr. Ganguli	185
The Unconscious in Sri Aurobindo	192
Levels of Experience in Normal Personality	194
Teaching of Psychology in Indian Universities	206
The Indian Psychologist in Search of His Soul	211
Swami Pranavananda Eastern and Western Psychology Lecture for 1985	216
The Structure and Dynamics of Personality in Integral Yoga	220
Progress of Freudian Thought	243

CONTEMPORARY PSYCHOLOGY AND ITS CRISIS

Psychology is today a most active science. In recent times it has been talked about a great deal and a vast psychological literature has actually been produced during a relatively short period. Since the rise of modern natural science in the 16th century, man had principally occupied himself in investigating the physical universe and later in the 19th century the biological phenomenon. His attitude was objective. But of late his attention has turned upon himself and he has wanted to study his own mind and nature. He has changed over to the subjective attitude. This withdrawal of man from objective nature to himself is in itself an important cultural event in the evolution of human interest in the West.

Psychology originally and etymologically had meant the science of the soul, which was understood as a metaphysical reality, the various activities of mind being its manifestations. But natural science as a discipline of knowledge rules out metaphysical realities and confines itself to the investigation of phenomena. Psychology, therefore, when it came to be regarded as a natural science, had to modify its standpoint. Soul was no longer permissible. It, therefore, simply posited that mind and its activities as such existed and that it was no concern of the natural science of psychology to inquire or consider whether an ultimate substratum to mind was necessary.

'A Psychology without a soul' was thus conceived and born and the scientist now felt free to apply his method of inductive investigation to the varied phenomena of mind. The scientist has since then been empirically investigating, collecting instances and making generalisations regarding the various modes or activities of consciousness like perceiving, remembering, imagining, thinking, etc., as also the personality as a whole. The modern man has thus, through the new way of inductive science, returned to the old seeking of knowing oneself. This is, perhaps, the cultural significance of the rise of psychology in the West in the recent past.

But psychology today is, in fact, no single science concerned with the investigation of a definite field of subject-matter. It presents such a diversity of points of view regarding the nature of the subject-matter as also the method and aim of investigation that it is very much more correct to consider it as a group of sciences aiming at the study of man from relatively different angles. The standpoint of natural science, which is stated above and which is shared by physics, chemistry, botany, zoology, etc., is considered inappropriate for psychology by thinkers like Dilthey and Spranger, W. James and Titchner, who can be taken as the best representatives of the natural science ideal for psychology. All valuations and judgments of human utility and purpose must be taken away and mind should be investigated structurally with a view to discovering the qualities of existence possessed by it and the laws regulating its behaviour, just as physics, irrespective of the practical usefulness or otherwise, studies the various kinds of material phenomena as pure existence and seeks to determine the laws of its behaviour.

For Dilthey and Spranger, this standpoint is altogether unreal. Mental phenomena, they urge, are not at all co-ordinate with the material. A mental activity has always a personal reference, it is always somebody's. A table, a chair, a plant, a stone, do not necessarily possess that reference. Mind and mental phenomena belong, they say, to the cultural world, to which mutual interaction of human subjects (individuals) is essential. Psychology is, therefore, rather a cultural or a social science. The nature of mind is here differently conceived and the method of investigation also has, therefore, to be different from that employed by natural science generally.

But even where people are agreed that psychology must adopt the model of natural science, they are disagreed as to the nature of the subject-matter and the aim and the method of psychological study. Titchner, for example, takes consciousness as the subject-matter and introspection as the method, and these are for him the first necessary concepts of the science. He represents the so-called introspectionist school in psychology.

Directly opposed to it stands Watson, the leader of Behaviourism, who affirms that consciousness does not exist, introspection is superfluous, and that psychology is really concerned with the behaviour of the human individual. Physics is his ideal for psychology and he aims at making psychology an experimental objective science. Thinking is to him simply sub-vocal speech and so are memory and other mental processes certain forms of bodily behaviour. But both of them want psychology to be a perfect natural science.

And one might easily observe that though these standpoints are sharply opposed to each other, they still seem to possess a complementary character, since the positive elements of the two standpoints can be harmonised into a science of psychology aiming at an empirical study of the human individual in the twofold expression of its activities, mental and bodily. A constructive synthesis of the conflicting standpoints of present-day psychology is perhaps not impossible; but contemporary psychology, however, presents the conflicts without the much wished-for synthesis.

There are yet other standpoints. Gestaltism is a school of psychology which has made a strong impression. Its one idea is that the 'whole' is not the mere sum of its parts, that there exists a thing like the Gestalt quality, the quality of the 'whole', as a distinct feature by itself. Unities and wholes, therefore, become to it concrete realities. The method of analysis, much honoured in empirical science, is found to be utterly defective as it tends to make the parts substantive realities.

A method competent to apprehend the complex whole as such will alone be the adequate scientific method. Analysis may, however, continue to be used as a supplementary technique. Psychology, to this school, is the study of the psycho-physical organism of the human individual. Mind-Body is one whole and a sundering of them is unscientific.

A striking contribution of the school is the explanation of the perception of movement. Movement, it affirms, is not constructed out of fixed positions given in successive moments of time, but is a direct perception of sense. In other words, it is not inferred as held hithertofore, but directly apprehended.

Introspectionism, Behaviourism and Gestaltism, all are points of view falling within the purview of the general stand of natural science psychology. But another one, which makes purposiveness of mind as its pivot, Hormism of McDougall, also belongs to the same group. Working according to some end, conscious or unconscious, as contrasted with the mechanical operation of physical nature, is regarded as the essential characteristic of mind.

The last to mention, and in a way the most important of all the schools of psychology, is psycho-analysis. Freud, the author of the school, was a neurologist by profession and used to treat nervous and mental disorders by the method of hypnotism. However, in the course of his practice, he made the happy discovery that if a patient was allowed simply to relate and, as it were, mentally relive his past experiences, he felt greatly relieved in his troubles.

He called it the talking-out method and started using it in place of hypnotism.

The use of the talking-out method soon revealed to him that experiences of past conflicts and frustrations continue to persist. Therefore the subconscious is a fact; otherwise how could we suppose the past experiences as persisting. And he was soon led to think that the subconscious is relatively the larger part of our personality; in fact, as he later chose to put it, the nine-tenths of personality.

But in the employment of the talking-out method, he discovered that the past experiences did not always easily come up. In fact more often many of them were held back. That observation revealed the great psycho-analytical fact of repression. But how does repression take place and what is the mode of its operation? The investigation of the mechanism of repression constitutes indeed the main line of work for psycho-analysis; that is its chief contribution to science as well. The symptoms of the mental disease are meaningful facts. They are willed by the patient in the sense that they afford a partial satisfaction to repressed wishes.

The normal behaviour of the individual too is in many ways influenced by his repressions. The slips of the tongue and other small errors of behaviour like forgetting, mislaying, etc., are also subconsciously determined by our repressed wishes. These repressed wishes, he was led on, by his experience of the mental patients, to consider as sexual in character. He felt that repression consists in the forcible suppression of sexual wish by the social and moral sense of the individual. But it is necessary in this connection to say that sex is to Freud co-extensive with the whole of the pleasure-seeking propensity of man. And he, therefore, traces the development of sex from birth to adolescence.

The development of the sex instinct which thus becomes to him the most fundamental instinct is something characteristic of psycho-analysis. Every activity, even religious, moral or artistic, is simply a modification of the original sex propensity.

Interpretation of dreams is another important contribution which psycho-analysis has made. Dreams probably betray the subconscious as nothing else and it goes to the credit of Freud to have affirmed that dreams are not a fantastic and meaningless play of imagery. In his ultimate scientific formulation, he maintains that all dreams are wish-fulfilments. The repression in disguise or otherwise seeks gratification in the dreams. The hungry man of the day sees himself in the dream-imagery of the night sitting at a grand feast.

This is very briefly the psycho-analytical doctrine and with it we have given a short resume of the contemporary major psychological thought-currents. Of late, some modifications of these have naturally appeared.

To these must be added Experimental Psychology which has lately become the most popular, in its form of normal scientific pursuit as also in its applications to industry and other spheres of life. The attempt here is to determine in quantitative terms, under controlled conditions, correlations of psychological facts. It is a study of reactions of personality in precise terms. The utility of this approach has been demonstrated well enough. But it is a matter of reactions and behaviour of personality itself; we do not get an insight into the inner working of personality here.

The above picture of contemporary psychology is quite a puzzle. The different schools and standpoints are so divergent that it is impossible to discover any scheme or system in the facts and theories of contemporary psychology. We know of differences of opinion regarding facts as well as theories in every science. In psychology the trouble is that the nature and character of the subject-matter itself is thrown into dispute. In behaviourism consciousness is inadmissible, for introspectionism, behaviour is hardly of much account and for psycho-analysis, the subconscious is the principal fact of psychological subject-matter. And then there are a number of distinctive approaches which further complicate these differences. Is the psychological data essentially characterised by a "Wholeness" quality or that of "purposiveness" or any other? Or, is the subject-matter of psychology fundamentally different from that of the natural sciences, since it involves a knowing feeling and a willing subject, which necessarily qualifies its facts of perceptions, images, emotions, thoughts and sentiments?

This situation constitutes what is known as the crisis in psychology.

A number of attempts have been made to elucidate the situation and reconcile the conflicting standpoints of the different schools. But the best of such attempts says no more than that each school, in its own way, is contributing to the growth of psychological knowledge and that in course of time a consolidated science of psychology is bound to emerge.

But that merely expresses a faith and as such it is excellent. It, however, throws no light on the possible inner connections among the conflicting schools and does not show a way out of the crisis.

But a way seems to be suggested by the yogic approach to human life and experience. Our ordinary psychological approach to experience consists in observing the facts of experience and then systematising and trying to explain them. The yogic approach is normative and practical. It seeks to take forward our experience to progressively higher and higher forms of synthesis and integration. In its attempt to do so, it discovers a plane and a form of consciousness characteristically different from our general mental consciousness. This new consciousness is found to be marked, among others, by the qualities of depth, spontaneity and wholeness, whereas our general consciousness operates through the mechanisms of a number of polarities.

Now, in the absence of a knowledge of this new consciousness discovered by the yogic approach, our ordinary polarities of sex and morality, the conscious and the unconscious and the oppositions of our likes and dislikes become insoluble. The fact is that their true reconciliation exists in a principle higher than themselves and that being not known, the data collected by the different schools looks so disjointed.

The Self-poised Consciousness of the Gita too virtually presents a state of consciousness higher than the mental and a full appreciation of the character of this consciousness can give a perspective which will enable us to see the vast and the varied data of contemporary psychology in a new light.

Indian yogic psychology has received, at the hands of Sri Aurobindo, a detailed and elaborate treatment and the body of psychological principles thus evolved shows clearly enough that the present-day difficulties of psychology are by no means insurmountable. Once we are able to ascertain the larger evolutionary setting and purpose of human nature, we will begin to recognise that what we today affirm as ultimate is, in fact, only a stage and a phase. Instinct was a stage for man and his reason and morality too may be a stage for something higher.

Without that higher state, we are surely handicapped in our understanding of reason and morality and our present mentality as

INTEGRAL PSYCHOLOGY 91

a whole. No wonder that in such a state of knowledge, we should regard sex as final, mechanism as final, purpose as final, interaction of the individual and the environment as final and a number of such other terms in the same way.

THE YOGA AS THE PURSUIT OF INTEGRAL PERSONALITY

Indian culture has a strong strain of Psychology in it. Ideas of growth, evolution, individual variation, levels of development, personal faith and worship, toleration and understanding for others' faith and ways of life, various pursuits of perfection and liberation are all grounded in the psychological conditions of life of the individual and society. The 'Adhikarabheda', the 'differential capacity', is the familiar Indian concept representing these ideas. A man's duty, work, faith, worship, education, pursuit of perfection must necessarily take account of it, be based on it, if an individual or a social unit is to have a true and effective growth in life. If this is ignored, we shall not have growth, but a superimposition, a formal structure, which will tend to create an external uniformity of behaviour, but not a genuine enrichment of experience. And the result will be a deep inner conflict and dissatisfaction. The ideas of reincarnation, of the classes or castes in society, the *varṇa*s or the four *āśrama*s or stages or divisions of life are founded on profound psychological insights and actual experience. The growth of the soul, the spiritual fact of life, is the real thing and our ordinary mental, moral, aesthetic growth and its experiences are contributory factors to this basic growth. And this basic growth needs long stretches of time, which can only be possible through repeated incarnations. Life is essentially an adventure of experience aiming at an infinite enrichment of itself. And we pursue it through fresh births and varied situations of life.

Psychology is thus a basic trend of Indian culture and deeply embedded in the religious and philosophical thought and life of the country. But in the latter-day traditional phase of our life, it has not been there as a living fact and, therefore, got encrusted with fossilised matter. Our organisation of knowledge has followed a different scheme from that of the West. It has had its own advantages and disadvantages, laying a greater emphasis on the unity of the 'whole' than on the separation of the disciplines and branches of knowledge. Hence psychology figures in our literature in a form of its own. It is there in the works of philosophy (Darshanas), of literary criticism (Rasa Shastras), of medicine (Ayurveda) and in many other kinds of writings. But the vast literature on Yoga is primarily a psychological creation. Yogic writing is all comparable to modern psychology, whether it exists in the contexts of philosophy, religion, literature, medicine, etc., or in independent treatises of Hatha yoga, Raja yoga, Bhakti yoga, Jnana yoga, Karma yoga, Tantra and other innumerable unnamed Sadhanas uptill *The Synthesis of Yoga* of Sri Aurobindo.

However, its standpoint is not exactly that of modern psychology. Its standpoint is that of practical pursuit of self-perfection, or self-fulfilment, from different points of view and by different techniques and processes, physical, physiological, social, religious, philosophical, psychological. It considers what man is, what he can become and how he can reach his fullness. And in doing so it assumes all freedom, it accepts no limitation on its search and research. Such has been the daring, the courage, the vision displayed by the explorations in this field throughout the long history of our cultural life that we can truly call this our people's most favourite line of work and achievement.

And is the same not the real business of human culture? That is, to become more and more what it can become, to achieve an increasing enrichment of itself or a progressive realisation of its potentialities and possibilities. This is exactly what education too needs. The problems of one state of growth can always be solved through the development of higher capacities or the unfoldment of new potentialities. Do our contemporary culture and education, through their state of chronic crisis, not seem to call for the growth of new capacities, and does yoga with its insight into the deeper potentialities of human nature not suggest an answer? Here is, indeed, an inviting and promising avenue for exploration.

Now, what is human personality as we come to know it from the varied researches of yoga? Indeed, most varied have been the approaches of yoga and most varied the pathways to self-perfection. But there is a wide agreement among them so far as the conception of personality is concerned. There is the ordinary form of it, which consists of the body, the numerous impulses of life seeking varied ordinary satisfactions and the thinking activity, which attempts to organise life and environment and even contemplates ultimate truths. All this form of personality is outward-turned *(i.e., bahirmukha)* and is environment-dependent and environment-involved. This is the normal outer personality of yoga. But when an individual, through a long process of self-detachment from identifications with things external, seeks an inward growth, he ultimately contacts a self-existent, deep, inner core of consciousness, which is innately luminous and delightful. This inner or really inmost consciousness is a complete new world of thought, feeling and will, possessed of self-existence, independence, creativity, mastery of body, life and mind and the environment. It opens up a life of intrinsic values, a life of positive pursuit and enjoyment of these values and thus gives to the life of external values a perspective altogether new and different. This is the essential and central personality of yoga, which sets off the outer personality in the role of outer instrumentation.

This deeper personality is an integrated fact and primarily attuned to the perception of the wholeness of things. Unity is to it a spontaneous fact, not a matter of inference or a high ideal. Positive pursuit of unity and its progressive realisation is its natural activity.

In between the two lies a region of mind, life and body, which is not so particularised and limited as is the normal outer personality, but much wider, tending to be universal and capable of freer contact and communication with other minds, lives and bodies. Telepathy, telekinesis and the like are the capacities belonging to this part of personality. This is truly the inner personality in relation to the outer, but not really the self-existent personality. It is yet environment-dependent and environment-involved and subject to the ordinary dualities of life.

The inner and the inmost personalities are two wide realms or domains of the integral personality of man which one discovers through a persistent effort of inner penetration and exploration. And they bring into concrete reality and enjoyment most interesting new values of life, giving to the ordinary values of life a new context.

However, if one follows a line of upward growth from within one's normal consciousness, one discovers ascending ranges of consciousness, wide, full of peace and unity, increasing in luminosity and commanding universal existence. These ranges possess a striking largeness and universality and over-all direction and command. Their values are again characteristically their own. These fields together constitute the superconscious of yoga.

'Samadhi' ordinarily consists in ascending to it with the intention of accepting it as the sole truth and of rejecting the ordinary consciousness of external reality. But this intention is not essential to the discovery of the superconscious. One can also seek it to illumine, to re-orient and to transform the ordinary personality. However, there is also a Samadhi in the region of the heart. That Samadhi too can be sought exclusively for its own sake as well as for a transformation of the outer personality.

In addition to these major domains of personality, the outer, the inner, the central and the higher, there is also a lower domain, the realm of the subconscious and the unconscious. This is much marked by obscurity, disorderliness, self-will and obstinacy and it exercises an extensive determining power over conscious life and behaviour. It is a large storehouse of all past experiences, greatly influencing our present and future experiences.

Such is the large picture of our personality as clearly elaborated and explained and widely supported by ample data of yogic experience as expounded in the writings of Sri Aurobindo. But in different forms, implicit or explicit, and in parts these are present in all yogic pursuits and all attempts at exceeding the normal personality and achieving something higher and greater. Sri Aurobindo in his *The Synthesis of Yoga*, has achieved a coherent systematization of the various discoveries and realisations of the different yogic pursuits.

It may also be stated here that this conception of Integral Personality is based upon positive facts of experience, which have been confirmed repeatedly in different individuals in contemporary experience at the Sri Aurobindo Ashram, Pondicherry and elsewhere.

Western psychology is a young science but a highly progressive science. It has followed the models of physics, chemistry, biology and tended to become experimental and quantitative. But all that has led to a situation in which a representative psychologist, Gardner Murphy, feels impelled to say that we know a great deal about the reactions of personality, but practically nothing as to what personality by itself is. Now, obviously, such an observation reflects the awareness that psychology needs to know personality as it really is. This is, in fact, a favourable circumstance for a mutual appreciation of each other by both Western psychology and yogic psychology.

Freud has added a completely new dimension, that of the subconscious, to Western psychology; and between psychoanalysis and yoga there are many interesting points of contact, though the fundamental approaches are, in fact, opposed. The psychoanalytic doctrine that the symptoms of the disease are willed by the patient is matched to the yogic principle that nothing happens to a person unless there is a basis for it in his will. Again, the principle that the psychoanalyst must first be himself psychoanalysed before trying to psychoanalyse others is parallel to the yogic ideal that one who is not himself liberated should not try to liberate others. The opposition in the basic standpoints too is as strong as the similarity in the above points. To psychoanalysts, the subconscious is the basis, the cause of the disorder and the cure too is to be found or achieved through an exploration of the same. To yoga, the superconscious is the focus of interest and it is through a contact with it and its collaboration that perfection and harmony in life have to be achieved.

It is, however, in Jung that Western psychology comes nearest to yogic psychology. His affirmation of a 'centre' of personality on the basis of dream analysis, particularly what he calls the Mandala dreams and certain other facts, is strikingly similar to the yogic conception of the central psychic or spiritual personality. This 'centre', Jung affirms, is other than the normal ego-personality and its various dualities. His book, *The Integration of the Personality*, gives a lucid and convincing account of what this 'centre' of personality is.

Recent Western developments of para-psychology and experiments in telepathy show many further points of contact between the two systems of psychology.

William McDougall, an eminent Western psychologist, once observed that if telepathy came to be proved, then psychology will have to be rewritten. Western psychology is all based on the assumption that consciousness is a function of the brain and, therefore, necessarily dependent upon physical instrumentation of the sense-organs. In telepathy, consciousness becomes a fact by itself, capable of acting on another consciousness by itself, independently of physical instrumentation. For yoga, it is the outer personality or its consciousness which is dependent on the body. So is also the subconscious. But the inner personality comprises wider functions and the central and the higher domains of consciousness are independent facts.

All this raises a great prospect of a wide and integrated knowledge of personality, of a psychology slowly taking shape but yet to emerge into its full form.

Now let us contemplate how such a fuller psychology is likely to affect human life and culture and, in particular, the problems of education and mental health.

What is exactly the nature of the crisis that our life as a whole is facing today? The crisis takes on many shapes, political, economic, social, educational, etc., but is it not a fact that at the root, it is all a matter of certain values of life, which we cling to but which are not as abundant as we would wish them to be and even when they are abundant, they are not wholly satisfying. The values we seek and cling to are the values of the outer personality, the values of the wherewithal of life, material, social, intellectual, aesthetic, or the values of the body, life and mind. Now these are, in their nature, limited and the satisfactions they afford are superficial and transitory. But not knowing the intrinsic values of life, the values of the spirit, which are, in their nature, unlimited and which satisfy too in a profound manner, we take the extrinsic values of body, life and mind as entire and ultimate, and hence arise all the struggle, the interminable conflict and the persistent dissatisfaction of life.

The contemporary crisis is virtually a crisis of personality: the surface personality being cultivated too exclusively, being taken as the whole man.

The yogic psychology of personality clears up the entire situation in a surprising manner. We have, in our recent culture and civilisation, laid too exclusive an emphasis on the outer personality and its life. But there are other domains and dominions of personality and other systems of values too. And if they are taken note of and duly cultivated, then new values would emerge, which would afford larger and deeper satisfactions and give to the extrinsic values a new modest proportion in life as a whole.

The contemporary crisis is a matter of great perplexity to us today and it is extremely interesting how clear and convincing the whole situation becomes if we look at it in the light of a fuller view of human personality.

The problem of education has, at this time, become particularly serious because it involves a widespread dissatisfaction and revolt in the youth the world over. In exasperation we talk of a radical change in education. But the radical change needed is really not in outer forms, processes and the content of education so much as in the approach and the total perspective of it. That is, we need to keep in view the fuller personality, accord to the essential personality of intrinsic values its proper first place and give to the outer personality its own due place as the instrumentation of life. With this new radical revaluation of personality, we need to think out and organise our entire educational life. This too is made amply clear by a yogic view of personality.

However, of all contemporary problems, the most serious is perhaps that of mental health or the fear of becoming unsound in mind on a large scale. This fear has not yet assumed serious proportions, but its possibility is completely in view and that is of all things the most dangerous since it pertains to man's sanity itself. There cannot be a more damaging commentary on a civilisation than that it is tending to drive man insane.

Here again yogic psychology has something clear and convincing to offer. If the outer personality is the whole man, the numberless desires, which are the governing fact of the outer personality, become all important. And these desires are very self-willed, insistent and mutually contradictory. Inner conflict, anxiety, tension, frustration become unavoidable. It is only when deeper and more abiding inner satisfactions of the self-existent joy within, of love and beauty and goodness become available that we are able to take a relatively freer and non-insistent attitude towards our desires, their satisfactions and non-satisfactions. Thus as a wide preventive measure, we need to bring to the fore in our public life the vision of the essential central fact of human personality and its intrinsic values and their limitless satisfactions. Such a general trend will minimise the importance given to desires, make desires easier of management and reduce inner conflict and tension.

In the matter of the treatment and cure of mental disorders too, yogic psychology has a capital idea to contribute. Now the problem here is to restore inner peace and harmony to the patient. What we ordinarily do is to find out the causes of conflict and tension and then try to eliminate them. The strict psychological procedures try to raise the unconscious conflict to the level of consciousness and then let a new relatively wholesome orientation to life's situation come about or otherwise help the patient to take a more reasonable and less insistent attitude towards life and its problems. The various physical procedures adopted, *e.g.*, shock therapy, ignore the psychological causes and try to bring about certain neurological conditions, which tend to put away the mental symptoms concerned. But this does not bring about the mental synthesis needed for a proper guidance of life. The diversion therapy diverts attention to other unharmful channels.

They all have their relative values and serviceability. Now, the contribution which yogic psychology can make is this. There are domains of consciousness in man where peace and harmony obtain as normal qualities and functions. If their influence and action could be made available to the disrupted outer personality, then peace and harmony could come into it and in a more effective form and may be more quickly too.

We may now conclude that yoga, as the most devoted and dedicated approach to personality and its perfection, without any assumptions and limitations and with its great tradition, is perhaps the most promising pursuit of the study of man and his true and full nature. And our conception of man determines the character and the quality of our cultural life as well as our educational pursuit. Besides, the problems of one part of personality can best be solved by a reference to the other parts of personality. An exploration of the largest resources of personality is, therefore, of the utmost importance.

May Yoga and Western psychology come closer together soon. They would enrich each other by doing so and help in the emergence of the psychology of the integral man.

THE INTEGRAL PERSONALITY

(In the words of *Savitri*, Sri Aurobindo's Epic poem)

The World of Matter

When earth was built in the unconscious Void
And nothing was save a material scene,
Identified with sea and sky and stone
Her young gods yearned for the release of souls
Asleep in objects, vague, inanimate.
In that desolate grandeur, in that beauty bare,
In the deaf stillness, mid the unheeded sounds,
Heavy was the uncommunicated load
Of Godhead in a world that had no needs;
For none was there to feel or to receive.
(Savitri, Book II, Canto 3)

The World of Life

There was a writhing of half-conscious force
Hardly awakened from inconscient sleep
And tied to an instinct-driven Ignorance,
To find itself and find its hold on things.   (II, 4)

The Emergence of Mind

This was the first means of our slow ascent
From the half-conscience of the animal soul
Living in a crowded press of shape-events
In a realm it cannot understand nor change:
Only it sees and acts in a given scene
And feels the joys and sorrows for a while.
The ideas that drive the obscure embodied spirit
Along the roads of suffering and desire
In a world that struggles to discover Truth,
Found here their power to be and Nature-Force.
Here are devised the forms of an ignorant life

That sees the empiric fact as settled law,
Labours for the hour and not for eternity
And trades its gains to meet the moment's call:
The slow process of a material mind
Which serves the body it should rule and use
And needs to lean upon an erring sense,
Was born in that luminous obscurity.
Advancing tardily from a limping start,
Crutching hypothesis upon argument,
Throning its theories as certitudes,
It reasons from the half-known to the unknown,
Ever constructing its frail house of thought,
Ever undoing the web that it has spun.... (II, 10)

*

The infant laugh that rang through time is hushed:
Man's natural joy of life is overcast
And sorrow is his nurse of destiny.
The animal's thoughtless joy is left behind,
Care and reflection burden his daily walk:
He has risen to greatness and to discontent... (II, 4)

A Spark of God

In this investiture of fleshly life
A soul that is a spark of God survives
And sometimes it breaks through the sordid screen
And kindles a fire that makes us half-divine. (II, 4)

The Soul and the Mind

A conscious soul in the Inconscient's world
Hidden behind our thoughts and hopes and dreams,
An indifferent Master signing Nature's acts
Leaves the vicegerent mind a seeming king. (VII, 2)

*

This mind no silence knows nor dreamless sleep,
In the incessant circling of its steps
Thoughts tread for ever through the listening brain;
It toils like a machine and cannot stop. (Ibid.)

*

The hurried servant senses answer apace,
To every knock upon the outer doors,
Bring in life's visitors, report each call,
Admit the thousand queries and the calls
And the messages of communicating minds
And the heavy business of unnumbered lives
And all the thousandfold commerce of the world.
Even in the tracts of sleep is scant repose;
He mocks life's steps in strange subconscient dreams,
He strays in a sublime realm of symbol scenes,
His night with thin-air visions and dim forms
He packs or peoples with slight drifting shapes
And only a moment spends in silent self.
Adventuring into infinite mind-space
He unfolds his wings of thought in inner air,
Or travelling in imagination's car
Crosses the globe, journeys beneath the stars,
To subtle worlds takes his ethereal course,
Visits the gods on life's miraculous peaks,
Communicates with Heaven, tampers with Hell.
This is the little surface of man's life. (Ibid.)

*

Unknown to himself lives a hidden king
Behind rich tapestries in great secret rooms;
An epicure of the spirit's unseen joys,
He lives on the sweet honey of solitude... (Ibid.)

The Integral Personality

All the world's possibilities in man
Are waiting as the tree waits in its seed:
His past lives in him; it drives his future's pace;
His present's acts fashion his coming fate.
The unborn gods hide in his house of Life.
The daemons of the unknown overshadow his mind
Casting their dreams into live moulds of thought,
The moulds in which his mind builds out its world.
His mind creates around him its universe.
All that has been renews in him its birth,
All that can be is figured in his soul.
Issuing in deeds it scores on the roads of the world,
Obscure to the interpreting reason's guess,
Lines of the secret purpose of the gods.
In strange directions runs the intricate plan;
Held back from human foresight is their end.
And the far intention of some ordering Will
Or the order of life's arbitrary Chance
Finds out its settled poise and fated hour.
Our surface watched in vain by reason's gaze,
Invaded by the impromptus of the unseen,
Helpless records the accidents of Time,
The involuntary turns and leaps of life.
Only a little of us forsees its steps,
Only a little has will and purposed pace.
A vast subliminal is man's measureless part.
The dim subconscient is his cavern base.
Abolished vainly in the walks of Time
Our past lives still in our unconscious selves
And by the weight of its hidden influences
Is shaped our future's self-discovery.
Thus all is an inevitable chain
And yet a series seems of accidents.
The unremembering hours repeat the old acts,
Our dead past round our future's ankles clings
And drags back the new nature's glorious stride,
Or from its buried corpse old ghosts arise,
Old thoughts, old longings, dead passions live again,

Recur in sleep or move the waking man
To words that force the barrier of the lips,
To deeds that suddenly start and o'erleap
His head of reason and his guardian will.
An old self lurks in the new self we are;
Hardly we escape from what we once had been:
In the dim gleam of habit's passages,
In the subconscient's darkling corridors
All things are carried by the porter nerves
And nothing checked by subterranean mind,
Unstudied by the guardians of the doors
And passed by a blind instinctive memory,
The old gang dismissed, old cancelled passports serve,
Nothing is wholly dead that once had lived.
In dim tunnels of the world's being and in ours
The old rejected nature still survives;
The corpses of its slain thoughts raise their heads
And visit mind's nocturnal walks in sleep,
Its stifled impulses breathe and move and rise;
All keeps a phantom immortality.
Irresistible are Nature's sequences:
The seeds of sins renounced sprout from hid soil;
The evil cast from our hearts once more we face.
Our dead selves come to slay our living soul.
A portion of us lives in present Time,
A secret mass in dim inconscience gropes;
Out of the inconscient and subliminal
Arisen, we live in mind's uncertain light
And strive to know and master a dubious world
Whose purpose and meaning are hidden from our sight.
Above us dwells a superconscient god
Hidden in the mystery of his own light:
Around us is a vast of ignorance
Lit by the uncertain ray of human mind,
Below us sleeps the Inconscient dark and mute.
   But this is only Matter's first self-view,
A scale and series in the Ignorance.
This is not all we are or all our world.
Our greater self of knowledge waits for us,
A supreme light in the truth-conscious Vast:

It sees from summits beyond thinking mind,
It moves in a splendid air transcending life.
It shall descend and make earth's life divine.
Truth made the world, not a blind Nature-Force.
For here are not our large diviner heights;
Our summits in the superconscient's blaze
Are glorious with the very face of God:
There is our aspect of eternity,
There is the figure of the god we are,
His young unaging look on deathless things,
His joy in our escape from death and Time,
His immortality and light and bliss.
Our larger being sits behind cryptic walls:
There are greatnesses hidden in our unseen parts
That wait their hour to step into life's front:
We feel an aid from deep indwelling Gods:
One speaks within, Light comes to us from above.
Our soul from its mysterious chamber acts;
Its influence pressing on our heart and mind
Pushes them to exceed their mortal selves.
It seeks for Good and Beauty and for God;
We see beyond self's walls our limitless self,
We gaze through our world's glass at half-seen vasts,
We hunt for the Truth behind apparent things.
Our inner Mind dwells in a larger light,
Its brightness looks at us through hidden doors;
Our members luminous grow and Wisdom's face
Appears in the doorway of the mystic ward:
When she enters into our house of outward sense,
Then we look up and see, above, her sun.
A mighty life-self with its inner powers
Supports the dwarfish modicum we call life;
It can graft upon our crawl two puissant wings.
Our body's subtle self is throned within
In its viewless palace of veridical dreams
That are bright shadows of the thoughts of God.
In the prone obscure beginnings of the race
The human grew in the bowed apelike man.
He stood erect, a godlike form and force,
And a soul's thoughts looked out from earthborn eyes;

Man stood erect, he wore the thinker's brow:
He looked at heaven and saw his comrade stars;
A vision came of beauty and greater birth
Slowly emerging from the heart's chapel of light
And moved in a white lucent air of dreams.
He saw his being's unrealised vastnesses,
He aspired and housed the nascent demi-god.
Out of the dim recesses of the self
The occult seeker into the open came:
He heard the far and touched the intangible,
He gazed into the future and the unseen;
He used the powers earth-instruments cannot use,
A pastime made of the impossible;
He caught up fragments of the Omniscient's thought,
He scattered formulas of omnipotence.
Thus man in his little house made of earth's dust
Grew towards an unseen heaven of thought and dream
Looking into the vast vistas of his mind
On a small globe dotting infinity.
At last climbing a long and narrow stair
He stood alone on a high roof of things
And saw the light of a spiritual sun.
Aspiring he transcends his earthly self;
He stands in the largeness of his soul new-born
Redeemed from encirclement by mortal things
And moves in a pure free spiritual realm
As in the rare breath of a stratosphere.
A lost end of far lines of divinity,
He mounts by a frail thread to his high source;
He reaches his fount of immortality,
He calls the Godhead into his mortal life.   (Ibid.)

*

But for such vast spiritual change to be,
Out of the mystic cavern in man's heart
The heavenly Psyche must put off her veil
And step into common nature's crowded rooms
And stand uncovered in that nature's front
And rule its thoughts and fill the body and life.   (Ibid.)

THE VERIFICATION OF THE TRUTHS OF INTEGRAL PERSONALITY

Yogic Truths and Verification

The demand for the verification of truths of Integral Personality is a legitimate one. Of course, the verification has to be adapted to the nature of the facts and truths concerned. Where the facts and truths are of the physical nature, standards of verification will be of one kind. But where they are of the mind and consciousness, they have to be appropriate and effective for them. Now, introspection is the method for the direct observation of mental processes and other deeper facts of consciousness. The same method, under controlled conditions, which too will have to be primarily inner – of conscious motivations and attitudes – and only secondarily external, physical, will and can provide verification for the facts and truths of consciousness.

As compared with the criterion of physical science, this criterion will, of course, be difficult. But shall we then, for reason of difficulty, give up the investigation of consciousness and its pervasive facts? If we do so, we then shrink from the essential fact of human living since consciousness is our being and without it we are just unthinking matter.

The writer here has no hesitation in affirming that the pursuit of Integral Yoga and the practice of introspection, in a deliberate and persistent manner since 1940, has afforded him repeatedly a deep joy whenever he found in his own experience affirmations of Integral Yoga, now one, now another, *as really true*. This is the verification which he has had and which gives him a sense of clarity and certitude regarding the basic truths of integral personality.

The approaches and the processes of verification can, in fact, be varied and they have to be adapted to the temperamental conditions of seeker and inquirer. We give below one, the most common and the most effective.

A preliminary apprehension of the truths of Integral Personality need not prove difficult if verification is pursued in a spirit of whole-hearted search for truth. A realisation of them or making them normal experience of life is a different matter, needing a great length of time.

Introspection, a correct introspection, to yield satisfactory verification is also not easy. It has, in the first instance, to overcome the normal out-gazing nature of mind. Our mind is capable of self-consciousness rather occasionally in its best moments of consciousness. This capacity has to be developed to a degree that we can, with ease and freedom, look at ourselves within indefinitely. With that should go a sincere will and attitude to see things in the best possible spirit of truth. 'To see things as they are' again is not an easy capacity. The partialities and prejudices of personal disposition and social suggestion have to be guarded against. The yoga is, in fact, ruthless in its demand for objectivity, i.e., 'seeing things as they are'.

Introspection would thus need cultivation. But it perfects itself through exercise. The exceptional convenience in this case is that it can be practised all the time and in the midst of all the activities of life, which means carrying on those activities self-consciously not just consciously and self-forgetfully. That is useful for those activities too, if self-consciousness does not involve forgetfulness of the external as it can when it is not strong enough.

McDougall, the well-known psychologist, it appears, tried to practise introspection. He has said somewhere that he could not distinguish between the sensation of hunger and that of thirst. On getting some sensation of one or the other, he would first take a glass of water. If the sensation disappeared he would feel sure that it was thirst. If the sensation persisted, then he would conclude that he was really hungry.

This is an extremely interesting introspective report. A very honest and frank one. The reader, a psychologist or a layman, may check for himself whether McDougall's observations of his inner states of thirst and hunger were correct or not.

Introspection, a reliable one, is evidently the first thing. This given, verifications and confirmations of inner conscious facts can be easily hoped for.

Now, Sri Aurobindo's delineation of the line of verification, which has been long used in India's spiritual history and which stands supported by contemporary yogic practice is as follows:

"If one stands back from the mind and its activities so that they fall silent at will or go on as a surface movement of which one is the detached and disinterested witness, it becomes possible eventually to realise oneself as the inner Self of mind, the true and pure mental being, the Purusha; by similarly standing back from the life activities, it is possible to realise oneself as the Self of life, the true and pure vital being, the Purusha; there is even a Self of body of which, by standing back from the body and its demands and activities and entering into a silence of the physical consciousness watching the action of its energy, it is possible to become aware of a true and pure physical being, the Purusha. So too, by standing back from all these activities of nature successively or together, it becomes possible to realise one's inner being as the silent impersonal self, the witness Purusha."

"The Purusha has to become not only the witness but the knower and source, the master of all the thought and action, and this can only be partially done so long as one remains on the mental level or has still to use the ordinary instrumentation of mind, life and body. A certain mastery can indeed be achieved, but mastery is not transformation; the change made by it cannot be sufficient to be integral; for that it is essential to get back, beyond mind-being, life-being, body-being, still more deeply inward to the psychic entity inmost and profoundest within us – or else to open to the superconscient highest domain."

This approach of self-detachment from the superficial uppermost thoughts and feelings and impulses to action for an access to the deeper states of consciousness is really a wonderful technique. It affords freedom from the superficial facts, correct appraisal of them, in addition to the discovery of the deeper facts of consciousness. This exercise is truly stimulating as it affords further and yet further discoveries of delight, awareness and effectivity. Introspection becomes rewarding for psychology as for life.

Apart from this technique of self-detachment, yoga and yogic psychology provide another verification too. They are result-oriented, i.e., they aim at a state of wholeness, integration, spontaneity, simplicity, freedom from conflict and tension, peace, harmony, joy, etc. The progressive growth of these qualities is itself a test and a criterion of the psychological foundations of yoga and yogic psychology.

One may also consider that India has a strong tradition of spiritual pursuit and enjoyment of spiritual life. Could this tradition have been built up, if generation after generation had not been able to verify and confirm the truths of life and personality affirmed earlier?

Of course, the present generation has to seek and discover its own criterion of the traditional truths of personality.

CONTEMPORARY PSYCHOLOGISTS AND PERSONALITY

Introduction

Contemporary Psychology is predominantly Experimental Psychology which is emulating the Natural Science model and wants to be quantitative and mathematical. It is showing fine results and utilities.

This approach tends to take man as a fixed quantity and then study its relations to the environment. But personality is essentially a dynamic fact and all the business of education and culture is to promote higher qualities. For that the unexpressed possibilities of nature are more important than the expressed ones.

What personality essentially is then becomes more important than the study of its reactions. And there is a lot in Contemporary Psychology on this issue too. Here we have a representative assortment of views on the subject. They do show the direction in which this investigation is moving. There is a view of personality as a fact of 'Self-actualisation' supported by many psychologists. There is also a recognition and appreciation of the search and the realisation of 'Who am I? Jung's perceptions regarding the deeper and fuller nature of personality are the most interesting and most influential too. They show a close sympathy to the Indian yogic and mystic perceptions. What is really interesting is that the qualities of 'wholeness', of 'harmony' within as with the external world are appreciated as the essential qualities of personality. Even Freud had a feeling for the mystic practices and what they could possibly achieve.

Selected Original Statements

1. *Sigmund Freud*: "It can easily be imagined, too, that certain practices of mystics may succeed in upsetting the normal relation between the different regions of the mind, so that, for example, the perceptual system becomes able to grasp relations in the deeper layers of the ego and in the id which would otherwise be inaccessible to it. Whether such a procedure can put one in possession of the ultimate truths, from which all good will flow, may be safely doubted. All the same, we must admit that the

therapeutic efforts of psycho-analysis have chosen much the same method of approach. For their object is to strengthen the ego, to make it more independent of the super-ego, to widen its field of vision and so to extend its organisation that it can take over new portions of the id. Where id was, there shall ego be." (*New Lectures*, 1933, p. 106)

2. *C. G. Jung*: Founder of the School of Analytical Psychology:
(A) "All the usual little remedies and medicaments of psychology fall somewhat short (of explaining personality) just as they do with the man of genius or the creative human being. Derivation from ancestral heredity or from the milieu does not quite succeed; inventing fictions about childhood, which is so popular today, end – to put it mildly – in the inappropriate, the explanation from necessity – he had no money, was ill, and so forth – remains caught in mere externalities." (*The Integration of the Personality*, 1940, p. 299)
(B) "If we survey the situation as a whole, we come to the inevitable conclusion – at least in my opinion – that a psychic element is present that expresses itself through the tetrad. This conclusion demands neither daring speculation nor extravagant phantasy. If I have called the centre the 'self', I did so after ripe reflection and a careful assessment of the data of experience as well as of history." (*Ibid.*, p. 198)
(C) "The centre acts like a magnet upon the disparate materials and processes of the unconscious and, like a crystal grating, catches them one by one." (*Ibid.*, p. 197)

3. *Gardner Murphy*: "Nobody knows anything much about the nature of man. We are in a position to raise a great many questions, to raise questions perhaps so grave and so fundamental that we begin to wonder if we even have a method for approaching an ultimate solution." (*Main Currents of Modern Thought*, Vol. 9, No. 2, N.Y.)

4. *Kurt Goldstein*: "The traditional view assumes various drives which come into the foreground under certain conditions. We assume only one drive, the drive for self-actualization of the organism; but we are compelled to concede that under certain conditions the tendency to actualize one potentiality is so strong that the organism is governed by it. Superficially, therefore, our

theory may not appear so much in conflict with others. However, I think there is an essential difference. From our standpoint, we can understand the latter phenomenon as an abnormal deviation from the normal behaviour under definite conditions; but the theory of separate drives can never comprehend normal behaviour without positing another agency which makes the decision in the struggle between the single drives. That means: Any theory of drives has to introduce another, a 'higher' agency. We must reject this auxiliary hypothesis as unsuitable to solve the problem. 'The tendency of the organism to actualize itself' always confronts us with the same answer. We do not need the drives." (*The Self*, Clark E. Moustakas, New York)

5. *Presscott Lecky*: "Let us think of the individual, therefore, as a unified system with two sets of problems – one, the problem of maintaining inner harmony within himself, and the other, the problem of maintaining harmony with the environment, especially the social environment, in the midst of which he lives. In order to understand the environment, he must keep his interpretations consistent with his experience, but in order to maintain his individuality he must organize his interpretations to form a system which is internally consistent. This consistency is not objective, of course, but subjective and wholly individual.

"The personality develops as a result of actual contacts with the world, and incorporates into itself the meanings derived from external contacts. Essentially, it is the organisation of experience into an integrated whole." (*Ibid.*, p. 91)

6. *Carl R. Rogers*: "I have however come to believe that, in spite of this bewildering horizontal multiplicity, there is a simple answer. As I follow the experience of many clients in the therapeutic relationship which we endeavour to create for them, it seems to me that each one has the same problem. Below the level of the problem situation about which the individual is complaining – behind the trouble with studies, or wife, or employer, or with his own uncontrollable or bizarre behaviour, or with his frightening feelings, lies one central search. It seems to me that at bottom each person is asking: *Who am I, really? How can I get in touch with this real self, underlying all my surface behaviour? How can I become myself?*" (*Ibid.*, p. 196)

7. *A. H. Maslow*: "The lack of meditativeness and inwardness, of real consciousness and real values, is a standard American personality defect; a shallowness, a superficial living on the surface of life, a living by other people's opinion rather than by one's own native, inner voice. These are the other-directed men who live, or rather are directed by publicity campaigns, by testimonials, by majority vote, by public opinion, by what other people think. They do not really know what they want, what they feel, what they themselves think right and wrong. Mind you, when everything goes well these are the adjusted people. They feel fine. They never go to the psychotherapist for help, thinking until it is too late that they need none. And yet they are sick, deep down sick, for they have lost their individuality, their uniqueness. They have become robots." (*Ibid.* p. 239)

8. *G. Bose*: An eminent Indian Psychologist, Head of the Department of Psychology, Calcutta University, wrote in his 'Progress of Psychology during the Last Twenty-five Years', published by the Indian Science Congress in 1938, the following:

"India's ancient learned men had a genius for introspective meditation and the Indian Psychologist has that heritage. In this respect he enjoys an advantage over his colleagues in the West. If this faculty is properly cultivated, problems requiring deep introspection such as those of thought processes, higher cultural inhibitions, etc., will be successfully solved. The mystic experience of saints and yogis should form the subject-matter of psychological research and India is the best place for this study."

9. *B. Kuppuswamy*: Formerly Head of the Department of Psychology, Mysore University, writes in an article, entitled "Yoga and Self-actualisation", as follows:

"The normal tendency in the West is to draw conclusions about the inner world from the outward impressions on the basis of the principle that 'nothing is in the mind which was not previously in the senses'. But Carl Jung started a new line of thinking in psychology regarding the problem of self and personality. According to him the ego is brought into being in childhood and firmly established in adolescence. Personality, as the expression of the wholeness of man, according to Jung, is an adult ideal, whose conscious realization through individuation is the aim of human development in the second half of life.

"The influence of Jung has brought about a new trend in the theories of personality in modern Psychology."

10. *C. M. Bhatia* in his presidential address entitled, "The Nature of Psychology and its contribution to Human Welfare", at the Psychology Section, Indian Science Congress, Calcutta, 1980, said:

"Unless Psychology is willing to deal with the heights to which human individuals have risen or shown themselves capable of rising, growth of psychology would be stunted. Many more facts are at present known than modern Psychology cares to acknowledge, perhaps again in a defensive mood to accept only facts which it is able to explain within its present frame-work. Man in his heights is the subject-matter of Psychology, whether it is his mystic experiences, his creativity, his destructiveness or the concomitant Psychological functioning of his body in respect of these experiences.

"To fathom the mysteries of nature not directly encompassable by the human mind, becomes more a central problem to Psychology than to other sciences. To be able to go beyond the human mind ultimately becomes the problem of Psychology.

"Psychology is not an elementary science. It is an ultimate science if ever there could be one. The study of Psychology, whether in the universities or outside them, must be attuned to this position if the study of Psychology is to be worthwhile and meaningful."

11. *H. C. Ganguli*: Head of the Psychology Department, Delhi University, in his elaborate study of 'Meditation' says:

"Meditation is a late entry into the research field but the interest it has aroused in investigators is most gratifying and this for several reasons. Firstly, there is substantial evidence by now that meditation leads to distinct therapeutic gains and alleviation of suffering. Secondly, there is the enticing prospect of gaining more knowledge about the nature and functioning of consciousness through interdisciplinary research and arriving at a unified model of consciousness that will be useful for an understanding of the cognitive processes. Lastly, there is a possibility, a fond hope perhaps, that meditation research may show the way to enhance the capacity and range of functioning of the human brain. This last possibility is exciting and can be, if attained, looked upon as a major scientific breakthrough. (*Meditation: An Altered State of Consciousness,* MS. p. 5)

"For the modern man meditation not only seeks to provide a non-invasive, non-pharmacological device for symptom relief, but also serves as an aid for attaining a higher level of self-actualization and psychological maturity." (*Ibid.*, p. 26)

12. Here are a few further passages of Jung representing his insights of later years too:

(1) "...The unconsciousness is not just evil by nature, it is also the source of the highest good: not only dark but also light, not only bestial, semi-human, and demonic but superhuman, spiritual, and in the classical sense of the word 'divine...'" (*Collected Works*, Vol. 16, p. 192)

(2) "...the ever deeper descent into the unconscious suddenly becomes illumination from above..." (*Ibid.*, p. 281)

(3) "...The individuation is psychically a border-line phenomenon which needs special conditions in order to become conscious. Perhaps it is the first step along a path of development to be trodden by the men of the future..." (*Ibid.*, Vol. 8, p. 225)

THE PURSUIT OF PSYCHOLOGY

A Plea for a Larger Orientation

Most of our universities now have full-fledged independent departments of psychology and they are fairly prosperous in the sense that they attract students and there is plenty of activity in the departments. But we might reflect a little on the overall position of the pursuit of psychology in the country and consider what contribution it makes to the cause of advancement of knowledge in the field. In this connection, the question arises whether our pursuit of psychology should or should not relate itself to the traditional Indian psychological knowledge as embodied in the various yogic systems and elsewhere.

To facilitate consideration of this issue, a draft on 'Psychology and Yoga' is presented here as also a few comments.

Psychology and Yoga

Western psychology is a vast body of knowledge regarding human mind, behaviour and personality, normal and abnormal, individual and social. There is a branch dealing with the mind and behaviour of the animal too. This is general scientific psychology, which limits itself severely to the empirical facts and seeks to be experimental. But there is also a powerful trend of psychological investigation represented by Freud and Jung which explores the unconscious and its effects on the conscious life of man. Jung explores also the fields of religion and yogic experience. There is also parapsychology coming into prominence, which seeks to explore phenomena like telepathy, memories of a previous birth, premonitions, apparitions, etc., etc. Telepathy has been taken up even for experimental investigation and it is becoming an important issue. Suggestology, a further recent branch, seeks to study the working of suggestion in various forms.

Western psychology is, indeed, a most active science and fresh issues and lines of investigation are ever coming up. What is, in fact, more important is the phenomenon of a general psychological way of looking upon life as such, war, peace, normal human dealings – personal, national and international.

But the most influential part in this pursuit is that of scientific psychology, which limits itself to empirical facts of mind and behaviour and seeks to be experimental. Lately, it has turned more to behaviour, which is more amenable to experiment.

The substance of achievement of this body of psychological knowledge can best be represented in the words of Gardner Murphy, an eminent contemporary psychologist. He says, "Nobody knows anything much about the nature of man. We are in a position to raise a great many questions, to raise questions perhaps so grave and so fundamental that we begin to wonder if we even have a method for approaching an ultimate solution."[1]

In India, Yoga has been the counterpart of Western psychology, and the research in this field has been enormous. Self-knowledge or *ātmajñāna* has been the characteristic objective of Indian cultural pursuit and again and again new approaches and processes were discovered and evolved for the realisation of a perception of the spiritual truth and reality. Apart from these, various forms of Yoga are well-known. They are Hatha Yoga, Raja Yoga, Jnana Yoga, Bhakti Yoga, Karma Yoga, Tantric Yoga and certain yogic forms called Vidyas in the Upanishads and other spiritual practices less known. In the wake of these has come the contemporary creation in this field – the Integral Yoga of Sri Aurobindo, as embodied in his systematic and comprehensive writing *The Synthesis of Yoga*.

All these yogic systems involve psychological systems of distinctive qualities with much common knowledge. These psychological systems have a standpoint of their own. They seek the essential truth of personality and a mastery of the empirical part of personality and not just an intellectual understanding and explanation of them. That means a sure and verified knowledge of personality. They do not separate the empirical from the essential and do not limit themselves by any assumptions in their pursuit of the knowledge of personality. The contemporary Integral Yoga deliberately seeks the most comprehensive approach and the integral psychology which it embodies is a most comprehensive account of personality.

The method in these Indian schools of psychology is primarily introspection, a direct observation of the states of consciousness, which is cultivated with great perseverance and dispassionateness

---

1. Main Currents of Modern Thought, New York, Vol. 9, No. 2.

over long years of training. Introspection is, no doubt, a difficult process, but this is the only one which gives a proper appreciation of the reality of the facts of consciousness and a direct knowledge of them. A greater reliance on objective observation in Western psychology has easily led to a failure of appreciation of the reality of mental processes and psychology has tended to become a study of behaviour. And this means a miscarriage of psychology as a science of mental life, with the result that we know a great deal *about* personality but almost nothing *of* personality.

In Western psychology, Jung, on purely empirical grounds through a study of the dreams of normal persons and a survey of religious experience, has come to affirm that there is a 'centre' behind the apparent dualisms of mental life. This 'centre' is comparable to the 'Atman' of Indian psychological systems, with the difference that in yoga it must be made, at the end, a fact of experience and not retained as an inference.

If we take the two bodies of knowledge, Western psychological knowledge of personality and Indian yogic knowledge of personality, do they not fall into a coherent form, yielding a surer feeling as to what personality is and what its outer form and reactions are? Indian psychology, as it were, fulfils Western psychology and Indian psychology gets a fuller and detailed knowledge of the outer form of personality. The knowledge of the essential part is indispensable. That is what lends uniqueness and wholeness to personality and is, therefore, most important for educational and therapeutic purposes.

Western psychology has been, one might say, rather unfortunate in emulating the example of other sciences. In the 19th century, while seeking recognition, it sought to become 'a psychology without a soul'. Then it sought to be like physics and again like biology and further like physiology and lastly experimental and mathematical in order to be a perfect science. The spirit of experiment is a correct approach, but to seek experimentation like that of the physical sciences is a different matter. It is interesting to note that Dilthey and Spranger in Germany reminded that its subject-matter was not like that of the physical sciences and, therefore, it should rather be itself than something other than itself. Ebbinghaus and Kulpe sought to apply introspection to the higher mental process – memory, thought and imagination – and it yielded promising results. But the direction neither of Dilthey and Spranger nor of Ebbinghaus and Kulpe succeeded in giving an effective new turn to the science. If it had, the situation today might have been very different and Western psychology and Yoga might have found themselves closer to each other.

Since independence, India has naturally sought to feel, live and act in her own selfhood more or less. This trend has had its effect in the field of the pursuit of knowledge too. India has had a high tradition of the pursuit of knowledge and scored great achievements in many fields. Mathematics, astronomy, medicine, literature, philosophy, religion and yoga are some of the most important ones In these, in particular, the Indian scholars have sought to recover their traditional roots and by doing so they felt well reinforced in their present pursuit of the same. But the process of discovering this selfhood continues and in psychology too a beginning has been made here and there. However, here India has much to contribute to world knowledge and the world demands it of us and appreciates it too when we are able to do so. Let us hope that our research is able to deliver to us, in a modern form, the psychological knowledge of the yogic systems more and more and also that the sum of world knowledge of psychology becomes more confident of human personality and its varied dimensions and domains.

Comments of a few Leading Indian Psychologists

I fully agree that we Indian psychologists should be conversant with the yogic systems and make use of the knowledge thus gained to realise our main objective. The distinction you have made between knowing *about* personality and knowing *of* personality is a crucial one.

Before making further observation on the point raised by you, I should like to tell you first what I told Prof. Durganand Sinha when he interviewed me a year ago to know my assessment of the work of the Indian psychologists. I do not remember the exact language I used but the following is the substance of my opinion: "The contribution of the Indian psychologists has not been such as we can justly be proud of. In the beginning when the scientific study of modern psychology, i.e., experimental psychology was taken up, we made a few studies which won recognition in the academic circle here and abroad. These studies were based upon introspective analysis of experience under controlled conditions. Apart from those, a few studies on unconscious mind, thanks to the genius of G. Bose, were regarded as contributions to the advancement of knowledge. I do not know what else we have to our credit. Of course there are several good theoretical essays; but these are little read, less understood and have the least impact on professional psychologists and laymen alike. We honestly cannot complain if our work on mental tests, personal selection, industrial relations and social surveys are regarded as second-rate. We have not the financial resources, man power, state or public support for a high measure of success in such work. No wonder that in the community of world-top-rank psychologists, we are relegated to the position of second-class citizens, so to say. Working in the same field in which the Western psychologists have excelled, we cannot aspire to stand shoulder to shoulder with them. But there is one field in which we, too, can excel. That is the field of introspective analysis of mental experiences."

From the above, you will see that I am for developing introspective psychology. In the beginning of my career, I was initiated to introspection by Dr. N. N. Sengupta, and then Dr. G. Bose made me go through the rigours of mental discipline to acquire ability for deep introspection. Training for introspection involving concentration and sense-control might be helpful in being trained for yogic practice. (My work as an introspectionist ended when I joined the War Service. After the War, I did not take it up again as I had to work in industries. That work was rewarding from the material point of view but not self-satisfying.)

I agree that knowledge of theory and practice of yoga will be of advantage to the Indian psychologists in the pursuit of study of their subject. Acceptance of this view by many of our younger psychologists becomes difficult because they have a vague notion of the meaning of the term yoga. I have been told by our bright young lecturers with Ph.D. degrees in Western psychology that they are confused in their minds about the meaning and implication of yoga. Almost impossible physical feats, occult power, mystic influence, means of gaining salvation, mental discipline for unification of the self with the supreme soul and such other ideas are associated with yoga. They say that yoga belongs to the realm of philosophy, not psychology. I do not claim to have understood the true connotation of yoga. For my purpose, I accept the teaching of Patanjali that yoga "does not mean union but only effort" (Radhakrishnan). It is a search for the divine and eternal part of our being, but it signifies strenuous endeavour. My knowledge of yoga is poor indeed. I read in books about various yogic practices, but I would not say that I could have a clear grasp. I believe one has to learn it the hard way through practice under proper guidance. In the ordinary sense, I take it that yoga implies concentration and sense-control; it helps to increase physical and mental capabilities. It leads to our perception of the objective character of a thing merging into our realization of its essence. To me the state of deep introspection is something akin to it, though in a much smaller degree.

You are very right when you say that we know about personality and not of personality. I agree that we need psychologists trained in yoga. You have truly said that "Atmajnana has been the characteristic objective of Indian cultural pursuit." That is in our element. If we cultivate it, we shall succeed. Knowing will be a revelation; sensing will be a feeling. I am glad you are taking up the problem of 'Psychology and Yoga'. You are the right person for it. The task is difficult. I may tell you that very few of the younger members of our discipline will be initially interested.

Prof. S. K. Bose
Formerly, Head of the Department
of Psychology, Calcutta University

I consider it a privilege to react to your article – "The Pursuit of Psychology – A Plea for a Larger Orientation" – enclosed with your letter of 17.8.80. We also received your subsequent letter of 22.9.80 addressed to my daughter, Mrs. Ira Das, and thank you very much for the same. It has taken a long time for me to recover. I am now almost all right.

I fully agree with the general approach of your paper, particularly that Introspection should not only be not tabooed, but that it is the only way of getting into the innermost working of our minds. Whoever have been able to portray human character deeply have delineated the inner introspective working of the mind, be they novelists, poets, psychologists or Indian Yogis. Therein one goes to the source of mental functioning. I have also never been able to understand why, when one introspects, the mental process itself changes. I also agree with you that "Objectivity" in observation has been made a mess of in Western Psychology. Western Physics has come to recognise the contradictions in the concept of "objective observation", but strangely enough not Western Psychology. I further quite agree with you that this has led "to a failure of appreciation of mental processes" and meant the miscarriage of Psychology as a Science.

This much is conceded. But the difficulty of "Indian Psychology" or "Indian Yogic Knowledge of Psychology" has been, as I see it (because I am no authority on Yoga) that Yogic Knowledge has not been connected with "material Knowledge". This has been my general criticism of "spirituality" also. Spirituality is being talked about without the "bases of Spirituality", which are, to my mind, 'material', thus giving the impression that 'Spirituality' stands up, almost hanging away from the physical reality of our everyday life. I hope I am clear. I see no dualism in the mental and the material nor the spiritual and the mental. It is the problem of connecting "Yogic Knowledge" with the physical realities of life that to my mind needs to be worked out or, if already worked out, to be re-affirmed. This will enable the Yogic Knowledge to make its contribution to the totality of human experience. A whole structure has to be worked out. May be it is already there in the Yogic system, for the Indian mind is very logical. But not being a student of Yoga, I am not specifically aware of it. If it is there, it has to be refurbished.

Needless to say that I shall be most interested in your project and very willing to actively participate in it, should you decide upon it.

Dr. C. M. Bhatia
Recently President, Section of
Psychology, Indian Science Congress

There is no doubt that psychological studies and research in India should be linked up with the rich heritage in the psychological field of the ancient Indian thinkers.

However, the difficulty is that we do not have any treatise dealing with the psychological aspect of ancient Indian thought. Nor is there a comprehensive text-book which could furnish a map of the problems and conclusions of the ancient thought.

Psychological studies have to be based on empirical work today. Neither faith nor fascination can promote objective studies.

It is true that there is considerable material of psychological interest in *Yoga*. It is certainly necessary to initiate a number of researches on the assumptions and the techniques and the results of Yoga. Recent studies of ASC – Alternate States of Consciousness – have opened out a new field. To my knowledge, attempts have not been made in Indian Universities to study Yoga from this standpoint.

I must frankly admit that it will not be wise to get involved in telepathy, memories of previous birth, premonitions, etc. The various attempts over the last three or more decades in the field of so-called *Parapsychology* have not borne fruit, in my opinion. Faith rather than intellectual interest has been the motive force in these studies in India and abroad.

Certainly the influence and limitation of suggestibility need serious pursuit, particularly in the light of millions who follow Godmen.

I firmly believe that psychological studies should be empirical and experimental. Any abandonment of these techniques and outlook will only lead to its devaluation.

While acknowledging that it is necessary to have empirical and experimental studies on religious behaviour and religious experience, particularly with respect to the relation between personality structure and the four yogas, I wish to emphasise that the clinical approach should be utilised and verifiable facts ascertained, so that repetitions could be attempted to confirm.

With respect to the observation "Western Psychology has been rather unfortunate in emulating the example of other sciences", the following warning by Sri Aurobindo, on the fate of the science of comparative philology is quite relevant...:

"...Conjectural science means pseudo-science, since fixed, sound and verifiable bases and methods, independent of conjecture are the primary condition of science." (*The Secret of the Veda*, 1971, p. 552)

While agreeing that ancient Indian thought has much to contribute to the growth of knowledge in Psychology, it must be clearly and firmly borne in mind that the immediate need is to present the discoveries of ancient Indian sages and thinkers in a form which enables assimilation in the modern context.

I fervently hope that this task will be undertaken as early as possible.

Dr. B. Kuppuswamy
Formerly Head of the Department of Psychology, Mysore University, has published many studies on Indian Psychology and is bringing out a systematic book entitled *"Elements of Ancient Indian Psychology"*.

Concluding Remarks

The foregoing responses of three important psychologists are extremely interesting. They show a clear recognition and appreciation of the tradition of psychological knowledge in India and yet do not know how to recover that tradition in the present situation and bring it into an adjustment with the Western approach which is now the established fact with us. This feeling of difficulty is a happy thing and if we sincerely face it, solutions will begin to emerge.

Dr. G. Bose in Calcutta and Dr. Gopalaswami in Mysore had fine original minds as psychologists and their contributions are always an inspiration to us. Dr. H. C. Ganguli's pursuit of 'Meditation' as a psychological study is also a fine attempt.

Introspection is finding repeated recognition at our hands and, once we whole-heartedly recognise its essential value for psychology, our main line of research and contribution will become clear to us. The Indian psychologist seems to be discovering his soul, his true identity and individuality, though yet faced with hesitations, inhibitions and ambiguities.

Dr. Kuppuswamy's insistence on verifiability is very relevant, but in respect of introspective data new criteria of verifiability will have to be evolved.

Indian psychologists pleading ignorance of the psychological facts involved in the yogic and the religious experience is too poor a defence, because none outside India will accept it.

THE SEARCH FOR A THEORY OF PERSONALITY IN CONTEMPORARY PSYCHOLOGY

Psychology is a Western science and it has grown up in the atmosphere and with the attitudes of other sciences of nature such as physics, chemistry, biology, etc.

It is essentially a study of man as an object of nature. It is, therefore, a study of man from the outside, externally. 'Self' has been a topic of study as phenomenon observed from the outside. "What am I?" has not been the issue of this Western science of man. And a study by inner exploration, as done in yoga, is also not recognised as a valid approach up to this day.

William James was a great recent American psychologist whose influence still persists, apart from psychology in philosophy as well as in religion. He treated of 'self' as consisting of 'a material me', 'a social me', 'a spiritual me'. These were the three components of the empirical me or self and besides these he affirmed a transcendental me, which however did not stimulate 'inquiry'. In fact, in another context it was denied. While considering the nature of thinking and thinker, he said 'thoughts themselves are the thinkers', each preceding thought thinks the succeeding thought.

To a superficial and external handling of self or personality, Freud added a depth, which was not of inwardness but of past experiences carried forward in the subconscious. Jung added to this dimension of past experiences the possibilities of the future as sometimes reflected in the dreams of the normal person and in mystical experience and in the religious life in general. However, the approach was external. An approach of introspection for the study of the human psyche, as done in yoga, was not recognised by him, even though he studied yogic texts deeply and interpreted them so well.

Western science is essentially analytical. Analysis of facts into simpler parts and tracing them to preceding happenings has been the secret of its understanding of things and its power of invention at the physical level. But as the limitations of the analytical method emerged, the quality of wholeness has been recognised more and more. There are trends even in physics that 'wholeness' is a distinct recognizable quality apart from what the parts possess. It is more widely appreciated than before that a whole is not just the sum of the parts. In psychology, it can more easily be appreciated that a person is not just a sum of the traits of his character. There we have a wholeness, a uniqueness, which is the characteristic quality, the essence of the fact of personality and which cannot be explained in terms of the parts.

This really opens up a new horizon in science, it takes science beyond the method of analysis. Beyond analysis, parts, specialisations and imbalances of life, it begins to see wholenesses, integrations, unities and harmonies. This really amounts to reason coming to see its own limitation, of its favourite capacity of the analytic function. Analysis is indeed a great power. When we are able to identify the parts of a thing, we feel clear about it. But the thing as a whole is a distinct fact. A personality seen and felt as a whole is one thing and the same seen as a sum of traits is another.

But mind involves divisions and partialities and we spontaneously turn to parts. It is the spirit in man which is integral, a conscious unified fact and which spontaneously turns to wholes. The mind can recognise its limitation and can conceive of wholes, but it is the soul in man which spotaneously appreciates and enjoys wholes. This is the essential point which we have to clarify to ourselves.

Jung, among the contemporary scientists and psychologists, has somehow come to this appreciation. His view of human personality is really large and comprehensive. Man's normal working personality is the ego, a self which distinguishes itself from the rest of existence and seeks adjustments with it. It is characterised by the qualities of "exclusiveness, selection, discrimination". It has to adjust itself with the external reality, physical and social, with the demands of morality and religion as represented within himself by a conscious and unconscious formation called the superego and with the claims and pressures of the vast unconscious, personal and racial.

This is the overall make-up of man. Jung studied this make-up through direct observation of mental working, through the interpretation of dreams, and as reflected in the various socio-cultural phenomena of religion, mysticism, etc. Through all this study he discovered the working of a number of polarities or dual opposing facts or propensities and in the midst of them a unitary existence which he has called the Self. His own words are clear and categorical:

"Is there anything more fundamental than the realisation 'This is what I am?' It reveals a unity which nevertheless is – or was – a diversity. No longer the earlier ego with its make-believes and artificial contrivances, but another 'objective' ego, which for this reason is better called the 'Self'." (*Collected Works*, Vol. II, p. 199)

However, the yet more important discovery of his is the process of individuation, i.e., of progressively becoming an integrated whole. Man in his present form is a divided phenomenon, a play of opposing propensities, a suppressive and a repressive superego and a vast impetuous disorderly libido of the unconscious. However, there is also the Self, which represents a wholeness in the individual. This is evidently the spiritual factor in the composition of personality. In Jung's later years, this became more prominent and the Jungian analysts in their practice of Jungian psychology stress it a great deal. Individuation or becoming whole is the way of cure as well as of progress in life.

Jung's concentration on a full and proper theory of personality was the primary one. His studies of types, of dreams, of the religious phenomena were all contributory to this central issue. What is personality and what is its essential trend? His answer is clear. He gives an empirical account of the diversities involved and the wholeness it is tending towards. And indeed his influence on contemporary psychology has been definite. In the midst of the fashion of creating ever more testing scales, psychologists have been conscious of the need of a proper theory of personality as the basic explanatory principle for different kinds of reactions to environmental stimuli. We shall presently mention some of these attempts.

We might, however, first consider Freud's "anatomy of personality", to use his own phrase in this connection. Psychoanalysis with some modifications here and there is a popular therapy for the problems of stress and strain so common in the present-day world and with that goes Freud's view of personality. Ego, Superego, Id are the three components of personality. Ego and Superego are broadly the same as in Jung, Id consists of the untamed passions and does not include the racial unconscious of Jung and the archetypes identified by him. What is particularly important is that the energy of Id is basically sexual and that the intellectual, aesthetic, moral and religious motivations of life are sublimations of the sexual libido of Id. A relative balance between the forces of Ego, Superego and Id means mental health. When this balance is disturbed we get mental ill-health. To restore the ordinary balance is the purpose of psychotherapy. Freud does not contemplate individuation or transformation of life.

In America, in particular, we have now a school of psychology called Transpsychology, of which Ken Wilber is an important representative. The main idea here is that beyond the normal personality, there are ranges of consciousness which too belong to man. Wilber identifies ten such levels or planes which, for brevity, he reduced to five: body, life, mind, soul and spirit. The last two are the higher spiritual planes of life. These five he equates with the five *koṣas* or Sheaths of personality of the Upanishad, the *annamaya*, the *prāṇamaya*, the *manomaya*, the *vijñānamaya* and the *ānandamaya*, the body, the life, the mind, integral (*holistic*) knowledge and bliss. Wilber has developed this concept and then tried to interpret the phenomenon of religion with great cogency, with the aid of such a larger personality. He has developed this concept with great pains and collected wide evidence in support of it. And it is indeed able to meet many difficult situations of knowledge and culture. He argues that the rational level has had a pre-rational level and so is there a post-rational level too, where wholeness is the governing principle.

This is a rising conception of personality, which holds out a great promise for knowledge and culture as a whole. It is comparable to the integral personality of Integral Yoga.

In the strictly academic field, we have naturally the old traditional views of personality still persisting with modifications more or less. W. James is remembered a good deal. Titchner's influence too can yet be traced. But the more influential views represent a biological-genetic base and trend.

Gardner Murphy has written a big volume called *Personality* (a thousand pages strong) and he can be taken as a representative of the academic views on the subject. The first few sentences of the 'Foreword' are a frank confession of the present state of knowledge of man so far as psychology is concerned. Says he, "To write about personality in such a way as to help in clarifying the little that we know and to show its possible relations to the vast and confused domain that we do not yet understand – this is my aim." (P.X) Further he says "Throughout the volume the approach to personality is made chiefly in terms of origins and modes of development on the one hand, interrelations or structural problems on the other. It has not been possible to do justice to the quantitative problems revealed by psychometrics, by factor analysis, by ratings, and by questionnaires, or to personality tests or therapeutic and educational problems" (P.X). "It is simply an attempt at evaluation of data on how personality grows" (P.XI). That shows how academic psychology broadly stands at present and what its interests are. An explanatory theory of personality is not attempted.

The author takes man as an organism which grows up in interaction with the environment. It has its needs and is subject to external moulding influences. 'Situationism' and 'Field Theory' are the preferred terms of personality and, regarding its growth, 'Situationism" stresses the external situation and 'Field Theory' takes the organism and the environment as one fact. The Individuality of the individual is not appreciated in either. The book, referring to the vast empirical investigations carried out, offers an elaborate account of the external influences. Consciousness as a distinct fact is not entertained. The organism is psycho-physical. But after all the elaborate handling of the problems and aspects of personality, the conclusion at the end is sceptical. Gardner Murphy writes, "The future course of personality research will plainly be governed not so much by the continuation of the methods borrowed from psychoanalysis, Gestalt psychology, physiology, and cultural anthropology, to which emphasis has been given in this book, as by altogether new modes of attack" (Pp. 926-6). Again, we are told, "The psychology of personality as it exists today will be crushed and pulverized and a new creation made from the debris, not because of the wisdom inherent in criticisms of it but simply because in grappling with the problems of man it will be weighed in the balance and found wanting" (P. 925).

Murphy did not himself think of a new mode of attack. However, his scepticism is surely not the prevalent mood in the field of psychology. Transpersonal psychology has positive ideas. Jungians have in view a large orientation of life and its transformation. The Freudian movement is in a creative form and there are other academic psychologists too with creative ideas.

Prof. B. Kuppuswamy, among the Indian psychologists, was much interested in a sound theory of personality. He was profoundly impressed by Jung's study of the subject and the influence he has exercised on other psychologists. He was also appreciative of the work of Maslow, Allport and Rogers in this field. He appreciated their affirmation that the highest need of man is 'self-actualisation'.

Gardner Murphy, in his *Historical Introduction to Modern Psychology* (1932), sums up the position on the theory of personality in the following words:

"Those who have occupied themselves with the measurement of personality traits have in general been even less concerned with the theory of personality than most intelligence testers have been with theories of intelligence" (P. 386).

"Among psychologists whose interest is chiefly empirical, personality has therefore come to mean simply the aggregate of the organism's capacities" (Ibid.).

"The notion of such an aggregate nevertheless varies widely. For certain psychologists the term 'sum' would be roughly a correct description of the relation of the whole personality to its constituent parts. For the Gestalt School and the behaviourists such arithmetical summation is not sufficient. Personality depends upon the organization and structure of the components. This conception is very characteristic of the outlook and method of Kantor and the "organismic" school...." (P. 386-7)

Most thinking is of the organismic type. That is Murphy's own position too in his 'personality'. However, the Self-actualisation idea with a stronger feeling for the deeper selfhood is also there.

This is broadly the American situation. In Germany, there is a 'Cultural Science Psychology' insisting on a subject of experience in the individual. That has a significance for a deeper theory of personality.

However, in the entire field of Western psychology the best idea on the subject one finds in Jung. And his position is very definite. We can close this discussion with his words: "If we survey the situation as a whole, we come to the inevitable conclusion – at least in my opinion – that a psychic element is present that expresses itself through the tetrad (the four primary functions of the Psyche). This conclusion demands neither daring speculation nor extravagant phantasy. If I have called the centre the 'self', I did so after ripe reflection and a careful assessment of the data of experience as well as of history." (*The Integration of the Personality*, 1940, p. 198)

Jungian psycho-therapeutic practice is progressively building up evidence in support of the Self. Transpersonal psychology too is doing the same in its own way. Western psychology and Yoga seem to be coming closer.

PERSONALITY, ITS DEVELOPMENT AND 'THE INNER VOICE'

A STUDY IN JUNG

What Can Integral Psychology Contribute?

C. G. Jung gives an interesting study of the process of individuation in his book entitled *The Integration of the Personality*. Consciousness and unconsciousness are, according to him, the two aspects of life. But they 'do not make a whole when either is suppressed or damaged by the other'.[1]

There is a conflict which means also collaboration, actual and possible, between 'the reason and the self-protective ways' of the conscious and 'the chaotic life of the unconscious'. But the yogis who are to him pastmasters in the art of attaining wholeness of life, aim at samadhi, 'an ecstatic condition that seems to be equivalent to an unconscious state.' 'In their case,' states he, 'the unconscious has devoured the ego-consciousness.' 'The universal consciousness', alleged to be attained in samadhi, he asserts, 'is a contradiction in terms, since exclusiveness, selection and discrimination are the root and essence of all that can claim the name of consciousness.'[2] 'An accurate application of the methods of the Pali-canon, or of Yoga-sutras,' he is prepared to grant, 'produces a remarkable extension of consciousness.' But the content of consciousness loses in clearness and detail with increasing extension. In the end, consciousness becomes vast but dim, with an infinite multitude of objects merging into an indistinct totality, a state in which the subjective and objective are almost completely identical.[3] But this is not the solution to be 'recommended north of the Tropic of Cancer where people believe firmly enough in the ego-consciousness.'

The above opinions are bound to interest a student of psychology and yoga. The objective of the realisation of 'a unique, indivisible unit' or 'whole man', that ideal of personality as Jung puts it, can be, on the whole, accepted on behalf of yoga. Both are also agreed that the human nature as such involves a conflict which has to be made good. Now Jung believes that the yogi does attain

---

1. C. G. Jung, *The Integration of the Personality*, 1940, p. 26.
2. *Ibid.*
3. *Ibid.*

to a wholeness of life, though he achieves that, says he, by reducing the conscious to the unconscious. But it passes comprehension how 'wholeness', which implies a single principle of organisation in all the elements of life, can be accounted for by the unconscious, which is recognised to be 'chaotic' in character. This single principle cannot be a moral rule, however universal, since by its very conception a moral law involves opposition to sensibility and impulse, which it seeks to govern. Thus the wholeness, implying as it does a transcendence of all conflict, cannot be explained with reference to any term of the unconscious or the conscious. The relative unification of wholeness, ordinarily realised in life, can surely be accounted for by the evolution of the moral sense, but the wholeness here visualised is the complete harmonisation of life and therefore that single principle must be a supra-moral principle; a sub-moral could give only the wholeness of an animal.

The concept of a supra-moral principle is bound to cause difficulty since we are ordinarily so much accustomed to treating moral life as almost the highest reach of man. Without going into a fuller discussion, we will content ourselves at present with just the affirmation that a life of conflict between good and evil with an increasing ability to choose the good does seem, of necessity, to imply something beyond it: a life of spontaneous righteous activity. That is the concept of spiritual life, which involves a definite transcendence of the moral or the human level of consciousness. The conflict of moral life cannot be final as no contradiction can be. If contradiction on the intellectual side presupposes a position of synthesis and reconciliation, the conflict of moral life can also be understood only against the possibility of spiritual fulfilment and consummation of life.

Now such a supreme principle, which can afford to take up and harmonise the whole of the mental life of man, is obviously man's highest potentiality and possibility. The unconscious, collective or individual, has been pretty thoroughly investigated by the psychoanalysts. And they all agree in regarding it as almost a mass of impulses seeking their individual gratifications. This new highest possibility of man, though an unconscious content, is obviously not a content of unconsciousness. It is also not a content of our ego-consciousness. Does it then not necessitate the positing of another sphere or aspect of our consciousness which, implying as it does a mode of consciousness higher than the moral, as-yet-unrealised, may be called the superconscious? Our subconscious is the dynamic retention of our racial and individual history. Our consciousness is adapted to the practical requirements of our life in relation to the environment. That is the essential biological and evolutionary function of it. But as in the animal at its higher levels indications of the beginnings of the rational level of consciousness can be noticed, so in man there are, as there must be, indications of the future evolutionary development. Such indications are factors in human nature qualitatively different from the subconscious, which is a record of the past, and the conscious, which concerns itself with the present.

But to Jung, what we are not conscious of belongs to the unconscious and no superconscious can really exist. He says, 'I am unable to separate an unconscious below from an unconscious above, since I find intelligence and purposiveness below as well as above.'[1] Our superconscious is surely unconscious to us except for certain extraordinary experiences, which betray its intrusion into the normal waking consciousness. But the unconscious can only have intelligence and purposiveness of an order which deserves at the human level the description of being chaotic, while the intelligence and purposiveness of the superconscious is of an order higher than man's present status.

The samadhi of the yogi, which Jung describes as unconscious, cannot really be unconscious in the sense of the chaotic unconscious of our life. It is surely not conscious in the sense of the ego-consciousness. But what necessity is there to suppose that 'exclusiveness, etc.' are the root and essence of all consciousness. Surely our normal human consciousness is such. But we know well enough that the entire extent of consciousness is so wide and varied that it may be a mistake to insist too categorically on the conditions of one mode of it being binding on all its forms. In particular when we know that the yogi himself far from seeking to lapse into unconsciousness tries to rise to a state of higher concentration and delight.

It should further be noticed that there are, in fact, many systems of yoga, with distinct aims and ideals. Some yogas, no doubt, wind up with samadhi. But the Integral Yoga of Sri Aurobindo cares for

---

1. *Ibid.*, p. 16.

samadhi just as an instrument for raising the level of the general consciousness and not for its own sake. And the main principle of the practice of it is to become increasingly more and more conscious of the subtle inner workings of life. Evidently a process of yoga proceeding by becoming ever more conscious of one's total being cannot end in dark unconsciousness. Still the unconsciousness which the yogi ultimately attains is different from the ego-consciousness. That is exactly the superconsciousness of yoga.

Jung says that everyone's ultimate aim and strongest desire lies in developing the fullness of human existence that is called personality. 'Education to personality' has become the slogan of modern pedagogy. But he complains, 'in general, our approach to education suffers from a one-sided emphasis upon the child who is to be brought up and from an equally one-sided lack of emphasis upon the deficient upbringing of the adult educator.' It is necessary that 'whoever wishes to educate must himself be educated'. In order to rear children to personality, it is the first thing that the ordinary parents, instead of being 'partly or wholly children' as they are, should themselves be personalities.

The ideal of personality is laudable, but for children it must not be overdone, because properly speaking it is an ideal of adulthood. Jung says, 'I suspect our contemporary pedagogical and psychological enthusiasm for the child of a dishonourable intent; people speak of the child, but should mean the child in the grown-up.' For there is in the adult an eternal child needing care and fostering, which is the part now wanting to complete itself. Modern man, he means, 'darkly divining his own defect, seizes upon the education of children and fervently devotes himself to child psychology'. 'This purpose,' says he, 'is praiseworthy, to be sure, but it comes to ship-wreck against the psychological fact that we cannot correct in a child a fault we ourselves still commit. Children, of course, are not so stupid as we believe. They notice only too well what is genuine and what is not.'[1] 'If there is any thing', he further says. 'that we wish to change in the child, we should first examine it and see whether it is not something that could better be changed in ourselves. Our enthusiasm for pedagogy may, in fact, be a cloak to hide from our view the uncomfortable feeling that we are ourselves still children and need up-

---

1. *Ibid.*, p. 284.

bringing'. 'Definiteness', 'fullness' and 'maturity' are the three characteristics, which if forced upon the child too soon will make of him a 'pseudo-adult', and that would be a sheer 'educational monstrosity'. And where the parents fanatically want to do their 'best' and 'live only for the children' the tragedy becomes serious indeed. The result is that unfulfilled ambitions of the parents are loaded on to the child.

Then what is the solution? 'No one can educate to personality', he unhesitatingly declares, 'who does not himself have it' and it is 'only the adult who can attain personality' and 'the achievement of it means nothing less than the best possible development of all that lies in a particular, single being.' And for this 'a whole human life-span in all its biological, social and spiritual aspects is needed.'

'Personality is an act of the greatest courage in the face of life,' and that means 'unconditional affirmation of all that constitutes the individual, the most successful adaptation to the universal conditions of human existence, with the greatest possible freedom of personal decision.'[1] This is, indeed, an inspiring sentence. But to educate someone to this is 'surely the heaviest task that the spiritual world of today has set itself' and 'a personality as a complete realisation of the fullness of our being is an unattainable ideal.'

As we have stated before, personality does not admit of foreign impositions, being in fact the realisation of the fullness of one's own being. Therefore personality must first unfold itself before it can be subjected to education. We do not know how and in what direction a budding personality will shape itself, and our hasty goodwill to mend the child early enough will easily reduce the natural growth of personality to an 'individualism', *i.e.*, a partial tilted sort of growth of personality.

Is one then to give no direction to the unfolding life of a child? That is not the intention of Jung. We have been trying to understand certain principles of the growth of personality. And we will do well to recapitulate them here. First, the parents or teachers have to make sure that they do not themselves suffer from the defect that they want to remove from a child. In doing so, it is necessary to suspect in oneself all kinds of subtle self-deceptions which one must seek to get over. In a word, one has to become

---

1. *Ibid.*, p. 286.

oneself a truly growing personality. That is the first condition favourable to the growth of personality in the child. Secondly, personality in each child is something unique, which must first be identified in him, before he can be helped to grow along that line.

'Fidelity to the law of one's being' is the mystic principle which governs the development of personality. 'A loyal perseverance and trustful hope' or 'the attitude which a religious man should have to God,' is exactly the meaning of the term 'fidelity' here. In clearer terms, the above principle means that 'personality can never develop itself unless the individual chooses his own way with conscious moral decision. Not only the causal motive, the need, but a conscious, moral decision must lend its strength to the process of the development of personality. If the first, that is, the need is lacking, then the so-called development would be mere acrobatics of the will; if the latter is missing, that is, the conscious decision, then the development would come to a rest in a stupefying, unconscious automatism. But a man can make a moral choice of his own way only when he holds it to be the best. If any other way were held to be better, then he would live and develop that other personality instead of his own. The other ways are the conventions of a moral, social, political, philosophic, or religious nature. The fact that conventions always flourish in one form or another proves that the overwhelming majority of mankind chooses not its own way, but the conventions, and so does not develop itself, but a method and a collectivity at the cost of its own fullness.'[1]

We are likely to forget that imitation is inimical to the growth of personality. But this does not mean that a growing individual will not learn from others. He will selectively and through assimilation make others' qualities his own. He will not seek formally to reproduce the incidents of a great man's life in his own and merely wish to become like him. The youth will, however, always read biographies with benefit primarily to stimulate the aspiration of the will to become great in life or rather to rise to one's own true and whole status of life and being.

Further, if 'fidelity to one's being,' is the supreme law and no objective standard of conduct given by social convention is to guide, then how is one to distinguish the passing fancy of the

1. *Ibid.*, p. 289.

sense-impulses from it? Jung does not entertain this difficulty. To him evidently fidelity to one's being, though apparently a subjective principle, is, in fact, for the individual, an objective one in the highest degree. As later, in connection with the inner voice which reveals the law of one's true being, he clearly states that it is inexorable and absolute and unconditional. And when this law of one's being is once discovered, it tends to take up the whole of life and govern it. It introduces a single purpose which will, if nourished, tend to grow all-powerful.

Jung next expounds more fully the meaning of convention and its place in society. Primitive life was 'exclusively a group life with a high degree of unconsciousness in the individual'; so too has the later historical development remained a collective matter. That is why 'convention is a collective necessity'. 'It is a makeshift, not an ideal, whether in respect to morals or religion, for subjection to it always means repudiation of wholeness and a flight from the final consequences of one's own being.'[1]

Further, 'to undertake to develop personality is in fact an unpopular venture, an uncongenial deviation from the 'high way', an idiosyncracy smacking of the recluse – or so it seems to those who stand outside.' But what is it then that enables a man to choose his own way against the heavy weight of convention? 'It cannot be necessity', says Jung, 'for necessity comes to many and they all save themselves in convention. It cannot be moral choice, for as a rule man decides for convention.' What is it then that determines the decision?

'It is,' according to him, 'what is called vocation: an irrational factor that fatefully forces a man to emancipate himself from the herd and the trodden path. True personality always has vocation and believes in it, has fidelity to it as to God, in spite of the fact that, as the ordinary man would say, it is only a feeling of individual vocation. But this vocation acts like a law of God from which there is no escape.'

Vocation is here obviously used in the true and proper sense of the word. It is not anything that one undertakes to do as an occupation in life for his livelihood. It is, in fact, something to which, in spite of what the convention and standards of one's society might have demanded, one feels called by an inexorable

---

1. *Ibid.*, p. 290.

inner voice. The vocation is further mentioned as an 'irrational factor' determining life. It is irrational because no known or knowable psychological condition of personality can explain its nature and character. Vocation is obviously, as here visualised, the call of one's truest being, which is non-empirical or metaphysical; it is the soul's own impulsion.

'Now, vocation, or the feeling of vocation' – he continues – 'is not perchance the prerogative of great personalities, but also belongs to small ones.' 'The smaller the personality is, so much the more unclear and unconscious it becomes, till in place of the inner voice appears the voice of the social group and its conventions, and in the place of vocation the collective necessities.'[1] A man of genius too need not have personality. And 'in so far as every individual has his own inborn law of life' he can develop personality and achieve wholeness by seeking it out and living according to it.

The value of personality to society is tremendous. Society lives by conventions which keeps it in a routine, but when new conditions unprovided for by the old conventions arise, a sense of danger and fear seizes the people. It is then that personality, which has all conventions and fears behind it, plays its part of emancipating the people from that fear. 'The group,' Jung maintains, 'because of its unconsciousness, has no freedom of choice, so that within it psychic life works itself out like an uncontrolled law of nature.' A personality which possesses true freedom within it is, therefore, able to rise above the mechanism of convention and lead the people out of its inadequacy for a particular situation.

'The deification of great personalities exactly shows the valuation that humanity puts upon the ideal of personality. And though at present a collectivism seems to be more popular, the ideal of personality is an indestructible need of the human soul.'

Most interestingly, in Jung, who is an empirical psychologist, we find a metaphysics too. 'Psychic life,' he affirms, 'is a world power that exceeds by many times all the powers of the earth... when this objective psychic fact, hard as granite and heavy as lead, confronts the individual as an inner experience and says to him in an audible voice, "This is what will and must happen," then he feels himself called, just as do the social groups when a war is on, or a

---

1. *Ibid.*, p. 292.

revolution, or any other madness.' Incidentally, wars and revolutions are conceived as psychic epidemics and 'the gigantic catastrophes that threaten us are not elemental happenings of a physical or biological kind, but are psychic events.'[1]

There is a further interesting sentence that gives the reason for the existence of an objective universal mind, as it were. 'Certainly,' declares Jung. 'All human beings resemble one another, for otherwise they could not succumb to the same delusions; and the foundation of the psyche upon which individual consciousness rests, is universally the same, beyond a doubt, for otherwise people could never reach a common understanding. But since life can only exist in the form of individuals, the law of life in the last analysis always tends towards a life that is individually lived.'[2] However, there can be one exception to this mode of expression of the universal psyche. That is 'when it seizes upon the group; but in that case it leads by rules of nature to a catastrophe, and for the simple reason that it acts only through unconscious channels and is not assimilated by any consciousness so as to be assigned its place among all other conditions of life.'[3] 'It is only the man who is able consciously to affirm the power of the vocation confronting him from within him that becomes a personality.'[4]

The above two paragraphs give in the ample words of the psychologist a most unexpected statement of the reality of an objective psyche and an individual consciousness. However, the character of the objective psyche is not discussed and, judging from his previous discussions, it would be identical with his unconscious. But this unconscious evidently seems to contain within itself a double character. In nature it works unconsciously and when it seizes the group it produces catastrophes, but when a man is able consciously to affirm it in the inner voice of his vocation, it raises him to the supreme status of wholeness and personality. Does this not seem to lend support to our sugestion, made earlier in the essay, that Jung's unconscious appears to involve both the unconscious working as in nature and the superconscious as in the possible higher ranges of experience to which man may attain?

1. *Ibid.*, p. 293.
2. *Ibid.*, p. 296.
3. *Ibid.*
4. *Ibid.*

We will next turn briefly to what Jung calls the 'problem of the inner voice.' The inner voice, we have already observed, is for him the call of the vocation. It is the demand for an 'absolute and unconditional' realisation of a man's own particular law. It also presupposes an objective psyche, whose subjective manifestations in each man are unique.

Now in connection with the psychic experiences involved in the inner voice, we have, says Jung, 'the eternal doubt whether what appears to be the objective psyche is really objective or whether it is imagination after all.' He explains the phenomenon, which is of such great importance to students of personality, by reference to facts of psycho-therapy. Let us say a man suffers from a delusion. He sees a persistent figure. He asks the doctor: 'Is it really there or do I merely imagine it?' And even when told that it is just his imagination, he still must ask: 'But why do I then imagine it?' Now the fact is, explains Jung, that 'a psychic' growth is taking place in the man's unconscious without his being able to make it conscious. And before this inner activity he has a sense of fear. 'Neurosis is thus,' concludes Jung, 'a protection against the objective, inner activity of the psyche, or rather it is an attempt dearly paid for to escape from the inner voice and so from vocation.'[1]

The fear or delusion is, therefore, genuinely objective. It is extra-conscious, not accessible to the individual's understanding and will. It is, of course, not objective in the sense of a socially verifiable phenomenon.

The neurotic has evidently failed in the full realisation of the will of his being, the fear that he suffers from is a restriction of his consciousness. And 'in so far as a man is untrue to his own law and does not rise to personality, he has failed of the meaning of his life.'[2]

The exact character of the inner voice is rather complex and varied. 'The inner voice is the voice of the fuller life, of a wide, more comprehensive consciousness.' 'The development of personality is synonymous with an increase of awareness.' But the fear that the majority of men have before the inner voice is justifiable. The contents of the inner voice that come to a limited consciousness 'as a rule, spell the very danger that is specific to the

1. *Ibid.*, p. 300.
2. *Ibid.*, p. 301.

individual.' 'The inner voice brings to us whatever the whole suffers from.'[1] Further, 'the inner voice brings forward what is evil in a temptingly convincing way, so as to make us succumb to it.'[2] But the last word that Jung has to say about the character of the inner voice is disappointing though utterly frank and honest. 'In a most unaccountable way,' he says, 'the lowest and the highest, the best and the most atrocious, the truest and the falsest are mingled together in the inner voice, which thus opens up an abyss of confusion, deception and despair.'[3]

His last word about personality, though not so confusing, is still very unsure. 'Personality is a great and mysterious question.' 'All that can be said about it is curiously unsatisfactory and inadequate.'

'All the usual little remedies and medicaments of psychology,' he frankly confesses as a psychologist, 'fall short in this connection, just as they do with the man of genius or the creative human being. Derivation from ancestral heredity and from the milieu does not quite succeed, inventing fictions about childhood, which is so popular today ends, to put it mildly, in the inappropriate; the explanation from necessity – "he has no money, was ill" and so forth – remains caught in mere externalities. Something irrational, that cannot be rationalised, must always supervene, a *deus ex machina* or *asulum ignorantiate* – that well-known superscription standing for God. Here the problem seems to extend into an extra-human realm, and this, from the beginning, has been covered by some of the names of God.'[4]

This is how a most searching investigation of human personality by the profoundest of contemporary psychologists ends. It is really revealing how an avowedly empricial standpoint, in its analysis of personality, finds itself pressed on beyond all terms of observable experience to posit, nay, definitely affirm, the working of an ulterior and a basic fact, which our author can only call an 'irrational' factor. This mystic note uttered by an empirical psychologist regarding the truth of personality accords so well with the similar 'mysticism' of the modern physicist regarding the nature of the physical universe outside us. As here, in psychology, it is something beyond the empirical terms which is the basic

1. *Ibid.*, p. 303.
2,3. *Ibid.*
4. *Ibid.*, p. 299.

reality, so there, in physics, it is not the observed phenomenon of hard and extended matter, which is real, but something beyond it, an indeterministic energy in a whirl of movement or perhaps 'consciousness under a mask'.

Jung and Integral Psychology

The irrational factor felt by Jung in the scheme of personality is clarified in another passage of the same book. Says he, 'If we survey the situation as a whole, we come to the inevitable conclusion – at least in my opinion – that a psychic element is present that expresses itself through the tetrad (the four primary functions of the psyche). This conclusion demands neither daring speculation nor extravagant phantasy. If I have called the centre the "self" I did so after ripe reflection and a careful assessment of the data of experience as well as of history.'[1] Further, 'The centre acts like a magnet upon the disparate materials and processes of the unconscious and, like a crystal grating, catches them one by one.'[2]

The mixed-up position, regarding 'the inner voice' and overall make-up of personality, is really due to Jung's inability at this stage to distinguish between the unconscious and the superconscious and their opposite kinds of contributions to personality. His identification of the different elements of personality is beautiful, but their sources are not identified and hence the perplexity of the paradoxical statements. The later work of Jung clarified things, and his followers, the Jungian Analysts, carry on the process further.

However, Integral Psychology, through its steady and detailed inner explorations, has achieved clarities on personality, its various domains and their workings. This could be a useful contribution to Jungian thought and practice. Integral Psychology appreciates the general findings of Jungian psychology. But it asks: 'How are these findings going to be put into practice?' Integral Psychology has an Integral Yoga for its actualisation. Does Jungian psychology not need a Jungian Yoga?

1. *Ibid.*, p. 193.
2. *Ibid.*, p. 197.

PROGRESS OF JUNGIAN THOUGHT

A Study in Jungian Analysis

All suffering is taken as evil, though evolutionally considered, it is an incentive for progress, for a fuller adjustment and integration, making good in some degree the inadequacy of the situation of suffering. Physical suffering is more easily recognised and looked after. However, the inner suffering is more serious, since it is not easily recognised and not duly looked after too even by the individual himself. But its consequences are deeper and much more harmful.

Religions have offered a healing touch to the ailing souls, but recently Psychology has evolved techniques for the difficulties of the human psyche, the inner conscious and unconscious life. Freud and Jung are the two foremost psychologists, whose methods are at the present most prevalent and they offer a most welcome approach and solution to the problems of mental health. Freudians seek to restore to the mentally disturbed the normal working condition. Jungians do that on their orientation of personality and by their techniques, but they also open up a vision of 'wholeness' in personality, if the patients care to pursue the path of self-integration. The Jungian path is for the mentally disturbed, as also for the mentally healthy.

"Jungian Analysis" edited by Murray Stain (published by Shambhala, Boulder and London, 1984) is a fine joint venture by leading Jungian Analysts and seems to present a wide coordinated picture of Jungian Analysis today. The essays deal with the history and practice, the aims and goals, the structure and dynamics, and the varied methods of Jungian Analysis. There are also chapters dealing with children and the aged and the role of the gender, the sex. Two chapters deal with the training of the Analysts. All the essays are fine studies and they all together present a comprehensive picture of Jungian Analysis, the progress this work has made and a greater success it looks forward to.

Jung's psychology has a wide span. It takes man comprehensively, what he is in his present ego-formation, what he has been and has carried forward in the unconscious, individual and racial, and what he is tending towards, i.e., a 'wholeness' of personality. All these factors have been elaborately dealt with in the extensive writings of Jung, availing of personal observation of inner dynamics and the expression of these dynamics in dreams, mythology, alchemy, mystic practices of the East and West and general religious life.

The most important discovery in all this extensive work is that there is in man a 'self' besides the ego and the polarities of the conscious and the unconscious, the male and female and the others that the ego involves. This self is an integrating, unique centre and a wholeness of life is the objective. This overall framework of personality is very good. Evidently in this framework, the 'self' and the 'wholeness' visioned are the most important factors, on which inner healing and inner perfection depend, but these are the factors that have yet to be investigated. Jung discovered them and did so effectively. But their nature, character and working need to be known as best as possible. They are most important for the process of individuation or transformation of life. We should know them well and should be able to mobilise them for mental health as well as for the perfection of life. Jung's emphasis remained on the ego up to the last. Should our emphasis not shift to 'self', if Self is to be given its full chance of integration and if 'wholeness' is to have its full play? If we persist in our insistence on the ego, then we refuse full play to Self and Wholeness, which can really overcome all unconsciousness and its fragmentation of archetypes. Such wholeness, oneness, unity is what the best traditions of Chinese and Indian Yoga aim at. The Samadhi state is, in fact, not the aim of spiritual life. 'Integrated living and action' is the aim. This is what the Gita substantiates in its teachings. However, there are systems of yoga which aim at Samadhi, which however is a highly conscious state. The unconscious Samadhi is an aberration. The egoistic state of exclusiveness and discrimination is not essential to consciousness. Consciousness is illumination and the higher unitary states are states of oneness, of indefinite extension and increasing brightness. History of mysticisms, Eastern and Western, amply bears this out.

The Integral yoga of Sri Aurobindo and the Mother as practised at Sri Aurobindo Ashram, Pondicherry, of which the writer has personal experience, bears out happy parallelisms with Jungian psychology and its practice, in many respects. The soul is here too the unitary and the unique centre in man, which commands body, life and mind and their dualities or divided opposing reactions and seekings. This soul is the evolving soul which they call the psychic being to distinguish it from the soul, which is the abiding individual spiritual reality as held by religions and philosophical systems. The psychic being is a spiritual principle, a representative of the metaphysical soul, involved in man's evolutionary history. Ordinarily, it stands apart, acting from behind, whereas body, life and mind constitute the apparent personality of man.

The yogic pursuit consists in seeking a contact with the psychic being and making it the dynamic and dominant principle of life. This one does by progressively dissociating oneself from the activities of body, life and mind, and by dedicating them to a disinterested purpose as service. That loosens the egoistic knot of life and a contact with the psychic being becomes possible. This contact, in the beginning, is occasional and fleeting. In course of time, it becomes steady and abiding. Then it begins to act in full power on the dualities, divisions and incongruities of outer life and harmonises them. A sense of wholeness in the normal working of life, in eating and drinking and all things, becomes a vivid experience. Of course, this needs an entire dedication of life to the yogic pursuit. But in the process, all complexities of life get bit by bit simplified. Ego then gets merged in the psychic being or the latter overwhelms the former and gives a new form of unity and wholeness and spontaneity to life.

The psychic being in due time becomes aware of a corresponding spiritual reality in the universe as the all-commanding fact of existence. The individual's life then acquires a wide universal dimension.

This growth is facilitated by a contact of deep inner rapport with a teacher, a Guru, who has gone through the length of the yogic pursuit previously.

The parallelisms between the practice of Integral yoga and that of Jungian psychology are evident. Jung's approach is that of an empirical scientist and, as such, he went the farthest one could go. And indeed he achieved the highest truths.

The yogic method is essentially that of inner exploration without the limitations of the assumptions or postulates of empirical science. The yoga is thus able to achieve ultimate certitudes as facts of experience. However, the ultimate spiritual reality is infinite and the yogic perceptions of it too can be much varied, but they all carry a degree of certitude which inferential knowledge cannot possess.

The writer confidently hopes that Jungian psychology will in the future elaborate its concepts of Self and Wholeness, in fact, discover the existential facts behind them and then mobilise the same in practice. At that stage Integral yoga and Jungian psychology will get much closer. Integral Yoga has a wide literature, so has Jungian psychology and a comparative study of the two is highly rewarding. It brings in a greater clarity and certitude regarding the profundities of life. The concept of the unconscious is a vast and a rich concept in Jung. At one time he characterised it as chaotic. Later he attributed to it even the higher possibilities of life. His position was that all that is not known to the ego-consciousness is unconscious. Here are his own words in this connection.

(1) "In talking about the unconscious we have always to talk in paradoxes.... We know just as well, and can rely on the fact, that the unconscious is not only chaos but also order..." (Collected Works Vol. 11, pp. VI-VII)

(2) "...the ever deeper descent into the unconscious suddenly becomes illumination from above...." (Ibid., p. 281)

(3) "Is there anything more fundamental than the realisation. 'This is what I am'? It reveals a unity which nevertheless is – or was – a diversity. No longer the earlier ego with its makebelieves and artificial contrivances, but another 'objective' ego, which for this reason is better called the 'Self'...." (Ibid., p. 199)

Now should we not distinguish between what is carried over from the past and represents partial integrations and what constitutes future possibilities and which represents higher integrations? Integral Yoga prefers to call the one the unconscious, the other the superconscious. The one is essentially chaotic and obscure, the other essentially organised and luminous, though to the ego both are not known.

A clarity was emerging in Jung progressively. However, a full clarity on this point seems to be called for.

In the end, it is a pleasure to cite from the thoughtful, inquiring, open-minded studies of the Jungian Analysts, a few statements as representative of the entire book. These statements represent the important ideas of Jungian Analytical thought and practice:

(1) "A significant aspect of Jungian treatment, however, is not described so well by the term analysis. This is the experience of the

Self that often occurs in, or as a result of, Jungian therapy. Jungian analysis results not only in Self-knowledge but also in a new kind of Self-experience. People who enter Jungian analysis may do so because they wish to know more about themselves, but if the analysis actually works, they come to experience themselves in a way that was previously not possible. This new kind of Self-experience takes place as the rigidities of ego-consciousness dissolve, and as the unconscious responds and is acknowledged within the security and understanding of the analytical framework. What actually creates the therapeutic effect in Jungian analysis is the increasing amplitude of a person's experience of the Self. This experience, moreover, usually brings with it an influx of energy and vitality, so that one common result of analysis is more creativity in one's responses to life and its challenges." (pp. 30-31)

*

(2) "Jungian analysis takes place within a dialectical relationship between two persons, analyst and analysand, and has for its goal the analysand's coming to terms with the unconscious. The analysand is meant to gain insight into the specific unconscious structures and dynamics that emerge during analysis, and the strcutures underlying ego-consciousness are meant to change in their dynamic relation to other, more unconscious structures and dynamics." (p. 29)

*

(3) "Jungian analysts, unlike their Freudian colleagues, do not generally engage in a meticulous reconstruction of childhood. Nevertheless, a certain amount of remembering childhood and adolescence does commonly occur in Jungian analysis. It is typical for considerable time to be spent tracing the history of various personal complexes from infancy to the present and becoming aware of how they have affected ego-consciousness in the past and continue to do so in the present." (pp. 37-38)

*

(4) "Coming to terms with the unconscious means: mastering

the personal complexes to some extent on the one hand, while grasping the symbolic meaning of emerging archetypal contents on the other. Analysis creates an ongoing dialogue between the ego and the unconscious (Jung 1966a, p. 80), which produces a dialectical tension of opposites within ego-consciousness, between ego strivings on the one hand and unconscious disturbances and archetypally based demands on the other. This dialogue is mirrored in the dialectical structure of analysis itself. This dialectic, in turn, reflects the Self, which actually consists of dialectical play of the opposites. For ego-consciousness to come to mirror the Self more completely is another way of expressing the goal of analysis." (p. 38)

The Education of an Analyst

(5) "The education of the analyst extends beyond anything that can be verbally expressed. It is, more than anything, an experience of transformation in which one comes to know one's own soul and to befriend it In the process, it is hoped that one may become what one really is." (p. 367)

*

(6) "There is, inevitably, the sense of vocation. Something in the person of the applicant is profoundly attracted to the mystery of the human soul, is fascinated by its complexity, and finds nothing more entrancing than to explore its labyrinthine paths." (p. 369)

*

(7) "One senses: here is a person who can take strain and stress, suffer disappointment and loss, endure embarrassment and shame, yet not crumble. Analysands will feel that this is a person they can trust, one to whom they can be fully open, who will not take advantage of them, and who will not break down under the burdens that they may bring. Analysands want to feel that the analyst can stand the dirt and stench of another's life and not turn away." (p. 371)

*

(8) "Jung never meant his writings to be regarded as sacred dogma. He often expressed his awareness that theories are workable for a while, then pass away or are superseded. I believe he intended that his writings would inspire those who came after him to revise and reinterpret his ideas in ways consonant with other times, other situations. People who are training to become analysts are encouraged to see how Jung's ideas apply to their own times, their own analytic cases, and, of course, themselves. While Jungian analysts tend to be individual in their approach, it is necessary that Jung's original perspectives and thoughts be mastered in the process of finding one's own way." (p. 376)

*

(9) "The individuation process is a lifelong journey and the analyst is at first a pilgrim, then a guide: but analysts never stop being pilgrims either. For it is well known that people cannot lead others further than they have travelled themselves.

...To find a creative balance between the personal and the collective aspects of the psyche and the world is the essence of individuation. To become an analyst means to take on the struggle against the lack of that balance, when it is observed, and to hold firm to the conviction that one can work toward its restoration." (pp. 377-8)

*

(10) "The study of religion is part of the education of the Jungian analyst. Foremost in Jung's psychology is the acknowledgement of the archetype of the Self as the principle of wholeness, the universal principle. The Self functions as an ordering principle, but since it is all-inclusive, it also embodies the opposite of order – that is, chaos. The Self, as overarching arhetypal power, is eternally engaged in making order out of chaos, only to watch the other dissolve again into chaos, and to reorder it, again and again. Religions, whatever else they may be, are expressions of the human need to relate to the ultimate source of being, the guiding power of the universe." (pp. 379-80)

*

These are inspiring words. The Jungian Analysts are not only bringing relief to the mentally suffering humanity, restoring better composition of personality, but much more than that they are opening up a way of perfection. Indeed, a prospect: we wish them all joy in the pursuit.

FREUD AND PERSONAL INTEGRATION OR DEVELOPMENT

Limitations of His Approach

Freud's Psycho-analysis is principally a psychiatric discipline and that is why the Psycho-analytical literature is full of cases of mental patients. But its contribution to normal psychology too is valuable. It is interesting to hear from Freud himself in his 'New Introductory Lectures' (1933): "I have told you that Psycho-analysis began as a therapeutic procedure, but it is not in that light that I wanted to recommend it to your interest, but because of the truth it contains, because of the information it gives, about that which is of the greatest importance for mankind, namely his own nature." (p. 214) We too are here interested in Psycho-analysis just for the understanding of our own nature, particularly to improve it, as it is primarily in that way that our nature is 'of the greatest importance to us.' Now in what respects has Psycho-analysis enlarged and deepened our knowledge of human nature?

Undoubtedly the idea of the unconscious was not unknown before but it had been left over to Psycho-analysis to prove the existence of it on the basis of extensive empirical evidence gathered from clinical practice. What is more, Psycho-analysis has unveiled the various mechanisms by means of which it works under the varied circumstances of mental life. Projection, Introjection, Identification, Rationalisation, Displacement and Conversion are a few most important specialised techniques of the operation of the uncosncious and each one of them means a definite contribution to our understanding of human personality.

The above techniques are, in fact, different modes of 'defence reactions' on the part of the individual. The idea of a 'defence reaction' is itself a happy discovery and involves a valuable contribution to the science and art of personal development.

A 'defence reaction' is an exaggeration in one's conscious behaviour of an action opposite to that which we may be conscious of having suffered in our inner life. That is how a cynic is a sentimentalist at heart, the bully a coward and the unromantic bachelor very affectionate and tender. Those who suffer from inferiority complex often develop an expression of vanity and conceit. The prudishness of old maids is really an expression of a long continued suppression of sex desire. Projection is the assignment of the mind or mental content to a location outside the mind. A man who is vain himself sees vanity everywhere and condemns it. Rationalisation is the production by the mind of 'reasons to explain conduct or belief which have no relation to the actual psychical causes of the conduct or belief in question.'

Next to the unconscious, the most important Psycho-analytical discovery is the fact of repression. It is important not only for explaining neuroses and their symptoms, but also for the understanding of much of the behaviour of the normal man. The mental operation of repression just consists of forcibly pushing out of the conscious mind some unacceptable feeling or objectionable experience.

The study of repression has been, in fact, the chief undertaking of Psycho-analysis and it is interesting to follow the devious ways in which repressed desires seek expression and gratification. Each one of the defence mechanisms above referred to, in fact, represents a manner of expression of a repressed desire. The ordinary slips of the tongue, pen or similar errors of behaviour were formerly considered to be just accidental occurrences. But it is now most interesting to know that they are in fact highly significant facts, as they reveal unconscious motives. The symptoms of neurosis have become significant only in the light of the discovery of the fact of repression.

Dreams have become altogether a new phenomenon. The discovery of the fact of symbolism in dream and neurosis mean in fact the acquisition of a new language, conveying valuable meanings of some of the deeper facts of life. We today definitely recognise that a dream is not altogether a wayward and phantastic aberration of mental life, but an expression and a safety valve of psychical life. It thus serves as a useful means of discovering the repressions of healthy as well as neurotic persons.

The problem of personal development is progressive integration, and for that we have to discover conflicts, seek to remove them and thereby establish harmony in the mind. The same is the method of attaining greater efficiency in life. Conficts inhibit and retard action. It is relatively much easier to deal with conscious conflicts. We know the trouble. It is such conflicts that have generally been recognised by the various practical systems of personal development. But Psycho-analysis has made a great advance upon them by showing that the worst conflicts of the mind are always those which are more deeply laid in the unconscious and of which we are not aware at all, and that they can be best detected through an interpretation of dreams. Thus has Psycho-analysis, for the aspirant of personal perfection, revealed a new field of psychical existence which harbours conflicts, the true causes of anxiety, worry and frustration, and which he only blindly sought to fight against so far. In the dreams, in fact, he has now a practical means of detecting the most intractable causes of disharmony in his life.

We have above referred to the repression and dream interpretation as valuable contributions of Psycho-analysis to a science and art of personal development. But they actually tell us nothing more than what the realistic picture at a particular stage of our development may be. One would ask, "Has Psycho-analysis got anything to offer for improving human nature? For making man happier and more harmonious within himself?" This is a very important question to ask of Psycho-analysis.

Obviously self-knowledge is a necessary pre-condition of self-development and in as much as Psycho-analysis acquaints us with the actual state of ourselves in the larger and the more difficult sphere of the unconscious, it meets the indispensable precondition of self-development. To the problem of positive self-development, its sensational answer is that a knowledge of the real circumstances of the origin of the conflict itself leads to a resolution of the conflict. Freud explains "that the pathogenic trouble does not exist between conflicting impulses all of which are in the same mental field. It is a battle between two forces of which one has succeeded in coming to the level of pre-conscious or conscious part of the mind, while the other has been confined to the unconscious level. That is why the conflict can never have a final outcome one way or the other, the two meet each other as little as the whale and the polar bear in the well-known story. An effective decision can be reached only when they confront each other on the same ground. And, in my opinion, to accomplish this is the task of treatment." (Introductory Lectures, p. 362) To make the un-conscious conscious is all the task. And that effects the cure. You would ask for proof, and Freud replies that "success in the main justifies our claims." (Introductory Lectures, p. 366)

One might here feel curious to ask how does the Psycho-analytical method compare with the time-honoured methods of

Suggestion and Hypnosis of curing diseases. A detailed examination of these methods cannot fall within the purview of this study. But one thing is clear that psychologists cannot agree to suppressing the unconscious. We must rid the unconscious of conflicts, as otherwise a positive integration of personality is not possible. Freud himself characterises the difference between his own method and that of suggestion and hypnotism in these words: "Direct suggestion is a suggestion delivered against the forms taken by the symptoms. a struggle between your authority and the motives underlying the disease. In this struggle, you do not trouble yourself about these motives, you only require the patient to suppress the manifestation of them...." Hypnosis is not regarded as different from suggestion as "suggestion is the essence of the manifestation of hypnosis." In further clarification of the same, says he: "The hypnotic therapy endeavours to cover up and, as it were, to whitewash something going on in the mind, the analytic to lay bare and remove something. The first employs suggestion to indict the symptoms; it reinforces the repressions,... analytic therapy takes hold deeper down the roots of the disease, among the conflicts, from which the symptoms proceed; it employs suggestion to change the outcome of these conflicts." (Ibid., p. 377) This gives the main point of difference very clearly and it may be noted that in one form suggestion is involved in Psycho-analytical procedure.

Some take too exclusive a view of the psycho-analytical procedure of treatment. But suggestion is involved in it and it may be that suggestion and hypnotism are entitled to a more respectable and legitimate place in psychotherapy. In fact, Ferenczi, in his *Active Therapy*, gives them a better place and so have Jung and Adler done. In the *New Introductory Lectures* too, there are a few interesting sentences bearing upon the subject. "As a psycho-therapeutic method," says Freud, "analysis does not stand in opposition to other methods employed in this branch of medicine; it does not invalidate them nor does it exclude them." (p. 208) "But, compared with psycho-therapeutic procedure," he claims, "psycho-analysis is far and away the most powerful and as a form of therapy, it is one among many, though certainly *primus inter pares*." (Ibid., p. 218) Therefore, obviously an exclusive psycho-analytical therapy is incorrect.

Our treatment of psycho-analysis has tended to give a moral value to it. But there are many who would say that psycho-analysis has tended to debase and degrade man and to speak of its contribution to the problem of personal development is outrageous. The psycho-analytical habit of talking about sex matters in perfect frankness is also considered to be vulgar. And then since it has so often to show the harmful effects of repression, it is held to be an advocate of 'free living'. Against such charges, psycho-analysis is very widely believed to be indefensible.

We feel that psycho-analysis, by discussing the details of sex life frankly and dispassionately, has rendered a service to man in as much as it has promoted self-knowledge, which is so essential for self-development. In considering sex, says Freud, "psycho-analysis sees no occasion for concealments or indirect allusions and does not think it necessary to be ashamed of concerning itself with material so important; it is of opinion that it is right and proper to call everything by its true name, hoping in this way the more easily to avoid disturbing suggestions." (Introductory Lectures, p. 129)

The best service of Freud has obviously been a general encouragement of the spirit of mental analysis and the investigation of varied and complex motives of our actions.

Regarding his theory of sex, the reader can still voice his protest. It is obviously not possible to go into the pros and cons of this much disputed theory here. But Freud as a scientist was much more interested in the realistic side of life than in its idealistic aspect. As against the right of morality and religion which had been much overdone, he felt called upon to justify the right of instinct. Among human instincts, undoubtedly, the sex instinct is the most important, but Freud did over-generalise it. But it is the instincts, the 'Id', which has been so far investigated by psycho-analysis; the 'Ego' and the 'Superego' of psycho-analytical personality have yet to be fully investigated. Freud's investigations were obviously limited by the phenomenon of mental disease and his essentially scientific, realistic temperament. His attitude was not dererminerd by the objective of human perfection, as it is in *Yoga*. But this attitude of perfection is a legitimate extension of psycho-analysis. From mental disease to mental health has been the programme so far and now one can easily contemplate the extension from average mental health to superior grades of mental health and happiness. This is exactly the problem of personal development. There are, indeed, some indications in Freud as to the nature and character of *a higher life* and we might now consider them. In his *New Introductory Lectures*, in the chapter entitled 'The Anatomy of Mental Personality', we come across a number of sentences which make a most interesting reading. "Superego, ego and id are the three realms, regions or provinces in which we divide the mental apparatus of the individual." (Ibid., p. 102) However, "you must not imagine sharp dividing lines" (Ibid., p. 110) between them. The superego "is the representative of all moral restriction, the advocate of impulse towards perfection," and "what people call the higher things in life." (Ibid., p. 95) "We have allocated to it the activities of self-observation and conscious holding of ideals." (Ibid., p. 94) This recognition of 'impulse towards perfection,' and 'ideals' in human personality is obviously interesting. He also clearly affirms that the "so called materialistic conceptions of history err that they underestimate this factor." (Ibid., p. 95) He continues to say that "Mankind never lives completely in the present, the ideologies of the superego perpetuate the past, the traditions of the race and the people, which yield but slowly to the influence of the present and to new developments, and, so long as they work through the superego they play an important part in man's life, quite independently of economic conditions." (Ibid., p. 96) Thus, a conscience, which is here recognised as superego, is not denied. But the psycho-analytical account of its genesis is repugnant to many. It is here held to be the heir of the emotional tie called the oedipus complex, and the sexual relation, which binds the child to the parents. However, "the superego is constantly becoming more and more remote from the original parents, becoming as it were, more impersonal." (Ibid., p. 92) And "It is also the vehicle of the ego ideal, by which the ego measures itself, towards which it strives, and whose demands for ever-increasing perfection it is always striving to fulfil." (Ibid., p. 93)

The 'id' is the sum of the instinctive desires which impulsively press for their individual satisfactions. "These instincts fill it with energy but it has no organisation and no unified will, only an impulsion to obtain satisfaction for the instinctive needs in accordance with the *pleasure principle*." (Ibid., p. 104) The logical Law of Contradiction does not hold good in this realm of mind as 'contradictory impulses exist side by side.' (Ibid., p. 104) "Naturally, the id knows no values, no good and evil, no morality." (Ibid., p. 105)

Now what is the ego? The ego is "a coherent organisation of mental processes." "What, however, especially marks the ego out in contradistinction to the id, is a tendency to synthesize its contents, to bring together and unify its mental processes, which is entirely absent from id." In the ego, the instincts tend to become 'subordinated to a large organisation,' and find place in a 'coherent unity.' The ego is, in popular language, 'the reason and circumspection', while the id stands for 'the untamed passions.' (Ibid., p. 107)

But how does this ego develop in us? Ego is essentially the principle of reconciliation between the instincts and the external world or reality, and one can, in fact, say that the ego is that part of the id which has been modified by the influence of the external world. "The ego has", we read, "taken over the task of representing the external world for the id and so of saving it; for the id blindly striving to gratify its instincts in complete disregard of the superior strength of the outside forces could not otherwise escape annihilation. But the ego has the most difficult task to achieve." (Ibid., p. 106) "Goaded on by the id, hemmed in by the superego, and rebuffed by reality, the ego struggles to cope with its economic task of reducing the forces and influences which work in it and upon it to some kind of harmony." (Ibid., p. 109)

It may here be incidentally observed "that the ego (including the superego) does not by any means completely coincide with the conscious, nor the repressed with the unconscious." (Ibid., p. 96) We have before us the empirical fact that a patient under analysis may not be conscious of his resistance. That would definitely mean "that the parts of both the ego and the superego themselves are unconscious." (Ibid., p. 98) Thus the unconscious in Freud is not identical with the repressed as is often held to be the case.

We just said that the ego seeks to achieve 'some kind of harmony' between the forces of the superego, of reality and of the id. Here are a few sentences where Freud grows enthusiastic about 'harmony', and the idealistic element of his thought comes out more vividly. He says that "it can be imagined that certain practices of the mystics may succeed in upsetting the normal relations between the different regions of the mind, as, for example, the perceptual process may become able to grasp relations in the deeper layers of the ego and in the id which would otherwise be inaccessible to it." "The therapeutic efforts of psycho-analysis," he admits, "have chosen much the same method of approach. For their object is to strengthen the ego, to make it more independent of the superego, to widen its field of vision and so to extend its organisation that it can take over new portions of the id. Where id was there shall ego be. It is reclamation work like the draining of the Zuyder Zee." (Ibid., p. 111)

It would be very consoling to the idealist to learn that the id is to be transformed into the ego. But he may not relish the statement that the ego has to be 'more independent of the superego.' The difficulty is due to the fact that we do not easily see the harmful effects to a man's growth if the moral ideal is pitched too high. Psycho-analysis advocates, properly speaking, a gradual raising of the moral ideal. When Freud speaks about education, this becomes perfectly clear. What is the primary business of education? Freud answers: "The child has to learn to control its instincts. To grant it complete freedom, so that it obeys its impulses without any restriction, is impossible. The function of education, therefore, is to inhibit, forbid and suppress and it has at all times carried out its function to admiration. But we have to learn from analysis that it is this very suppression of instinct that involves the danger of neurotic illness... Education has, therefore, to steer its way between the Scylla of giving the instinct free play and the Charybdis of frustrating them. Unless the problem is altogether insoluble, an optimum of education must be discovered which will do most good and the least harm. It is a matter of finding how much one may forbid, at which times, and by which method. And then it must further be considered that the children have very different constitutional dispositions, so that the same educational procedure cannot be equally good for all children." (Ibid., p. 203)

The same exactly is the problem of personal development. Each individual has to strive for a particular "optimum" of moral development at a particular time and it serves no useful purpose to tune up the superego and the ego or the id and unnecessarily intensify the sense of guilt. But, there is here evidently no preaching of the gospel of 'free living', since the demand of the superego has really to be reconciled with the claim of the id. One cannot simply allow the id to have its own way. That will be no solution of one's troubles. The frustration of the superego can cause as much trouble as that of the id. The idea of an optimum, for each individual and for each stage of development, is definitely the word of highest moral wisdom.

As in regard to moral life, so to religion all that Freud denies is the divine origin of the thing. As in morality so in religion a psychological account is attempted. Psycho-analysis "has traced the origin of religion to the helplessness of childhood and its content to the persistence of the wishes and needs of childhood and maturity." (Ibid., p. 299) But Freud affirms that "this does not precisely imply refutation of religion." And in fact it need not. Not even the divine origin of morality and religion. For all that psycho-analysis does is to characterise the psychological circumstances attendant upon the progress of the growth or development of our idea of morality and religion.

In this connection one might raise the question, whether a theory of non-moral origin of morality and religion, evolutional or psychological, must needs be disparaging to the nature and character of the moral or religious life? Virtually, the dignity of either primarily lies in the form of its present character rather than in the aristocracy of its birth. Psycho-analysis makes valuable contributions to our ideas of both morality and religion, in as much as it has shown the psychological and the deeper psycho-analytical processes involved in their origin and growth, and one might affirm that, as a result of these contributions, our notion of morality and religion will become clearer and purer. Whatever the origin of morality or religion, divine or otherwise, what we today prize in moral and religious life are certain qualities of character, such as, conscientiousness, sincerity, frankness. Now it is most interesting that psycho-analysis, with all the wealth of the most convincing empirical data, shows the necessity of these qualities for a man in the interests of his mental health. The modern man in general has imbibed quite a lot of the scientific spirit which has ever been on the rise in Europe since the Renaissance and, therefore, sermonising to him to be moral and good has little effect.

Heaven, as an objective, does not much attract him as hell does not frighten him, but he knows the consequences of mental ill-health, the worry, the anxiety and the more serious disorders of mind and, therefore, prizes mental health as a real value in life. Now, psycho-analysis shows how sincerity, frankness, conscientiousness and correct self-knowledge are absolutely essential to it.

But how does psycho-analysis show the need and justification of the moral qualities of conscientiousness, frankness and sincerity in life? Conscientiousness is the desire and attitude to do one's duty in every situation of life. And what is Duty? Duty is an absolute, unconditional command of the moral ideal to the actual in man to live up to it. Conscientiousness, above all, is a recognition of the supreme value of the inner life of man. Now psycho-analysis has, in recent times, promoted the spirit of examining one's motives, conscious and subconscious, and thus discovered for the modern man a new value in his inner life. But in the determination of one's duties, psycho-analysis takes fully into account the facts that an over-strung conscience causes, in many cases, serious mental disorder, ruining life altogether, much less promotes development. Therefore, it considers that the voice of the conscience, "the moral ideal", must be more realistically adjusted to "the actual" of a man. That is to say that the optimum of education, referred to above, has to be discovered and that will represent to man his attainable moral ideal at a particular time. This view of duty involves the recognition of the relative right of the instinct considered earlier.

Now about the qualities of sincerity and frankness. Hypocrisy is certainly the direct negation of moral life. And what has psycho-analysis discovered in this connection, in its investigation of the etiology of nervous disorders? Just this that the repressed wish, through devious mechanisms of the unconscious, is the cause of the disorders. Now the characterisation of the various forms of the unconscious mechanisms which are, in fact, so many ways of self-deception, is the principal achievement of psycho-analysis. Moralists complain of the superficial hypocrisy. Psycho-analysis has revealed unsuspected operations of hypocrisy and thus made tremendous contributions to the development of a purer moral life.

And then what does psycho-analytical therapy aim at? It does nothing more than asking the patient to be perfectly frank and sincere with himself. He must be true to himself. He must face, at the plane of consciousness, the repressed wish and accord due recognition to it. Psycho-analysis thus makes a fine positive contribution to the moral development of man. "Our best hope for the future" declares Freud, "is that the intellect – the scientific reason – should in time establish a dictatorship over the human mind." "And the very nature of reason is a guarantee that it would not fail to concede to human emotions and to all that is determined by them the position to which they are entitled." (Ibid., p. 234) From the rational standpoint, this is high idealism.

Freud's commitment to neurotic patients and their sexual complications became somewhow a prepossession with him. In the idealistic trends, which are also clearly and definitely present in him, particularly in his conception of optimum education, how much to repress and when to do it, etc., he modified his position considerably. And this modified position needs to be taken note of and duly further developed. The original sexual theory will then undergo a change. Sex is a basic trend of human nature, concerned as it is with the continuity of the race. But surely it is not the all-determining trend of nature. Further, for a theory of human nature as a whole, do we not need to observe it as a whole? How can we build up a valid conception of human nature on the basis of the data supplied by the analysis of neurotic patients alone? The revisionist schools of psycho-analysis have changed things a good deal.

In the terms of Integral Psychology, sex belongs to the lower vital, the essential biological factor, common between man and animal, concerned with the perpetuation of the species. But besides this there is reason, recognised by Freud, and also the spiritual soul, for which harmony and wholeness are spontaneous facts. For a sound and a comprehensive view of human nature, we have to take note of all these facts.

It can, however, be said that in a state of civilisation and in individuals or a class of individuals sex may become dominant, but then there are also individuals who live in their souls and feel freedom from sex. Those who live in their reason and rational activity would also find sex a secondary factor.

What Can Integral Psychology Contribute?

Freud delved deeply into the unconscious and discovered the devious ways of its working. The defence reactions in the forms of Projection, Introjection, Identification, Rationalisation, Displacement and Conversion are valuable discoveries and they do contribute to the realisation of a clearer and purer personal life. Above all, he sets up an ideal of becoming conscious of oneself more and more and of taking a non-moralistic attitude towards the instinctual urges. He recognised the three major components of personality and their respective functions: the ego and its adjustment to the objective reality, the super-ego and its peremptory moral, social and religious demands and id and its untamed passions. And then try to seek and maintain the best possible working balance among them. He even sensed that the mystics achieved through their practices a perfect unification in life. But this possibility he entertained and left the matter at that. For practical purposes, a working balance is all that he aimed at.

Now, the 'Psychic Being' of Integral Psychology is a thing of simplicity. It is essentially conscious and harmonious, capable of exercising a harmonising action on the diverse components of personality. Is this fact of personality, ever verifiable in yogic practice, relevant to Freud's aim of achieving a working balance in life or not? In fact, dealing with the complexities of inner life, its divisions and conflicts, its repressions, is a difficult and often an inconclusive affair. On the other hand, to take an attitude of detachment towards them all and to turn to the unitary Psychic Being and seek its wholeness is relatively simple. And if a sincere approach is taken and a contact made with this deeper fact, even weak and occasional, a wonderful effect may be achieved. This is, in fact, the best contribution that can proceed from Integral Psychology to Freud's conception of human nature.

The Psychic Being is self-existent delight and is the central fact of life and it can progressively bring about a domination of its own quality. The id's sex and untamed passions, super-ego's uncompromising demands and ego's precarious adjustments get steadily and firmly reshaped into a realistic wholeness of spiritual living.

This single fact added on to psycho-analysis will give a new consistency to its thought and a new effectivity to its therapeutic practice. Naturally this fact, when scientifically ascertained, will require a rethinking of other ideas and a reformulation of the view of human nature and the process of therapeutic cure. Theories are often all tentative approaches to truth and they always need readaptations.

(The main part of this paper was presented at the Freud Memorial Meeting in Calcutta in 1939.)

CULTURAL SCIENCE PSYCHOLOGY AND INTEGRAL PERSONALITY

Science is systematic knowledge and though the classification of sciences has been variously attempted, we might here distinguish them into natural and social or cultural sciences, corresponding to the German division of *Naturwissenschaften* and *Geisteswissenschaften* or *Kulturwissenschaften*. The former are best exemplified by physics and chemistry and the latter by economics, politics and ethics. Natural sciences are concerned with the objects of nature, and their procedure is to observe facts, describe them and seek to find out their mechanical and causal explanations with the help of the methods of Analysis, Experiment, Induction, Deduction, Hypothesis and Generalisation.

The *Geisteswissenschaften*, on the other hand, are concerned with the facts and the products of the social life of man, like art, religion, science, language, history, law, custom, etc. Now these are all essentially the products of inter-subjective intercourse and possess a trans-subjective validity. But they are understandable without the individual subjects, which have developed them and also recognise them. That gives a basic difference between the two groups of sciences. The work of the *Geisteswissenschaften* begins only there, says Windleband, where a willing and a knowing subject is essential to the phenomena. Or, in the words of Dilthey, *Geisteswissenschaften* are the sciences which are concerned with the historic-social reality.

For a reasoned statement of the standpoint of the natural science psychology, we cannot do better than turn to Titchener. He says that "If Psychology is to fill a chapter in the history of science, it must be because the facts and laws of Psychology are strictly co-ordinate, formally interchangeable with the facts and laws of established sciences. (Titchener, Systematic Psychology, Prolegomena, p. 27). Further, the data of science... are, stripped of meaning. They are to be "scoured clear of... evaluative accretion." (Ibid., p. 32) This is the existential type of Psychology which, Titchener thinks, "can take its place as a pure science alongside of physics and biology." (Woodworth, Contemporary Schools of Psychology, p. 12) It will interest us much more to read from him that 'the subjective' factors, the emotive processes are taken in the same existential way, so that psychology is freed from any concern about judgements of value. It is true that these judgements have their growth in psychological soil, and that feeling is the basis of value. Psychology, nevertheless, considers the emotive process precisely, as it considers the ideas, it analyses them, or makes out their modes of interconnection. And the term 'subject' "if it is at all used is to be treated as a shorthand name for a group of phenomena, which in point of fact are just as objective as the phenomena of natural science." (Ibid., p. 107)

We might make a little digression here to consider Gestalt Psychology in relation to the question of the general nature of psychology and the main problem of science we have just been discussing. On the point of the chief problem of science, we know that Gestalt Psychologists are most pronounced in their opposition to the method of analysis. Von Ehrenfels had already shown how real in itself a "Gestalt-qualität" is. It is a quality which is possessed by an object by virtue of its being an organised whole and is not possessed by any of the parts making the whole. A melody possesses a quality which none of the component notes possesses. That quality belongs only to a certain arrangement, an organisation of notes. In fact, by changing over to another key, we get an altogether new set of notes, but the melody-quality may remain the same. The Gestaltists urge that by breaking up a whole into its parts we can never hope to get the essential character of that whole. Therefore the main problem of science is not analysis but the investigation of the properties of the organised wholes. And this is not only true of psychology; the Gestalt principle is sought to be extended to physics and chemistry too.

But while Gestaltism is opposed to Titchenerian Psychology as, in fact, to all science in regard to the main problem and method of analysis that it employs, it is in agreement with the natural science standpoint of Titchener for psychology. Mental facts are for the Gestalt Psychologist, as much as for Titchener, exactly like the facts of external nature. The only difference is that, whereas the one seeks to break up the complex mental processes into their elements, the other takes them as organised wholes, the properties of which it is the primary object of science to study. The "Ich-Bezogenheit", i.e., the subjective reference and implication of the mental processes is as much of no account to the one as to the other.

Cultural science psychology differentiates out from the natural science psychology first in the recognition that the facts of mental life are fundamentally of a different order from those of natural science. James Ward has pointed out this difference very clearly. He says: "The language of the physicist is simply: it is this or that, a,b,c, or d. But the psychologist cannot say there are such and such presentations or feelings or movements – as if they were independent entities." (Ward, Psychological Principles, p. 23) On the other hand, he has to say that "The individual experience has such and such presentations, feels thus and thus and acts in this wise or that wise." (Ibid., p. 24) A mental process is always somebody's process and to talk of a 'state of consciousness' divorced from its subjective reference, the 'Ich-Bezogenheit' character, is to see it in a mutilated form. Thus psychology must be 'the science of individual experience' (Ibid., p. 28) as Ward said, or 'the science of the individual subject' as Spranger put it.

Now other features of cultural science psychology are more or less derived from it. We investigate the nature of the subject and for Ward it possesses two things: one, the faculty to attend and act, and two, the capacity to feel. Spranger characterises the subject or self as *Sinnerzeugende* (meaning-creating) and *Sinnerlebende* (meaning-experiencing) and as definitely *Strukturiert*, that is, possessing a definite 'structure', which constitutes its individuality. Now this subject is in continuous interplay with the environment which is first social or cultural and then physical so far as our subject is concerned. Each subject, through its activity with the environment, continuously creates values of various kinds, economic, political, moral, religious, scientific, etc., and apprehends those that are already objectively given. Thus the cultural environment of art, literature, science, education, economics and politics, morality and religion, which is the primary environment for the subject, is permeated through and through by valuation and the essential nature of our subject too is value-creating and value-seeking. Now one might ask how could one hope to understand mental processes in their true character, if they were divorced from value. It is, therefore, that the concept of value has been considered to give the difference between the natural and cultural sciences.

The values of our cultural life as exemplified in art, literature, etc. have ultimately been created by the subjects. Thus the study of personalities becomes of fundamental importance for cultural science psychology. Hence we must understand the different types of uniqueness of personality-structures, because they hold the key to the understanding of the different objective manifestations of culture. Thus the cultural science psychology will tend to develop primarily an individualising tendency of the historian to study and classify uniquenesses rather than to discover general laws which the natural sciences do. "Natural sciences are," it is said, "nomothetic, cultural sciences idiographic." That is, the former seek causal connection, the latter uniqueness.

Here one comes very close to one of the important claims and also the tests of cultural science psychology. Dilthey had already affirmed that a cultural science psychology was of the fundamental importance to the *Geisteswissenschaften* so that it alone gave the proper foundation for their understanding. Störring rightly points out that the natural science psychology too has rendered much useful service to the understanding of the various cultural provinces. But obviously cultural science psychology will be more competent to do so, since it starts with the concrete given whole of the historico-cultural reality as its primary data, which it then seeks to characterise and analyse. Natural science psychology starts by rejecting all valuation-implications of experience and it should then be no wonder that it finds it at last difficult to explain 'meaning' or properly understand the cultural phenomena. If we divorce mental phenomena to start with from meaning, which is essential to it, then naturally later on we will feel forced to take recourse to some artificial devices to provide for it. And then how will 'unmeaning' sensations and images account for meaning? *Geisteswissenschaftliche* psychology scores a great point over the other type of psychology in its doctrine of meaning. A proper foundation to meaning is provided only when it is recognised as a fundamental tendency of the human mind to create meaning wholes, in which values find an objective realisation. "To produce an objective world of this kind out of itself is one of the most fundamental laws of mental life, depending upon its essential nature." (Saupe) The mind of man is, in fact, as we have said before, a meaning-creating (*Sinn-erzeugende*) and meaning-experiencing (*Sinn-erlebende*) principle of existence.

The method of investigation of the cultural sciences, aiming as they do at the apprehension of 'value' and 'meaning', has naturally to be different. Dilthey had declared fairly long ago, *"Die Natur erklären wir, das Seelenleben verstehen wir."* We explain nature, but we understand mind. Nature, says Dilthey, presents to us discrete events, which we seek to interrelate by making hypotheses and supplying causes. This is the method of explaining. But in the *Geisteswissenschaften*, the facts are directly given as interconnected wholes, as *Zusammenhänge*. These we simply seek to understand, i.e., determine the meaning or the value content of those facts. It may be observed that the peculiarity of the method of understanding is a consequence of the special nature of the subject matter of the cultural sciences. With Dilthey, 'understanding' was still a vague conception, a kind of an 'artistic intuition' and it is really Spranger's achievement to have developed it into a definite instrument of investigation. It is, says he, "the peculiar cultural science method of investigation by means of which the individual mind obtains connection with the objective mind, in that it apprehends the meaning of a concrete mental objectification." (Saupe) "The result of this understanding activity is then the apprehension of the meaningful." (Ibid.) That understanding activity possesses a creative tendency is apparent from the fact that we often give new objective forms to an understood meaning. Further, since all objective forms of spirit once proceeded from individual minds, therefore all understanding ultimately is the understanding of personalities, their 'structural' properties and the dominant value-tendencies. To take an example to illustrate 'understanding', we might contemplate a child at play. Now do we understand his activity when we have described the state of consciousness of the child at that time? In fact, we understand it only when we apprehend the meaning of the activity.

Spranger's characterisation of 'understanding' is not uniform throughout. At first he said "understanding" in the widest sense of the term means "the apprehension of the mental organisation in the form of objectively valid knowledge as meaningful." (Ibid.) Later he modifies it to say that "understanding" means "apprehending given facts in the relation of a whole as meaningful." (Ibid.) The meaning of the parts of a machine are determined by the meaning or purpose of the machine as a whole, i.e., the work that it does.

Sich hinein versetzen (to put one's self in) is the *conditio sine qua non* of all psychological understanding. To understand a particular social fact, one requires to imagine the type of personality and the mental act that it is a product of and then identify oneself with it. That is how one puts oneself in another personality to understand that social fact. But perhaps the two kinds of psychologies which we have been discussing are supplementary in character. Not that either this or that must be right and then the other necessarily wrong, but that they represent two different lines of approach to the same subject matter. And judged by the measure of success that both of them have had in the application of their doctrines, one feels encouraged to affirm that either of them possesses a measure of validity.

Nature can be taken as an impersonal reality, as a thing of structure and parts and qualities and of general laws and repetitive occurrences, but the human situation is a thing of intersubjective intercourse, of subjects or selves in interaction, of seeking goals, objectives and values. It is different from the physical, chemical, biological natural phenomenon. In the field of history, economics and culture, events have a quality of purposes and uniquenesses and our seeking is to understand the sense and the meaning of these uniquenesses and this is done by *sich hinein versetzen*, by a process of identification with it and not by superficial external observation. Mental processes are no impersonal facts; they are somebody's and his intention imparts meaning to the process. We do not understand it duly if we ignore this fact. The cultural psychology standpoint has, therefore, a truth in it. However, it is possible to ignore this meaning and treat the mental process as a structural fact and seek laws of mental behaviour. These have a serviceability. But the subject's intention, its meaning and value stand ignored.

Both the approaches, of natural sciences and cultural sciences, have a validity and they both can be applied to psychology, but we cannot afford to be ignorant of their merits and demerits. The natural science method of observation, induction and generalisation has been applied to history, religion and other social phenomena, but that surely involves an essential defect.

The issue of intention and meaning inspired Spranger to inquire into the ideal forms of personality based upon the essential motivations of life. These he identified as six: scientific, economic, aesthetic and religious and further of sympathy and of mastery. These types are really conceptual aids for the understanding of the historical cultural reality.

This psychological standpoint is specially useful in certain psychological fields, e.g., of folk psychology, religious psychology and the like. And, in psychological systems like Freud's and Jung's where the individual subject is central, this standpoint has its obvious validity. However, the two approaches, of natural science and cultural sciences, psychology, get mixed up.

It would be interesting and useful to see the sympathy of this approach to that of Integral Psychology. In integral personality, the 'psychic being' is the central and the all-commanding fact. It supports and progressively transforms all mental life. Cultural science psychology too has fastened upon the subject of experience as the essential fact of life. But what is more important is its method of knowing and understanding a fact by *sich hinein versetzen*, by putting oneself in. Is it not 'knowing by identity,' the favourite principle of Sri Aurobindo's epistemology and metaphysics?

The natural science psychology thinks of self and personality as a summation of mental processes and fails to account for its uniqueness, the essential quality of personality. If we fail to see and recognise an individual subject, how can uniqueness be explained?

The investigation of the nature of the subject too has been attempted and six fundamental interests have been identified. That helps in understanding the historico-cultural phenomena. But in integral psychology, we know of the psychic being a great deal. It is an evolving principle, conscious spiritual reality progressively integrating the disparities of mind and life. Further, that the uniqueness in an individual grows as the psychic being grows up. At the lower levels, the individual is a part of the mass and it is the mass life that is the fact, as in crowd-life even the present-day individual gets merged in the mass.

It is, indeed, a capital point that cultural psychology makes out in affirming the fact and reality of a subject, but it is important to know about its nature and the conditions of its development. The quality of uniqueness gets its full play only when the psychic being grows up to be the overt governing principle of life. Until then, universal nature of mind in varying degrees determines life.

(The main part of the paper was delivered as Presidential Address at the Psychology Section of Indian Philosophical Congress at Allahabad in 1938.)

THE URGE FOR WHOLENESS

(A Summary of the Presidential Address, Section of Psychology and Educational Science, Indian Science Congress, Jan., 1946)

What is the most basic urge or trend of human nature? Contemporary psychology gives many answers; sex, will for power, behaviour, reflex action, purpose and some other similar concepts. The variety of voices of these answers, so different and exclusive as they are, constitute the well-known crisis in the science of psychology today.

The question, what is really the first or fundamental urge of human nature, therefore, becomes an acute issue.

The author of this address would contend that an answer to this question can only be formulated by considering the whole phenomenon of human nature in all its ranges of experience, conscious, subconscious and the superconscious. Most of the existing answers are based upon an exclusive consideration of the nature of the subconscious or a bit of bodily behaviour or some other particular fact. The super-conscious experience affirmed by vast yogic, mystic and religious literature of the world and the modern yogic experience have so far not been seriously considered by the psychologist in evolving his view of human nature. And while evolution is recognised as a fact, we do not seem fully to recognise that for the understanding and explaining of a particular stage of the process, the stages antecedent to it alone cannot be sufficient. McDougall affirmed 'purpose' or 'goal-seeking' as the essential characteristic of mind, yet resorted to the antecedent facts of 'structural dispositions' to explain behaviour. The natural-science habit of looking for antecedents as causes seems to have influenced unconsciously even a deliberate purposivist like him.

Indian psychology has been in fact thoroughly purposivistic. To it the next higher form of consciousness possible to man has been the matter of the first importance. The end towards which an evolutionary process moves is by far the most important single factor to explain the nature of the process. The antecedents come only next to it. Indian psychology discovered and ascertained the reality of a form of consciousness, possessing the quality of wholeness, a consciousness in which the conscious and the unconscious operate not through mutual stresses and strains and an economic balance of the whole, but through an essential unity and harmony. If such a consciousness is a reality, then obviously our present view of mental action needs a re-orientation.

The author feels strongly persuaded to affirm that an evolving 'wholeness', a tendency to a progressive perfection of organisation is the principal trend not only of human nature but of organic evolution as a whole. This progressive perfection of organisation of life is more easily noticeable in the sub-human species, from the amoeba to the ape, in an increasing adaptation to and mastery of an ever more complex environment on the whole. In man, however, the situation becomes different. Through his power of thought, he rises to an immensely greater capacity of dealing with his environment. But through the development of self-consciousness, which makes thinking possible, he becomes conscious of deep inner discords whose harmonisation becomes the new direction of evolution. Simultaneously, he becomes conscious of the mechanism of projection, as a fact ingrained in his animal nature, and begins to recognise the true causes of happenings as belonging to the forces within the personality rather than to things outside. Now the yogic fact of a fulfilled consciousness, a consciousness whole, harmonious and balanced, called by Sri Aurobindo the Psychic Consciousness, experienced and enjoyed by many individuals in the past (to that the yogic, mystic and religious literature bears wide evidence) and which is today equally well experienceable by pursuing an intensive inner discipline of life, is a relevant evolutional fact. The fact, no doubt, occurs under rather exacting conditions of life, but when once its character is definitely ascertained, its effects for general consciousness will become easier to determine. But even otherwise the quality of the fact, so distinct and unique, representing a form of consciousness, in which the so-called fundamental polarities and dualities of the general human consciousness are made good, must irresistibly draw our attention.

Among contemporary psychologists, it is interesting to discover many direct and indirect recognitions of the fact of a whole and a harmonised consciousness. Even in Freud, we read a sentence as this: "It can be easily imagined that certain practices of mystics may succeed in upsetting the normal relation between the different regions of the mind, so that, for example, the perceptual system becomes able to grasp relations in the deeper layers of the ego and in the id, which would be otherwise inaccessible to it." Dr. G. Bose, the most eminent psycho-analyst of our country, while carrying the idea of polarity to the extent of positing a counter-wish to every wish, affirms himself to be a believer in "pure consciousness as distinguished from the consciousness of this or that." Further, in his theory of mind, he finds it necessary to admit a principle of unity as the 'guiding principle' of all mental action. This principle, according to him, reconciles the last polarity of subject and object too.

Dr. S. C. Mitra's hypothesis regarding the nature of mind possesses an obvious similarity to the view here defended, as he assumes that mind, to start with, is "in a state of perfectly stable equilibrium quite content and at harmony with itself." However, for us, such equilibrium is the evolutional goal, not the starting-point.

McDougall too contemplates a fully integrated personality under a single master sentiment.

However, Jung stands above all in having perceived clearly and distinctly the force and the power of the psychic consciousness. He finds the ordinary psychological explanations of personality as 'inappropriate' and, guided by his principles of analytical psychology, discovers a truly unique fact in personality. This he calls the 'centre' or 'self'. To activate the centre and live in the consciousness of the self is to live the life of wholeness. This consciousness is creatively synthetic, as it assimilates the disparate materials of our mental nature and reshapes them into a picture of wholeness. All this perception is superb. Yogic practice too, at its best, aims at nothing else but the activation of the psychic centre or the soul in its dynamic aspect.

But while the recognition of a unique centre is fine, Jung did not see that the consciousness of the centre, marked by a sense of wholeness, constitutes a higher plane than the ordinary mental consciousness. In consequence, he mixed up the superconscious with the subconscious and declared the Samadhi state a state of unconsciousness.

The hypothesis here presented thus commands an appreciable direct and indirect support from contemporary psychology. But it primarily relies upon its own strength and merit. It offers a theory of mind based upon the widest data of conscious phenomena, since it takes into consideration the evolutionary progress as a whole from the earliest beginnings to the stages which set the goal to the present human consciousness. It gives a coherent explanation of the normal and the abnormal consciousness. Above all, it gives a clear scientific meaning to the concept 'normal' and saves the term from being a changing social average. Lastly, affording a fuller perspective of mental life, it is capable of reconciling the conflicting standpoint of the schools of contemporary psychology. The fact of psychic consciousness is a supreme fact for psychology as it presents a form of consciousness higher than the mental and is, therefore, capable of showing the true sphere of validity of the facts of our ordinary consciousness. Sex, will for power, etc., cease to have the validity they ordinarily possess. The urge for wholeness, the trend towards a fuller organisation and harmony of life, as shown by the psychic consciousness, therefore, is the most basic trend of human nature. The other answers, possessing a partial validity as they do, can be accommodated as particular instrumentations of the trend towards wholeness.

Indian psychology has indeed a great promise but the value of its peculiar standpoint and the facts discovered by it have yet to be duly appraised by us for the benefit of our modern psychological knowledge.

THE PSYCHOLOGICAL SYSTEM OF SRI AUROBINDO

The rise of psychology in recent times can truly be called a phenomenon. In the 16th century, Francis Bacon had powerfully appealed to the European scholars to explore nature and build up power. And they responded admirably and created, within about three centuries, a remarkable state of civilisation. The mastery that it gave to man over the natural forces of land, sea and air was undoubtedly an astounding achievement. But an altogether objective attitude, directed to the study of the given facts of nature, involved a neglect of the human subject. The result was twofold. There was a lack of interest and knowledge regarding human personality and, therefore, lack of control and conscious direction of its energies. Secondly, an altogether objective attitude led to a cultural maladjustment with the external situation and hence neuroses of certain kinds.

The interest then grew in man and his personality difficulties, and psychology tended to become a living and an influential science. Freud, Jung and Adler became leaders of a great cultural movement, which sought to draw the attention of man from the objective fact to himself. And within a few decades, a large body of psychological knowledge grew up. The standpoint of these three luminaries of psychology was marked by a depth and intensity in the study of personality, which did not exist in the science before. Wundt had founded experiment in psychology, but his new method was mostly confined to the study of sensations. Kulpe had extended it to thought processes and Eibbinghaus to memory and it was a good advance. Yet the dominant outlook of the science was governed by the theory of associationism, which holds sensations as the primary data and explains memory, thinking, imagination and voluntary action as the result of different forms of associations amongst them. J.S. Mill in England and Condillac in France were the chief representatives of this way of thinking and they set the standard for the rest for a long time.

The various contemporary schools of psychology, Psychoanalysis, Purposivism, Gestaltism, Behaviourism and their subschools, arose in reaction to associationism and, in particular, to its intellectualism and atomism. All contemporary schools, howso divergent in their positions they may be, hold activity as more primary than sensations and ideas and insist on the unitary character of personality. All this is very good.

But the sum of our psychological knowledge is confined to the conscious mental processes of sensation, idea, memory, imagination, thinking, etc., and the subconscious, which is more or less the reservoir of our past experiences. These experiences, are, however, dynamic facts which by their own force tend to rise to the surface of consciousness and otherwise influence our thought and action. The exploration and the identification of the contents of the subconscious and their working will stand as a fact of scientific achievement to the lasting credit of Freud's Psychoanalysis. Jung, through his conception of the Racial Unconscious, has gone deeper and it is a further achievement of contemporary psychology.

The idea of evolution, since Darwin, has very rightly been a necessary idea of all knowledge in the West and some of the important psychologists make large use of it to explain mind and behaviour. But, even when it is made use of, man is conceived as a product of antecedent evolutionary conditions. This is natural, since the two principal drives of Darwinian evolution, the struggle for existence and the survival of the fittest, are mechanistic forces. But even a purposive and a teleological evolution, which has gained large ground in recent times, remains committed to mechanical causation and does not undertake to explore the ends and goals of evolution and their working.

This works most adversely, in particular in psychology, where mind is definitely recognised as teleological in its activities. The category of end remains really a name and the entire field of consciousness and behaviour is sought to be explained in terms of the antecendents of instincts and habits.

We have here sought to give the general framework of contemporary psychology, its overall situation. We will now try to give a broad perspective of the psychological system of Sri Aurobindo and also see in what measure it can make a contribution to the fund of our contemporary psychological knowledge.

Sri Aurobindo has not propounded a psychological system as a separate body of knowledge in the Western sense, but his writings on yoga and philosophy do contain one in an interconnected and a unified treatment of the issues of life and existence, growth and evolution, in the Indian way. It is, however, a complete view of mind and personality. It has a standpoint of its own, a methodology adapted to its standpoint and a large body of knowledge of its own. And the system is thoroughly psychological, since its emphasis is always on experience and not on any *a priori* reasoning. We will now consider some of the salient features of this system or body of psychological knowledge.

The first and the most important characteristic of the psychological system of Sri Aurobindo is its empirical standpoint. It rejects all *a priori* assertions about personality. Considering the general character of the system, in particular its emphasis on soul, one would feel inclined to call it a system of rational psychology like those of Spinoza, Leibnitz, Wolff and Kant. But in fact it is not so, because it insists on experience, though with the Western empiricists it does not agree to remaining confined to the experience of perception and its ideational elaborations. It seeks to widen the scope of experience and it seeks in particular new qualities of experience. The idea of evolution is even more strongly an element in this standpoint. But the evolution here contemplated is purposive and teleological, while it has no objection to accepting Darwin's principles of the struggle for existence and the survival of the fittest as mechanical factors determining the process at a stage. However, as evolution advances and consciousness grows stronger, the process tends to become larger and richer. Perceptual consciousness of the animal, which is all too fragmentary, limited to the given bits of space and time, tends to become a larger unity at the ideational and the thinking level of man. Here the larger unities of space and time can be comprehended and a more unified personality comes into being. All the same, the personality is yet a loose sort of organisation of its propensities and reactions to the environment. A self-conscious integration of them is yet another stage, which so far only some individuals represent in action, but that surely means it a clear general possibility for the future.

The incorporation of the idea of evolution into the standpoint of psychology would thus tend to make it practical, whereas scientific psychology seeks simply to observe, classify and explain facts. The issue of theoretical and practical standpoints, in fact, receives a most interesting kind of synthesis in Sri Aurobindo's psychology. Sri Aurobindo is not content to take human personality as a unit by itself, and then try to analyse and explain it. It belongs to a process of evolution and he insists that it must be taken as such. Its past, which has led on to its present form, must be considered, but more so must its future possibilities be considered, which are evidently dynamic influences determining its growth at the present moment. This standpoint is theoretical, since it aims at truth for its own sake. But if we insist on taking our stand on perceptual experience, we will not be able to appreciate the ideational or intellectual level of experience, and similarly if we take the intellectual as our final stand, then we will fail to comprehend the supra-intellectual levels of experience. We must personally persist in ascending further and further and then alone could we hope to understand the larger fields of personality. Thus the practical emphasis in Sri Aurobindo's psychology is thoroughly consistent with the theoretical aim of science. We have simply to remember that here the subject-matter of study is a process, which has a past and a future to it and, therefore, we cannot treat it as a finished product. And in unravelling the future more fully than is indicated now, we have naturally to grow ourselves to have that experience.

The standpoint of Sri Aurobindo's psychology is thus empirical, evolutional and of personal growth. The last characteristic is important since, in psychology, human personality, which is the object of study, is also the studying scientist, whose faculties of observation must grow *pari passu* with the widening and heightening of experience.

The methodology of psychology rightly prizes introspection as its primary method, as it alone gives an immediate knowledge of the psychological data, the experience. The other methods of objective observation of behaviour and experiement and the various forms of these rest upon introspective experience, without which they could not be operative. But introspection, as so far developed and used in psychology, is limited to the observation of certain sensory, perceptual and ideational experiences, as they play up at the surface of consciousness. The Free Association of Freud, which can be regarded as a kind of introspective report, is undoubtedly a most interesting development and extension of it. In this form, introspection becomes an observation of the deeper content of the subconscious.

Now Sri Aurobindo would demand of introspection to become an instrument of self-observation of such a form and quality that the individual is able fully to stand back as it were from himself and observe himself with complete detachment. This would involve at first a progressive self-detachment and self-discovery to such an extent that the individual attains to an identification with the inmost subject of experience within himself and the best possible detachment from what he calls *his*, this body and the possessions, ideas and opinions, emotions and sentiments.

The mastery of such introspection is a hard discipline, but even an appreciation of its nature and character would put the observer on guard against his *non-subject* identifications and thus enable him to eliminate them more or less. The moralistic and religious bias of 'oughts' and 'ought-nots' is one of the serious hurdles, since until a thoroughly objective and realistic attitude becomes well-ingrained, there is always the danger of being carried away by such persuasions in our observation of experiences. This introspection, when sufficiently developed, would be competent not merely to observe what plays up on the surface of consciousness directly, but also what is the subconscious and is exercising its influence on the conscious contents, and also the pull and the force of the dynamic goals of evolution acting on the present personality. This becomes possible in the measure the individual attains to the proper subject-identification and detachment from the projective posture of personality.

Such introspection is the main method of Sri Aurobindo's psychology and when this is developed, the objective observation too receives proportionate extension and depth in its study of other personalities. Experiment, as the principle of observation under predetermined and controlled conditions, admits of an application to both of the above methods, as is ordinarily possible, with of course some necessary modifications.

We can now proceed to consider some of the other salient features of this system of psychology. Before Freud, conscious experience was practically the whole of the data of psychology. Today we recognise that it is only about one-tenth of our mental life, whereas the nine-tenths of it is subconscious.

Jung's racial unconscious is a further extension of the same. Sri Aurobindo finds that the unconscious virtually goes much further so as to include our material body too. The intimate relation of matter and consciousness in our life, as well as the progressive evolution of consciousness from the beginnings of life to man, show that the two are not contradictories, as is believed, but that they constitute in essence a continuity. Thus there can be no unbridgeable gulf between body and mind for psychology and further, if the progressive growth of consciousness in evolution is any indication of the future, then the final object of evolution must be the achievement of the fullest consciousness and, therefore, a complete elimination of the unconsciousness. But in his conception of the Superconscious, he adds an altogether new dimension to human personality. If the evolution is a fact, then the future possibilities must be present in the organism as definite present potentialities. The animal, for example, does possess the rudiments of rationality of man, which we must say is a definite possibility of animal life. Similarly, in man his possibilities must be admitted as potentialities which may become actualities in the future. Knowledge, feeling and will of an integrated personality are not normal to man today. But they are surely indicated in him and can be regarded as evolutional possibilities. These do not belong to our past experience and cannot, therefore, be called a content of the subconscious. They have evidently to be regarded as another aspect of personality and this Sri Aurobindo calls the Superconscious.

For the growth of personality, the Superconscious is evidently the most important part of it and it is to this that Sri Aurobindo has devoted by far the largest measure of his energies. He has explored it, marked out its several successive ranges, characterised them and shown the relative influence of each on the normal mentality of man. This constitutes the most valuable part of the detailed working out of the psychological system of Sri Aurobindo.

It may be recalled in this connection that Freud had explored the Unconscious, formulated the laws of its working, brought out the fact of repression and practically shown how a subnormal personality could be brought to the level of normality. Sri Aurobindo's call was to the Superconscious, because he was primarily interested in the further growth of human consciousness. He then addressed himself to the realm of the Superconscious and has characterised the principal contents of it and evolved a technique by which a self-conscious acceleration of growth is made possible.

Jung in his otherwise most remarkable book (The Integration of the Personality) affirms that the so-called Superconscious of the yoga is no distinct fact from the subconscious. (Vide 'The Integration of the Personality', 1940, p. 26.) He explains that the yogi, by a special discipline, tries to universalise his consciousness, but in doing so the consciousness becomes dim and ultimately identical with the unconscious. This is, however, contrary to actual experience. By yoga, one progressively achieves freedom from the mind's fixations on the particular appearances of things and thus an indefinite extension is realised. But it is a highly conscious and luminous experience which is of great significance to the life as a whole. However, there are certain paths of yoga, which are in fact aberrations of the true yogic discipline, which seek release from the ordinary life into the unconscious.

In his reasoning of identifying the Superconscious with the subconscious, Jung in fact gets involved in a self-contradiction. He rightly recognised the yogi as a pastmaster in the art of whole living and this wholeness evidently comes to him through the new consciousness of yoga, the Superconscious. The unconscious is to him as to Freud chaotic in character. Now how could the two fields of consciousness, one chaotic and the other whole, be identified?

Besides the Superconscious, the subliminal is another new sphere of consciousness identified by Sri Aurobindo. The individual is surely a particular representation of the species. It possesses the general characteristics of the species in an individual formation. Now the subliminal self, or the subliminal sphere of personality, is exactly the meeting-ground of the individual and the universal. In that, the individual participates in the universal and is thereby able to exercise functions like telepathy, tele-audition and others, which involve a wider action than those of the normal personality.

Another important salient feature of Sri Aurobindo's system of psychology is the idea of levels or planes of consciousness. Two levels of experiences are a patent fact of common psychology, the perceptual and the ideational. Sri Aurobindo, the explorer of the Superconscious, unravels a number of others coming after them in an ascending order. Of these, the first he calls the plane of psychic experience. Our normal personality is, as the etymology of the term goes, truly a mask. It is a superficial organisation of our being meant for dealing with the external situation. This he calls the surface personality and is the sum-total of all the perceptual instinctive reactions of the organism and mental elaborations of thought and sentiment. The psycho-biological life as a whole is such a formation. In this connection, it is easy to recall Bergson's view of mind. He regards mind as an instrument concerned with external reality and which creates line, forms, figures and all the fixed positions of the external world so that the organism may be able to act on it and achieve the practical ends of life. The real fact of personality is to him a deeper flow, an *'élan vital'*, which we are able to contact when we dissociate ourselves from the superficial formations of the states of consciousness.

To Sri Aurobindo, the mind is an instrument of organisation and action and is all concerned with the external situation. It is a trasitional term of evolution and a secondary phenomenon, since it is in the psychic experience that consciousness comes to its own, which is, therefore, the primary fact. It is by an introspective penetration, a going within, that we land upon this plane of experience, which is characterised by markedly different qualities. This experience is, at the first instance, a whole consciousness, an integral fact and, therefore, free from the stresses and strains of the mental willing, which is always counteracted by some contrary willing, conscious or subconscious. It is marked by a greater clarity and a clearer and a surer joy. This experience is a whole in its own nature and exercises a harmonising function with regard to the rest of the personality.

This plane of experience is also an *'élan'* in the language of Bergson. It is a movement, it is a flow. Sri Aurobindo chooses to call it a flame, which tends to rise higher. But if we call it an 'élan', we will have to call it an *'élan conscient'*, since it is essentially consciousness in its urge or movement.

Ordinarily, our identifications are all with the formations and habits of our mind and body, the acquired reactions of the organism and we, therefore, remain limited to them in the use of the organism of personality. But the psychic experience does even normally, at times, emerge in our ordinary consciousness or we do sometimes spontaneously get on there. Even so far as the common perceptual and ideational levels are concerned, we do move up and down, sometimes living at the plane of sense-experience and at other times at so many other intermediate positions between them. If we could recognise when the psychic experience comes up and then feel its quality and efficacy for integrating the rest of the personality, then a distinct psychological action would be set up in us, an aspiration would arise, which would seek to bring the psychic to the front and make it lead the personality. That would be the happiest situation for the growth in integration.

The psychic experience is the first of the superconscious facts of our mentality. The subsequent ones, which Sri Aurobindo has clearly characterised, are even more powerful. But we cannot undertake a discussion of them here.

In connection with the fact of the psychic experience, Jung, the profoundest of the Western psychologists, provides an interesting parallel. We have already referred to his book 'The Integration of the Personality.' It pronounces an interesting judgment on the present stock of our psychological knowledge. Says he, "All the usual little remedies and medicaments of psychology fall somewhat short (to explain personality) just as they do with the man of genius or the creative human being. Derivation from ancestral heredity or from the milieu does not quite succeed; inventing fictions about childhood, which is so popular today, and – to put it mildly, in the inappropriate: the explanation from necessity – he had no money, was ill, and so forth – remains caught in mere externalities. (Ibid., p. 299) Finding all the available explanations of personality unsatisfactory, he persists in his own search for one and at last declares that there is a psychic centre of personality that is not identical with the 'I'. He thus affirms a centre different from the ego. And he ascribes to it a dynamic influence. Says he, "The centre of personality acts like a magnet upon the disparate materials and processes of the conscious and like a crystal grating, catches them one by one." (Ibid., p. 97) It thus has an integrating and a harmonising function.

The parallelism between the psychic being of Sri Aurobindo and the centre of Jung is most interesting. Even their functions are broadly the same. However, for Jung it is a hypothesis, whereas for Sri Aurobindo it is a fact of experience, which he characterises in great detail and even gives the method and the technique of bringing it more and more into the front.

The discovery of this new fact of experience, whole and integral in character, would obviously be of the deepest consequence for the science of psychology. Evidently, a full appreciation of it will lead to a reconstruction of psychology, since all our present explanations visualise the mind and its polarities as final. In view of the wholeness of the psychic experience, these polarities would naturally acquire a different meaning. Self and not-self is the most basic polarity of our psychological existence, as our self lives, moves and has its being in a constant relation with a not-self. Our mind depends upon and is correlated with the environment. But the psychic experience is a wholeness. It does not depend upon the environment, nor is it necessarily bound to it.

The psychic experience also sets up a new standard of mental health. Mental health is today 'on the whole' an economic balance among the stresses and strains of the various parts in the anatomy of personality, i.e., the superego, the ego and the id. It is not a state of complete inner harmony, which is revealed in the wholeness of the psychic experience and promised by its integrating and transforming action.

We had started in an ambitious way. We had announced a psychological system in the title. But we have barely given a few of the salient features of it. We hope they do make out that we have a system here, another orientation of personality, which can suggest new lines of research and make some contribution to our knowledge of personality.

THE SILENT MIND

(A discussion between Dr. H. C. Ganguli, Delhi University, and Dr. Indra Sen, Sri Aurobindo Ashram, Pondicherry)

1. H.C.G.: Dr. Indra Sen, of all the ideas developed in the writings of Sri Aurobindo, the concept of the Silent Mind appears to me, from the viewpoint of psychology, the most fascinating concept. As a psychologist, I would like to know your views on this. You have been at the Ashram for about four decades and before that, in the Delhi University. I feel that I cannot find a more appropriate person. If you agree, we can explore the matter in a question-answer manner.

   I.S.: I entirely agree that the Silent Mind is a concept which goes beyond modern psychology and is a new one propounded by Sri Aurobindo. I would, therefore, be glad to say what I can on it and certainly the question-answer approach economises time.

2. H.C.G.: What does Sri Aurobindo mean by Silent Mind?

   I.S.: Mind can be as still as the water of a lake when no wind is blowing. This is the traditional image of the mind for one who seeks his soul. The state of Silence has significance for the Science of Psychology in as much as it shows that the state of flux is not essential to mind, which is equal to saying that thinking is not essential to it.

3. H.C.G.: Is Silent Mind the same as what Patanjali calls Chitta Vritti Nirodha?

   I.S.: Yes, Silent Mind is a stage on the way to perfect Nirodha which is attained in Samadhi.

4. H.C.G.: Is Silent Mind the same as Pratyahara? By Pratyahara here, I mean a state of blocking of incoming sense-stimuli as well as blocking of non-voluntary thoughts or images.

   I.S.: Pratyahara is a corrective for externalised consciousness. It is a preparation for the Samadhi state. Silent Mind involves Pratyahara. In Pratyahara Silence is more or less involved. The two concepts are overlapping: however, they represent two different approaches to the problem of personal development. Silence progressively grows in a conscious manner from Pratyahara, the firm self-conscious stand, to Dharana and Dhyana (concentration and meditation) and perfects itself in Samadhi (perfect self-conscious self-existence) through identification with the Spirit which is basically calm and still.

5. H.C.G.: Is Silent Mind an end in itself?

I.S.: For some, like J. Krishnamurthy, it seems to be an end in itself. Krishnamurthy says he is not interested in anything beyond the Silent Mind. So happy he feels with the discovery and enjoyment of Silent Mind. But, I feel, he is in touch with the Reality beyond the Silent Mind.

6. H.C.G.: What is meant by Mind in the expression Silent Mind?

I.S.: Mind refers to the distinctive human consciousness, as different from animal consciousness. Mind in the Indian sense excludes instincts, etc., which are included in the Vital or Prana. As you know, we distinguish three levels of experience, the Mental, the Vital and the Physical.

7. H.C.G.: Is Silence of Mind a normal condition of the person who has attained it or is it present only during states of meditation?

I.S.: It is not a normal condition. But one can invoke or induce it at will, if one has achieved some proficiency. Normally he lives more quietly. The important thing is that he is not subject to compulsive thinking.

8. H.C.G.: What are the characteristics of thinking, feeling and acting of a person fairly proficient in Silence?

I.S.: Tranquilisation of emotions – greater harmony.
Such a state of emotions is both an effect and cause of mental silence. The two interact and go together. Thinking gets integrated and becomes increasingly more effective. There is a greater purposiveness in thought and it develops the capacity for receiving higher inspirations. In will, one enjoys an integrity and force one does not enjoy otherwise. There is a sense of power in the person.

The practical consequences of Silence are really wide and deep. Silence gives mastery over thinking. Compulsive thinking ceases to be a necessity.

For the issue of integration of personality too, it has its value. Integration cannot just be a canalisation of energies. That will not bring self-mastery and self-direction. The unity of the person must come to its own and command its diverse energies. That implies a Silence or non-insistence on the part of the energies to follow their own impulsions.

9. H.C.G.: In thinking, is greater use made of imagery as against language or words?

I.S.: As silence grows, commitment to images and words and their successive movements perhaps becomes less and seeing things as a whole becomes more. However, the quality of seeing things as a whole becomes a regular feature when the psychic being becomes active and operative. There is then a start in the direction of holistic seeing and thinking.

10. H.C.G.: What is the difference between the Silent Mind and the Psychic Consciousness?

I.S.: The first is a state of the mind which is the surface consciousness in man. The second is the deep Inner Consciousness in man, the Chaitya Purusha of the Upanishad, which is best represented by the "Centre", beyond all dualities or polarities of C.G. Jung, the well-known Western psychologist.

11. H.C.G.: Is Silent Mind equivalent to a state of Higher Consciousness?

I.S.: No. Silent Mind is the silent state of mental consciousness. Higher Consciousness is not the same as Silent Mind though Silence is innate in it. Mental consciousness is pale as compared with the Higher Consciousness which is more luminous. In Higher Consciousness, we have Psychic Consciousness as well as above-mind planes of Consciousness.

12. H.C.G.: What is the technology or device for developing the Silent Mind? Can we say it is meditation, repetition of a Mantra, or is it the devlopment of the Sakshi Bhava (the Witness attitude)?

    I.S.: All are useful and can be practised as the mood favours. When Sakshi Bhava is not possible, meditation or simple quietude is not possible, Mantra can be used. When Sakshi Bhava becomes easy, Mantra can be dropped.

13. H.C.G.: Can I ask you to elaborate on the technique of attaining mental silence?

    I.S.: Leave the mind altogether. Seek an identification with the Psychic Centre in the heart. Mental concentration involves great effort. Movement inwards (towards the Psychic Centre) or upwards (above the head) brings about mental silence more easily. If you remain on the surface of the mind, you may struggle with the agitation, the waves, but it is a difficult task. Go beyond the breakers or dive deep. Waves will continue but not affect you.

    Jnana Yoga (the Yoga of Knowledge), Karma Yoga (the Yoga of Action) and other forms of yogic practices will, each in its own way, involve silence of mind in its pursuit of integration of personality, as restlessness, vagrancy, revolts and egoisms of thoughts, feelings and volitions are inconsistent with a calm, self-possessed, unified personality.

    However, Vivekananda, Sri Aurobindo and the Mother have suggested processes of their own experience for achieving Silence. Vivekananda recommends the practice of the witness attitude. You watch the thoughts come and go, but do not get carried away by them, withhold your consent to them and they will tend to slow down and drop off.

Sri Aurobindo says, see where these thoughts come from. You will find them coming from outside, from the universal nature. This really involves achieving a distinction between oneself as the detached observer and the activities of general nature. This given, self-separation from ideas becomes easy. In the ordinary state, one is all identified with the activities and regards them as his very self. Then Silence becomes extremely difficult. This is, however, one of the methods given by Sri Aurobindo.

The Mother recommends what she calls the 'stand back attitude.' Says she, before speaking, eating or doing anything, stand back a little and that will give you control over your involvements and you will progressively build up a poise of self-mastery and mastery over circumstances.

14. H.C.G.: What is the role of attention in the acquisition of the Silent Mind?

I.S.: Practise going inward or upward. Look inside. Do not put too much effort. Do not struggle: then you get tied to the surface. For example, to go below the surface in water physically, one might just let the body drop down, not exert oneself unnecessarily. Effort is the straining of the surface mind. Dropping down is really relaxing with a will to go down. Intention to go up or down is indispensable.

15. H.C.G.: In Sri Aurobindo's Yoga, is there anything beyond the Silent Mind?

I.S.: Silent Mind is purely a mental state. One has to go beyond it to the Soul, to the Divine.

16. H.C.G.: If one does not believe in a spiritual life or in the Divine, but from a purely psychological point of view, is it possible for a person to attain a state of Silence?

I.S.: Of course, yes. But he will get only a relative state of silence. Not perfect Silence which comes in the spiritual condition.

17. H.C.G.: What would be the duration of practice sessions for a young man of college-going age?

    I.S.: I have a bias against mechanisation. One should practise according to his inclination. When the mind gets too unruly, has too many strong thoughts, then better stop practice. Secondly, one should not practise for 10 minutes and then forget about it. It is a 24 hour assignment, as it were. One should seek silence and quietude as a normal basis for activity. Then it works better.

18. H.C.G.: How does an outsider, say, a psychologist, assess the progress of an individual in the development of the Silent Mind? What are its behavioural manifestations, as distinct from the practitioner's subjective reporting?

    I.S.: An outer indication of self-composure is the minimum you can expect from one who has achieved some proficiency. A relative non-involvement in circumstances is also an important indication.

19. H.C.G.: How would you relate the concept of the Sthitaprajna (stable or tranquil Mind or Consciousness) of Sri Krishna with the Silent Mind of Sri Aurobindo?

    I.S.: Sthitaprajna is a higher stage than that of the Silent Mind. But Silent Mind is a necessary precondition of Sthitaprajna. No one can be a Sthitaprajna with a turbulent mind. The condition of a Sthitaprajna is elaborately described in Chapter II of the Gita.

20. H.C.G.: Thank you, Dr. Indra Sen. I feel that our discussion has been extremely interesting and illuminating. This concept of the Silent Mind is fascinating and I am grateful for your throwing light on this.

    I.S.: Thank you, Dr. Ganguli. The session with you has been really interesting, a good hearty contact as between friends. But it is more a contact between the modern science of psychology and the traditional yoga – as renovated and rejuvenated by Sri Aurobindo. As you know, I was also a psychologist, and again, like you, was the President of the Psychology Section, Indian Science Congress, a long time back. What I wish most for all inquiring psychologists and what I have deeply wished for you when you have come to Pondicherry, is a personal discovery and identification of the psychological fact of the Silent State of Mind.

(With acknowledgements to *Indian Journal of Psychology*)

THE UNCONSCIOUS IN SRI AUROBINDO

The unconscious is an enormous discovery of Freud and contemporary psychology. It has not only given an insight into the etiology of neuroses and a way of psycho-therapy but also added a new dimension to human personality and thereby deepened our sense and understanding of it. It has also overflown into the general cultural life and stimulated new trends of thought in literature and philosophy. The significance of the doctrine of the unconscious is, therefore, great both for science as well as culture and a critical appraisal of it seems to be much called for.

The unconscious, as it has passed on to the general cultural life, is the one Freud had originally characterised. It is synonymous with the repressed and the sexual. But the author had found facts to modify it later on.

With Jung, the unconscious becomes a much wider concept. It includes much besides the repressed and is not necessarily sexual. In fact, there is a racial unconscious too, consisting of the primeval human ways of thinking and acting besides the personal. But more important than these is his insistence on the forward-looking attitude of the individual, of his conscious, and his refusal to accept the natural science causation as determinant of pyschology.

To Sri Aurobindo, the individual is an evolutionarily growing factor and, therefore, the conscious and the unconscious are dynamic in character and, on the whole, directed towards goals of progressive organisation. The unconscious – rather the inconscient, as he calls it since it is not the contradictory of consciousness – is to him the general substratum out of which only a fragment has managed to become conscious. And "the subconscient is the Inconscient in the process of becoming conscious..." (*The Life Divine*, Birth Centenary Library, Vol. 19, pp. 734-35) The terms 'inconscient' and 'subconscient' are specially coined by him to convey the essential dynamic character of these ranges of personality. The 'unconscious' and 'subconscious' convey states rather than processes, besides the former implies a denial of consciousness and not a lower grade of consciousness. But whereas to Western psychology all that is not conscious becomes unconscious, to Sri Aurobindo the inconscient and subconscient constitute only the evolutional past of personality. The evolutional future too is a present potentiality and constitutes a distinct aspect, in fact the more relevant aspect for the understanding of the teleological trend of our mental life. This he calls the Superconscient and regards it correlative to the subconscient, in the sense that to grow into the Superconscient is the most effective way of growing out of the subconscious and the inconscient, or becoming conscious of them. Given the proper approach, it is possible to verify these two important ranges of personality in experience by their distinctive characteristics.

Now, so far as the inconscient and the subconscient are concerned, Sri Aurobindo distinguishes three ranges of them. These pertain to the three principal factors of our personality, the physical, the vital and the mental. Ordinarily, we identify consciousness with mental awareness. But Sri Aurobindo says that "if we separate the mind as witness... we can discover that life and body, – have a consciousness of their own..." (Ibid., Vol. 18, p. 558) This is no doubt a submental consciousness. Now, the subconscient is below the conscious in the mind, in the vital and in the physical. "The true subconscious is other than this vital or physical substratum; it is the Inconscient vibrating on the borders of consciousness, sending up its motions to be changed into conscious stuff, swallowing into its depths impressions of past experience as seeds of unconscious habit and returning them constantly but often chaotically to the surface consciousness..." (Ibid., Vol. 18, p. 559) The inconscient is the yet lower substratum of personality and, in the main, constitutes the mechanical necessities of our nature and its inertia.

This view of the unconscious and the subconscious is perhaps capable of explaining the widest range of facts of the normal and the abnormal behaviour of human personality, as also of bringing them into line with the facts of general evolution. Besides, through the correlative fact of the Superconscient, it is able to offer the most effective way for the organisation and the integration of the subconscient and inconscient. The cultural consequences of it too will evidently be the more balanced and harmonious.

LEVELS OF EXPERIENCE IN NORMAL PERSONALITY

The rise of biology in the 19th century influenced knowledge as a whole and the ideas of development, evolution and organism came to be looked upon as almost universally valid. Psychology also tended to take them up as necessary to mental life and adopt biology as its very model, giving up its former models of physics and chemistry. And thus the idea of development became integral to psychology and we find in recent and contemporary psychology many ideas of the stages of development as levels of experience. In the eighties of the last century, James Ward clearly formulated two levels of experience in normal personality which he called the "pre-sensational continuum" and the "representational continuum." The same were called by Stout the "Perceptual" and the "Ideational" and availed of with great success in the characterisation of the varied processes of mind. McDougall also followed the same plan. The classification of mental processes into perceptual and ideational, those that are essentially determined by sense-perception and those that primarily consist of an inner activity of ideas, gives very great facility in understanding and relating mental processes to one another. Sensation, perception, instinct, emotion, imitation, etc., all come in one class and memory, imagination, thinking, volition, etc., in the other. And these two levels broadly correspond to the animal and the human levels of evolution and have, therefore, a sound biological and evolutional basis.

However, contemporary psychology presents to us many other schemes of the stages and levels of development. Psycho-analysis, e.g., gives us the conscious and the unconscious as the two primary levels and then an elaborate scheme of several stages in the development of the sex life of an individual, which are really stages in the development of normal personality. These stages, in the normal personality, come in succession at different times in the chronological life of the individual, yet as unconscious facts they continue to exist all the time since abnormal circumstances can always cause a regression to any earlier stage lived through previously. Jung's Analytical Psychology specially presents a level of experience called the "Collective Unconscious". Similarly, other psychological schools present, in some form, the idea of development in mental life.

Typology is an important branch of contemporary psychology, which treats human personality as consisting of different types. Jung's introversion and extraversion have become famous and they represent two psychological attitudes, those of outward-directedness and of inward-directedness, regarding the external events and things or internal experiences as the real or primary values of life. Spranger, from the point of the Cultural Science Psychology, distinguishes six fundamental types, the theoretical, the economic, the aesthetic, the social, the power-seeking and the religious. Here six values or ideals of life are the basis. Kretschmer makes physique the basis of psychological types. These are, however, a few principal attempts at classification of personality into types. Evidently, we have here a variety of standpoints, each of which has a sphere of validity, but we cannot discover a scheme to relate them together and bring typological knowledge into a coherent form.

This treatment of personality is related to that of the levels of growth and experience. The introvert lives largely at the ideational level and the extrovert a great deal at the perceptual. And then, in fact, everybody is both and there can be a change from the one to the other. In a sense, all the types and levels, as possibilities of human nature, are present in everybody. Those that occur in succession in the natural order of growth we call levels of experience and those that appear as relatively fixed forms of trends we call types. But the growth can get halted at an earlier level or there can be a regression to a previous state.

Here the aim is not to go into the exact relationship between two approaches to the study of personality but just to show that they are connected and that in the treatment of both of them, we have a variety of standpoints amongst which a systematisation seems to be almost impossible.

The essential thesis of this paper is that with the discovery of the primary constituent factors of human personality and their mutual relationships, a right base for the levels of growth and types of personality could be found and that might show a way of relating and systematising the various standpoints and classifications of the levels of growth and the types of personality. Sri Aurobindo, in his treatment of human personality, offers a plan which is distinct from all the rest and which is supported by strong facts and reasoning. Basing himself upon the facts of general evolution, he affirms that human personality is a synthesis of three factors: matter, life and mind. The original suggestion in this connection came to him from the Upanishads, where *anna* (Matter), *prāṇa* (Life) and *manas* (Mind) are referred to many times in connection both with cosmic nature and with the individual human personality. He, however, elaborates it into a vision of evolution and an original view of personality and, in doing so, he principally relies on the facts of his observation and introspection.

Now, Matter, Life and Mind are recognised by Modern Science too as the three principal steps or stages or emergents of evolution; and man, as the last product of the continuous process, is surely a synthesis of them all and, therefore, must of necessity partake of the characteristics of all. This argument based on the facts of evolution is supported by the facts of introspection too. Ordinarily, we regard all consciousness as mental. Mind and Consciousness are considered identical. Sri Aurobindo says that this is a consequence of confining our introspection to the surface movements and actions of consciousness. There they are all mixed up. But if we try to seek the origination of these movements and actions, we shall discover three broad kinds of consciousness. One, the Mental, consisting of thinking, remembering, is all ideational, essentially motivated by thought. Two, the Vital, involves activities of instincts, emotions and other adaptations of organic life. Three, the Body Consciousness, a pervasive abiding sense of our physical existence, which fills us out to the frontiers of our skin. These do, of course, run into one another in the life of the adult person and give rise to processes of a composite character. But they are qualitatively distinguishable and, when distinguished, contribute to a clearer understanding of the psycho-physical activities of personality and to their more effective direction, control and modification.

Let us illustrate it with concrete introspections. Food-seeking is a fundamental impulse of all life and a most familiar experience to everyone of us. Now it will be interesting to ask how it works at the adult human level. Obviously, its working is not so simple as it is at the animal level. Here, besides the animal vital impulse for food, we have a whole mass of hygienic, medical, social, aesthetic ideas and opinions, which are present in the situation. McDougall has admitted that he could not always distinguish between hunger and thirst and that to decide in cases of doubt he would take a glass of water and if that satisfied him then he regarded it as a case of thirst. Surely, the inner situations of these experiences are complex and it needs a careful and a dispassionate observation to be able to disengage the mixed strains of our personality. Now in our behaviour of food-seeking, three situations would probably be recognisable. One, that of craving and restless seeking for food. Two, that of a sense of need in the body for food. Three, that of a calm and detached feeling that you should take food. The first is the most common experience and appears to have a strong visceral reference. The second has no restlessness about it, nor a special visceral reference. It is a steady pervasive feeling of the body as a whole. The third, though believed to be a common experience, is in fact not. The ideas and opinions are availed of by the vital craving for its own justification and satisfaction. The presence of craving and restlessness in the situation, when we believe we are guided by a medical or social 'ought', will show up the true and the *primary* determinant of that behaviour. Craving can also turn up in a situation where the body consciousness seems to ask for food.

Here all the three consciousnesses above considered are represented in our normal food-seeking behaviour and a failure to distinguish among them will surely lead to confusion and disappointment in practical life. Craving is not hunger or need, and it can easily be pampered and the consequence will be strain to the digestive system. The local references of these consciousnesses in the body are a great help in their identification. In a confused situation of food-seeking, it is possible to suspect the presence of craving and try to dissociate oneself from the strong visceral sensations. After some practice, this becomes quite easy and, when that element has thus been in a measure eliminated, one can at once recognise if there is a real hunger present. Similarly, by eliminating the vital element we can find out if we are truly determined in a situation by our ideas and opinions of what would be right food under certain circumstances. By distinguishing these three consciousnesses, we can also become aware of a conflict we might be creating or labouring under in regard to our food-seeking impulse.

Now what is true of the food-seeking behaviour would be true of many other activities. Under the influence of the social and ethical standards of life, we normally ascribe our behaviour to certain justifiable 'oughts', but actually we are determined by instinctive urges of the vital factor of our personality. That evidently means inner division and conflict and with that go the consequences of the same. But what is more regrettable is the case where we sincerely want to be determined by an 'ought', to live by reason or impersonal objective truth and, therefore, strengthen the 'ought' and the reason in us by our adhesion to it and in consequence cause a suppression of the vital drive and then believe that we are determined by reason, whereas in fact we continue to be determined at least partially by the same desire, though now from its subconscious quarters. A more rational handling of the situation would be a clear recognition of the mental factor, the reason we want to live by and also of the vital factor, what we want to be relieved of and then steadily dissociate ourselves from the latter and more and more identify ourselves with the former. This kind of handling of such a situation will not lead to suppressions and repressions.

In this connection, it will be worth examining how the Free Association method of Psycho-analysis works out its cure. The method is supposed to consist of a free revival of ideas. The patient is asked to speak out whatever occurs to him, in particular what occurs to him in connection with the symptoms of his disease. And the becoming conscious of the original causes of the disease is supposed to effect the cure. Now the cause of the disease, according to Psycho-analysis, is always some inner conflict and the cure must consist in the removal of the conflict, i.e., in the reintegration of the divided will. And the Free Association method is virtually a process of revival of the previously lived emotions and attitudes involving a recognition of what has been repressed and partially dissociated from the self and thus reintegrating it into the central will of personality. Thus psycho-analytical work is not primarily one of ideas, but of emotions, instincts and attitudes, these divisions and conflicts and their reintegrations. Primarily all this belongs to the vital factor of our personality and the id, ego and the superego are all in greater part distinctions within the vital being.

Now if Matter, Life and Mind are the three main stages of the general evolution, and then man, who is a product of the same, must evidently consist and partake of them; and if the same factors seem to be verifiable in the workings of personality by introspection, then they must naturally constitute the basic references in the treatment of personality. That is to say, in our classifications of processes, they must be our best guide and right basis. But before attempting a substantiation of this point, it will be necessary to characterise the three basic factors of Matter, Life and Mind a little more fully.

Considering them as terms of general evolution, Matter is inertia and repetitive mechanical action, Life is impulse and activity expressed in self-preservation and self-propagation and Mind is ideational activity serving as an aid to Life and trying to raise it to impersonal objective truth. In personality it is very interesting to observe that there is a positive impulse to inactivity, continuing to be in the same state, inertia. It is also recognisable in all our repetitive behaviour. This is different from that of rest and sleep, though the latter may involve it. It is positively recognisable as such and is a conscious state though the vividness of consciousness is much lower than that of normal ideational activity. The various goal-seekings connected with self-preservation and self-propagation constitute a class by themselves and this is our life factor. They all are conscious seekings, more conscious on the whole than the impulse for inactivity or routine activity. These seekings by themselves are able to maintain a fair balance between the organism and the environment, which is very well represented in animal life. But the ideational activity in man brings into being an idealised world, which seeks to impose a new order on these seekings. Out of a conflict of the two arises the trouble and tragedy as well as the progress and the greater possibilities of human life. The ideational activity is essentially the mental life. It represents, on the whole, the highest degree of consciousness and at its highest presents to us a vision of impersonal objective truth. But it enters into compromises with the vital, which is strongly individualistic, self-assertive and self-aggrandising and the super-ego is perhaps the most important resultant formation. The super-ego is intolerant, aggressive and egoistic like the vital impulse, but it acts in this form in the name of society and objective truth. Obviously the super-ego is primarily a vital formation. The true reason and objective truth appear in our experience as free, comprehensive and dispassionate but they are a very small part of us. Thus what we call mental life consists of mental consciousness, vital consciousness and bodily consciousness and, of these, the vital is the predominant. Contemporary psychology treats them all as one mental phenomenon and that certainly does not contribute to clarity in understanding our behaviour and, in particular, in trying to modify it in education and self-culture.

All concrete processes of psychological personality involve all the three consciousnesses; the difference between one and another is the way these consciousnesses combine and in the degree they do so. It is possible to conceive of all the activities as constituting a series, with the most physical at the one end and the most mental at the other, and the rest arranged between them in increasing degrees of consciousness. Evidently, the processes with the physical factor predominant like reflex action, habit and routine thinking will fall together, the goal-seeking activities connected with the preservation and propagation of life come in another class, thought and imagination concerned with impersonal objective truth lie in still another. And these classes will be distinguishable by progressively greater degrees of consciousness present in them. And that suggests also the way of correctly handling them in the modification of behaviour. Where the consciousness is the least, it is mechanical repetition that changes behaviour. Habits cannot be changed by changing opinions. A changed opinion in the mind is a favourable circumstance and no more. Essentially one has to re-train the vital and the physical consciousness and for that one has to resort to methods appropriate to them. So far as the physical element is concerned, repetition of the new act is the way and for the vital consciousness a breaking of the old identification and the formation of a new one has to be achieved and this is sometimes done suddenly too.

Thus we have here a plan of the levels of normal experience, the physical, the vital and the mental, recalling the *anna*, the *prāṇa* and the *manas* of the Upanishads, which offers a new approach to the study of personality. We have already seen that it is strongly supported by the parallelism of the stages of general evolution and the facts of introspection confirm it. It also gives a practical advantage in handling personality. For failure to distinguish among them and their true natures, Psycho-analysis ascribes to mental ideas and their revival what really belongs to emotional and instinctive attitudes of the vital. A direct recognition of the true psychological factor will obviously be an advantage, besides constituting the appreciation of the truth in the matter.

Now we wish to undertake comparison of this plan with some of those obtaining in psychology and see their relative merits and demerits. The distinction of the perceptual and the ideational levels broadly corresponds to the animal and human levels and this has an emotional basis. It does serve admirably in the classification of the different processes of personality. But there is a thinking which merely serves instinctive ends. It simply justifies what we vitally desire. And then there is the thinking which consists of sheer mechanical rounds. And there is also the true thinking which is purposive, directed to the solution of intellectual problems and the discovery of dispassionate truth. All these varieties of thinking on this plan will be put together since they consist of trains of ideas. But the essential energies in them are different even though the apparent form is the same. And in consideration of these energies, it is more rational to regard them as predominantly physical, vital and mental processes and handle them accordingly. Similarly, habit and instinct are put together at the perceptual level, since they have a sensory determination. Firstly, on this basis, habits of thought and feeling have to be separated from habitual action and, secondly, the conscious accompaniment in instincts is rich, whereas in habits it is scanty.

The psycho-analytical treatment of the stages of development is all a matter of growth of the vital consciousness. It marks out the various steps it traverses to reach the normal ego-life of adjustment with reality for one of more or less pure wishfulness. Thought and the higher ideals are, indeed, in a measure used by the vital as means and they are there no more than canalisations of the vital energy. But reason, as the perception of dispassionate objective truth, too does exist and in his later series of 'Introductory Lectures', Freud does recognise it clearly, when he says, "our best hope for the future is that intellect – the scientific spirit, reason – should in time establish a dictatorship over the human mind," and the aim of scientific thought is "to arrive at correspondence with reality. that is to say, with what exists outside us and independently of us and, as experience has taught us, is decisive for the fulfilment or frustration of our desires." The ego grows through a perception and recognition of reality. But its purpose is practical and its intention and method are to find the successful ways of the fulfilment of its desires. In this process it does modify its desires, but its essential nature and spirit is not that of letting the reality govern it, of surrendering its own desires to reality and seeking all its satisfaction in reality as it is independently of us. The ego is thus egoistic even when it adjusts to reality. But the true vision of science and our last hope for the future is different. That really requires and holds up a level of experience where the objective truth will entirely rule us. How the transition is to take place, how the growth is to proceed to that plane of experience, Freud did not undertake to characterise. He confined his researches to the growth from the state of rank wishfulness of the id, the uncultivated vital, conscious and subconscious, into that of the relatively controlled and modified wishfulness of the ego, the relatively cultivated vital. But he truly recognised that the hope of the future lay in a complete transcendence of personal wishfulness and the achievement of the plane of impersonal objective experience.

It is exactly this part of the growth that has interested Sri Aurobindo and his method of Integral Yoga is an account of the theory and the practice of this growth. The other part, which occupied Freud almost exclusively and which he, in effect, made the whole of personality, comes in for a treatment at the hands of Sri Aurobindo as a lower rung of the ladder. This lower rung shows how man, the natural vital being, becomes a social vital being with thought as a servant of life. But the latter stage seeks to show the way of rising to the level of true objectivity, objectivity at the practical plane as also that of truth as such. If the first be called growth from the natural to the normal, the second may be called growth from the normal to the real, since here reality and truth become true determinants of personality. In characterising this process, Sri Aurobindo distinguishes many stages and steps between the normal mind and the supermind when the consciousness becomes truly constituted of Truth. However, those levels are not the subject of treatment here. Just now we are concerned with the levels of experience of the normal personality and in that connection we have attempted to show that there are, in fact, three distinct levels – the physical, the vital and the mental, progressively increasing in consciousness, possessing special characteristics and local references in the body. A failure to recognise them leads to confusion in Psycho-analysis. We have just now seen that all the stages of development of the so-called mental life characterised by it are, in fact, all of the vital consciousness, the mind recognised by it was mostly that which is dominated by the vital and that the true mind, which reveals itself in a measure in scientific work in its perception of objective truth, is envisaged only as a future hope of humanity without attempting to explore the ways and means of attaining to it. In consequence, Psychoanalysis has tended to make the vital the whole of man, which is an obvious misstatement of human nature and personality.

The Jungian collective unconscious, the new level of experience discovered by him, can also be more adequately accommodated in our threefold scheme. Sri Aurobindo adjoins the three consciousnesses of the physical, the vital and the mental to recognisably distinct subconscious and unconscious ranges, which tend to carry forward in the individual the racial and the universal history of the evolutionary process. This is perfectly consistent with his general evolutional standpoint and approach. The collective unconscious of Jung would here be coincident with those ranges of the unconscious which embody the racial history. Here there would yet be further lower ranges embodying pre-racial universal history. But the more important thing is that it would primarily consist of the vital unconscious, since life was then lived at that level. To talk of the archetypes of the collective unconscious as 'ideas' unknowingly introduces the mentalist and intellectualist prejudice falsifying the true facts, which must be of the nature of self-assertive urges of a general character.

We have probably shown sufficiently that the physical, vital and mental are the truly fundamental planes of experience and that the other schemes of development get into their right perspectives only when they are properly placed in them. We should also like to consider them in relation to the study of types of personality. The conception of mind in contemporary psychology is not at all clear and that is a source of many confusions. Freud showed that instinct rules our life, not mind, thought or ideals.

In that he saw the force and power of the vital consciousness and also rightly observed its true nature of self-assertion and self-affirmation in its wishfulness. Besides it, he also noticed the true 'reason' and its function. But yet he used the term mind as covering both, which tended to obliterate a real distinction. Had he clearly kept the distinction in view, he might have been spared most of the over-generalisations of the vital consciousness and thus given a truer picture of personality. The same applies to Western psychology as a whole. The animals have a consciousness which is, properly speaking, a sub-mental consciousness. It is the consciousness emerging from and growing with the biological phenomena of 'life'. It is rightly the vital consciousness. Mind is a new emergent in man and the mental consciousness is the true characteristic of the mind. Certainly most of the human consciousness is vital consciousness, the consciousness of 'life'-phenomena, which it shares in common with the animal. Contemporary psychology is supposed to have given up its intellectualist bias, but by using the term 'mind' too widely it is unconsciously perpetuating it.

The modern treatment of types of personality suffers from the same bias. Introversion and extroversion are essentially dispositions or attitudes of the vital, the life-impulse thrown upon itself. In the abnormal cases, it is more clearly recognisable as such. The gratification sought, in one case, is that of control, management and domination over other forces and in the other case, that of one's own force. But the play is primarily of the vital force and consciousness. In normal life, however, where mental and intellectual activity exist as a strong trend, the true case of introversion, i.e., a real interestedness in ideas and higher emotions, is noticeable. In melancholy, e.g., the individual is introvert but the interestedness in ideas and ideational activity is not for itself, it is rather as means for the self-gratification of the vital force, which has met with frustration at the hands of the external forces. To base personality types on the physique, as Kretschmer does, is to affirm that the body is the determinant of the vital and the mental consciousness. A more correct basis would perhaps be to recognise the physical, vital and mental consciousnesses as the primary modes and their relative domination in personality as the determinants of three primary types and their various combinations of the sub-types in between them. The idea of the physical, vital and mental consciousnesses is connected with the well-known Indian idea of the three gunas: *tamas, rajas* and *sattwa*, the three primary qualities of the entire phenomenal existence. And on their basis, we come across in the Gita and elsewhere a plan of personality, a *tamasic*, a *rajasic* and a *sattwic* personality and *tamasic-rajasic* or *tamasic-sattwic* or *rajasic-sattwic* and so on. *Sattwa*, light or consciousness, is, in fact, the quality of mind, *rajas*, activity, that of life and *tamas*, inertia, that of matter. Thus the *sattwic* personality may be called a mental personality, the *rajasic* the vital, and *tamasic* the physical, and among these the various combined types will exist.

This treatment of types has a surer basis than any other and would possibly afford a scheme to accommodate the various typological schemes that exist today. It would firstly place them where they exactly belong in the personality's mental, vital and physical strata and then give them the right total perspective.

In the end, we would venture to suggest that this plan of levels of experience and types of personality could give a new approach in psychiatry too and might even provide a wider base for its various psycho-pathological schools and therapies to discover their mutual relatedness. The somatic therapy, the hypnotic method and the various forms of analytical and psycho-analytical treatments base themselves on partial data of personality, on which they lay an exclusive emphasis. Each one of them has to its credit a proved record of serviceability and success. A fuller view of personality may indeed provide a scheme for their harmonisation.

TEACHING OF PSYCHOLOGY IN INDIAN UNIVERSITIES

In modern scientific knowledge, psychology is perhaps still the youngest but a most influential science. Its growth in recent decades has been phenomenal. Its ramifications into subsidiary disciplines and applications to life have been large and wide. It has virtually given a new turn – the psychological turn – to the human mind as a whole. Sociology, politics, economics, and literature bear abundant testimony to the impact of psychology. The responsibility of psychology to truth and human culture, therefore, becomes obviously great. And it is being felt by important representative psychologists that psychology, in its present state, is hardly equal to its responsibilities. Its so-called schools, which had contributed so much to its growth during the second and the third decades of the century, yet continue as unsynthesised approaches to human personality. And, in fact, new ones continue to emerge and assert themselves in an exclusive sort of way, without a perspective of the total truth of personality. Further, all our psychological knowledge, enormous as it seems to be, is for the most part limited to the relations and interactions of the human personality and the environment. As to what personality is, its nature and constitution as a fact, we have not had sufficient curiosity, nor exploration and systematic study. Jung's observation in this connection is well-known. He says, "All the usual little remedies and medicaments of psychology fall somewhat short (to explain personality) just as they do with the man of genius or the creative human being. Derivation from ancestral heredity or from the milieu does not quite succeed; inventing fictions about childhood, which is so popular today, and – to put it mildly – in the inappropriate, the explanation from necessity – 'he had no money, was ill', and so forth remains caught in mere externalities."[1] Gardner Murphy too has substantially said the same thing. He says, "Nobody knows anything much about the nature of man. We are in a position to raise a great many questions, to raise questions perhaps so grave and so fundamental that we begin to wonder if we even have a method for approaching an ultimate solution."[2]

1. *The Integration of the Personality*, 1940, p. 299.
2. *Main Currents in Modern Thought*, Vol. 9, No. 2, New York.

Modern scientific psychology has thus many problems to face. It has yet to evolve an established psychological approach to the study of personality as physics has done regarding the study of matter. That really means that it must overcome the necessity of the growth of more or less philosophical schools in psychology. Further, it cannot continue to remain content with the study of the reactions of personality alone. It must squarely face the problem of the nature and constitution of human personality. And it must also integrate, into its body of knowledge, the true psychological insights of, in particular, India and China, the two non-European countries which have possessed traditional interest in human personality. In the pursuit and realisation of these objectives lie the real hope and prospect of a proper universal science of psychology.

As things stand, modern scientific psychology is a product of European history and culture. Its assumptions, its objectives, its methodology are all grounded in modern European naturalistic rationalism and the Aristotelian tradition of knowledge. Indian psychology, on the other hand, is grounded in a perception of unity of all knowledge and existence and other principles peculiar to the Indian inspiration regarding knowledge and culture. Indian psychology has thus a form all its own. Its content of psychological insights and perceptions is a matter of long experience and of repeated verifications after its own standards. Its greatest strength is its surprising agreement, in spite of all sorts of other differences, regarding the essential nature and constitution of human personality. Mind is, to practically all schools of Indian philosophy and psychology, the outward-directed consciousness, besides which there is a self-existent consciousness called the *puruṣa*, the *ātman*, the *jīva*. And this is affirmed as a fact of experience, though philosophical systems adduce speculative reasons too to prove its existence.

The mutual adjustment and integration of the two bodies of psychological knowledge is a most challenging problem for the psychologists in India, as well as Europe and America. But, evidently, it is the Indian psychologists who can and who would be expected to contribute their Indian share to the growth of a proper universal body of psychological knowledge. If that is so, then the teaching of psychology in India must follow a line of its own – a line which will enable it to discover, recover, assess, evaluate and contribute the Indian psychological values to our growing world fund of psychological knowledge. That means, our standpoint and our courses should take a due cognisance of the traditional psychological talent of the students so as to develop it in the best possible measure. This must in fact be done even when the aim be to achieve the best possible growth of the psychological capacity in the students.

Standing as we do in the modern stream of life in India at the present moment, the Western books on psychology are our best aids for psychological training. But considering the traditional introspective talent of the country and the general character of Indian psychology, the introspectionist school of the West should be preferred and other approaches used additionally. And with this should go a sufficient introduction to the Indian psychological knowledge. This may constitute the basic psychological training for a pass-graduate taking up psychology as an elective subject. At the Honours and the M.A. levels, a wider and deeper acquaintance and understanding of Indian psychology and its original sources (though translations) should be afforded. At the completion of studies, an M.A. in psychology of any Indian University should command a fair confidence of a good training in Western psychology and adequate acquaintance with the character of Indian psychology and its sources. If the teaching of psychology in India is adjusted to this form, then for purposes of research the whole field of Indian psychology, of the Yoga-shastras, the Rasa-shastras, the Ayurveda and other fields, will become available. These subjects will command for the Indian psychologist an originality which other subjects cannot easily do. This body of psychological knowledge is India's obligation to the world too.

The principal contribution of Indian psychology will perhaps be towards the building up of a proper theory of personality, a comprehensive view of human nature. And this might facilitate the emergence of an integrated conception of the contemporary body of psychological knowledge which suffers, at the moment, a great deal from dispersion, division and lack of unity.

All this directly applies to the field of general psychology. But psychology has determined the basic approach to life as a whole in Indian culture. The idea of *adhikārabheda*, an individual's capability by virtue of his status of growth, has been a pervasive idea of Indian life. The *varṇas*, the fourfold division of society, and the

Ashramas, the fourfold demarcation of stages in an individual's life, have all been conspicuously influenced by this sound psychological idea of the growth of an individual or social group as their true title to fresh opportunities of life. Under these circumstances, one could infer that all aspects and relations of life must have received a psychological consideration and manipulation. One could then expect some insights concerning our other fields of psychology too.

Regarding the field of capitalist and labour relations, one fact could be specially mentioned. We have today a society ruled by the spirit of law and the principle of contractual relations. And these determinants of our relations tend to grow intenser and wider in life. Indian life, so far as its cultural leaders were concerned, has persistently subscribed to the ideal of unity and love as the true determinant of life of an individual as well as society. This means a difference in the basic reference of life. And this fact can be an important psychological truth affecting the entire practice of our social applications of psychology.

Indian psychology has been progressively coming up in the minds of Indian psychologists, but its movement has been slow, and now, at times, even a keen frustration is expressed that we are not able to represent Indian psychology as we should and as is expected of us by the world. Dr. G. Bose, in his article on psychology contributed to "The Progress of Science in India during the past Twenty-five Years" published in 1928, wrote: "India's ancient learned men had a genius for introspective meditation and the Indian psychologist has that heritage. In this respect he enjoys an advantage over his colleagues in the West. If this faculty is properly cultivated, problems requiring deep introspection such as those of thought processes, higher cultural inhibitions, etc. will be successfully solved."

Since Independence, almost all scientific disciplines have been trying their utmost to recover and evaluate India's contribution in their respective fields. And under these circumstances, psychology too has felt the same urge and even seen that, in this field, the contribution of India has been particularly great. Many presidents of the Psychology Section of the Indian Science Congress in their addresses have stressed the urgent need for work in this field.

But yet the process to discover and recover Indian Psychology has not acquired the proper momentum. And it is indeed desirable that the psychologists of the country make up their mind clearly and fully regarding Indian psychology and decide upon pursuing the matter until the present situation of our psychological teaching and research is brought into the form that it should be.

THE INDIAN PSYCHOLOGIST IN SEARCH OF HIS SOUL

In recent years, many times organised attempts have been made to consider the Indian contribution to psychology. Undoubtedly, Indian psychologists have been anxious to find out what has been their country's contribution to psychology. Growth of international contacts in recent years have actually created a demand on us. We are repeatedly asked, what is the Indian contribution to psychology? Or what the Indian viewpoint on this or that psychological issue would be? And the philosophical, cultural and yogic trends of Indian life and history encourage others to expect some real psychological insights from us.

But most of us, when placed in such a situation of high expectations and special distinctions, find ourselves in an unenviable position. We feel extremely uncomfortable and do not know what to say. The fact is that Indian psychological things have nowhere figured in our education or research and, therefore, we are not even aware of the existence of the Indian perceptions, conceptions and judgments regarding the nature, constitution and working of human personality.

But, lately, the urge to find these out has been steadily increasing, it has been finding some expressions at the Psychology Section of the Indian Science Congress and certain other psychological conferences and now the Madras Psychological Society has given a pointed and concentrated expression by calling a conference solely to consider this issue. We are sure this conference will prove a distinct advance in the Indian psychologist's search for his soul.

The Indian psychologist has virtually a soul much maturer and richer than any other Indian scientist. But it is a strange irony of things that whereas an Indian physicist, botanist or even an anatomist has facts to claim old Indian contributions to these modern disciplines, the Indian psychologist finds himself the poorest in the learned company. And how untrue it is! Right from the time of the Vedas, wonderful insights and concepts regarding personality and its working are to be found. In fact, many elaborate systematic expositions of personality as a whole are there. The Rig Veda had a characteristic perception in regard to personality, which it expressed in the word *vakra*, the crooked. This expressed all maladjustments and disharmonies of consciousness and behaviour. And the Veda seems to have a spontaneous appreciation and admiration for the *ṛju*, the straight. The straight and the crooked will correspond to our contemporary wholesome and unwholesome personality and how sufficient and how original is this perception to represent personality as a whole and its varied functions and their mutual relationships.

The Upanishads present the celebrated view of the five *kosha*s or zones of personality, the fourfold division of conscious states (the waking, the sleeping, the dreamless-sleeping and the supernormal), threefold levels of normal personality (the body, the life and the mind: the *anna*, the *prāṇa* and the *manas*) and a lot more which is highly challenging. Consider the last one. Is human personality just body and mind, whereas in cosmic evolution we recognise Matter, Life and Mind as the three distinct steps? Is man not the product of them all? And then should there not be all three recognisable in him and determinant of his life and behaviour? Consider also the fourfold division of conscious states. For a comprehensive view of personality, is it not necessary that we should take into account the experiences of the waking, the sleeping, the abnormal and the supernormal? The waking states alone are only a part of the personality.

The Gita presents a complete psychology of personality. It treats of the essential nature of normal personality, the principal determinants of its working, the problem of division and conflict that beset it, the way of resolving the conflict, the form and quality of the ideal and integrated personality and many other issues that go with these.

The various yogic systems are avowedly disciplines for the perfection of personality. The Hathayoga, the Rajayoga, the Tantra Yoga, the Bhakti Yoga, the Jnana yoga and the Karma Yoga are well-known and each one of them has a complete system by itself, with a theory and an application of the normal personality and its growth into higher integration.

The works of literary criticism offer interesting theories of emotions and sentiments.

Ayurveda has its own contribution to make.

In recent times, Sri Aurobindo has contributed well about 3,000 pages all dealing with human personality and its innumerable facets, under what he has called the system of Integral Yoga.

These are barest mentions of a few salient features and ideas from the long history of Indian psychology. If we would plough our entire field carefully, we can be sure of a marvellous harvest which might enrich our modern psychology wonderfully. But we have first to discover our field and ourselves as the happy and proud heirs of it. How otherwise could we own it, joyfully plough it and confidently look forward to a rich harvest?

In this process of discovery, the most important thing is the approach. A wrong approach can seriously handicap our entire effort. It is necessary that we do not impose or insist upon any of our contemporary preconceptions regarding the character and methodology of psychology. The aim too should be conceived in an elastic way. We may look for judgments about human personality, its nature, constitution and working in the context of society and existence broadly. Having found these judgments, we can classify and rearrange them in a new way. And then proceed to test them by modern techniques wherever possible or seek new techniques where necessary. In this way, we may be able to get quite a great deal.

The approach to the subject of our present conference can serve as an illustration. Our subject is 'Indian Contribution to Modern Psychology'. The direct suggestion of the subject is to look for things of the nature of modern psychology in Indian thought and literature and this is what we have tried to do whenever we have wished to find something in the nature of Indian contribution. But has this approach itself not been the cause of our disappointment? Modern psychology is a recent product of a long cultural history. It is qualified and determined by the attitudes and interests of that history. Indian cultural history has enjoyed some other distinctive attitudes and interests. How could then the products of two distinctive processes be identical in form and character? However, man and personality are universal human interests and both the West and the East have been interested in them though in characteristic ways. Thus the right thing would be to ask for the Indian knowledge of personality, but not for things of the nature of modern psychology.

If the argument commands some force, our deliberations at this conference will reorient themselves so as to conceive the subject as Indian Thought and Human Personality. We will then more easily get some useful things for modern psychology under this approach. We could then break up our subject as follows:

1. The Veda, the Upanishad and Human Personality
2. The Epics and Human Personality
3. The Six Systems of Philosophy and Human Personality
4. Ayurveda and Human Personality
5. Yogic Systems and Human Personality
6. Jain and Buddhistic Thought and Human Personality
7. Dharma Shastras and Human Personality
8. Traditional Indian Life and Culture and Human Personality
9. Recent and Contemporary Indian Thought and Life and Human Personality
10. Indian Psychology and Modern Scientific Psychology

At the conference, we will not have the time to explore these fields. At best we can consider a few representative ideas of these varied fields. But if committees of competent persons could be appointed to conduct studies in these fields and submit the fruit of their labours at a successive seminar, we would definitely then find ourselves in a happier situation than we are today.

This conference has evidently been called with a serious purpose. The inspiration of it seems to have aimed at achieving something. It called upon each participant to formulate, as perhaps an upshot of the deliberations of the paper, two or more problems for research and also outline the methodology for studying them.

We append here a series of judgments of Indian psychology, which are highly challenging and promising. They can all be interesting subjects for research. And the methodology can be a theoretical study of literature, a comparative study in Indian and Western psychologies, a correlation and synthesization. There can also be questionnaire studies on many of the issues. Observational studies are also possible, where the judgments refer to data available in contemporary Indian life. Original experimental approaches too are quite possible in a few cases.

These judgments, broadly stated, are as follows:

1. That atmosphere is the most effective educational influence.

2. That given an open-minded attitude towards oneself, unsuspected capabilities can develop in a person through aspiration and under the stress of circumstances demanding those capabilities.

3. That normal personality is essentially a play of the principle

of inertia, energies and harmony (Tamas, Rajas and Sattva).

4. That normal personality is a synthesis of mind, life and matter and not merely mind and body.

5. That integration of personality can best be promoted by the spiritual principle, which is in its nature unitary and integrated, rather than by mind, which is divided.

6. That Ananda is the only self-existent emotion. All others are derivative.

7. That knowledge can only be possible when the cognising consciousness becomes silent. An agitated and restlessly active consciousness will know things as seen under the stress and character of the compulsive activity.

8. That whole-willing is the real perfection of volitional life and this means self-dissociation from fragmentary or partial willings, which is the case with all normal willing, perceptual or ideational. Without whole-willing, there is no integrated personality and this is achievable by a steady and persistent rejection of the partial willings involving want, anxiety and eager clutching at results accompanied by an aspiration for whole-willing.

9. That anxiety is the root problem of human life, normal and abnormal. And this is inherent in ego-selfhood. The remedy lies in the progressive softening down of the intensity of its self-assertiveness and ultimately a complete denial of it and espousal of the calm, the whole and joyous soul-selfhood.

10. In the educational field, there is a judgment. *Sā vidyā yā vimuktaye*: Knowledge is that which makes for liberation, i.e., promotes the growth of a free personality.

Are these judgments not challenging? But we do not recognise them as such and yet they have enjoyed and do continue to enjoy the authenticity of the experience of Indian life. The academic psychologist of the country, however, has yet to ascertain the truth of these. And we are assembled here exactly in response to the challenge of these judgments and resolved to know them and to know by the clear and rational consciousness of the scientific method, to the best of its expanding capacities.

(The Chairman's paper for the Section of 'Indian Philosophy and Modern Psychology', at the Madras Psychological Society's Seminar, long ago.)

SWAMI PRANAVANANDA EASTERN AND WESTERN PSYCHOLOGY LECTURE FOR 1985

Subject: THE PSYCHIC BEING OF INTEGRAL YOGA OR THE 'CENTRE' OR 'SELF' OF JUNG

(We give here the detailed Contents of the full Paper and an Abstract thereof.)

Introductory

(1) Swami Pranavananda's Inspiration
(2) East and West, in Approaches to Personality – Complementary
(3) New fields of Research

Part I

(4) Jung's Pioneering work
(5) Jung's 'Centre' or 'Self' – Varied Evidences adduced
(6) Progress of Jungian Thought
(7) Transpersonal Psychology
(8) Academic Psychology of America
(9) Rise of interest in Meditation in the West
(10) Jung's 'Centre' or 'Self' – How will it affect Psychology?

Part II

(11) The Psychic Being of Integral Yoga, Its Quality and Character – How to Ascertain Its Existence?
(12) Its Growth as Personally Gone Through
(13) Its Psycho-therapeutic Working
(14) Its Expression in Some Children
(15) Its Effects on Personality Generally
(16) Psychology as a Science of Man and Personality, Free and Unhampered
(17) Fields of Application
(18) Concluding Observation: Jung's 'Centre' or 'Self' or Psychic Being of Integral Yoga is the central fact of personality, essential to our conception of it and all its reactions. It is really the most important subject for research.

Abstract

Swami Pranavananda's inspiration to promote comparative study of Eastern psychology and Western psychology has been really fine. The two approaches have been, in fact, complementary. The one from the outside treating man as an object in nature like a plant, an animal or a physical object. This has been a study of the reactions of man. And this is done under the self-imposed limitation of Natural Science to study the phenomena alone. The mass of psychological knowledge thus produced, in various fields, has been immense. But this is all *about* man, not *of* man himself.

The other approach has been of direct introspective investigation of the nature of man in a true, full and unhampered manner, with no postulate or assumption admitted. This leads to a clarity as to what man by himself is.

Are the two approaches not complementary, either approach needing the knowledge acquired by the other?

Gardner Murphy, an eminent contemporary psychologist, frankly admits, "Nobody knows anything much about the nature of man. We are in a position to raise a great many questions, to raise questions perhaps so rare and so fundamental that we begin to wonder if we even have a method for approaching an ultimate solution." (*Main Currents of Modern Thought*, Vol. 9, No. 2, N.Y.) Further says he, among psychologists whose interest is chiefly personality, it has come to mean simply the aggregate of the organism's capacities. (*Historical Introduction to Psychology*, p. 386)

However, there are trends in Western psychology which are definitely trying to exceed the empirical limitation to explain the phenomena of personality. Rise of interest in the study of meditation is a promising approach. Transpersonal-psychology too is interesting. However, C.G. Jung, who started as a psychiatrist with Freud and later diverged as a free explorer of the nature and character of the human psyche and its diverse manifestations, is by far the best example. And his conclusion is that behind conscious and unconscious activity of the psyche, at the back of its diversities, exists a unitary 'Centre' or 'Self', which progressively tends to integrate and create 'Wholeness' in life. This fact he affirms repeatedly and it is further confirmed by the Jungian Analysts, his followers, with ever new clinical data. Says Jung, "All the usual little remedies and medicaments of psychology fall somewhat short (to explain personality) just as they do with the man of genius or the creative human being. Derivation from ancestral heredity or from the milieu does not quite succeed; inventing fictions about childhood, which is so popular today, and to put it mildly – in the inappropriate, the explanation from necessity 'he had no money, was ill, and so forth – remains caught in mere externalities." (*Integration of Personality*, 1940, p. 299) Further says he, "If we survey the situation as a whole, we come to the inevitable conclusion – at least in my opinion – that a psychic element is present that expresses itself through the tetrad. This conclusion demands neither daring speculation nor extravagant phantasy. If I have called the centre the 'self', I did so after ripe reflection and a careful assessment of the data of experience as well as of history." (Ibid., p. 198)

The 'Centre' acts, he adds, "like a magnet upon the disparate materials and processes of the unconscious and like a crystal grating, catches them one by one." (Ibid., p. 197)

And say his followers: "A significant aspect of Jungian treatment, however, is not described so well by the term analysis. This is the experience of the Self that often occurs in, or as a result of, Jungian therapy. Jungian analysis results not only in Self-knowledge but also in a new kind of Self-experience. People who enter Jungian analysis may do so because they wish to know more about themselves, but if the analysis actually works, they come to experience themselves in a way that was previously not possible. This new kind of Self-experience takes place as the rigidities of ego-consciousness dissolve, and as the unconscious responds and is acknowledged within the security and understanding of the analytical framework. What actually creates the therapeutic effect in Jungian analysis is the increasing amplitude of a person's experience of the Self. This experience, moreover, usually brings with it an influx of energy and vitality, so that one common result of analysis is more creativity in one's responses to life and its challenges." (*Jungian Analysis*, Shambhala, Boulder and London, 1984, pp. 30-31)

Thus this fact of a 'Centre' and 'Self' in personality is highly challenging and must be seriously investigated by academic psychology.

On the other hand, Integral Yoga as developed and practised at

Sri Aurobindo Ashram, Pondicherry, also affirms a central spiritual principle, evolutionary in character, localised in the region of the heart, which commands and progressively harmonises the diverse tendencies of the mind, life impulses and the body. It is different from the soul, perhaps a reflection of it. But it is embedded in the evolutionary life and is a part of it. It is called the Psychic Being. It is a self-existent, conscious and joyous principle. The outer personality of mind, life and body is egoistic in organisation, i.e., self-centred and much divided. When through self-consecration and dedication to a disinterested purpose, it becomes attenuated in its self-centredness, then the psychic being gets a chance to come up and act more overtly and lend its joy, consciousness and unity to the outer personality.

This is the nature, the quality and character of the psychic being.

The evidence adduced are manifold. The first is the narration of personal experiences of it during a long period of yogic preoccupation with it. These narrations are records of empirical facts, which show a slow growth in discovery and progressive clarity in perception of it. Then there is the narration of the present state when almost at will a contact can be made with it. What effects this has made on the personality as a whole is also narrated. The joy, the wholeness, relative independence of circumstances and a spontaneous feeling for truth, goodness and beauty as palpably better perceptions.

Study of it in children is another line of evidence. Then its working in cases of depression is also considered.

One section of the paper is devoted to the various fields of its application, viz., personal development, abnormal psychology, education and others. These applications afford much confirmatory data.

The conclusion of it all is that Western psychology and Indian psychology are complementary in their approaches and, therefore, needed by each other. And that there are also trends in Western psychology which run parallel to Indian psychology.

Further, that the 'Centre' or the 'Self' of Jung and the Psychic Being of Integral Yoga present the most challenging subject for research.

(The full text of the Lecture with the Appendices is over 40 typed pages and will be published by the Psychology Trust of India, under whose auspices it was delivered in Delhi, on Jan. 6, 1984 and carried the Psychology Lecture Award for 1985.)

THE STRUCTURE AND DYNAMICS OF PERSONALITY IN INTEGRAL YOGA

Personal Search for the Central Fact
Empirical Snaps of the Process at Different Stages

Note:
The Ashrams in Indian history have been seats of intensive cultural cultivation and nurseries of personality development. And many have been the qualities of a cultural life and of the personality development pursued by them in different times and different places. But mostly the spirit was the objective, though with variant emphases.

In the present case, the structure and dynamics of personality development at Sri Aurobindo Ashram, Pondicherry, a contemporary institution with worldwide contacts since 1926, is taken up for study and investigation.

In the extensive paper, at first its broad cultural orientation, its philosophy and psychology of life is briefly stated. The personality consists of body, life, mind, the subliminal and the psychic being, the inmost spiritual fact. Each part contributes its own structural or constituent, and dynamic or functional elements. To harmonise them into an original and creative form and quality of personality is the purpose of the pursuit at the Ashram. This is done through aspiration, i.e., a steady willing for the aim, through rejection of the recalcitrant elements and through a progressive self-opening to the aim of harmony, integration and perfection as felt and conceived at different stages of growth. All faults, defects and difficulties are taken as imperfections of nature, which are to be made good. Social, moral and religious inhibitions and prohibitions are to be seen in this light.

The psychic being, the central self-existent, joyous, spiritual fact is the true harmonising factor of life. The same has to be sought and activated.

The reality of the same is shown in many ways. First of all, through the writer's personal individual pursuit of it and its experiences at different stages. This is done through introspective reports of experiences lived through. The quality of psychic consciousness is also sought to be demonstrated through its expression in some children, in their inner joyfulness, simplicity, spontaneity, harmony and striking attractiveness. The wholeness and joyfulness of the psychic being is further shown through its psychic therapeutic action in cases of depression, anxiety, worry, etc., etc.

Further, there is a broad characterisation of the community life of the Ashram in its pursuit of personality development. Some problem cases of the community are also considered.

Thus the adventure of the Ashram is shown as representative of the essential Indian interest in the Spirit – in its purity and fulness – reconceived and reformulated in the light of fresh spiritual experience.

Sri Aurobindo Ashram, Pondicherry, is a nursery of personalities of a particular quality, where individuals expose themselves, as best they can, to the special overall influence and grow up slowly in an intended quality and form. In fact, each Ashram does that, each in its own way. The form of the personality and the process leading to it are obviously of deep psychological significance and of value for education and the general guidance of life.

Now, the structure of personality in Integral Yoga is briefly this. The normal personality of man is made up of three parts, Body, Life and Mind, which represent in synthesis the three stages of general evolution – Matter, Life and Mind. The Body represents the physical organisation, the organs and the systems of the body, their functionings, their over-all relative unity as also their individual natures and disharmonies. The Life represents the biological part that man has in common with animals, the urge to live, the instinctive adaptations to the environment and modification in habits achieved through experience. The Mind represents thinking, primarily in its function of serving the instincts and habits, but also at its best as an instrument of seeing truth as such.

Thus normal personality involves three levels of experience and their principal factors, the physical, the vital and the mental, and they are continually availed of for identifying the problems of personality at each stage of growth and for seeking their solutions.

These three levels and factors correspond to the principles of *Tamas, Rajas* and *Sattva*, inertia, activity or restlessness or agitation and balance or harmony. This basic standpoint is found to be extremely helpful in handling personality and achieving progressive harmonisation.

The identification of these parts is a job, as they normally all get mixed up at the empirical level, at the surface of consciousness. But prolonged self-observation and an attempt to go to the root of motivations progressively leads to the identification of the three factors separately, which is exhilarating in discovery and extremely helpful in the control and re-direction of the inner motivations.

Of course, this involves a training in learning to observe oneself objectively, see things as they are, unhindered and unhampered by social, moral and religious inhibitions and prohibitions. One has to learn to regard all faults, however grievous and serious, as imperfections of nature and all as remediable. A sense of sin or of guilt is irrelevant as every fault is an imperfection which can be made good. A will for wholeness and wholesomeness should naturally be there.

Evidently, it takes time to get this attitude settled in the mentality but, as it is done more and more, it facilitates the identification of motivations. Even the right attitude firmly taken is a great help.

The aim is the harmonisation or integration of all the three parts, the body, life and mind. In other words, a general sense of peace and joy, a whole-hearted dedication to the work, the pursuit of a knowledge and well-being as a whole, individually and in collectivity. Yet, in other words, the aim involves a seeking for the self-conscious joyous spirit or soul or psychic being in oneself and a Supreme Spirit, the Divine or God, in universal existence or the world or society. This implies a sense and an urge for the depth in oneself and in the external reality, whatever name and form it may take with individuals at different stages of their growth. In this matter, an openness of attitude is advised and is found most helpful. Any formal belief is a limitation; growth in consciousness, in depth, in width and in height is the thing that matters.

The aim is evidently of the first importance. With that goes an attitude of self-observation and identification of the motivations of thoughts, attitudes and actions. And a constant attempt to reject the inharmonious, the recalcitrant and the egoistic or self-assertive elements and to aspire for the peaceful and the harmonious trends and a maintenance of general openness to supreme harmony, truth and unity under any name and form. This constitutes the basic dynamism of personality in Integral Yoga, which goes with the basic structure of it as stated earlier.

Ordinary personality is acquisitive, self-regarding or self-separative. This involves a basic conflict with the not-self and an essential insecurity in the self. The personality in Integral Yoga aiming at a general peace, harmony and unity proceeds in a self-consecrating way. The basic approach and attitude towards life and existence has to be of self-consecration, of dedication, of increasing oneness and unity with it. This creates in the wide realms of body, life and mind progressively an attitude of self-surrender to supreme harmony in place of the individual and divergent self-assertions in body, life and mind as they normally are.

Our self-observations will soon reveal to us that we are a most imperfect sort of unity, among all kinds of self-assertions everywhere. The tongue cares for the immediate taste and not the reaction of the stomach or the general well-being of the body. The life's impulses go in contrary pairs, are very many and each is self-assertive. And the ideas and opinions of the mind show a similar sort of confusion. A harmonisation or integration of this vast diversity is an enormous task. But it is clearly a necessity and it has to be pursued and lived and enjoyed. Life will be very imperfect and ineffective, if it continues to be divided and full of conflicts and tensions.

A sadhak of the Ashram progressively builds up this faith and frame of mind, while consecrating himself in some work of the Ashram. Along with that go his meditation and study and music and other cultural activities, as also physical education through games, gymnastics, etc., – all converging on an integral self-opening to the higher unifying spiritual influences of life.

Among these influences, the place of the spiritual guide and the guru is a pivotal one. With him, the sadhak seeks an inner relation of trust, confidence and reliance. Something of this quality can be seen in our contemporary psycho-therapies too. Freud insists on a rapport, a relation, between the psycho-analyst and his patients. And it was necessary that the analyst should have been previously psycho-analysed himself so that he became conscious of his own repressions and complexes.

The Jungian analysts are equally emphatic on the nature and quality of this relationship. Here are a few words of theirs on the subject.

"Analysands will feel that this is a person they can trust, one to whom they can be fully open, who will not take advantage of them, and who will not break down under the burdens that they may bring. Analysands want to feel that the analyst can stand the dirt and stench of another's life and not turn away." (*Jungian Analysis*, p. 371)

The Buddha too had observed to the effect that nobody should try to liberate others who is not himself liberated.

Evidently, for reconstructing personality this relationship is of the highest importance.

In Integral Yoga, in this connection we have one great simplification. It is that of progressively turning the unconscious into the conscious under the influence of the Superconscious. All fragmentation, all diversity, all egoisms are due to unconsciousness. As consciousness increases, a progressive unification automatically comes about. A sadhak's task is, therefore, to become more and more conscious of himself and his doings. The ego personality, in Freud's judgment, is nine-tenths unconscious. The conscious and the unconscious is the basic division of normal personality. With Jung, the unconscious is a vaster and a more complex reality. His unconscious too is chaotic, but it also has the archetypes and the principle of wholeness. Jung's 'Tetrad', the four primary functions of the psyche, include intuition, which means the faculty concerned with the future possibilities of life.

The Superconscious in Integral Yoga is the future possibility of full consciousness, of wholeness, of unity, of perfection. To let the Superconscious penetrate and transform the conscious and the unconscious is all the task of achieving harmonisation or integration in personality.

The structure and the dynamics of personality in Integral Yoga, in fact, need further elaboration. The individual personality is a particular fact with a particular body, a particular life and a particular mind. But these particular body, life and mind are specimens of Universal Matter, Universal Life and Universal Mind. As such, the two must be somehow intimately connected. Empirically, if an individual withdraws or dissociates himself from his identifications with his particular body, life and mind persistently, he can land in a wider consciousness. This consciousness is the fact involved in phenomena like telepathy, telekinesis, hypnosis, where a supra-sensory action is indicated. This is called the subliminal in the language of Integral Yoga. The subliminal exercises an influence on the particular personality more or less and is a factor in the dynamics of personality.

However, if we withdraw, through slow progressive self-dissociations, more and more inward, as though from the periphery to the centre or the outer crust to the core, we reach ultimately the inmost consciousness as a distinct fact, qualitatively different, more luminous, joyous, unitary and self-existent, i.e., uninvolved in the environment. It stands contrasted to the ordinary mental consciousness, which is involved in the environment and is less luminous. Integral Yoga calls this the Psychic Being, localised in the heart and involved in the evolutionary process with the body, life and mind but spiritual, i.e., self-existent and abiding. Soul is, on the other hand, a substantive spiritual reality commanding individual existence but independent of evolutionary development. The Psychic Being may be taken as a reflection of the soul in evolution.

This inmost fact of the Psychic Being is the central fact of personality, the self-existent individuality, the basis of uniqueness in personality.

The sadhak of Integral Yoga would evidently have a deep seeking for this fact and would seek a progressive inward penetration to contact and realise this inmost luminous and joyous fact of life. When this contact comes about, the Psychic Being becomes directly the all commanding dynamic fact of personality, harmonising and integrating the diverse elements of personality.

The seeking and the discovery of the Psychic Being and letting it act directly is, therefore, the central motivation of a sadhak under Integral Yoga.

So far we have stated the structure and the dynamics of personality under Integral Yoga as a matter of the psychology and the philosophy of life as obtaining at the institutional life of Sri Aurobindo Ashram, Pondicherry. Now, the more important two issues are (i) the empirical ascertainment of the quality and the character of the Psychic Being and (ii) the form of the personality achieved under its influence and the discipline of Integral Yoga as a whole.

The approaches to these two issues can be twofold. One, to the community of the sadhaks as a whole and the growth and the change of valuations taking place in it and the form of personality achieved in terms of peace, joy, equability, etc. With the community will go the problem cases, which are deviations from the main stream of life showing revolt, recalcitrance or any other form of self-assertion, direct or disguised. This would mainly be a work of the objective observation and would need delimitation to be precise and definite.

The other approach is of personal individual reporting of the process of growth and the form of personality progressively evolved. This approach is more definite as it leads to a clarity regarding the reality and existence of the central fact of personality, which is the most important issue in all personality studies. This is the most dynamic fact in personality and if this is mobilised, it can alter the correlations among traits and qualities of life or those between life and environment.

Now, here are snaps of a few salient occasions during a period of growth extending over life since 1940.

1. In 1940, the resolution comes to me to devote myself wholeheartedly to the Integral Yoga and aim at the fulfilment of life envisaged by it.

2. In 1941, December.

On one day, around 4 a.m., I experience a small circumscribed roundish luminosity in the heart or about there. I feel startled, I am aroused. The luminosity lasts a short time, perhaps a minute as recollection goes, but it leaves deep joy. It is a vivid recollection even today.

Its effect was a repeated recourse to the heart and joy in doing that. This was not the habit with me; my preoccupation normally was with thinking and the head.

3. In 1944, summer weather, afternoon.

I am sitting in my working room, am alone, have been so for a couple of hours, doing ordinary reading, writing. A sudden thrill of joy in the heart overtakes me. I get absorbed in it. It passes off but I remain engrossed in it, to the exclusion of other thoughts for sometime. The experience is a vivid recollection today too.

This further intensified my heart-awareness and induced concentration in the heart in addition to that in the head, which was normal with me.

4. Then I remember a period of time – a couple of years perhaps – when I would sit for hours, hovering as it were, for the peace and joy of the heart centre. I would then get occasionally palpable peace, which I longed to retain but could not.

5. Next, I recall a period of time when the mind was in much

agitation, which affected my sleep too and I would long for deeper peace. This peace was an object of intense longing and when it came, it was a cure for the agitation of the mind.

6. Further comes back to my mind the period of a few years when I used music a great deal to activitate the heart-consciousness. The music consisted of a record of Mira's songs, which I loved to play endlessly and which afforded me deep inner concentration and joy. Music is really of many kinds. There is a music which just excites. The music for the heart-centre has a quality of its own. Songs of Bhakti (devotion) are the appropriate thing.

7. At one stage, flowers began to strike me as particularly beautiful and I began to seek and enjoy them. A bed of fresh blooming flowers would be overwhelming and evoke the heart-consciousness and I would linger on with them as much as I could. Music ceased to be the impelling need that it was during one period, but flowers continue uptil now to be an inviting attraction. Flowers of pink colour in fresh bloom, in particular, spontaneously evoke a deep inner thrill and change the entire inner atmosphere even when there was previously a sadness or indifferent feeling.

8. Two experiences occurred around 1960 and these served to bring out the contrast and the distinction between the inner consciousness and the outer personality in a sharp manner.

(i) One was a very queer one. In a situation when I was asleep, possibly in a mid-day nap, I happened to find myself inwardly awake. I could see myself asleep in one part and awake in another. It was a striking experience without a precedent and without even knowledge and I felt really surprised and startled. It much separated the inner and outer and afforded the joy of a discovery.

(ii) The other experience was of smarting under an injury and an insult when I sudenly thought of turning to the psychic centre. I could do so and, I suppose, well enough and I landed upon deep joy. It was again thrilling to have joy deep within and acute pain outside. The inner and the outer got clearly distinguished.

9. Human nature gets easily perturbed. For 'Shrimad Bhagwad Gita', *samatvam yoga ucyate*, equal-mindedness is yoga and for the stoic philosophers in the West, imperturbability was a high idea.

Now, when I have got into a state of perturbation, for whatever reason, and I turn to the psychic being and its steady calm and can get into a contact with it, perturbation gets liquidated very soon.

This is an experience of great utility, frequent occurrence and vivid confirmatory value of the existence of the Psychic Being.

10. Besides the perturbed state, I have now almost a habit to turn to the psychic centre, when I find myself dull or indifferent in feeling, which is a disagreeable state of consciousness. With this turning, almost immediately a change of consciousness takes place and I get into a joyful state. However, sometimes a standing back or self-dissociation from the present identification takes a little time.

11. Similarly, when I can recognise, in a disagreeable state "oh, here an egoistic motivation is involved" and I turn to the psychic, I become free and the psychic joy springs up.

12. The Psychic Being now stands in my consciousness as the joyous resort for all difficulties or problems that arise in the ordinary mental consciousness, frustration, disappointments, resistances whether inner or of external relations. After getting to this resort and staying there in joy for sometime, I find myself equal to the problem I was involved in.

13. This really amounts to the emergence of another personality within me, joyous, free and confident. The ordinary personality now becomes secondary and less interesting. But it too is now more peaceful and less attached to and insistent on external objectives. However, it continues to be the ordinary way of life.

14. A further consequence of this inner emergence is the clarity and the certitude regarding 'what I am' and a clarity regarding 'what ordinary nature is'. This feeling comes to me as a fulfilment of my seeking as a psychologist, which was that of knowing man as he truly is.

15. The experience of the Psychic Being also gives me a real and a concrete sense of depth in myself, which works out a real sense of depth in the universal existence. This status of consciousness carries with it a sense of clarity all round, a deeper unity behind the apparent plurality and its anomalies.

This is so far as the approach of personal search of the central fact of personality and the appreciation of its quality and character and its relation to the ordinary personality are concerned. The reality and existence of the Psychic Being, as an abiding central fact, is a certitude, I avail of it repeatedly every day and like to stay there indefinitely at times.

Some confirmatory external evidences have also come about during the last several years when my personal experience of the psychic fact has been clear and available for a wider use. These evidences are as follows.

Our social life consists of contacts with others, which are agreeable, disagreeable and indifferent. With the emergence and activisation of the Psychic Being, contacts begin to occur which are particularly striking as they come sometimes in unexpected situations.

These contacts are felt as deep and they involve the heart. There is in them a felt sense of identity with the other person. Such contacts tend to become more significant than other contacts, they set a standard for other contacts, which then acquire a new orientation. And a tendency then comes into being to see whether in other contacts too the psychic quality can be evoked or not. In some cases, in fact very few cases, it can be done and then they become deeper, disinterested and more reliable. It really depends upon the psychic sensitivity of the other person too. These contacts can arise where the ordinary sympathies of social status, religion, culture, language, etc., do not exist. And they can be with men, women, children, young and old, beautiful or plain or even when apparently unattractive.

Under circumstances of psychic contact, communication of thought and ideas becomes easier.

I record below a few striking cases of this contact and quality.

(1) In 1985, in March-April, I am sitting at the shore in Pondicherry, as more or less usual, in a contemplative form with almost open eyes and not looking at anything in particular. My inner state was of meditation in the heart. Suddenly I get drawn out and see a group passing by, 2-3 women of the labour-class and 2-3 children 8-10 years old. This group as a whole gets drawn towards me and I am struck by their engrossment in me. I find each one of them, the women and children, individually drawn towards me too. I feel thrilled and surprised and deeply moved. The group does not halt there, but keeps hurrying forward, however lingering on in their look towards me. I remain drawn to them and feel with them a pleasant inner contact. They too show joy in their expression. I remain full of this contact even when they disappear from sight.

This case stands in my consciousness as a recent striking case of psychic contact at the collective level. Usually such contacts are individual.

(2) Another case occurring under similar circumstances also comes to mind.

Perhaps about a year earlier, in summer of 1984, evening time, I am sitting on the shore in a contemplative form with half-open sort of eyes. I have been sitting there for a long time. Suddenly a young man comes and sits by my side with freedom and even a sense of familiarity.

He asks me, "You are an old man, how do you find life?" I feel amused, look at him for a while and then say, smiling, "Very good, most enjoyable." He shows surprise. I then ask him, "And how do you find life, my young man?" He is pensive, makes no reponse and then goes away.

I continue to feel for him, wish he had stayed longer. A contact had come about with him. He had felt drawn to me. But response was not the one needed or it did not serve to console and encourage him.

But it was surely a case of a spontaneous deeper contact in an unexpected situation. I continue to feel for him, even though it was a very brief contact.

(3) Another striking case of such a contact was with an old man, which much surprised me when it came about.

I visit a friend in a rural home. I meet also his father who lives separately, by himself in a room. We did not have much in common to talk about and he is orthodox and rather rigid in his social prohibitions regarding his daughter-in-law in particular. I was seeking a relaxation in these rigidities of his. I try to get into my psychic form and evoke joy in him. I do not succeed on one occasion. I try again and he gives a striking response of spontaneous whole-hearted joy and it thrilled him and it thrilled me. After that, this contact became our normal contact and we began to enjoy meeting each other, even though we were otherwise so differently situated and poised.

This contact too stands out prominently in my consciousness, unexpected as it was.

(4) Another one with the son of our vegetable seller, whom everybody called 'Mullaji' at Jwalapur (Hardwar). When I first had this type of contact with the boy, he was about eight years old. Whenever we met, we had mutually a spark of joy. It went on year after year and the last time I met him, he was a grown up young man of about 14 years, self-conscious and self-important, doing

well at school and in his N.C.C. group. He still gave a spontaneous joyous contact of the heart but now with a difference.

I always thought that the state of development of the psychic being in him was good. Now, the external life of the boy was getting more engrossing to him and the psychic being was getting covered up by new interests.

The Psychic contacts are an interesting and a recognisable fact of life. They are marked by depth and tend to be more lasting. Their value for life is pretty evident.

Psychic Quality in Children

Some children show psychic sensitivity in a special measure. Some children at a very young age, about three to ten, before they get strongly projected outward show a striking inwardness, quietude, joyousness, and attractiveness. These children can be distinguished from the rest, who have ordinary outward playfulness, hilarity and attractiveness of child life. The latter category is a common phenomenon but the former is not. The children with psychic quality are striking in their sweetness, harmoniousness, joyousness and beauty. During the last about 15 years when my interest in the Psychic Being was strong, whenever I came across a child of this quality I observed him carefully and that year after year. I saw, as the child grew up, how this phase passed off and yet found him distinguishable from others in his qualities of joy, concentration and relationship with others, elders and companions. I know half a dozen such children and have observed them for a long time and have a deep appreciation for them. The youngest is now about 4 years and I saw his psychic quality when he was about 2. Then there are twins of a college lecturer now about 9 years old. I have watched them for 4-5 years. Then there is one Ashram boy, he displayed this simplicity when he was about 4. Now he is over 20. I have watched his growth all through. I remember when he passed out of that stage and began to show care and anxiety and yet displayed a wholesomeness which was striking. I enclose here in the appendix the pictures of a few children. There is here also a picture of Indira Gandhi's family group. Every face is happy and yet each one's happiness has a quality of its own. Please observe the young boy, about 8, sitting in the front. Does his joy not have an inwardness and depth and does he not have a charm about him? I have shown this picture to lots of individuals and groups and had interesting responses. Most of the people preferred that face even though they did not have any reasons to give.

These pictures were shown at the last Science Congress Psychology Session (Delhi 1986) and some of the responses were really striking. Some observers could spontaneously identify the psychic quality. One has to be calm and quiet and dispassionate and just wanting to know and feel the thing as it is. The ability to identify the psychic quality is an asset of life, an asset to see and recognise a quality, rather rare, but which represents peace, joy and wholeness, so central to personality and its future possibilities. This capacity would also be an evidence of the percipient's own psychic sensitivity and his possibilities of future integrations in life.

Psycho-therapeutic working with the Psychic Being

With the inner joy as a fact clearly in recognition and appreciation, I started applying this to others who approached me in depression or for consolation, or clarification in a difficulty of life. In the case of a depression, I would try to get myself in the psychic form, as best as possible, and then try to tap his heart-centre, while keeping him interested in a relaxed manner in any casual light-hearted talk. In some cases joy would come up in the depressed readily, in some a few days contact and action would be necessary. In one case, with the best effort no response could be had. The other person's responsiveness or receptivity is definitely a factor. In cases of doubt and difficulty in life and general lack of enthusiasm too, this method works. However, some general re-orientation of the situation too is given. The essence of the matter is that if the psychic centre can be tapped, joy comes up and everything changes.

Psycho-therapy is today a most important branch of psychology. It is also producing clinical data affording to psychology a deeper insight into the constitution of personality. The experimental psychology's contribution is primarily of tests and a quantitative assessment of mental qualities, which have found wide utility in education, industry and other fields of life. This work is essentially of determining correlations among phenomenal factors. The clinical work of Freudian or Jungian or general eclectic psychotherapies involves a deeper exploration into the working of the human psyche. The Jungians now talk a great deal of the 'self' in man besides his ego, the normal personality. Here are a few interesting sentences from a recent publication entitled "Jungian Analysis". (Boulder and London, Shambhala, 1984)

"The significant aspect of Jungian treament, however, is not described so well by the term analysis. This is the experience of the self that often occurs in, or as a result of, Jungian therapy. Jungian analysis results not only in Self-knowledge but also in a new kind of Self-experience. People who enter Jungian analysis may do so because they wish to know more about themselves, but if the analysis actually works, they come to experience themselves in a way that was previously not possible. This new kind of self-experience takes place as the rigidities of ego-consciousness dissolve, and as the unconscious responds and is acknowledged within the security and understanding of the analytical framework. What actually creates the therapeutic effect in Jungian analysis is the increasing amplitude of a person's experience of the Self. This experience, moreover, usually brings with it an influx of energy and vitality, so that one common result of analysis is more creativity in one's responses to life and its challenges." (pp. 30-31)

The self is evidently becoming prominent and as our knowledge of it increases, our conception of personality will undergo modification.

What is normal and what is abnormal is an old question. We have no sure standard of normality. The socially passable is a most variable standard.

The Psychic Being, as an ascertainable fact of experience, is in a position to give the much needed guidance on normality and some other problems of psycho-therapy.

The psychic consciousness is the unitary and unifying consciousness in man. It is essential wholeness, with no inherent conflicts and divisions. Will this not be the true norm for the wholeness and wholesomeness of ordinary life? Of course, it has to be investigated and ascertained precisely. And the Jungian Analysts seem to be proceeding in this direction in the clinical way. Integral Yoga, by its method of yogic introspection, knows it and is making use of it for general personality development as well as therapeutic purpose when necessary.

Being essential wholeness, the value of the Psychic Being for therapeutic purpose is the highest. If it can be mobilised, joy and harmony can be restored to a patient in a much shorter time and that more effectively. Freud never achieved a true liberation from a repression. Its acute working could only be brought to a level of social passability. All psycho-therapeutic procedures are prolonged dealings. Psychic action is very quick, when it gets a chance.

Here are a few cases personally handled, which yielded striking results.

(1) A gentleman around 60 had got into a state of continuing depression. Difficulties in business and in relations with the sons were ostensibly felt as the cause. Nothing seemed to help him. He turned to spiritual life for solace and comfort. He came to me and I encouraged him in his attempt to spend time at his favourite Ashrams in Hardwar.

In my contacts with him, I sought to stimulate, to activate his heart centre. Overtly I also tried to give him a new orientation regarding his situation. That the sons should be given their independence when they were grown up and felt responsibility for the work; and that the labour did make ever new demands and pressed for them through protests, strikes, etc. But in this new orientation, I sought essentially an attitude of detachment rather than an intellectual understanding of things. The main reliance, however, was the psychic joy of the heart and the same I tried to evoke in him, whenever he came to me. Our contact slowly grew and he began to rely upon me more and more. Along with that, the joy also grew and, in a year or so, his depressions left him, joy came up on his face and he could play his limited part in his business. In this process, his contact with me grew to be strong and intimate and he became a spiritual seeker forever more at peace within. The embarrassments he had from his sons and business became manageable.

At one time, I followed the Freudian Free Association Method with the patients whom I took up as a hobby, while I was a teacher in Delhi. Then I naturally used to delve into the past and unearth the repressed experiences. And as a repression rose to consciousness, the patient would show immediate relief.

But under Integral Psycho-therapy, I have found that the hunt for repression is not necessary. If peace and joy increase in the patient, a re-organisation of experiences within begins to take place. The repressed elements would sooner or later arise and get re-adjusted under the guidance of higher influences of peace, joy and unity which are being promoted, through the patient's or seeker's contact with teacher or helper. This contact has, of course, to be maintained over a length of time.

My work has been essentially one of arousing normal persons to a sense of higher possibilities of life, of greater integrations, of peace and joy, of the aims of higher spiritual realisations. But this certainly includes anxiety, defeatism, pessimism, worry, sleeplessness, boredom, lack of interest in life and the like. Two cases of schizophrenia too have come my way.

In all these, getting into a good contact, a contact of trust and reliance is the first thing which must be promoted more and more. Then a general orientation of faith in recovery, of patience and perseverance and of the goodness of life and existence have to be built up through repeated contacts, meetings and general discussions. And in and through all these, to seek to tap the psychic joy of the person, to infuse one's own psychic joy into him and to invoke higher peace in him. This done over a length of time, the recovery and joy and hope in life can be confidently expected.

(2) Another striking case is of a lady who has had many deaths in the family and this had created in her a deep-seated fear for death and almost killed her joy in life. She had become a depressed person with practically no hope in life. We got into touch with each other and developed a mutual responsiveness. I sought joy and brightness in her life and she showed some responsiveness. Our contacts steadily grew up and we sustained them. I kept up my working of Integral Psychotherapy through meetings once or twice a year and correspondence. She got over her fear of death in a few years and it was such a satisfaction, to her and to me, when she wrote saying that another death among relations came off and she took it with equality, without the old depression she used to have.

Now her form is of a spiritual aspirant seeking the highest realisation and fulfilment of life. Her case is a matter of deep satisfaction as she has arisen from a subnormal state to a supernormal one.

(3) Another case of psychicisation. Two of our relations, a lady and her daughter, 37 and 15 respectively, were on a visit with us and they were unhappy and I felt concerned about them. As a part of my approach, I proposed to ask of them a question to which

they were to answer with the first word that occurred to them. Others present in the house were also asked to join the experiment.

The persons who participated were these: (1) the lady, 37 (2) the girl, 15 (3) another lady, 50 (4) an elderly lady, 75 (5) a gentleman in business, 55 (6) a boy of 12.

The question was:
How do you find life?

The answers were:
1. Terrible.
2. Oh, terrible. This is my honest answer.
3. Very interesting (quite emphatically).
4. Interesting and useful, but at times complex.
5. It is useful.
6. O.K. (with distinct joy).

These answers were obtained on 30-12-83. The lady and the girl, who were finding life terrible, became my subjects and I sought a change in their feeling for life and I followed the approach of Integral Psychotherapy, while maintaining with them my best daily contact.

On 29-1-84, another occasion presented itself and the experiment was repeated. The additional members were a little different.

The question was the same –
How do you find life?

The answers were:
1. The lady (37): tolerable.
2. The elderly lady (75): tiring, satisfied with inner change.
3. Another lady (50): very interesting.
4. An Ashramite lady: quite good.
5. An Ashramite gentleman (55): interesting.
6. An Ashramite young lady (40): fine.
7. An official: complex.

On 2-4-84

The lady in question (37) reported life as "Better and Pleasant".

On 14-5-85

The lady in question (37): Good and Promising.
The girl in question (15): Fine.
The boy (12): Fine.

With that, my quest ended. The lady and the girl who in December '83 were finding life terrible, now in '85 were finding it good and fine.

No digging into the past was done. Orientations to life too came about incidentally through informal contacts and talks. But I was persistently seeking, for them, a joy in the heart ever more and making them laugh too off and on.

Life is complex and normal, varied impacts of life too provide correctives for wrong attitudes and a happier change can come about. The girl had, during this period of '83 to '85, a stay at a new boarding school, which was helpful. But the lady had three visits to us and her situation otherwise remained the same. In her case, it can be more definitely said that the change in her was induced by the impacts she received here.

It is hardly necessary to give more cases. Through psychic action, ordinary anxiety, worry, lack of interest in life and the like can be tackled really effectively. But it has, of course, its own conditions of working.

The Psychic Being

Its Value for the appreciation of "wholeness" in Science and Philosophy and for Peace and Unity in the Individual and Society

The wholeness quality is a rising perception and conception in science and philosophy. Analysis and the atomic view of life and existence are increasingly felt as inadequate. Mind is essentially an instrument of knowledge, whose power lies in breaking up and seeing the parts. Its synthetic function is secondary. Today mind, through prolonged analytical activity, seems to have come to see the limitations of analysis and inquires into the wholeness of things in science as well as philosophy. This is extremely interesting. It is a new prospect for knowledge and life. Now, the psychic being is the form of consciousness unified, not divided like the mind and it spontaneously sees wholes – and wholes within wholes. Its power is intuition, going straight to the unity inherent in its object of knowledge.

In science, there are individual thinkers who are beginning to find the ordinary scientific method, of collecting instances and of generalisation, cumbersome and so often unfruitful and are talking of intuition as an alternative approach.

If a deeper poise of consciousness were cultivated and the Psychic Being tapped, intuition could become a utilisable instrument of knowledge. Of course, this is a possibility for investigation and precise ascertainement.

Our general life today seeks collaboration and peace. Our conflicts and divisions in life, individual, social, political, international, are so acutely and insistently felt and widely enough. But our mind is capable of partialities and finds safety in parts and an exclusive sort of living. It seeks collaboration but cannot see and feel it as the real truth of life. If we live at the surface of things, we are attached to diversity and distinctness of things. Unity of things is not a source of direct joy.

Learning to live at a deeper level and contacting the deepest psychic consciousness easily brings the sense of unity, peace and collaboration. Our practical necessities of life do insist on an inquiry into this possibility.

The Ashram Community as a Whole

We had undertaken an inquiry into the structure and dynamics of personality in Integal Yoga in the situation of Sri Aurobindo Ashram, Pondicherry. We stated at first the general cultural character of this situation. And then attempted to delineate the form and the quality of the personality slowly coming up in that situation and the influences at work there. The approach taken was that of personal pursuit and we tried to characterise a few stages in the process of growth. This approach of individual personal experience or introspection has the unique advantage of direct perception of facts and the certitude that it carries. This certitude of direct perception is not possible otherwise. Other methods involve inferential elements and that affects the certitude of knowledge obtained.

The certitude of direct personal experience was then sought to be confirmed by the expression of the psychic consciousness in some children and by its application to psycho-pathology. And in both cases, actual instances were cited. We also considered what psychic contact is, with some illustrations.

We may now consider the fact of psychic consciousness in the light of the communal life of the Ashram, the life of the collectivity of Sadhaks. The Ashram life is virtually a psychic-centred life. To seek, to achieve and manifest the psychic consciousness is the essential purpose of the Ashram environment and organisation. With individual psychic consiousness goes a collective aspiration for the same; as also a sense and feeling, as the highest objective, for a universal spiritual consciousness in and behind the world phenomena.

The Ashram as a whole, does seem to facilitate a particular form and quality of personality stressing and representing progressive growth in consciousness, a joyful dedication to work, whatever it be, a toleration, understanding and sympathy for others in their individual approaches to issues of life and work and an emphasis on inner values of joy, freedom, good will, love, etc. This life also shows self-confidence, reliance on higher dispensation of life, relative freedom from moral and religious prohibitions, adaptability to changing situations and a hopefulness as to the future.

That is broadly the general quality and character of life in the Ashram. But the ordinary equipment of life as one enters the Ashram is different and it takes a long time to get into the mainstream. During this period, the recalcitrant elements come into a reactionary play too and that gives rise to interesting psychological cases, which require individual handling. In fact, most cases present different kinds of difficulties at one time or the other and they have to be handled individually.

The recalcitrances, discordances, egoisms, revolts open and disguised, can take on very many forms and they can persist too quite long. Leaving the undertaking of yogic life in the middle, one can go away, give up one's assignment of work, get into a melancholic mood, protest against things in various ways, get into a quarrelling relation with others on trifles, etc., etc. All this stuff has to be cleared up so that one gets into a state of simplicity, joy and harmony. But that is exactly the task of recreating personality. It is an enormous task, but surely of the highest value. In Jung's words: "Personality is the highest realisation of the inborn distinctiveness of the particular living being. Personality is an act of the greatest courage in the face of life, and means unconditional affirmation of all that constitutes the individual, the most successful adaptation to the universal conditions of human existence, with the greatest possible freedom of personal decision." (*The Integration of the Personality*, 1940, p. 486) And regarding "Individuation", the process of becoming personality, Jung's words are even more interesting. Says he:

"It must be a genuine process of purification where all superfluities are consumed in the fire" and the basic facts emerge. Is there anything more fundamental than the realisation "This is what I am"? It reveals a unity which nevertheless is – or was – a diversity. No longer the earlier ego with its make-believes and artificial contrivances, but another "objective" ego, which for this reason is better called the "Self". (Collected Works, Vol. 16, p. 199) For Yoga, such attempt and realisation, of becoming personality, is the very sense and purpose of human life.

As illustrations of the difficulties experienced by some individuals and the help given to them to overcome the problems posed by their natures, the following cases may be considered.

(1) A person was in a pretty disordered form. He would become violent and indulge in destructive activities. He became unmanageable at home and was sent on to Sevagram Ashram during Gandhiji's time. With all the sympathy shown to him there, he did not improve. He was then advised to go to Pondicherry Ashram. The Mother accepted and began to give special attention to him. He was provided for in the Ashram and given some work at the Dining Room. She gave instructions that if he indulged in destructive activity, throwing about utensils, etc., he was not to be reprimanded or interfered with. In some time, he tended to become more and more calm and began to behave tolerably well. In a few months, he was almost like others in his behaviour.

Here it is relevant to consider a process of yogic action too. It is that of inducing in a person, by an act of will, higher peace, the peace of a unified consciousness. This person was going to the

Mother, as others were, occasionally and was receiving the attention for himself individually. And the Mother's action was, according to him as to others, of the impact of a harmonious and a harmonising consciousness. The general atmosphere of the Ashram too was friendly and sympathetic. The result was that his inner impulse of gross self-assertion and violence was pacified and a general harmonisation came about in him.

This person lived at the Ashram for long years, more than 20, and is now no more.

(2) Another person, an energetic young man, felt drawn to the yogic pursuit and decided to live at the Ashram. But his approach had an element of violence in it. He was not prepared to pursue personal recreation in a steady way. He wanted it quick, very quick. In fact, he insisted that it should be done in six months. He was all enthusiasm for the pursuit, in his service as well as study. But he soon got into difficulties with some fellow sadhaks. That was not much by itself. He could have avoided those frictions. But the task of inner reconstruction, facing oneself, was proving too much. The Ashram situation, which involved that pressure, tended to become unbearable and he went away. His life outside was a hard one, but he preferred those external hardships to the one of inner self-confrontation.

(3) Another similar case was of a person who had a strong spiritual seeking, an appreciation of inner values, but also a strong attitude for external satisfactions. He came leaving a good position outside. He was happy but, after a few years, the external adjustments and pressure became too much and he went away even though he was in difficulty in finding a satisfactory work for his livelihood.

He was unhappy outside too. His spiritual seeking asserted itself more and more and in a few years he wanted to come back. The Mother accepted him again and gave him the best facilities. He was happy. But in a few years, the other impulse, the extrovert side, got the upper hand and he began to complain of the external situation and again went away to face life outside, which had its own problems.

This was an interesting case of a seesaw movement between the Ashram and the world. He will have to resolve it and become single-minded. But for the present, it was left to the future to resolve this inner division.

The Ashram is full of such cases. Each sadhak has an interesting case history, which shows the inner workings of the human psyche in its slow growth towards a wholeness in life.

Concluding Observation

Hinduism does not have a distinctive creed. It embodies an urge and a trend for the Spirit in man and the universe under whatever belief and form of worship it might find expression. These beliefs and forms of worship represent different levels of development too. But an awareness of the Spirit, however crude or however refined, is the pervasive and the persistent feeling of Indian life. And the Spirit is all-inclusive, all-accommodating and a persisting existence. This accounts for the toleration, the persistence and the synthesisation of Indian cultural life.

Islam and Christanity have distinctive creeds. But in India, they have tended to acquire a variant form and colour. It can definitely be said that Indian Islam and Indian Christianity have a quality of their own which is easily recognisable in the masses. At the level of the masses, it can be said that the Indian life has a common distinctive quality, more or less the same all over.

Now this distinctive quality, in its purity and fullness, is the objective of the pursuit of the personality development of the Ashram. As such, it is representative of Indian life in its essential quality, creatively reconceived and reformulated in the present context of world life.

This is as I understood the adventure of Sri Aurobindo Ashram to be and the same I have sought to consider here as a psychologist for a scientific purpose. However, for this field of experience, new methodologies are needed. This is just the first attempt.

(Contributed to a research journal in psychology)

PROGRESS OF FREUDIAN THOUGHT

A Study in Freudian Rivisionists

Freud was a strict theorist, even though he modified his positions a few times when new facts obliged him to do so. He was a scientist and a realist to the core, yet idealistic trends of life were not ignored altogether.

He was as though born to justify the claims of instinct against morality and religion. In his neurotic cases, he was led to see by his teacher Charcot the hidden working of sex. Thus repression was discovered and it became a pillar of psycho-analytic structure of thought. Pleasure seeking and instinct were identified and then all pleasure seeking was turned into sexual activity. The thumb-sucking of the child became sexual activity and the whole concept of Infantile Sexuality came into being. Repression, Sex, Infantile Sexuality, tracking back conflicts to childhood and Free Association Method became the salient features of Freudian working. During waking hours, social inhibitions are more effective. But during sleep and in dreams, repressed elements can play up better directly or in disguised form to evade the action of the inner censor or the unconscious Superego. Thus dreams and their interpretation to detect the repressions and resolve secret conflicts also becomes an important process in psycho-analysis.

Freud then became or at least acquired the reputation of an advocate of 'Free Living', a life without 'repressions' and without a sense of guilt in life. 'The sense of guilt' is an uncomfortable feeling and it is a common fact of life and all due to the inhibitions imposed by morality and religion. Morality and religion, therefore, come in for severe strictures at the hands of Freud. So does civilization, which is essentially determined by these.

But can life do without morality, religion and civilization? Can life be all a matter of pleasure-seeking or instinct uninhibited by an 'ought' of morality, religion or civilization? Freud came to recognise the force and value of these forces and then modified his original positions. His writing, "Jenseits des Lust-Prinzips" (*Beyond the Pleasure Principle*), was a virtual bombshell for Freud's disciples, as it changed his basic stand. Pleasure was no longer the all-governing basic position. And, while discussing education, he propounded that wisdom consists in discovering the 'optimum' for an individual, i.e., when, by what means and how much to repress and suppress. He thus admitted that repression and suppression were necessary to life, that pleasure and instinct could not be given a free play, but they must be dealt with discreetly.

And while discussing in the "New Lectures", in the chapter entitled "The Anatomy of Personality", the mutual relations of Ego, Id and the Superego, the ordinary externally adjusted personality, the untamed passions, conscious and unconscious and the moral and religious controls and the directives of morality and religion, he affirms that psycho-analytic treatment aims at an "economic balance" among these three factors of personality. However, he admits that mystic practices may possibly be achieving more, a greater harmonisation among them.

This is psycho-analysis as it was with Freud. But Freud's colleagues and followers have, in different countries, under varying historical situations and the experience of psycho-analytic practice and individual thinking, modified Freud and a wide literature of deviant and revisionist thought has come into being. And to understand Freud today, one must consider along with the original thought of Freud, the thought of the Deviants and the Revisionists too.

But before we venture upon other facets of psycho-analysis, we may consider it in relation to the major deviant trend of Jungian thought in particular. Jung affirms an inherent trend for wholeness in the human psyche. This is the essential function of the 'Centre' or the 'Self' in personality. The Jungians, his followers, appear to be, as it were, tapping in their therapy an experience of the Self. However, they yet seek "to come to terms with the unconscious" in and through their therapeutic processes, which are different though in essential approach allied to those of Freud. Jung's attitude is all turned to the unconscious and its contents of the archetypes, as Freud's is all turned to childhood memories and complexes. Jung has a futurist orientation towards a wholeness not just that of a working balance. Yet the racial archetypes, which are things of the past, figure so prominently. Will a clear and whole-hearted futurist attitude be not more helpful for the realisation of the wholeness possible in a case? The contents of the unconscious will unavoidably come up and seek harmonisation under the will for wholeness and they will have to be brought under a scheme of conscious reorientation. But that is different from a conscious approach of directly coming to terms with the unconscious. In a full futurist approach, we would intensify our will for wholeness and let the unconscious contents come up as they may and get readjusted. The unconscious is largely a field of autonomous formations and they are disorderly. Should one not let them take their time for entering into a scheme of harmonisation?

Even in Freud, in Free Association, if the patient gets indulgent in his recollections, a release does not come about. Recollections should afford a progressive detachment, an objectivity, then alone a relative freedom from repressions can come about, not otherwise. This implies a will for health and well-being coming to its own more and more.

These points are of value for appreciating the true character of the curative process.

The Indian Yoga, in its various forms, directly aims at a conception of perfection, a wholeness, a well-being. This is pursued through all the practices of a discipline and the recalcitrant elements get progressively harmonised. There is no doubt that some disciplines of yoga take a suppressive and repressive attitude towards the recalcitrant elements. That is not helpful. These elements should be welcomed for disposal and harmonisation, but not hustled in the process. It is more helpful to attune oneself to the futurist possibility of wholeness, perfection and well-being of life.

With this little digression of reference to Jung and Yoga, we may return to Freud and his revisionist colleagues and followers. Jung was, at one time, a disciple and colleague of Freud's and so was Alfred Adler. But they ceased to be so and developed their independent approaches, independent therapies and independent views of human nature and of life generally. They are, therefore, not Freudian revisionists, they deviated from him rather radically. Freudian revisionists are those who continue to be Freudians, but have sought to reinterpret him or have differed from him in certain ideas or theories of his.

Freud died in 1939 in London. He was born in 1856 and lived and worked in Vienna all his life. His "New Introductory Lectures" published in 1933, a few years before his death when he was ill, embody his own revisions and expansions. His two series of lectures, the early and the new, taken together give a fine exposition of the psycho-analytic thought in original form and in later developments in Freud's own words. His two followers and colleagues Ferenczi and Rank, have given the development of psycho-analysis, which embodies the revisions which generally came about. More recently, a cultural or interpersonal school of revisionists has come about which is influential. This has much changed Freud's position. Besides these, there is much of an eclectic character, which shows how widely some ideas of Freud have spread out in the fields of psychiatry and psychology. But in the midst of all this, there are orthodox Freudians everywhere, who seek to remain close to Freud's thought.

"Great Ideas in Psychology", edited by Robert W. Marks, presents in original words modern psychology and it represents well the contemporary position of psycho-analysis. Freud's own later modifications are given here in a chapter, "The Dissection of the Psychic Personality" taken from his "New Introductory Lectures", written in 1932, which are critical revisions of earlier lectures and enlargement of the field. "The Development of Psycho-analysis" by Ferenczi and Rank gives the development of the movement, its present position and the future trend. This will give us an authentic idea of the subject to enable us to appreciate that psycho-analysis has been an actively growing doctrine from the very beginning and it continues to be so and that it is more than a technique for handling neurotic cases, – it is rather a view of human nature, an interpretation of life as a whole. We have referred to some of the modifications which Freud made in his theories. To those, we may add here that with Adler he had agreed to recognise that "non-sexual factors might produce an unconscious conflict".[1] And the experience of war neuroses had obliged him to accept that "His earlier theories were not sufficiently developed to deal with all the facts."[2]

Here we want to understand, in particular, the later developments of psycho-analysis.

Says Marks, the editor, regarding Freud that "his critical approach to his own thought was dynamic and extensive; consequently, each period of his activity contained revisions of earlier developed thought, or a change in emphasis on specific issues."[3]

1. Robert Thomson, *The Pelican History of Psychology*, p. 252, Penguin Books.
2. *Ibid.*, p. 253.
3. Robert W. Marks, *Greater Ideas in Psychology*, p. 33, Bantam Books, New York.

Now Ferenczi and Rank represent the development of the psycho-analytic technique in this that a mere unwinding of libido and its phases is not the objective. That is unnecessary. Through active intervention, the patient should be led to the reliving of the oedipus situation (the situation of the Oedipus complex or the Electra complex, of the son's or daughter's incestuous wish for the mother or father and the guilt and conflict in it) and getting enlightened on all his neurotic situation of the present. This much shortens the treatment. The book sums up the present position of the working of the psycho-analytic technique as follows.

Psycho-analysis, starting from the impression of the first surprising insight, reached a phase of understanding of the working of the cure. The cures so startling in the beginning became, with the rapidly increasing knowledge of the common mental mechanisms, comparatively less satisfactory, so that one had to consider how to bring the therapeutic ability into harmony with the newly acquired knowledge, which had progressed so far ahead.

Our own presentation, described from this point of view, represents the beginning of a phase which we should like, in contrast to the previous ones, to call the phase of experience. Whereas formerly, one tried to obtain the therapeutic result as a reaction to the enlightenment of the patient, we now try to place the knowledge obtained by psycho-analysis directly in the service of our therapy, by directly provoking the corresponding personal experience on the basis of our insight, and explaining to the patient only this experience which is naturally directly evident to him also.

"The knowledge on the basis of which we are able to intervene at the right place, and in the requisite degree, consists essentially of the conviction of the universal importance of certain fundamental early experiences – as, for example, the Oedipus conflict, – the traumatic effort of which, in the analysis, like a provocative treatment in medicine, is kindled again and, under the influence of living through the experience consciously for the first time, is brought to a useful ending".[2]

Ferenczi and Rank recognise that, previously, proving and disproving of certain theories was considered more important and cure was then neglected. Now the position is different. The

1. *Ibid.*, pp. 74-75.

authors say: "The theoretic knowledge, in itself indispensable, of the development of the normal mental life, the theory of dreams, the sexual theory and so forth, must be used in practice only insofar as they help to make possible the desired reproduction of the Oedipus relation in the analytic situation, or to make it easier."[1]

That means that the theoretic edifice is not indispensable. However, perhaps the Oedipus and the Electra complexes are. But we might observe that it is perhaps the conflict and the guilt feeling of an earlier stage that is determining and contributing to the present neurosis. To recognise it and relive it with relative detachment and freedom under the guidance and the help of the free mind of the analyst is the essential thing. It brings about a reorientation in the patient and repression is disposed of and the patient becomes a normal person. This is perhaps the real truth of the matter, which needs to be appreciated more and more.

The authors do also affirm that "Theoretic results must be applied mechanically to the theory much less frequently than heretofore, but a constant correction of the theory should result from the new insight gained in practice."[2] And they recognise that "cures can be made with all psycho-therapeutic measures."[3]

They are conscious that in the beginning of the psycho-analytic movement, they achieved wonder cures and later these became less frequent. That was due to the fact that the proper relation between theory and practice was not properly understood. We took certain parts of theory "too literally or too generally".

This is a fine realization even though by a few. Facts discovered by psycho-analysis under certain circumstances are not challenged. It is the generalisations based on them that cause difficulty. The foregoing position of Rank and Ferenczi represents them and their adherents, not Freud and his orthodox followers. Psycho-analysis has become vast and covers very many ramifications.

These developments of Rank and Ferenczi in psycho-analysis are happy. But the goal remains generally an 'economic balance' in personality, a socially accepted normality of life. And all the emphasis on the future, on the wholeness trend and the Self and its activation in analysis are additional trends. However, in Yoga, as

1. *Ibid.*, p. 74.
2. *Ibid.*
3. *Ibid.*, p. 72.

we have said before, the wholeness is not merely an imagined ideal but a fact amenable to experience in the individual, as well as in existence. To turn towards them, to seek their influence, to get into touch with them is the most effective way of achieving wholeness, simplicity and spontaneity in life. Of course, the past burdens of conflicts, repressions, fixations, etc., have to be got rid of. But for Yoga, the will for wholeness should lead to the reconstruction of personality.

The cultural schools of revisionists in psycho-analysis have tended to develop a fuller possibility of personality. Their emphasis is on "Total Personality", on "optimal development of a person's potentialities and the realization of his individuality."[1] And personality is an interpersonal or social product and adjustment to the environment is the essence of the matter. Analysis is seen as an interpersonal process, in which "the analyst is seen as relating to his patient not only with his distorted effects but with his healthy personality also. That is, the analytic situation is essentially a human relationship."[2]

It is said: "Freud grossly underrated the extent to which the individual and his neurosis are determined by conflicts with his environment." Freud's 'biological orientation" led him to concentrate on the phylogenetic and ontogenetic past of the individual: he considered the character as essentially fixed with the fifth or sixth year (if not earlier), and he interpreted the fate of the individual in terms of primary instincts and their vicissitudes, especially sexuality. In contrast, the revisionists shift the emphasis from the past to the present, from the biological to the cultural level, from the constitution of the individual to his environment. "One can understand the biological development better if one discards the concept of libido altogether and instead interprets the different stages in terms of growth and of human relations."[3]

These revisionists are many and quite influential too. But they should be seen with the position represented before by Ferenczi and Rank and the group of orthodox Freudians. Anna Freud, Freud's daughter, was an eminent psycho-analyst, who collaborated with Earnst Jones in England in psycho-analytic work.

---

1. Herbert Marcuse, *Eros and Civilization*, p. 235, Vintage Books, New York.
2. *Ibid.*, p. 229.
3. *Ibid.*, pp. 226-27.

Abraham was an early collaborator of Freud and a creator of the analytic theory. Jung too stands in close sympathy with Freud even though his overall standpoint is different. Adler too was an early colleague of Freud, though he later deviated from him and developed a different standpoint.

But the revisionists of the cultural or inter-personal schools represented by Erich Fromm, Karen Horney and Harry Stack Sullivan have adopted a new basic standpoint, a social and a cultural one, in place of the biological and genetic one of Freud.

Regarding sex in life and neurosis, here is an explicit denial. Says Fromm: "Sexual problems, although they may sometimes prevail in the symptomatic picture, are no longer considered to be in the dynamic centre of neuroses. Sexual difficulties are the effect rather than the cause of the neurotic character structure. Moral problems on the other hand gain in importance."[1] The Oedipus complex too is now interpreted as a desire to be protected, secure – a child, and no more an incest wish for mother or father. Thus the 'Cultural School' of revisionists are professedly revisionists, but they take up a standpoint and an approach of environmental determinism of life in place of one of the unconscious conflicts and repressions. And this makes them look so different from Freud, different in the very spirit of the matter.

Psycho-analysis has been undoubtedly a powerful movement of thought, which started as a technique of cure for mental disorders, hysteria, anxiety and others. But it developed into a view of human nature and then of civilisation and culture. Its earliest formulations had their excesses and over-generalisations. Those were progressively modified by Freud himself, by his brilliant original colleagues and later by his followers. The cultural school among his followers has changed Freud's position drastically. But it is a powerful movement of thought, ever throwing up new ideas.

But it has not had an impact of Yoga. Jung's Analytic Psychology has had that impact and of deeper spiritual experiences expressed in religious life and otherwise, as his thought and the work of the Jungian Analysts show. Jungian Analysis helps mental patients to recover social normality but it also shows the way to life's perfectibility. Psycho-analysis has yet to contemplate this larger dimension of life seriously. That will mean a very great

1. *Ibid.*, p. 246.

enrichment of its thought and capabilities, when that comes about.

Freud wrote "An Autobiographical Study", which is a plain, matter-of-fact account of his life and work. It ends on a modest note as follows: "Looking back – over the patchwork of my life's labours, I can say that I have made many beginnings and thrown out many suggestions. Something will come of them in the future, though I cannot myself tell whether it will be much or little. I can, however, express a hope that I have opened up a pathway for an important advance in our knowledge."[1]

Surely, Freud opened up a pathway which has yielded knowledge of the antecedents of neurosis and many other facts. But is purpose not the more important thing in life and existence? And is it not relevant to the understanding of facts? Sri Aurobindo has asked, does the secret of the lotus flower exist in the mud from which it rises or the form and the beauty it embodies?

Supplement

CHANGES IN FREUD IN HIS OWN WORDS

Freud's views underwent modifications repeatedly and then there have been deviations and revisions too. Hence it is not easy to know Freud's final position definitely. His "Autobiographical Study", published in 1935, four years before his death, gives a clear statement of the changes, in his own words, which is extremely helpful. It is given below. Also another passage, which shows that Freud was temperamentally not given to speculation.

(1)

"There is no more urgent need in psychology than for a securely founded theory of the instincts on which it might then be possible to build further. Nothing of the sort exists, however, and psychoanalysis is driven to making tentative efforts towards some such theory. It began by drawing a contrast between the ego instincts (the instinct of self-preservation, hunger) and the libidinal instincts (love), but later replaced it by a new contrast between narcissistic

---

1. Sigmund Freud, *An Autobiographical Study*, pp. 129-30, Hogarth Press, London.

and object-libido. This was clearly not the last word on the subject; biological consideration seemed to make it impossible to remain content with assuming the existence of only a single class of instincts.

"In the works of my later years (*Beyond the Pleasure principle, Group Psychology and the Analysis of the Ego*, and *The Ego and the Id*), I have given free rein to the inclination which I kept down for so long to speculation and I have also taken stock of a new solution of the problem of the instincts. I have combined the instincts for self-preservation and for the preservation of the species under the concept of Eros and have contrasted with it an instinct of death or destruction which works in silence. Instinct in general is regarded as a kind of elasticity of living things, an impulsion towards the restoration of a situation which once existed but was brought to an end by some external disturbance. This essentially conservative character of instincts is exemplified by the phenomena of the compulsion to repeat. The picture which life presents to us is the result of the working of Eros and the death-instinct together and against each other."[1]

(2)

"I should not like to create an impression that during this last period of my work, I have turned my back upon patient observation and have abandoned myself entirely to speculation. I have on the contrary always remained in the closest touch with the analytic material and have never ceased working at detailed points of clinical or technical importance. Even when I have moved away from observation, I have carefully avoided any contact with philosophy proper. This avoidance has been greatly facilitated by constitutional incapacity. I was always open to the ideas of G.T. Fechner and have followed that thinker upon many important points. The large extent to which psycho-analysis coincides with the philosophy of Schopenhauer... not only did he assert the dominance of the emotions and the supreme importance of sexuality but he was even aware of the mechanism of repression... is not to be traced to my acquaintance with his teaching. I read Schopenhauer very late in my life. Nietzsche, another philosopher

---

1. *Ibid.*, pp. 104-5.

whose guesses and intuitions often agree in the most astonishing way with the laborious findings of psycho-analysis, was for a long time avoided by me on that very account; I was less concerned with the question of priority than with keeping my mind unembarrassed."[1]

---

1. *Ibid.*, pp. 109-10.

PART THREE

INTEGRAL PERSONALITY AND LIFE

CONTENTS

Section I

Integral Personality and Life

Integral Personality and its Great Possibilities for Man and His Culture	259
Yoga, Science and Man	264
Human Resources and Reserves of Energy: Their Full Extent, Their Mobilisation	270

Section II

Integral Personality and the Pursuit of Philosophy, Social and Political Life, Culture, Religion and Science and Technology

The Individual, the Universal and the Transcendent: The Three Key Terms	273
The Philosophical Issue	275
The Social and Political Thought	278
The Cultural Issue	282
The Religious Issue	287
Science and Technology in Environmental Management	290

Section III

Integral Personality and Bodily Health and Excellence

Health and Happiness	292
The Ideal of Physical Education	295
Physical Culture and Spiritual Progress	299

Section IV

Integral Personality and Mental Health and Excellence

Yoga and the Pursuit of Health and Perfection of Life	301
Integral Psycho-therapy	308

Section V

Integral Personality and Education

What should be our Philosophy of Education? And our View of Man, the Whole Man?	313
Integral Education: The Revolution It Seeks	316
Educational Psychology	318
Education as a Normal Social Function	321

Section VI

Integral Personality and Creative Activity ... 323

(In Art, Literature, Music, Crafts and Life generally)

Section VII

Integral Personality and the Future ... 333

Section I

INTEGRAL PERSONALITY AND LIFE

INTEGRAL PERSONALITY AND ITS GREAT POSSIBILITIES FOR MAN AND HIS CULTURE

Sri Aurobindo's view of personality is both a systematisation and an elaboration of the past Indian views on the subject and, being supported by fresh yogic exploration and experience, it acquires a great significance for the present. To Sri Aurobindo too, the mind is an outer formation, produced by nature and adapted as an instrument of action on nature. The real personality is the spirit within. However, while the past Indian philosophy has regarded it as an unchanging soul, Sri Aurobindo affirms it as a fact of evolution and calls it the psychic consciousness. This psychic consciousness is, according to him, slowly growing up as a potentiality and is due for expression as an actuality in life in the normal course of things. This makes a great deal of difference so far as the previous position is concerned. The spirit is not indifferent to and detached from our normal life, but involved in it and seeking to express itself in it. This spiritual principle, which is of itself seeking expression, would naturally admit of an easier realisation or at least would be directly helpful in the transformation of existing life. Soul as substance, detached and independent, however, is not denied but that is affirmed as another fact of personality serving as its static basis. The psychic being is the dynamic counterpart of it. This is one capital point in Sri Aurobindo's view of personality.

Another is the relation of the unconscious, the conscious and the superconscious. Evolution, cosmic and individual, is a basic principle with Sri Aurobindo. All nature is moving up towards higher and higher levels of consciousness: out of unconscious matter has emerged life and out of subconscious and semiconscious life has emerged the mind of man. The unconscious is, therefore, progressively becoming conscious and the conscious rising to higher degrees of consciousness, which are now superconscious to us. The whole process is determined teleologically, by a pull and attraction of the superconscious states. However, the growth of consciousness is a difficult and slow process since the unconscious offers resistance and seeks to persist in its own action. This is the principle of operation in personality, by the fact that a progressive growth of consciousness does take place and that at the higher stages of growth, the attraction of the superconscious states tends to become clearer, the chief causal factor of personality are the ends and goals of the superconscious. This gives a new orientation and movement and thereby accords to the 'teleological determination' and 'goal-seekingness' its full validation.

Western psychology normally does not even recognise the fact of the superconscious. A psychologist like Jung too, who has made illuminating studies of yogic practice and affirms progressive integration as almost the law of personality, contends that the 'wholeness', of which admittedly the yogis are 'pastmasters', is reducible to the unconscious. But the unconscious, which is essentially 'Chaotic' in character, could not in the same breath be credited with the quality of wholeness. Besides, in an evolutionary process, if there is a past and a present, there must also be a future, unless we affirm that the process has entirely run its course. The human consciousness is, in fact, a superconscious state to that of the animal and likewise there must be states of yet higher order to the present human consciousness. The yogic discipline is able to demonstrate these in individuals and what is achieved in such cases is surely indicative of racial possibilities.

The superconscious has been the special field of exploration and mastery for Sri Aurobindo and he has identified many successive levels of it reaching up to that of the completest integration, which he has called the Supermind. The significance of this work is really tremendous. It gives a new basic orientation to personality, releases new forces for the growth of human capacity and character and creates new prospects for the cultural advancement of the race as a whole.

Sri Aurobindo has also identified a further part of personality and yogically demonstrated its reality as a fact. This is what he has called the subliminal in personality. The normal personality, which plays up in interaction with the environment, is a self sharply set against a non-self. It is a finite particular in the language of philosophy. Now if an individual, by a progressive self-dissociation, separates himself from this finite self-hood, he may discover within himself a form of consciousness which is felt as widely continuous with others. Here we participate in the universal consciousness and then get into direct contact with other minds. This consciousness is not superconscious to our individual mind, but is of the same level and order though universal in character. Extra-sensory phenomena of psychical research and parapsychology, which are causing so much perplexity, are to Sri Aurobindo primarily the behaviour and action of the subliminal in human personality. This part is, in some personalities, normally more active and therefore they are able to display extra-sensory capacity. But it admits of cultivation as the superconscious states do.

This is a broad outline of the view of human personality, which Indian philosophy, in the person of Sri Aurobindo, has contributed to the subject. This view, by virtue of its wide comprehensiveness and due appreciation of the different aspects of personality, can truly be called the integral view of personality. It can easily accommodate, within its broad scope, the Western science of psychology as a most useful body of knowledge of the outer personality, of the environment-dependent mind and of the subconscious. And in doing so, it will give it the larger perspective of the integral personality – in particular, the determining orientation of the superconscious. In this, the gain of the integral view too would be great. It will get annexed to it a vast body of detailed knowledge of the interrelations of the organism to the environment.

Evidently this is a posibility of a great and wide synthesis in the knowledge of human personality. A corresponding synthesis in the objective life of human culture will also go with it. And that will mean a reorientation of whole life through a reorientation of human personality.

For vividness, a spontaneous wholeness of perception, we may represent Integral Personality diagramatically as follows:

The terms Superconscient, conscient, subconscient and inconscient are preferred by Sri Aurobindo in place of the terms Superconscious, conscious, subconscious and the unconsciousness to denote the dynamic character of the facts concerned. The Inner Being is the same thing as the subliminal behind or inside of the body, life and mind, three large concentric zones, – and the True Being may be put next to the central circle, the inmost fact of the Psychic Being. It has the quality of the psychic being and therefore it is called true being. The outermost zone represents a consciousness, ordinarily not cultivated and developed, which envelops the individual and through which environmenal influences must pass to enter into it. A disease can sometimes be felt as 'coming in' though yet outside. If the envelope is awake and active, the disease may be counteracted more easily while it is yet outside.

We are ordinarily conscious in a very small part of ourselves and are, therefore, not able to command the larger resources of our personality. We also look outwards and our dealings are with the environment. We have become conscious at least scientifically though not individually and also look backwards or past-wards and we also talk of tapping the unconscious, which is no doubt a real accession of strength to the personality. For the discovery of the central fact of personality, the psychic consciousness, which is the true integrating factor corresponding to Jung's 'Centre', we have to cultivate an inward look, the *Antarmukha* of Indian philosophy. The resources that this inward look and the centre yield are revolutionary to psychology, as then consciousness and personality become self-existent and the environment-dependent consciousness an outer part of it for external adjustments. For the discovery and appreciation of the superconscious, an uplook, a future-orientedness, a hope for new integrations of life has to be cultivated. This involves a progressive disassociation from dependence on the past, the unconscious, and the hard mechanism of life. This dimension of the Superconscious holds the highest and the widest resources of life, of universality and transcendence. This holds the key to the future progress of man, individually and collectively.

The integral personality is the most important basic contribution of Sri Aurobindo to psychology and thereby to human knowledge and culture as a whole. Ultimate Reality stands unknown and unknowable to most of Western philosophy. This has to be no doubt so, if the discursive mind is the only faculty available to man. But ultimate reality is not unknowable to the psychic being and the superconscious range of personality. It is most interesting how the discovery of integral personality shows the way of solving the so-called insoluble problems of philosophy.

This discovery also helps overcome partialities or limitations in other fields of knowledge and life.

It can show to science its rightful place in life as a pursuit of the laws and resources of phenomenal reality through reason, a pursuit which must be subordinated to the good of the integral man, to the overall unifying ultimate reality behind the phenomena. Science is a part of life, but without the context of the whole of reality and the whole of man, it becomes an aberration of life.

Culture is the dearest asset of man. But cultures have different qualities involving a predominant emphasis on some aspects or aspect of personality. Now integral personality raises the possibility of an integral culture of man towards which all particular cultures of human history can become valuable contributions.

Again, religions have presented to man a serious problem and the problem becomes specially acute, since each religion claims an absoluteness for itself. And there is a real truth in this position, since each experience of the Absolute would have the quality of absoluteness. But this happens to the limited finite mind of man. This limited mind gets overwhelmed by the least touch of the Absolute. But the integral personality has a much larger capacity. It can see the truth of each such perception and yet asks for an integral perception of the Absolute. What a possibility is here opened for appreciating the truth of each religion and showing the possibility of a fuller experience of God, the absolute existence.

For education, the conception of integral personality is immediately indispensable, since it alone can show how integration of personality, the actual ideal of education today, is possible.

Thus integral personality is a supreme value for man and all his pursuits. But this needs the harnessing of the resources of yoga to ordinary life. Ordinary life has to be enlarged, widened, deepened, heightened. Then alone can the greater resources of life become available.

YOGA, SCIENCE AND MAN

Yoga

Yoga is the science and art of self-perfection, of bringing forth the deepest and the largest potentialities of man, of the realisation of the highest, the supreme fact of existence – God, Truth, Ultimate Reality. The approaches to the Infinite must necessarily be infinite and indeed many have been the yogas and the lines of sadhana with distinctive approaches, but all aiming at some higher possibilities of man and his life.

In the contemporary life, the interest in yoga grows phenomenally strong both in India and the world. We see an increasing number of people turning to yoga and experimenting with its physical and psychological practices.

In the West, apart from the interest in yoga, many new trends in philosophy, science, literature, art and socio-political life have appeared, which represent a seeking and appreciation of the deeper and psychological truths of life. The rise of psychology and the psychological values is almost universal. The appreciation of the "Gestalt" and the "Whole" is interesting. Parapsychology and telepathy are striking. "Silent diplomacy" was a wonderful innovation. Detente and reconciliation are highly impressive. Appreciation of the necessity of world unity too is undeniable. And there is much more otherwise. All this creates a climate favourable to the pursuit, realisation and enjoyment of the spiritual values of life and gives a new positive direction to the life of the people.

Yoga is really a search into the deeper facts of conscious life. It is, as Sri Aurobindo says, "a plunge into the profundities of the soul." As such, it gives a methodology for the investigation of all human problems, whether of psychology or philosophy or religion or therapy (physical or mental) or socio-political behaviour. The reason is that consciousness and attitudes are involved in all these and one can take a superficial and an external view of things as also a deeper and an inner one. A deeper view, which can go to the root of the matter, will evidently have a better chance of controlling the phenomenon. The motivations and attitudes much influence and determine our thinking. Now, ideas by themselves present one kind of picture under logical considerations, but quite another when viewed in the light of the conscious and subconscious motivations of the person concerned. But what is more important in the methodology of yoga is that it reveals planes of experience other than those of sense-experience and rational thought. And the problems of these planes, proving almost insoluble, find an easy solution in the light of a higher plane and its experience. Problems of philosophy and of religious creeds, found baffling and embarrassing at the rational level, can be found so simple in the light of the unitary spiritual experience.

Even in science, the approach of a deeper poise is a matter for serious trial in contrast to that of external superficial observation. The deeper poise can give an inner identification and feeling for a vaster field and lead to fruitful suggestions, which could then be tested by analytical observation.

Yoga, as method of approach, is a powerful instrument, not much tried so far except in the spiritual field, but full of promise for the future.

Science

Science, as a cultural trend of life, arose in Europe in the 16th century in reaction to religion and asserted the right of human 'reason' to seek and know truth on its own. Religion had peremptorily demanded faith in the supra-physical. Science, in revolt, affirmed the physical (external nature) as the sole valid field of knowledge and Reason as the sole valid instrument of knowledge. The spirit of free inquiry was a joy to the suppressed soul of Europe and it spread quickly. Sensational discoveries and inventions opened up a large new vision of life and uptill the First World War, the faith in science was a rising tide – "Science can solve all problems." The First World War shook that faith and the Second raised fears of total annihilation and brought about a chronic state of crisis in general life. Even after the Second World War, great new discoveries and inventions have been made. Space exploration, landing on the moon, advances in medicine, genetics, etc., are striking examples. But the general life is stricken with fear ever so much.

Science has been so far mainly interested in the physical, chemical and the biological phenomena and it is only in physics that it has reached far enough to touch almost the ultimate. Rise of psychology was a new departure in science, the attention, instead of being directed on 'the other' and 'the external', turned upon itself: man sought to know himself. Of Matter, Life and Mind, the three great facts of nature, science knows matter well enough, life not yet enough and mind and consciousness the least. Our contemporary civilisation is primarily a representation of our capability regarding matter. When life gets known better, things are bound to change and when mind gets known in its turn, things will take on another character.

Scientific inquiry suffers from serious limitations. It limits itself to the phenomenon and to sense-observation and rational activity and does not even yet recognise that the phenomenon cannot be divorced from the noumenon, the ultimate reality, and that intuition can be a valid instrument of knowledge. It seeks a larger synthesis but stands committed to analysis and division. Integrality of things escapes it and it gets involved in imbalances of things.

Sri Aurobindo sums up the work and the final position of science in these words:

"Man has created a system of civilisation which has become too big for his limited mental capacity and understanding and his still more limited spiritual and moral capacity to utilise and manage, a too dangerous servant of his blundering ego and its appetites. ...Science has put at his disposal many potencies of the universal Force and has made the life of humanity materially one; but what uses this universal Force is a little human individual or communal ego with nothing universal in its light of knowledge or its movements, no inner sense or power which would create in this physical drawing together of the human world a true life-unity, a mental unity or a spiritual oneness.... Reason and Science can only help by a standardising, by fixing everything into an artificially arranged and mechanised unity of material life. A greater whole-being, whole-knowledge, whole-power is needed to weld all into a greater unity of whole-life." (*SABCL*, Vol. 19, pp. 1053-55)

But the spirit of free inquiry and dedication to truth and objectivity of science have been a great training for man and it has now advanced far enough almost to step into the realm of spiritual facts, of a soul in man, and a will and consciousness in the universe. And yoga is, indeed, a link between science and spirituality. Religion seeks to lead the masses towards spiritual facts and has to make all sorts of compromises with ordinary human nature. But yoga seeks soul and God and perfection and peace as objective facts of experience and is easily separable from religious faith and ritual and social observances. Psychology and yoga are, therefore, the natural culmination of the growth of the scientific spirit. Already science shows signs of discovering more effective ways of knowledge, which are quicker and more integral in their grasp of truth. Yoga, scientifically pursued and developed, could bring a wonderful fulfilment to science and contemporary scientific civilisation.

In the field of psychology, Jung's affirmation, on scientific grounds, of a 'Centre' in personality apart from the normal ego-personality, an integrating force, is a perception comparable to the yogic affirmation of the spirit or soul in man. And Sir James Jeans' affirmation of a universal will behind matter is comparable to the yogic affirmation of a universal spirit. But, to Jung and Jeans, their affirmations are inferences, even though well founded, whereas, to yoga, soul and God are facts of verifiable experience.

Man

Man's acutest problem today is his inner conflict and lack of confidence in life, i.e., absence of meaning in self-existence and joy in the pursuit of life. He feels vague, unsure, without purpose and a positive feeling for life. The existentialist philosophy with its emphasis on anxiety is a reflection of the contemporary mood of man. We blame education, we blame society and the cultural situation for our deep discontentment and try many alternatives hoping to get a solution of the problem. But the alternatives, even when achieved with great difficulty, soon wear out and the discontent persists as before. But yoga has an interesting insight to offer. It knows that human personality is a vast and a varied fact. It has a surface consciousness, which is concerned with the surface impressions of the environment and is dependent on them for its satisfactions. Now this consciousness basically lacks security and self-existence. It is all dependent on the fleeting impressions of the environment. When we are predominantly identified with this consciousness, then we are much subject to insecurity and anxiety. But if we try to live more deeply and draw back from our projectionist posture, our feeling about our self undergoes change. We feel an inner assurance of existence, as it were. And if we go deeper still we can ultimately land upon a sure ground of self-existence, which entirely changes our orientation of life and makes it a delightful adventure.

What an insight it is! Is it not a real answer to the existentialist philosopher? And it is thoroughly verifiable. We argue without end and come to no clarity and yoga says: practice deeper poise within yourself, restrain yourself from too projected a posture of life and you will discover all the joy of your existence. Our education and culture are landed today in great perplexity. But yoga is sure and clear. It says: your posture of consciousness needs correction and then the whole world will acquire a new meaning. Your life will become meaningful and so will the world around you. It also says: try and see it for yourself. Yoga can very well be said to be the key to our life. It opens up to us our own inner hidden treasures of joy, which enable us to discover corresponding hidden treasures of joy in the external world and then all existence becomes wonderful. When we live too superficially, try to control and enjoy things superficially, we feel insecure and lost.

Persistent anxiety, insecurity, inner conflict and tension have created in our contemporary cultural life its very worst symptom, in the form of a wide incidence of mental disorder. This phenomenon is the worst commentary on our contemporary living. Modern psycho-therapy is rendering considerable help, but the problem is awfully challenging and the remedy is difficult and partial. Right here yoga has a special possibility. The problem of the mentally affected person is inner peace and harmony. Now, yoga particularly affirms a core of inner peace and joy. The ordinary psycho-therapeutic practice seeks to eliminate or reduce the intensity of the subconscious conflict by raising it to the level of consciousness. A degree of detachment is thus brought about. But if a spirit of indulgence operates, then free association or reliving of the past experience does not succeed. But yoga claims to be able to activate the deeper core of peace. Now that could be a strong positive factor to restore harmony. A psycho-synthesis could thus come to the aid of a psycho-analysis or even act by itself. This possibility could also be considered in connection with the problem of public mental health.

On the preventive side, yoga offers even a more important possibility. Mental disorder is ultimately rooted in desires, their frustrations and their conflicts. If we are able to manage our desires intelligently, then inner difficulties can be much obviated.

Yoga, in fact, suggests in the pursuit of innner peace a progressive detachment from desires. That really creates a way of life which can prevent mental disorders. This aspect is even more important for realising a more enjoyable state of cultural life.

Science had, at one time, opened up a new horizon of life, of free inquiry and of mastery over nature. The charm of that vision is now almost exhausted and its attraction has become dubious. We now need another horizon and prospect of life. And yoga offers such a one. It says, it is possible to develop in ourselves marvellous new attitudes and capacities of knowledge, love and will, and create for ourselves an infinitely richer world and happier living. This vision has to become a vivid feeling and it will surely release a vast creative energy in the world.

HUMAN RESOURCES AND RESERVES OF ENERGY: THEIR FULL EXTENT, THEIR MOBILISATION

(A Contribution to a Symposium)

Man is made up of many parts and each part has its own resources and reserves of energy, original (by birth) and cultivated. The body, the biological life part and the mind. Each has an original endowment and then a cultivated asset. And then how these stand in their individual and collective organisation, harmonious or burdened with inner conflicts and tensions.

Then there is a contact with the deeper individual and the larger universal spiritual resources of life and their contributions of peace, harmony and inexhaustible resources of energy.

Such is the overall picture of man and his resources and reserves of energy.

The normal personality of body, life and mind, or familiar personality, is basically environment-dependent and therefore the conditions of the environment, favourable and unfavourable, do affect the mobilisation of its resources of energy. The inner composition of personality, its harmoniousness, its wholesomeness is a basic fact favourable to the energy assets of a person. To that come the inner contacts with the spiritual facts of life and existence.

All this is much demonstrated by the following facts of life, which are easily available.

1. A peaceful and a calm person is ordinarily capable of a larger output of work. Fatigue does not come to him easily and when it comes, he is able to overcome it soon. And he is able to work continually without needing intervals of rest for recoupment, as is usually necessary.

Such a person can more easily develop his inner spiritual contacts and then his capacity of work and resources of energy would increase a great deal.

2. Violation of the above conditions leads to numerous consequences of the contrary type, which too can be easily observed. For example:

(a) a person with dissatisfaction with himself and the environment, official or familial or otherwise, i.e., in a state of conflicts and tensions, will get tired soon and lack concentration in work.

Such a person would be wasting his energy in inner conflicts and tensions and would be having less energy for work.

(b) Talkativeness can be observed as dissipation and wastage of energy. On the other hand, silence and quietude as helpful to concentration and conservation of energy and effectivity.

(c) People who often look tired are persons lacking in inner peace and quietude. And there are also people who look fresh even after a whole day's continuous work.

One can also consider how the energy resources of a person may be increased. A high purpose in life has an integrative influence, it creates harmony and conservation of energy. Ordinarily, we try to give incentives. They give a bit of purpose, but it feeds the demanding attitude and leads to more demands by the worker. A disinterested high purpose works differently.

To create a state of civilisation favourable to the creation of a harmonious personality capable of spiritual reinforcements is a wonderful possibility both for the individual and the society. It is difficult to achieve but that surely sets the goal to human living.

Jung's *The Integration of the Personality* throws a most interesting light on the 'wholeness' quality of personality, the limitations of the ego-personality, its polarities, its conventions, its archetypes of the unconscious and also on the possibilities of transcending them. All that would clarify a good deal of our subject.

Freud's investigations into the repressions and suppressions of a life show how life's energies get jeopardised.

By the side of these studies of man as he is, stand the approach and working of the varied yogic disciplines as to what man is capable of becoming and the process involved in that.

We talk of tapping the unconscious today. And indeed that means much additional energy. To harness the energies of the unconscious of the individual and more so of the society is a wonderful possibility for development and general progress. But to be able to tap and harness the superconscious is a greater secret which needs to be duly considered and utilised.

Our present position of scientific progress gives us primarily the energies of 'Matter' and in a limited way of 'Life'. Our knowledge of Mind is yet mainly of its reactions to environmental conditions. When psychology comes to its own and is able to give a confident knowledge of mind and consciousness, our life is bound to undergo a radical change. The resources of the unconscious and the superconscious would add immense energies to those of our present superficial personality, which is also too dependent on the environment and subject to external conditions.

The existentialist philosophy, which seems to give to the present world its orientation of life and existence, unfortunately takes man as he finds himself in the much mechanised industrial life of rush and competition, involving anxiety and lacking in freedom. But this predicament is of the superficial ego-personality. The larger resources of personality offer a different possibility, a possibility of peace and quietude in the midst of activity, of inner detachment and freedom and of independence of circumstances.

"Human Resources Management and Development" is a new subject for science and even for psychology. Its possibilities are unlimited and it needs to be pursued and deeply investigated.

Section II

INTETGRAL PERSONALITY AND THE PURSUIT OF PHILOSOPHY, SOCIAL AND POLITICAL LIFE, CULTURE, RELIGION AND SCIENCE AND TECHNOLOGY

THE INDIVIDUAL, THE UNIVERSAL AND THE TRANSCENDENT: THE THREE KEY TERMS

Life and existence, when taken comprehensively, appear to involve three terms or dimensions – the finite individual, the universal nature, and the transcendent Reality. The finite individual, a stone, a plant, an animal, a human being are familiar facts of normal experience. They constitute our world. But the vast nature comprising the physical phenomena, the animal kingdom, and the human society, is less frequently contemplated but is a reality in its own right, a universal reality, of which the finite individuals are particularisations representing the same universal reality in individual nuances.

But the individual and the universal realities show many gradations of being, broadly represented by matter, life and mind. And there is a clear indication of a process, a movement, an evolution in these. And mind, by no means, seems to be an end-term, a finished organisation. It is deeply marked by division and conflict and points to a state of unity, a harmony, a more perfect organisation. Evidently, there must be 'a higher', 'a possible', 'a more perfect', and perhaps 'the most perfect' as a definite side and dimension to the individual and the universal.

The nature and the being of these three and their mutual relations is the crux of the matter in the understanding of the diverse issues of life. A true appreciation of the nature of the individual, the universal, and the transcendent, and a harmonious and balanced relationship between them can be the yard-stick with which to measure and assess the success and achievement of a philosophical system and of a cultural status and growth. It is a most interesting pursuit to study philosophical systems, Western and Eastern as also the cultures of the world, past and present, with this perspective of three dimensions of experience and existence. There are systems which show a high appreciation of the universal, almost to the neglect of the individual and the transcendent and they tend to become pantheistic or monistic of a particular type. There are then those that are preoccupied with the truth of the individual: a pluralism is then the natural consequence. There are again those to which the transcendent is almost the whole and the essence of existence. The individual and the universal there get undermined and the empirical reality becomes a problem.

The cultures too have had their emphasis on the one or the other and even the same culture might exercise different emphases at different periods of its history.

Indian culture, from its foundations in the Vedas, has shown a vivid appreciation of the transcendent as the real reality dominating and determining the rest. The empirical life, however, is much appreciated in Vedic times and a fine balance and proportion seems to have been achieved among the individual, the universal and the transcendent. But the Upanishads become fairly marked out in two lines, one emphasising and carrying forward the Vedic balance and the other getting more preoccupied with the transcendent and showing a relative lack of appreciation of the individual and the universal. The latter philosophical thought of India has predominantly been more drawn towards the transcendent. However, there have been philosophical systems which have represented the other trend of the Upanishads too.

Indian cultural life, in its long history, has had naturally many different emphases according to the conditions of its inner urge and aspiration and the external socio-political circumstances. Recent Hinduism, since the time of Dayananda Saraswati and Ram Mohan Roy, reinvigorated by many other outstanding spiritual and religious personalities, has been reorienting and recreating itself and getting into a fresh form of faith and confidence regarding the entire situation of life.

The major line of recreation has been the growth of an attitude and interest in empirical life, the world, the individual, the amelioration of circumstances, the civic and political life, the general social conditions. The impact of the West has been the dominant influence in all this. However, under the present circumstances, the Indian values of the individual and the universal have also been coming to the fore. Dayananda, for example, recaptured and forcefully represented the Vedic balance.

THE PHILOSOPHICAL ISSUE

The real issue for Indian philosophy, covering most of the influential schools exercising a living sway over Indian minds, is a clear thinking out of the relation of the transcendent with the individual and the universal. The transcendent is no doubt the absolute reality, but the empirical fact cannot be outside it and must be in some way intimately connected with it. This is the essential position to get clear about. If the empirical is in some way intimately connected with it, then the empirical can lead on to That as also be a medium of its expression. And in the empirical field, the individual and the universal have again to be clearly inter-related. The individual is a particularisation of the universal. The particularisation is a clear fact and so is also the universality of the phenomenon. The individual has, therefore, to live and grow in his individuality and uniqueness, but with a clear sense of solidarity with the universal. And the two together live and grow, in an increasing measure, in a sense of solidarity and relationship with the transcendent.

These are the philosophical issues progressively taking shape in Indian thought and mind, but needing to be elaborately stated and worked out in our relation to science and technology, international relations, national life and other issues of contemporary living.

Various Approaches In Philosophy

Man must seek the Real and be himself a vibrant Reality. That is an inalienable urge of human nature even when expressed in a few persons. The quality of this urge has a wide uplifting influence on humanity generally. However, this urge is difficult and not easy to sustain continually. The moods of pragmatism, positivism, agnosticism and the like are natural. But the urge for the Ultimate, the Absolute, the Final and the last in existence does assert itself again and again in the individual as also in humanity.

The Greeks had thought of philosophy as the search for wisdom, but in Plato, the representative figure, it did culminate in the search for the Real, the world of ideas.

Hegel called philosophy 'the thinking consideration of things'. But why should the philosophical urge to know things be subjected to the limitation of 'thinking'? Is this urge not of an absolute kind, of knowing things in whatever way and degree we can? The very touch of the Real is necessary to feel and enjoy Reality ourselves. Thinking is, after all, a phenomenal activity in man, directly serviceable for dealing with the universal phenomena. And the Real, the noumena, may well be not responsive to 'thinking'. Did Kant not say that we can 'know' things-in-themselves but cannot think of them since the categories of understanding are inapplicable there. Even in ordinary sense-perception, we know, we are aware of things and we may not think of them. So philosophy may be a deeper awareness of things, but not a 'thinking consideration' of them.

Wittgenstein has, in recent times, taken a stand that the philosophical judgments are not expressible in language, hence philosophy is not possible. An influential school of Logical Positivism has in consequence come up, which has made a useful study of the capabilities of language. This is all fine, but can we eradicate the human need for the Real, the urge to know and to be that? And is the expression in language, adequately, a necessity? Is the satisfaction of the human need not the essential fact? And in the past, has the attempt not been made to express the Real, the Ultimate, the Infinite and recreate a language and a symbolism for the same? For a mood of positivism and agnosticism, logical positivism has, no doubt, a justification.

Let us seriously consider whether philosophy, as an unhampered and free search for the Real, can possibly harmonise all the varied approaches to philosophy or not, and also restore to philosophy a rich creativity in recognising the possibility of infinite approaches to the Infinite and infinite elaborations in thought and language, however inadequate they be. If there is at the core a certitude of perception, it will certainly afford a deep satisfaction and all creations will be enrichment of our knowledge of the Infinite, the Ultimate, the Real.

What is man? – and who is it that philosophises and seeks to know the Real? Is man just mind plus body or something more? The Gita regards 'body', 'mind' and 'soul' (śarīra, prāṇa, manas and ātman) as the major factors in human personality. The Upanishads affirm five sheaths or levels of being in man – body, life, mind, vijnana (the plane which directly knows the truth) and delight (the essential joy of existence). Here is a much larger conception of personality. Sri Aurobindo has elaborated this in great detail into a form of integral personality. Now, in this integral personality, there are parts which, when cultivated, give us an intimate experience of the Real in the individual as in the universe. The mind, in this conception of personality, is an instrument of help for the organism's adjustments with the environment. It is a form of consciousness adapted to external organisation of life, not for apprehending truth of things. The deep-lying unifying spiritual self-existent consciousness is really the principle for knowing the inner unifying truth of things. Thus what remains speculation or inference to mind can be clear direct knowledge to the inner spiritual consciousness. We cannot, therefore, afford to remain ignorant of the more competent parts of our personality for the solution of the anomalies of our mental handling of things.

Sri Aurobindo has contributed a capital idea to contemporary thought for the consideration of man and existence. It is that three terms – the individual, the universal and the transcendent – represent three essential aspects of man and existence, and that all these aspects need to be considered for a due appraisal of both. Man has an individuality, it is in solidarity with the society and general nature, and it has also an aspect of a potentiality of further 'becoming' or a course of future evolution. All the aspects are involved in man and that makes his personality a rich and a complex fact. Similarly, society, nature and existence have to be considered in this fuller manner.

Man becomes thus a transitional being to be evolutionally exceeded and transcended, and so mind has a function with a purpose – for a stage of growth. For the deeper purposes of philosophy, one has to seek other parts of the integral personality capable of intuition and an integral perception of things.

THE SOCIAL AND POLITICAL THOUGHT

In regard to the social thought, the first thing to recognise is that human society, as an empirical fact, which is sustained, supported and inspired by a transcendent Reality, is a field of realisation and manifestation of the same. And that the individual is in unity and essential solidarity with the society as a whole, so that through its growth, it contributes to the good of the whole society, as also is benefited by the state of growth of the whole society. A separation of the individual from the society can be only a limited and partial affair. It cannot be an absolute fact. In body, life and mind, we share in the nature of the universal and an individual does not possess them as absolutely original facts. His soul or the spiritual element is of the same essence and nature as the supreme spirit, which covers and includes all existence. There too, the individual as individual is not an absolute fact. An advanced individual is always limited by the level of the society and it is only as the society advances that more advanced individuals can come into being.

Thus an individual must grow individually, universally and transcendentally, i.e., in his personal unity and integration, in his inner oneness with others, and in his contact and interchange with the transcendent. The society as such must grow in its self-awareness as a social unity, with individuals growing as unique personalities and increasingly expressing the higher consciousness of the transcendent in terms of unity, harmony and mutuality.

In this connection, it will be interesting to observe that individual salvation, the 'moksha' of our philosophies, needs a reconsideration. A liberation from involvements in external nature is the very foundation of spiritual living. A life of desires and involvements is a life of subjection to the objects of desire to which one feels attached and is dependent on. This life is indeed a poor life. But is the liberation or can it ever be, while in life, truly complete and absolute? The liberated person discovers his true identification with the free spirit within him or above him and he enjoys enormous freedom and happiness. But does some identification, limited and secondary though, with his own imperfect body, life and mind, and with the body, life and mind of the universal nature of which he is a part, not continue to persist? And if that does, then our moksha is of a particular degree and quality which needs to be defined. It can be argued that moksha gets perfected only on the soul leaving the body. But a moksha, which is realisable in the body, may also be perfectible in the body. In fact, a mode of existence which offers the opportunity of spiritual freedom would suggest the possibility and inherent intention of spiritual perfectibility. And that would lead to another spiritual possibility, that of collective liberation and perfection.

The actual social thought as it is developing in India at the moment is determined by the ideals of Western democracy. Liberty, equality and fraternity are indeed high ideals. But egoistic pluralism is the wrong foundation for the realisation of these. An egoistic pluralism affirms a basic social reality of a number of self-seeking individuals, without an essential and a basic unity. The unity achievable in such a case can only be a weak and a fluctuating one, dependent on the compatibility or otherwise of diverse and contradictory interests of the individuals.

The reconstruction of social thought suggested above involves an affirmation of the individuality of body, life and mind recognising itself as part of the universal matter, life and mind and the spiritual element as part of the supreme universal Spirit. The egoistic separative selfhood, therefore, is not affirmed as the real truth of life. It is a condition and a circumstance through which the true individuality in its process of growth has to pass. But the more important part of our reconstruction is the relationship with the transcendent, which gives direction and character to our future progress, individual and social. The unity of the transcendent is the unity of the supreme Reality, which is the highest self of all and, therefore, accords to all their highest fulfilment. The egoistic self-seeking personality in its self-giving attention to the universal and transcendent attains qualitatively distinct fulfilments, which are far superior to the satisfactions of the desires which the ego-personality normally seeks. The deeper individuality is in relation of unity with others and intrinsically carries a self-satisfaction in itself. Thus a threefold satisfaction of an abiding quality comes to an individual. A threefold development, individual, universal and transcendent, brings a threefold fulfilment in three essential dimensions of personality and existence.

Western social thought stands on egoistic pluralism, so far as democratic thought is concerned, and socialistic monism, so far as communism is concerned. Of course, the two can be combined in varying degrees and that is what is happening a great deal at the moment. But the normal egoistic personality is the basis in all these cases. However, reason and thought of the egoistic man are accepted as the governing principle of life and an order is sought to be realised through law and rule. But reason is a generalising and abstracting principle and it cannot comprehend concrete and unique wholes of life and deal with them adequately. It must always deal with individuals according to rules, ignoring the individualising factors. Thus an individual cannot in a rational ordering of society receive consideration as individual. The so-called freedom of the individual of democratic thought is really the freedom of the ego to indulge in its separative impulses within certain limits. But this separation inherent in the ego creates its own problems and as a reaction comes into being the socialistic thought which affirms the solidarity of the State as against the freedom of the individual.

The aim of Western social thought, whether democratic or socialistic, is power and material prosperity of life. Scientific research and education too are primarily geared to this aim. Morals and religion are additional and subordinate influences. Contemporary Indian social thought primarily rests on the egoistic pluralism of democratic thought, but combine with it is a strong emphasis of socialistic thought in its conception of a welfare state. The 'welfare' conception in her case is further qualified by the Gandhian emphasis of uniting ethics with politics. This constitutes an original quality in Indian social thought.

But the foundation in all this social thought, Western and Indian, democratic and socialistic, is the egoistic personality and it stands or falls by the merits and demerits of the egoistic personality.

If we take a larger view of Indian philosophy and cultural life and seek to work out a social thought for the present, competent to deal with the problems that confront Indian life and for which it must find a solution, a larger and a deeper conception has to be worked out. And the perspective of the individual, the universal, and the transcendent, and a right relationing of the three is offered here as a possible line of approach.

This perspective will primarily give a few new attitudes, which will mean new creative forces for the recreation of social life. The first is that the egoistic personality is a separative formation of life, serving a subordinate purpose, and not to be cherished as an intrinsic value. The individual selfhood to be cherished is the one that feels and enjoys its solidarity with others, and is sensitive of the higher, and which continually seeks to grow in its individuality as also its universality and its transcendent dimension. The second is that reason is a good organising principle of human consciousness, but incapable of appreciating the individual and promoting individuality and uniqueness and concrete wholes of life and existence. For that, a more integral function of consciousness, a deeper penetrative identification, and a larger synthesising sympathy and understanding are needed. The third is that society is a concrete whole and a unit of existence of which an individual is an essential and inseparable factor, involving a relation of mutual contributoriness in being as well as becoming, in status of existence as also quality of activity. The fourth is that the present statuses of the individual and society are extremely imperfect and that higher and higher qualities of existence lie above them, exercising a pull on them in their growth and development.

These are the basic new attitudes that this perspective of the individual, the universal, and the transcendent is likely to give to us. And it is perfectly possible to try to assess the new values of social living that they can usher in and the effectivity and power they can give to deal with the social problems.

Here we have considered social and political thought with reference to India. But it surely has a wider application to the general human situation.

THE CULTURAL ISSUE

Culture is man's highest possession; it is, in fact, the form of his being, what he has become and is tending to become. It is evidently of the greatest interest to consider its nature, its process, its differentiations and the mode and manner of its growth. Still more interesting is it to consider the life-histories of different cultures, their origin, rise to maturity, decay and death. In this study, one comes across a couple of instances, where through successive self-renewals the cultures seem to enjoy indefinite self-prolongation. The growth of cultures through mutual impacts, friendly or otherwise, is also most interesting. And the phenomenon of death among them through natural decay or through attack of one upon another is evidently very instructive.

A culture, the ensemble of the life of a people, its practical adjustments of life, its crafts, fine arts, literature, philosophy, morals and religion, its social structure and politics seem to constitute an organic growth, intimately connected with the character and the temperament of the people and its geographical situation and historical antecedents. It is in its motive and form as unique as the individual human personality. It is, in fact, the expression and the being of the personality of the people. And, therefore, each culture is a unique value and contribution to the general human culture, the totality of fundamental living wealth of man.

While all cultures are unique expressions of the personalities of the peoples concerned, yet they do admit of a relative evaluation on the basis of the qualities and the degrees of the growth of the personalities. But the individual is always the key to the understanding of the community and humanity. It is the microcosm which unlocks the secrets of the macrocosm, the universal existence. Therefore, we need to understand the individual human personality rather carefully.

The Human Personality

The individual human personality was the object of primary interest to the Upaniṣhadic seers of India, who in the nurseries of their Ashrams, laid the essential foundations of Indian culture. According to them, personality consists of three concentric formations – the material body, the vitality or the life-force and the mind, – the sharira, the prana and the manas – and a luminous centre, the soul or the Atman, which silently controls and directs them. Ordinarily, our identification is all with our body, the life-impulses and the mental activities and, therefore, the soul remains veiled. But the Upanishadic sages, through a profound introspective research, had found that the soul is, by its essential nature and character, its competence of self-existence, the master-principle, whereas the body, the vitality and the mind together constitute a dependent factor, an instrument of action on external nature.

This discovery of the soul as a fact of experience (not as an intellectual conception or a hypothesis), then naturally became the governing factor in the creation and regulation of the cultural life of the individual and community. And, obviously, if the soul is the true master-principle, if it is the true intrinsic value in our life, then its standards alone can guide and regulate the life and action of the body, the vital force and the mind.

We have, it may appear, made a long digression in discussing the nature and character of human personality. But in fact it is not so. Culture is a fact of the personality of man and, therefore, it is of the first importance that we should understand it properly. The ascending levels of body, life, mind and soul of the personality virtually give us a yardstick with which to comparatively evaluate different cultures and properly assess different elements of the same culture.

The perception of the soul, we have said, was the central inspiration of the ancient seers and on this they based Indian culture. The same essential outlook has continued to govern it through all the vicissitudes of its long life. That is why Indian culture has been commonly characterised as spiritual. Ancient Greek culture was primarily intellectual and aesthetic. And modern European culture, which has practically spread over the whole world, has succeeded in creating an enormous material equipment of life, our present paraphernalia of civilisation. Science, which has been the predominant activity of this cultural epoch, has primarily aimed at developing technology and the production of goods which minister to our comfort. That is why it is called materialistic. The source of its chief inspiration is pretty obviously the body and the life-impulse.

The consciousness, which is whole and entire, completely self-poised, is, on the other hand, of distinctly superior quality in all its functions of knowing, willing and feeling. It is not limited to the appearances for an impression of things. It can directly contact their essences. Its grasp is wider and deeper and can, therefore, know totalities and wholes. It is essentially synthetic and intuitive in its action. Its will is integral and its feeling is one of inherent and essential joy.

This consciousness, which has obviously a different quality, is the spiritual consciousness as distinguished from our normal mental consciousness. As an isolated and individual phenomenon, it is known to man the world over. All great mystics and religious leaders have possessed and displayed it in life. But Sri Aurobindo has, in our day, affirmed that the crisis in which mankind finds itself landed is an extreme consequence of the working of the analytical intellect, of mankind having come to identify itself too much with the external and mental consideration of things. And the solutions, which too we are attempting in the mental way, will also not lead us out of our difficulties. The real solution lies in recognising the limitations of our approach and seeking to rise to the larger way of spiritual comprehension of things. He, in fact, sees a purpose of Nature in the deep crisis that we find ourselves in. It is to show the full consequences of the mental way and thereby prepare humanity for further progress, for a step forward in evolution, for a transition from the mental to the spiritual. Thus, according to Sri Aurobindo, Nature herself is getting ready for the next emergence. Matter, life and mind, the so-far achieved terms of evolution, are going to be followed up by Supermind. Sri Aurobindo's call to man is to co-operate with Nature, to help in the realisation of her intention, to become a conscious and knowing participant in her cosmic mission. Thereby he would best find the solution of his problems and discover the true foundations of a new living culture, which will be as integral and whole as the spiritual consciousness is.

Now if a spiritual consciousness is our common human goal, then its wholeness and inclusiveness itself is a proof of the fact that the distinctive experiences of different nations must be complementary contributions to it. One nation can really have no fear of another, but what it seems to contribute by following its own individual development is a unique quality of experience, which must be an additional enrichment to that of the others. On the spiritual consideration, we can thus realise a true unity amidst real diversity. Sri Aurobindo puts the relations of the individual, the community and humanity with great clarity in just a few sentences. He says, "...the law for the individual is to perfect his individuality by free development from within, but to respect and to aid and be aided by the same free development in others. His law is to harmonise his life with the life of the social aggregate and to pour himself out as a force for growth and perfection on humanity. The law for the community or nation is equally to perfect its corporate existence by a free development from within, aiding and taking full advantage of that of the individual, but to respect and to aid and be aided by the same free development of other communities and nations. Its law is to harmonise its life with that of the human aggregate and to pour itself out as a force for growth and perfection of humanity. The law for humanity is to pursue its upward evolution towards the finding and expression of the Divine in the type of mankind, taking full advantage of the free development and gains of all individuals and nations and groupings of men, to work towards the day when mankind may be really and not only ideally one divine family, but even then, when it has succeeded in unifying itself, to respect, aid and be aided by the free growth and activity of its individuals and constituent aggregates." (SABCL, Vol. 15, pp. 63-64)

Here we have a complete scheme of a harmonious living for the whole of humanity with the freedom of the individual and the nations fully guaranteed. And it all rests upon facts of human nature and personality. Today when we seriously think of unity, we want uniformity, i e., sameness or similarity in external behaviour. But insistence on uniformity kills inner creation and therefore the force of life and existence. Uniformity for a time may itself give material for creative work, but the freedom of the spirit will before long assert itself and break up the shackles of imposed uniformity. Or else the spirit, failing to find room for its exercise, will withdraw and what we shall be left with is an uncreative community existing by no greater force than its physical inertia. A living and a creative unity has to be a unity in diversity and in the spiritual consideration of things, we can more easily appreciate, realise and work it out. In the mental way, uniformity is naturally the first suggestion, because reason is accustomed to classification and standardisation; without that, as it were, it cannot comprehend things.

The Separatist Tendencies

We also complain a great deal of the separatist tendencies today. They are again an interesting symptom of our cultural situation. They evidently show an exclusive instead of an inclusive way of looking at things. But imposition of uniformity is no solution. It is a reaction and is suppressive in effect. Separatist tendencies can surely be frivolous, just encouraged by egoistic fancy. But they can as well be real and when they are so, they naturally mean a demand for the expression of an individuality and a personality. And this demand must be conceded in the interest of the totality itself, because the part concerned may, through such development, be able to contribute something unique. However, the part must also recognise that it is a part and not the integer without which it would become unreal.

The foregoing exposition has primarily shown that the spiritual consciousness or view of life and existence, by virtue of its essential wholeness and integrality, seems to hold the key to the problem of an integral culture for the world and India. It has also shown how this wholeness implies independence and freedom and unity. However, this way and experience is no common possession with us. But if the general position rests upon a truth, essential and central to our nature, then our future culture at one time or another will have to base itself on it.

How can we practically set about creating this new culture and new orientation of life? The first thing evidently is to fully recognise the nature of the mental and the rational way of life, its sphere of efficiency and power and its limitations. That itself will, in some measure, create an expectation and appreciation of the larger spiritual way of our future culture. The next thing is to learn to seek and recognise the fact of spiritual consciousness, to encourage its cultivation and growth and create conditions for the same. If we succeed in creating a general aspiration for it, an increasing number of individuals will be drawn towards it for a practical cultivation and the new way will tend to spread.

THE RELIGIOUS ISSUE

Since the end of the First World War and more vividly after the end of the Second World War, a state of crisis has overtaken man and his entire cultural life. In this, the values of the past, which were so satisfying previously, are being felt more and more as inadequate. Intellectual, moral, aesthetic and religious standards all become shaky and life seems to lose the old supports, but discovers no new ones to hold on to.

Religion, the strongest of these holds, suffers perhaps the most. A vast communistic movement denounces it as an 'opiate', but otherwise too the allegiance to it becomes weak and formal. However, a seeking for an inner solace, comfort and peace, which is the essential function of religion, grows stronger.

The question is, what does this all mean? What is it that the human spirit now seeks? Why does it reject what it cherished for so long?

A spirit of universalisation seems to come upon man as a wide and a large phenomenon of the contemporary times. Science, technology, rule of law, ascendancy of reason, feeling for freedom seem to have contributed much to the growth of this spirit. A free inquiry and personal experience have, in consequence, become powerful motivations of human living.

Religion too is approached in the same way and the necessary beliefs and prescribed ceremonials are felt as irksome, but a free quest for soul and God and inner solace and peace are cherished.

What does this trend show as to the form religion might possibly take in the future? Religion as a phenomenon of human life consists of a number of factors. They are: (1) a seeking after God, the essential spiritual element; (2) a creed, a body of beliefs; (3) a system of ceremonial forms; (4) a church, a religio-social or religio-political system.

Our ordinary personality of mind, life-impulses and body and its outward orientation needs external aids of social organisation, ceremonials and beliefs for a religious exaltation. But they can easily become restrictive and oppressive for the inner soul in its free and spontaneous seeking for God and a spiritual relationship with the Supreme.

The contemporary cultural situation, with its spirit of free inquiry and personal experience, is precisely demonstrating an unwillingness to accept the external forms and shows a clear identification with the free and the spontaneous approach of the inner spirit to a higher reality.

If this attitude finds its fuller development, it seems fairly clear that the religion of the future might possibly be primarily a cultivation of the essential spiritual approach to the highest universal reality, the Divine. And that would mean a seeking, practice and enjoyment of spiritual life. Science will tend to systematise it into a universalised body of knowledge, in which differential psychology of temperament and personality as also the variations of environment and the value of ceremonial performance, creeds and general educational and cultural influences will find due recognition. We will thus have a comprehensive yogic system to guide the course of what may be called spiritual education.

If the practice of spiritual life becomes an educational scheme for humanity, it will indeed be a great day for human progress and fulfilment. And indeed a fulfilment for religion too, as then various religions will be lifted out of their egoistic narrowness and exclusiveness and all rendered into their universal form, which each seeks to achieve but is not able to do because of the persisting egoism in it.

In the history of man, whenever religion has become empty of its spiritual content or oppressive and intolerant, it has evoked reactions of various kinds. A Buddhism silent about God and seeking absolute tranquillity comes into being or humanity and state take the place of God as ideals of life. But the reality of God has a supreme value and satisfaction for man and the human spirit always turns towards that after every kind of reaction and revolt.

This account, however, is one primarily based on empirical or rational grounds. On a purely spiritual basis, one would affirm that as a result of an influx into our human consciousness from above – and this phenomenon is well-known to religious and mystic life – the spiritual consciousness may get intensified in man and he may then turn more effectively to the purely spiritual pursuit and accord to other aids and ideals their respective places. Sri Aurobindo and the Mother, in particular, affirm that the present juncture in human history, loosened from the holds of the past, is just the occasion for a high influx and a new creation. And they call upon man to see and recognise the contemporary situation rightly and act by it adequately, in the form of a readiness to respond to the new calls that might be made upon him.

Through a weakening of the formal parts of religions and an awakening and strengthening of the spirit of free inquiry and personal experience, the rise of interest in yoga as also in psychology, psycho-therapy and other allied studies, and a closer contact between East and West, – religion, as a general inner seeking for the spiritual satisfaction, is becoming more and more prominent. People, in an increasing number, seem to be drawn together to share a common spiritual seeking and a common fulfilment. This is evidently a powerful new factor contributing to the growth of human unity. Science and technology have been great forces in this direction. But unity is, at the foundation, a matter of the Spirit and not of community and satisfaction of interests. Religion, taking on the form of spiritual seeking and satisfaction and coming to look upon the different ceremonials and creeds as secondary aids, becomes a deep bond. Such religion will, it appears, give solidarity to the feeling of human unity, which in its turn will clarify and strengthen the true spirit of all religions.

SCIENCE AND TECHNOLOGY IN ENVIRONMENTAL MANAGEMENT

(The Focal Theme of the Indian Science Congress for 1985)

Science, as Bacon visioned and planned, was to study Nature and find out its secrets, and later technology devised the applications of it for a massive benefit to man. Bacon had said, "Knowledge is Power" and indeed it is so. But science gets handicapped, if it works only for power.

But this led to an exclusive sort of attention to the environment, intensification of human greed, multiplication of wants and attachment to comfort, overproduction, unemployment, and political domination in various forms.

Human quality was not equally attended to. Hence arose a host of problems – cultural, economic and political.

In particular, arose the imbalance between the power of science and technology and the capacity of man to use it for the good of all. The larger powers of nature needed in man larger capacity to use them duly.

In India now, we must not repeat this mistake and not pay an exclusive sort of attention to the environment, but pay even a greater attention to the development of human appreciation of the larger good of man.

Each discipline of science, while suggesting how it can contribute to creating a better environment, may also consider how man too needs to readjust himself to a new environment rightly.

Psychology, as the chief study of human nature, will be expected to contribute more on the side of man in this entire subject of man and environment.

Since Bacon's time, much water has however gone down the Ganga of science. Hence, science needs to be redefined and brought into due relation with a proper view of life and existence. India has a cultural history of its own and the study of nature will have a place of honour of its own here.

The West and the East have different appreciations of man and the external nature and there seems to be a complementariness here. Cultural consequences of science and technology, as witnessed in the West, which need to be carefully examined, are invading our life powerfully.

If our essential cultural values, the basic attitudes of life, are identified and cultivated and combined with science and technology, will the overall pattern of life be not a richer and a fuller one? And will this not be, for the West too, a new possibility?

Science and technology are good but a relative good like all other good things in this world and they should not undermine the quality of man's life. On the other hand, they should carry a sense that they involve new responsibilities and a new awareness of the whole. A sense and feeling for the integrality of life should be always there and science and technology should be in their due place in that context. Einstein, in view of the total situation of science and life, had pithily observed, "Morals must catch up with Science." This is a very true insight. We should, from the beginning, keep morals in good company with science. This really means that an equal attention should be paid to man as to environment. Or, in other words, as we seek to develop and cultivate the resources of the environment, so should we seek to develop and cultivate the larger and nobler energy resources of man too.

Postscript

The focal theme becomes the central issue of the Science Congress for a year. Each section or branch of knowledge considers it and makes its recommendations. These recommendations are consolidated by a central body and then passed on to a task-force appointed by the Government to implement them.

But all this is normally done with a one-sided emphasis on the external reality, the human element is more or less taken for granted. But are man and environment not a totality, needing a joint consideration of both? Environment needs improvement, but so is man too capable of improvement. Does the quality of human life not suffer when it becomes more and more attached to comforts and dependent on the environment? Should his 'will' of self-reliance, the 'will' of progressive mastery over the odds of life, the faith in a higher and a larger governance of life and existence also not be cultivated? Will that not help to build up a more confident and a happier nation?

Section III

INTEGRAL PERSONALITY AND BODILY HEALTH AND EXCELLENCE

HEALTH AND HAPPINESS

We all cherish health and happiness. They constitute the very essence of human living. With them, living is a joy, without them it easily becomes a burden.

But do we pursue them consciously and intelligently enough, knowing that in each one of our thoughts, feelings and acts, we deliberately aim at and intend our best well-being, our health, our happiness? Or, do we live and act rather conventionally, habitually, as others are doing, without individually examining, checking, scrutinising whether our thoughts, feelings and actions do really lead to health and happiness or not?

Our consciousness is normally poised externally. External situation of things and other persons and their external interaction is our primary world and reality. All our life, its aims, pursuits and achievements are governed by this fact. We become aware of ourselves only when we have pain somewhere, in the body or in mind. It is the experience of difficulty that makes us aware of ourselves and then we put in effort, more or less, to recover our normal well-being. Once we are back in our normal well-being, we return to our ordinary external pursuits and get lost in them.

Do we not need a constant self-awareness, a self-watchfulness of the bodily conditions and its interactions with the environment, in order that we may be able to maintain its well-being in good form and promote it to ever higher levels? This is exactly the issue of 'Bodily Well-Being as Sadhana'. This is the spiritual approach to the problems of health and happiness.

Our ordinary body is basically an unconscious organisation. We have no clear feeling of the body as such nor of its different parts and organs, nor of the varied processes and activities that go on in it, nor of the conditions of their harmonious working and continued progress. Evidently, we must constantly observe our body and its changing states in the whole and in the parts and firmly will their harmonious working and progress. If that is done, we will be able to prevent attacks by disease, achieve its cure more easily if it comes in, enjoy increasing well-being of the body and in later life effectively counteract the progressive invasion of the unconscious in the form of senility and hope for a prolongation of life.

To achieve this marvellous possibility, all that is necessary is that we persistently cultivate the right balanced posture of our consciousness. That is, to replace the tilted, all too outward posture of consciousness by one of self-aware other-awareness. That is to say, we should be aware of the external situation while remaining aware of ourselves. Other-awareness should not be one of self-forgetfulness or self-loss or of self-awareness with other-forgetfulness, or other-loss. Both the exclusive awarenesses have serious limitations and constitute an imbalance for an effective and successful living in the world.

To acquire this balanced poise, one needs to cultivate observation of the changing states of one's body as well as of the mind and of the conditions of those states and then try to guide, control and improve them for the future. Evidently, to observe the bodily states is the easiest thing to do. Such observation can lead to most interesting discoveries. First, of a pervasive consciousness which will enable us to pursue and promote the good of the body as a whole, harmonising its egoistic warring members. The tongue surely cares for the immediate satisfaction of its taste-buds, has no consideration for the difficulties of the stomach and absolutely no feeling for the well-being of the body as a whole. Body consciousness is a wonderful discovery to make. It harmonises all the parts into unity and spontaneously promotes the maximum well-being of the body. It is a spiritual fact, possibly a reflection of the unitary soul at the physical level. One feels it as filling out and enclosing the entire body.

Along with this discovery can come a further discovery, that of the soul itself, of the psychic centre of life, of a focus of joy and delight in the region of the heart. As this fact gets clear, one finds in it an abiding intrinsic joy of life and a ready resource for the recoupment of life, which shows altogether a new perspective and horizon for human living. The psychic centre is intrinsic happiness, always fresh, always bright, always young as it were, and sure of self-existence, knowing no end nor a beginning. One begins to feel indifferent to external satisfactions and dependence on circumstances. One begins to feel sure of himself, of deathlessness, of a happy destiny, and of a sure superiority over the external facts of life.

Is this not the right fulfilment for the ordinary life, which is all dependent on the environment?

With this discovery comes a yet greater discovery, that of a Universal Transcendent Consciousness commanding all existence. It is felt as a vast Presence above.

These two, the soul in man and the Higher Presence above, are the essential spiritual realities, immortal in nature and the source of all energy, all joy, all consciousness for the phenomenal existence of matter, life and mind. These can infuse into the body something of their own quality, a heightened well-being, a surer self-existence and a greater durability.

The bodily well-being can thus be limitless, if the body becomes aware of these resources, learns to rely on them and to draw its sustenance from them.

THE IDEAL OF PHYSICAL EDUCATION

Physical education, as a practical discipline, means a systematic development of the body, its health, strength and capabilities. However, there are many such disciplines and each one of them has a philosophy of life behind it. There are, for example, systems which regard the body as a complete fact in itself and then try to cultivate it as such and make it a more efficient physical instrument. There are also systems which regard man as not only a physical body, but as an active mind also. They seek to develop the body, but make use of the mind, its power of will, its suggestions and resolutions. a great deal in order to enhance and develop the health, strength and capabilities of the body. This standpoint is now becoming increasingly popular.

But man is, in fact, a spiritual reality, a soul, a 'Psychic' Being, with mind and body as its instruments. Obviously, the body could be cultivated as such and thereby given the benefit of the force and power of the deeper spiritual reality. And if that is done, it will more and more acquire the deeper equality of the soul, its forbearance, fortitude, endurance and invulnerability to external forces.

We can thus, it will appear, have a system of physical education which will seek to develop a spiritual quality in the body. This quality will naturally be different from the one where body is taken as the sole fact and also from that where body and mind are taken together. Here our aim is to create a conscious contact between the body, mind and the soul, to open out the body and the mind to the influence of the soul, to let the soul act on the body and the mind. The result is that the force of a higher order, the spiritual, is able to work more and more on the other members and thereby lend some of its own immortal qualities to them. The way to achieve it is to act in the best possible consciousness of these facts, i.e., to seek physical education in the awareness of oneself as being a spiritual reality with mind and body as its instruments. Or, at least, to pursue the activities of physical education in the best of one's consciousness, with the fullest available awareness, in the midst of best cooperation of one's will and the spirit of joy and harmony and all this as self-giving and consecration to the soul within and the Divine in the universe. This psychological situation progressively works out a change in the physical system of the body and makes it more and more open to the influence of the spirit, which begins to transform the essential being and quality of the body. The ordinary body is egoistically organised and it works and develops on the basis of the quantum of energy egoistically obtained and possessed by it. The changed psychological situation, involving self-giving and consecration, makes it open to the universal sources of energy and that means a new and a vast basis of life and energy. Evidently, the possibilities of physical perfection will then become much greater. In fact, this psychological approach initiates a process, which working through many grades of physical transformation, is capable of realising a new quality of body as a whole, which Sri Aurobindo calls the Divine Body. The divine body is a body human in form, but fully possessed of the qualities of divine consciousness. It has an awareness, a sense of delight and a will which are divine in their nature and character. In the highest sense, the realisation of such a body must be recognised as the ideal of physical education. But the way to it and the stages leading to it themselves afford a high foretaste of the great state ultimately aimed at. There is a clear and a growing sense of the increase in energy, well-being, health and capacity for physical performance.

Ordinarily, sportsmen achieve excellence by limiting their energy and application to one or two games. When physical education is pursued in the best possible consciousness as described above, then such a breadth and intensity develops in consciousness that a limitation of the object of attention to achieve excellence in it does not remain necessary. It becomes possible to command a many-sided excellence.

Such a pursuit of physical education, which involves the growth of consciousness in breadth as well as intensity, also becomes a means of the intellectual, moral and aesthetic growth of man. The reason is pretty obvious. Physical exercise and games are to be done with the fullest possible consciousness, i.e., with due intellectual, moral, aesthetic and spiritual appreciation. They would then naturally become means of these higher cultural aspects of life and by doing so would themselves occupy an important place in the integral education of man. And that is as it should be. The body is an integral part of total human personality and as such has its relation to other members of personality and, therefore, must be capable of making its contribution to their well-being, as they must be able to do to the well-being of the body. The body is not merely a mass of matter like any other. It is a matter that has been evolved and adapted to be able to bear the impact of human mind and soul and be their instrument and vehicle. As such, it has a hand in their being and working and, therefore, it can be so cultivated as to help and facilitate their growth and working, as it can also be a handicap and hindrance to them.

The ideal of physical education can thus be very high and large. It is not merely relative health, efficiency, strength and excellence in certain physical performances. Its proper aim is the growth and development of the body so as to make it a conscious participant in the full life of the integral personality. Our body is only imperfectly conscious of some of its functions. However, if the consciousness grows in it, we can become more and more conscious of them and then their power and efficiency improves. And if the integral personality also grows, that is, if we become conscious of our different parts of personality and being and achieve a proper unification amongst them, we begin to live a life which is not limited to our conscious surface but which comprehends the subconscious too and unites the subconscious and the conscious to the Superconscious. In this integral consciousness and life, the body-consciousness begins to take a place of privilege, so far as embodied existence on earth is concerned. Such a place of plenitude and perfection of the body is the legitimate right and ideal of physical education. And while directly aiming at this status of perfection, it does also make a contribution to the growth of the integral personality.

The Asanas are the highly developed and most varied postures of the body, which aim at an effective mastery of its functioning and its energy as a preparation for a spiritual realisation. They are also much practised these days for purely physical benefits. But if pursued in a larger way, in the setting of the future consciousness to which they belong, the benefits accruing to the student will be much greater. The same physical effort will produce much greater good and well-being of the personality.

However, there is yet a limitation that belongs to the basic approach and the philosophy of Hatha Yoga, i.e., of seeking to rise from the lower to the higher.

The Integral Yoga makes available a new approach, that of seeking to let the higher integrate and organise the lower. The lower, on its own too, must be progressively disciplined, but to that must come a growing openness to the higher. The higher already enjoys integration and can, therefore, more easily infuse its quality into the lower which lacks it.

In view of this yogic philosophy, physical education acquires a new meaning and, therefore, the Asanas, if cultivated with this orientation, will acquire a new power and, in fact, any convenient physical culture, if pursued thus, will turn to produce high spiritual benefits.

PHYSICAL CULTURE AND SPIRITUAL PROGRESS

'A conscious soul in a conscious universe' is the ideal in human living. We should feel ourselves as souls, conscious and blissful, and the world around us as pervaded and inspired by the Divine, the universal conscious Reality. That is the true and the right living. But, ordinarily, we live as minds, i.e., as partially conscious beings in a world of unconscious material objects and partially conscious other minds. In this state, our bodies tend to pull us down towards unconsciousness and our consciousness has always to work against the pressure of unconsciousness of our body and of the material nature.

To rise in consciousness progressively is the course of general evolution as of individual development. But our body is unconscious and it carries out its myriad processes unconsciously. The biological impulses of preservation, acquisition, propagation, etc., are a little conscious but basically they are passionate drives which for the time being possess the individual and serve a purpose largely unconscious. The activities of the mind, which are governed by these drives, are just partially conscious. There are some activities which are mechanical. But there are also those which are very conscious, the goal is clearly seen and intended and the means too seen and intended. This part of the mind is our reason and it seeks to bring about the best possible unification and harmonisation in our life. But its power is limited and what it can achieve is a loose sort of organisation involving adjustments among the impulses and some little control over the body and its functions. But the body is inert and unconscious and it blindly obeys the impulses as they become activated and seek to possess it. Mind is also able to impose its ideas and opinions on the body and they are often in conflict with the impulses. The situation thus becomes complicated. The need of the body is one thing, an impulse aims at another thing and the mental opinion may be a third thing. How is an inner harmony to be achieved and how is an overall well-being to be promoted and enjoyed?

We have, through prolonged inner observation, to learn to distinguish these three parts of personality and watch their actions with increasing freedom. Such daily observation is a most interesting and highly rewarding activity of exploration and discovery. During this process, we are likely to get sometimes a glimpse of the really detached, free and blissful soul deep within us. That affords the true vision of the inner situation leading to increasing freedom from the aggressive attitudes and actions of the mind and the vital nature. We are then also likely to discover that the body has a consciousness of its own behind its apparent unconsciousness. If the body consciousness underlying the myriad activities of the body can be felt and activised more and more and the same progressively freed from the tyranny of the vital impulses and the interferences of the mind, the need of the body then comes to determine the life and action of the body, enabling it to live and enjoy a wonderful well-being.

Physical culture and the exercises we practise under it would enable us to concentrate more and more on the body as a whole and its various parts and their functions. Under such concentration, if we seek to go deeper and feel the body as a whole, we are sure to discover and recognise the true need, the true hunger, the true thirst, the true fatigue, the true impulsion for activity and so on and, in a clear-sighted way, rightly use our body and enjoy its most faithful serviceability. Then the desire to eat or a hankering for a taste will not be able to mislead us nor any doctrinaire opinion as to when to eat and what to eat create a conflict or confusion in us. With the emergence of the soul, the Divine Presence will also emerge and that will bring about a true harmonisation and body-consciousness will become a more vivid reality. Thus physical culture will ultimately lead to the realisation of Soul and God and show that physical culture truly and fully pursued is a complete Sadhana by itself. It will not only bring health and physical well-being, but spiritual fulfilment of life too.

Section IV

INTEGRAL PERSONALITY AND MENTAL HEALTH AND EXCELLENCE

YOGA AND THE PURSUIT OF HEALTH AND PERFECTION OF LIFE

(Basic Document for the All-India Yoga Health Seminar, New Delhi)

1. Yoga is union with the Highest, the Supreme and the Ultimate in existence, the Divine. It is also the method, leading by progressive stages, to such union. It is, therefore, the science and art of self-perfection too, self-perfection conceived variously as the integration of the *prāṇa*, the life-force, of the *cittavṛtti*s, the mental activities and of the whole personality – the *śarīra*, the *prāṇa*, the *manas* and the *antarātman*, the body, the life, the mind and the Soul. It has involved an ascension in consciousness through one or another part of personality, the *prāṇa* in Hathayoga, the *manas* in Rajayoga and the *antarātman* in Integral Yoga. In the case of Jnana Yoga, Bhakti Yoga and Karma Yoga, the parts are respectively the knowing, feeling and willing aspects of consciousness. But yoga has also involved a descent of the Highest into the human *ādhāra*, the vessel, the instrument, and consequent transformation of it into the nature of the Highest as in Tantra Yoga and Integral Yoga.

The above characterisation is essentially psychological and it would cover practically all systems of sadhana and yoga, the Buddhist, the Jain, those of the Christian mystics, the Muslim Sufis and others.

2. Yoga is, indeed, the essential education, as it promotes the growth and perfection of personality and consciousness and not merely its enrichment through acquisition of information. Its aim is to develop the inherent capabilities of life and thus make life fuller, richer and more competent.

Evidently, like education, it is meant for all, though a few may be able to pursue it to its highest levels of perfection. A general atmosphere of yogic interest is bound to promote health and harmony of body, life, mind and the personality as a whole. It will necessarily encourage attitudes of sincerity, honesty and self-examination and thereby promote better social understanding and relations. In this aspect, it can in course of time begin to influence for good the international relations too.

In the Indian scheme of knowledge, the place of yoga-vidya has been the supreme, the first, as it seeks to improve and enhance the human knower's capabilities of knowing and thereby widen the sphere of the knowable. To it, the Absolute too is directly knowable, but only to greatened capabilities of knowing. The significance of this knowledge is inestimable, as it is this knowledge that can give true certitude to all our knowledge of the phenomenal. Without it, the most verified knowledge is, whether in its nature or use, necessarily stricken with doubt, ambiguity and vacillation.

Indian culture too has, accordingly, given to the yogic pursuit the highest value. This has held up standards of sincerity, honesty, self-reform and self-improvement. It has, however, in the past served the ends of individualism, since personal salvation was the supreme goal of life. But, in contemporary times, yoga has received a fresh extension. It has been affirmed that the entire evolution of life, from the animal to the human, has been a progress to higher and higher grades of consciousness and the present mental consciousness of man is further tending towards a more integral and spiritual consciousness. Besides, man is not only an individual; he carries in himself a universality too. He is a particular instance of humanity as a whole and, therefore, an integral part of it. His full development should, consequently, imply the growth of the true individuality in him, but also the universality he represents and that means the development of his kind, his fellowmen. As his fellowmen progress, he advances in his universal aspect of consciousness, otherwise he remains handicapped in that part.

This is a most interesting development in the history of Indian spirituality, as it gives it a direct socialistic turn in place of the old individualistic bias.

3. Yoga is, it may be reaffirmed, an integration of the essential energies of life. It is evident that an aim of life, as a whole, is essential to it. A clear aim steadily pursued is itself a great integrative force and all yogic disciplines do involve a definite aim. An aim gives, in fact, a whole philosophy of life. It is,

therefore, necessary to emphasize that a proper philosophy of life is a most helpful preparation for yoga and, really, an integral part of it.

4. As a further factor of the total outlook and perspective of yogic practice, it may be stated that yogic effort involves a twofold movement, a movement from below upwards, of the less organised to the higher integrations, and from above downwards, of the higher integrations to the less organised. The emphasis on the one or the other has varied from system to system, but here the truth of both of them may well be affirmed. It may also be affirmed that all effort, whether of professional work or social service or personal recreation, when made in a spirit of dedication and self-giving to a high and a noble aim, leads to a movement upwards and it evokes an action and response from above downwards too. However, the same effort can be made in a self-indulgent way; then it becomes a disintegrative force, the force of *bhoga*. When not self-indulgent, it may yet be self-acquisitive; then there can be an upward movement of integration but without a reciprocating action of the higher.

This principle is of great importance since, if rightly understood and followed, it can effectively turn all life into yogic practice and endow it with increasing yogic and spiritual benefits.

5. As to the concrete form of the practice, it follows clearly, in particular from the foregoing point, that the exercises must comprehend all the parts and planes of human personality. They must be physical, mental and spiritual. Under the physical or biophysical come the practice of Asana and Pranayama, under the mental the practice of concentration, pursuit of knowledge, devotion and selfless action and under the spiritual, the deepest inspirations and aspirations of life.

Surely, in an attempt to raise the essential standards of life in general or that of bringing yoga nearer to the life of the people and making its benefits available to them, a comprehensive system of exercises must be evolved and recommended.

A general education as to the meaning of yoga, its various systems, the aim of life and the attitudes of self-indulgence *(bhoga)*, of self-acquisitive discipline and of self-dedicating activity constitute the preparation for the yogic practice. Self-indulgence, self-control and self-consecration can be said to be the key words of the art of living. Self-indulgence is dissipation and disintegration, self-control is egoistic integration and self-consecration is the way to divine harmonisation, perfection and fulfilment. An understanding and appreciation of these truths is, indeed, the indispensable equipment for the yogic pursuit.

Under the physical or biophysical exercise, the practice of Asanas is, indeed, the most useful for a general application. They bring about an integration and enhancement of the *prāṇaśakti*, the vital force. They give to the body suppleness, endurance and immunity. The soundness of the biophysical part of personality, which the Asanas directly produce, also induces in a measure health and well-being of the mind.

It may, however, be stated here that other forms of physical exercise too, when done with a sense of conscious purpose and openness to the universal energies of life, can lead to the realisation and enjoyment of the yogic benefits.

Pranayama too is a biophysical process, but more directly instrumental to the control and discipline of mind and its vagrant activities. There are many forms of it, but the simplest consists of equal rhythmic movements of inspiration and expiration.

Among the other recognised biophysical processes are the various *kriyā*s, the more important being *dhauti* and *nauli*. These need expert guidance and, therefore, cannot be recommended for general practice without proper aid.

Under mental exercises come those of concentration, directed and purposive thinking, silence or the capacity to be quiet and free from thinking activity, equality or control and freedom from emotional disturbances and the training of will-power. These can have a great variety of forms. Concentration can be practised on an external object to start with, but one should aim at achieving concentration of consciousness in the head or the heart or both according to inclination. Such concentration leads to wonderful unfoldments of new capacities.

Among the mental exercises, the fundamental one, which inspires and moves all these and others of the kind, is the urge and force of aspiration, the will, eager and fervent, for things higher and nobler. The force of this will is the energy that makes for progress. The exercises which enhance aspiration are, therefore, the most important. And the chief among them is *satsang*, spiritual fellowship or association with aspiring persons, directly or through their word.

Further exercises under this head would be those connected with the right regulation of the basic functions of life, *viz.*, Food, Sleep, Activity or Work, Fatigue, Rest, etc. A clear understanding of the aim and the purpose of these in life, a recognition of their various qualities, an appreciation of their true qualities and of the method to improve them progressively and the ability of right adjustment of them to the peculiar needs of one's personality are a matter of great personal education and an enormous achievement in life. All this is basically yogic and truly meant for all. This is foundational to all progress in life — mental, moral, social, spiritual.

The right regulation of the basic functions of life primarily involves one exercise, *viz.*, that of cultivation of good habits. Ordinarily, when we want to form a new habit, we try to acquire a piece of behaviour. The whole approach is more or less external. But, in fact, it is a case of reintegration of the will in a particular matter. For that, an aspiration for the right will and right behaviour and a rejection of all interfering and refractory impulses are the process to pursue. And this pursuit, if done sincerely, leads to the acquisition of a habit more effectively, more smoothly and more expeditiously.

The practice of equality and freedom from emotional disturbances has already been referred to. In this connection, one should also consider the emotional refinement and elevation through the appreciation and enjoyment of poetry, music, painting, sculpture and other artistic forms and expressions. The highest in this direction is the practice of universal love and delight.

In the training of will, the most important principles are the awareness of one's desires and volitions, constant intention to organise and harmonise them, due care in resolving upon a thing and fidelity in its execution. When resolutions made are not disregarded but carefully executed, the joy of achievement leads to a sense of power and an increase in the ability to execute. At its highest, through self-consecration one can attain to identification with the Divine Will and a superhuman power.

Under spiritual exercises come the deepest inspirations and aspirations of life. These occur to almost everybody, though they pass off unnoticed and unrecognised for the most part. But even then their potency is the highest in life. It is they that guide and determine the direction and evolution of life. It is, therefore, extremely important to learn to recognise them through careful and persistent self-examination.

They constitute what is called faith in life and the Gita has effectively clinched the matter in the words यो यच्छ्रद्ध सः एव सः '*as a man's faith, so is he himself*'. Thus the practice and the growth of the power of faith is an essential spiritual exercise. This really means an increase in the awareness of the true, the real, the higher and the ultimate. In one word, it means awareness of the destiny of life and the divine guidance of all existence.

The attitude of reverence is intimately connected with the sense of faith. Reverence for the higher leads to a secret awareness of it, which constitutes faith or an inner acceptance of it even though reason has not yet confirmed it.

6. The exercises for the growth of personality are, in fact, inexhaustible. The more important thing to know and to remember is the aim and the objective, which is the increasing perfection of life in its different parts and aspects. If one does that, one will be able to plan and formulate one's own appropriate exercises for a particular stage of development.

As to the time in the day best suited for practice and the duration of time, the best general rule is the individual's convenience, capacity and effectivity in working. The effectivity in working of an exercise is relative to an individual's capacity to do it without getting fatigued and to assimilate its effects. For every new mastery, a state of freshness, lightness, joy and enthusiasm is obviously helpful. Therefore, early morning time, soon after refreshing sleep, is recommended for all kinds of exercises discussed above. Again evening time, after some refreshment and rest at the end of the day's work, is a favourable time. Some would find the time after the mid-day rest very congenial for certain exercises. The individual should aim at determining these points for himself as soon as possible, though in the beginning he may find it difficult to do so. But, in any case, these occasions and durations of exercise should not be entertained exclusively. All exercises are meant to change life as a whole and any violation and infringement of the right attitude in any exercise taking place at any time should be taken notice of and rectified.

7. Union with the Divine, perfection and fulfilment are today not very dynamic goals for man. In this pragmatic age, health,

physical and mental, and efficiency in work are the real moving ideals of life. Yoga, which aims at the highest perfection, does certainly include these empirical goals and provides for them as the basis and the preparation for the highest achievement. The Asanas and Pranayama are, indeed, invaluable aids to bodily health. They have a great preventive value. The Asanas have also a high curative value. They do always include a right regulation of the basic functions of life: food, sleep, work, rest, etc. Then their value for health becomes much greater.

As to the mental health, yoga provides a psycho-synthetic system of prevention and cure of disorders. Under its approach of integration of personality, it demands an increasing awareness of one's desires and volitions and a persistent attempt to organise and consecrate them. This leads to reduction and eradication of inner conflicts and tensions. And the most general cause of mental suffering are such conflicts and tensions. A right management of one's desires and volitions would inevitably be an effective prevention of inner tensions. For cure, a psycho-analysis, an analytical understanding and appreciation of the confused volitions of the past and a proper psycho-synthesis for the future would be needed.

The Asanas and Pranayama too, through the health of the body, contribute to mental health. The latter, however, has even a direct relation with the mind.

Efficiency in work too is a most cherished ideal today. We seek an increasing capacity for work, a comprehensive command over different aspects of a matter and an effective power of execution. All these are evidently related to the qualities of concentration and integration of personality. Yoga, which makes concentration and integration its very goals, must necessarily help the growth of efficiency in work.

It is perfectly possible to turn to yoga for health and efficiency alone. But yoga argues that a total and a comprehensive approach to life is able to mobilise the energies of life more completely and thereby effectuate these lesser achievements more easily. A high aim of life, we have said, is itself a great integrative force. It is, therefore, well worth considering whether to follow the full technique of yoga or avail of a partial aspect of it.

INTEGRAL PSYCHO-THERAPY

The Approach and the Stand-point

Mental health is the aim of all psycho-therapy, but integral psycho-therapy will have to aim at a wholesomeness of life and consciousness in appreciation of all the domains and dimensions of Integral Personality, in particular those where wholesomeness exists as a normal quality. It is with their help that wholesomeness would be more easily promoted in the afflicted or disrupted or oppressed and embarrassed parts.

The dimensions and domains of wholesomeness or wholeness are normally not dynamic, *i.e.*, not consciously available to us for practical utilisation. What is available is the ordinarily waking consciousness with all its diverse impulses working under diverse social, moral and religious prohibitions. A working wholeness of personality thus comes into being. It is a personality which is socially serviceable and, therefore, individually satisfying on the whole, but in fact it is not unified, not an effectively organised unit of life. The aim of social conformity and that of moral or religious obedience have to exercise a constant pressure on a host of diverse impulses, some co-operative, some recalcitrant and resistant, some hostile and defiant. When the inner divergence assumes the form of an acute conflict, anxiety becomes abnormal and life grows socially and individually difficult. Such disorders can be very many, but the basic situation perhaps remains the same.

What is to be done? When the disorder is such that it renders the person too helpless to seek to be well again and incapable of being collaborative in the treatment, physical methods such as electric shock have to be resorted to. But when the person has the will to get well again and seeks a cure, then at the waking level, one tries to console, assure and convince him that worry does not help. One tries to divert his mind to other things of the happier sort and so on. This might prove sufficient in some cases and a working feeling of life might return.

But it might not, and then a digging into the subconscious is done to discover the hidden, the old forgotten, the suppressed and repressed cause of anxiety. The person is asked to relax himself on a couch, turn to the past and let memories arise. This is done over a long time and the person reviews himself more or less as a witness. In course of time, the hidden thing comes up. He, as it were, recognises it and feels an immediate relief. But this process, though long and tedious, works only if the person reviews his past as a witness, *i.e.*, in a state of relative detachment. But when a person becomes indulgent in his past experiences, he strengthens his involvement in them, and the release does not come. Then Freudian Free Association does not produce the desired result.

The Freudian 'Anatomy of Personality' will be helpful to understand this working better. Id, Ego and Superego are the main parts of personality. Id consists of the untamed impulses, Ego of the adjustments arrived at with the external social and physical reality, and the Superego of the demands of the society and the moral ideal as to what the conduct should be. Between the Superego and the Id, a wide disparity exists. That is the field of constant conflict and tension. The Ego too is only relatively adjusted, not heartily reconciled. It has, on the whole, accepted reality, but it has not given up the essential wishing and willing of its diverse impulses. The overall picture of personality is thus one of lots of impulses, some of which have become moderated in their self-assertion and are more or less reconciled to external necessities, but persisted in their self-assertion in a subdued manner. However, the Superego stands above all these impulses, the untamed ones of the Id and the tamed ones of the Ego, uncompromisingly insisting on its own demands and creating or accentuating the sense of guilt each time they are not fulfilled. The insistence of the Superego and the impulsiveness of the Id between them constitute the warring factors of personality, and psycho-analysis, on the whole, tends to favour the Id, let it have a freer and fuller play and hold the Superego responsible for the conflict, the guilt feeling and the consequences that follow. In connection with the education of the child, however, Freud says that impulses have to be suppressed but that should be done discreetly. That is, indeed, very realistic.

The essential approach of psycho-analysis is that of analysing the subconscious and raising the repressed cause to the plane of consciousness. This done, a recomposition of personality comes about. The aim thus is a psycho-synthesis, a reorganisation or re-integration of personality. Now for Integral Psycho-therapy, psycho-synthesis is the dominant interest throughout the process of cure. It, therefore, stresses the will to get well; the hope and the joy of recovery, the faith in the success of the process. These qualities have, as it were, to be communicated to the patient by the Integral Psychologist. The sense of guilt is a handicap, which has to be worked off. Conflicts and tensions of life have to be seen realistically, *i.e.*, as facts of normal nature to be harmonised and pacified. Sex too has to be seen as a normal propensity of human nature intended to serve a purpose in the scheme of cosmic evolution.

Our normal personality is a superficial organisation of reactions to environment. It is egoistic, that is, self-centred in varying degrees. When the self-centredness is keen and strong, adjustments with the environment and objectivity become more difficult. The sense of guilt also tends to be more acute for failure to conform to external demands of physical reality, morality and religion. An appreciation of the universality of human nature, with its impulses of sex as well as other impulses, facilitates adjustments and reduces guilt feeling. This involves growth in wideness as a corrective to the normal or abnormal narrowness of the ordinary egoistic personality.

But there is another direction of growth which brings a real liberation from the problems of the superficial outer personality, which is our ordinary quality. That is growth inwards, in depth, behind the superficial formation of life. This is gained through a process of self-dissociation from the ordinary impulses, through an act of stepping back or of self-detachment. Such a process would sooner or later enable one to feel a deep inner consciousness, a personality by itself, of freedom and joy and peace. In relation to this, the outer reactions and involvements become truly superficial and secondary and the inner sense and feeling essential and real. That makes for liberation from the confusions of the outer personality as nothing else does.

In comparison to this direction of movement, the Freudian would be called a movement not in inner depth but rather downward into the past, toward what we have lived before, on which we stand, which is the foundation of the ordinary waking life. The inward movement involves self-dissociation, which brings real freedom from involvements. The delving into the past brings relative detachment, only if the reliving of the past experience is done with some objectivity, as if watched from a distance.

There is yet another direction of movement open to Integral Psycho-therapy. It is upward towards the Superconscious, the wide universal fields of wholeness and greater luminosity of consciousness. If some openness can be created to the Superconscious, it will mean a powerful therapeutic influence.

The Integral Psycho-therapist, who is a therapist working for a cure, is also a teacher who promotes growth in wideness, in depth and in height and thereby mobilises therapeutic influences of different qualities. He achieves a cure, but really opens up for the patient a prospect of a larger and a fuller life for the future. Evidently, he must, in some degree, himself wield these dimensions of personality or at least have an openness towards them and be able, through willing and overt expressed guidance, to create a sincere turning in these directions.

All nervous disorders are disorders of the superficial outer personality. They arise out of the divergences and contradictions of its impulses and the self-centredness of human nature. As a basic corrective of this. Integral Psycho-therapy would recommend an attitude of self-offering, self-dedication, self-consecration to the common good of all including his own, himself being one among many. Human nature through its self-centredness, its egoity, its acquisitiveness, ordinarily seeks its exclusive good and that creates conflicts and tension in the individual as also in society, because of the exclusiveness of the impulses and of the individuals. Now a general basic attitude of consecration to the common good, to the Truth, to Reality, to the Supreme Being would create the most favourable basic condition for mental health, for peace, for harmony for the individual as for society.

A further general attitude needed is of appreciation of human nature, its varied impulses, their insistences, their contradictions, etc. Above all, an appreciation that this character is universal.

A further appreciation that the faults and aberrations of nature are often hard facts and have to be handled with patience and sympathy. And that the attitudes of intolerance, anger and suppression do not help.

Further, that the faults are curable. Nothing is irremediable.

Further, that these faults are confined to the outer personality of contradictory impulses. The inner central personality and the higher Super-consciousness are joyous and harmonious. And that through their help, all faults of outer nature can be made good.

Further, that all faults are different involvements and fixations. A stepping back, a detachment, a contact with inner joy and the higher peace is the best way of release from the involvement and the fixation.

The role of the psycho-therapist or the teacher in all this process of cure or re-education is very important. He has to communicate new values of life to the patient. He must evidently be, in some degree, in possession of these values. He must also be free to vary his methods according to circumstances. The approach, the standpoint and the general principles are, of course, more or less fixed. But techniques can be employed or put aside as needed.

The foregoing is a preliminary statement of the approach, the standpoint and a few general principles of Integral Psycho-therapy as embodied in the Integral Yoga of Sri Aurobindo and the Mother and as found useful with individuals and groups in actual practice by the present writer. Public mental health is an issue intimately connected with that of individual mental health. The basic attitudes or valuations needed for the education of an individual for the recovery of mental health will obviously have a validity for general public mental health. And then the incidence of individual nervous disorders will tend to become less.

Section V

INTEGRAL PERSONALITY AND EDUCATION

WHAT SHOULD BE OUR PHILOSOPHY OF EDUCATION? AND OUR VIEW OF MAN, THE WHOLE MAN?

Why do we feel dissatisfied with our education? Why do our educated people not much command our respect? Why are the educated people themselves not much satisfied with themselves? How is it that, even after repeated attempts at reforms, we remain dissatisfied with our education? What is wrong with us or with our education or with both?

The fact of the matter possibly is that we carry within us a deep inheritance, a philosophy of life, a system of values, and the education which the British brought over from Europe and introduced here has a philosophy, a system of values of its own, and the two philosophies, the two systems of values are at variance, not matched to each other. Even after independence, we have not consciously and deliberately recognised the real problem and not attempted a real solution. Hence this persistent dissatisfaction with education and ourselves.

The same is virtually the problem of our cultural life in the context of the contemporary civilisation of the world as determined by the rise of science and the Western life. This problem is faced by other Eastern countries also and, in the West too, the inadequacy of mechanised life is now being felt increasingly and the need for inner peace, inner contentment, self-satisfaction, an essential joy and meaning in life, intrinsic or spiritual values, felt more and more.

Education and civilisation are thus faced with a problem at a wide human level. It is really a world problem. But for India, it is a more acute one because of the disparity, the divergence and difference in the values of traditional Indian culture and those of contemporary life. The work involved is one of cultural recreation in the context of present national and international life, not really one of preserving our traditional cultural values in an indifferent and hostile world. We, as Indians, must dive deep within ourselves, our history, seek inspiration from the great past creators of life, moral, spiritual, social, political and discover the essential strength of our living and recreate it in the present situation of new social, political and world impacts. In doing so, we will naturally dissociate ourselves from the 'name and form' (Nama-rupa) of our wide and vast cultural life of different previous epochs of our history. If we stick to them, we will be badly handicapped, since the present age needs its own appropriate outer forms. But our essential strength of life must be rediscovered and fully availed of for our own joy and success, and also as contribution to the general life of humanity.

Now, the education which has come to us through the British represents the philosophy of the Enlightenment, of intellectual Liberalism of the 18th century Europe, as also the temperament of the European people. This Intellectual Liberation stands for science, spirit of enquiry, intellect and man or humanism. And the temperament of Europe means external attitude, amelioration of the conditions of life and success in work. All this means the cultivation of the circumstances; utility and usefulness of things becomes the governing consideration. Essential worthwhileness of life and intrinsic values come in, in this scheme of things, in an incidental way only.

The traditional values of Indian life have primarily stressed an improvement of the quality of life, its peace, its harmony, its love and sympathy, capacity of enjoying truth, goodness, beauty for their own sake, of soul and God, the basic facts in man and the world, of seeing things as a whole and promoting good on the whole. This has involved simplicity in external life, but richness in inner life in terms of tolerance, understanding, sympathy, good will, spirit of sacrifice, a general selflessness and so on. This has ensured to the Indian people a good measure of inner peace, tranquillity, forbearance and self-satisfaction. This has also given them the capacity of repeated self-renewals, of putting forth great men of exceptional qualities again and again and enjoying a longevity equalled only by the Chinese.

Indian emphasis on the inner values of man has been, during certain periods, accompanied by a neglect of the conditions of life, which has been a weakness. The West, laying a predominant emphasis on the external conditions, has resulted in the multiplication of wants, attachment to comforts, increase of tensions and mental complaints. A sense of inner joyfulness is absolutely necessary as a corrective to the pursuit of external pleasure and resultant tensions. Obviously, here a mutual complementariness is present. We need to cultivate our environment, and the West needs to cultivate the inner resources of life.

Virtually, our life is not all environment-dependent. Our soul is a self-existent fact and it is the seat of inner essential joyfulness and of wholeness and integrality and deeper identity of oneness with others and all existence. Education should be of the whole man, the integral personality, of the environment-oriented part as well as of the soul, as also of the higher dimensions of universality and transcendence, of the highest common good (the *sarva-hita*), of Integral Truth and Supreme Beauty, the Divine Reality. Such education will afford to the individual deep inner satisfaction, a wide commanding power over the world and good practical efficiency to deal with the environment.

Such education will represent the profoundest philosophical and yogic realisations of India's past and be an adequate consolidated philosophy of education for the present and the future. This education will also meet the need of the West. It will give to it all the great inner resources of personality, of joy, tranquillity, peace, inner harmony, worthwhileness of life, etc. In this Indian philosophy of education lies the best promise of a true philosophy of life and a true philosophy of education for mankind. And in this Indian view of personality, in this Indian Psychology, lies the best promise of a comprehensive view of the whole man. A civilization based on this psychology of personality and this philosophy of education can well promise a unification and harmonisation of the human race and its varied cultural trends.

The Mother of Sri Aurobindo Ashram, Pondicherry, had in her message to the Kothari Education Commission, in a few words, beautifully stated what India and the West need in respect of education:

"India has or rather *had* the knowledge of the *Spirit*, but she neglected matter and suffered for it.

The West has the knowledge of matter but rejected the Spirit and suffers badly for it.

An integral education which could, with some variations, be adapted to all the nations of the world, must bring back the legitimate authority of the Spirit over a matter fully developed and utilised."

INTEGRAL EDUCATION: THE REVOLUTION IT SEEKS

The revolution which Integral Education seeks is that the Psychic Being, the evolving spiritual principle in man, is the master principle of his existence, capable of integrating the diverse and vagrant impulses and factors of personality. This should be intended and sought to be made dynamic in life.

But how to do it? That is the question. Through love and adoration of beauty and grandeur in nature and human living, in literature, in history and geography, in arithmetic, geometry and algebra, in fact in everything. And indeed, a greatness and a wonder is present in everything. It really means cultivating a new attitude, an attitude of looking up to the greatness and beauty in things, admiring them, opening ourselves to them and growing into their form and quality. This attitude is by itself a powerful educational force, which will progressively reduce self-assertion and egoism and division and promote a sense for the higher, create a will for the future, for unity, for harmony, for the ultimate Divine and the Supreme in existence.

And this spirit should be the inspiration of all the five factors of Integral Education, the Physical, the Vital, the Mental, the Psychic and the Spiritual. This being done more and more, the Psychic Being will be encouraged to exercise its influence more and more and the children would tend to grow into harmonious and wholesome personalities.

Man is not "mind plus body". Man is, as the Gita says, body, life, mind and soul *(śarīra, prāṇa, manas* and *ātman)*. The Atman, in its evolving form, is called by Sri Aurobindo and the Mother the Psychic Being, to distinguish it from the soul as the presiding spiritual fact. This is the revolution initiated and carried on by Integral Education. If sincerely carried out, it means a real revolution for ourselves in India and also the world.

A mind, partly conscious and much divided within itself, can at best be an inhibitive force for the unruly vital impulses of anger, hatred, destruction, etc. The essentially conscious and joyous Psychic Being, as an undivided whole by itself, can integrate and even transform personality, raise it to its own peaceful and harmonious quality. 'Mind plus body' formula, the idea of utility and the seeking for pleasures that fills our general cultural life has brought about a loss of values. An attitude of looking up to things higher, greater and more satisfying and which by being shared get multiplied, the spiritual goods of life, is the one thing needed. An Integral Education makes the psychic being central to all education and fills us with the vision of things great and beautiful. This is the solution of our contemporary cultural situation. It would be nice to check it up in personal experience.

May ever more men see the force of this solution and work for it sincerely, devotedly, for the good of all.

EDUCATIONAL PSYCHOLOGY

Educational Psychology is today the very foundation of education. To let the personality have a full flowering of its inherent capacities and capabilities is all the business of education. And that implies an appreciation of what personality is and what are the conditions of its growth. And that is really Educational Psychology, which is by itself a large body of psychological knowledge. Under Integral Psychology and Integral Personality, its form will be even more elaborate.

The following topics show its wide scope and with their help, it may be in a measure possible to contemplate this branch of psychology in the light of Integral Psychology, as treated earlier. Its full elaboration will come sometime in the future.

Frame-work of Topics

Part One

I. The various dimensions or levels of Human Personality (or the planes and parts of the Being):

 (i) the Mind
 (ii) the Vital
 (iii) the Physical
 (iv) the Subliminal – the Subtle Physical, Vital and Mental
 (v) the Psychic Being – the individual spiritual entity
 (vi) the Universal Spiritual Consciousness
 (vii) the Supramental Integral Consciousness

or

 (i) the Subconscious
 (ii) the Conscious
 (iii) the Superconscious

II. Their Capacities and Functions

III. The Growth of Character – of the normal outer personality of body, life and mind:

(i) Aspiration, rejection and opening oneself, as the three basic processes for promoting this growth
(ii) Practice of Self-consecration in works of service, concentration (study), meditation and devotion
(iii) Formation of new habits
(iv) Getting rid of old ones
(v) Habitlessness and spiritual mastery of life

IV. The Growth of the Integral Personality
   (i) Psychicisation
   (ii) Spiritualisation
   (iii) Supramentalisation

Part Two

I. Knowledge, kinds of Knowledge, Integral Knowledge
II. The Pursuit and Attainment of Knowledge – conditions of it – place of faith and doubt, Seeking and openness to Truth as the basic right attitude
III. Instruments of Knowledge – their purification and perfection – senses, intellect, intuition
IV. Communication of Knowledge – will to communicate – will to receive – we understand what we sympathise with. Methods of communication – Instruction, Example, Influence
V. Material of instruction – as means for the cultivation of the instruments or faculties of knowledge. Syllabus and curriculum not end in themselves

Part Three

I. The teacher as personality – a seeker and lover of Truth and Knowledge, with a will to share his experience with others and promote the same in others
II. The student as personality – a learner, seeking more and more to know things, himself and the world
III. Their mutual relationship – fellowship, full of love and reverence, in the adventure of knowledge and experience

Part Four

I. The fact of atmosphere – individual and institutional
II. Methods of conscious cultivation of the same
III. Its high educational value

Sources: 1. The Synthesis of Yoga – Sri Aurobindo
2. Letters on Yoga – Sri Aurobindo
3. Savitri – Sri Aurobindo
4. Collected Works – The Mother
   [in particular, Vol. 12 (On Education)]

EDUCATION AS A NORMAL SOCIAL FUNCTION

Contemplation of the Entire Concrete Social Situation as the True School

Future Possibility of a Self-conscious Evolved Society

Man by nature is a creature of impulses, which are very many, diverse and contrary, each insisting on its own immediate satisfaction, not caring for the larger good of man as a whole.

Education means building man up so that these impulses learn to take a longer and larger view of self-satisfaction, individually and socially.

Now, growing up in a social setting, the individual is under constant social persuasions, as also under the needs of inner self-gratifications and self-expressions. These motivations are constantly in action and the same are the most effective means for the growth of personality.

Education should really facilitate their working individually and socially and then it will be spontaneous and most effective.

When the urge for vocalisation and communication is strong, language learning is actively in progress and the environment should offer all the help for the same, which will be eagerly availed of.

Similarly, should the impulses of construction, destruction, imagination, reasoning be served. All learning should be a part of such facilitation and then it will not become arbitrary and no forcing will be necessary.

The setting of life itself will, under this view, have to be so considered that it evokes the best in the individual and serves its needs more and more. That will really be the simplest and the most spontaneous way of the essential education that a man needs.

To move in this direction of creating a self-conscious society as a school, we should recognise that even now the society and the street are imparting, in point of basic attitudes of life, more than the conventional school does. If we do that, then we will try to make the society and the street conscious of what it is doing. If that consciousness comes about even in a small way, we will be anxious, at the first instance, to reduce and eliminate the negative and the harmful influences. That will surely go a long way in giving to the growing generation an easier educational chance.

(In this connection, we may recall that the Mother named a school that was being opened at Auroville as 'The Last School'.)

Section VI

INTEGRAL PERSONALITY AND CREATIVE ACTIVITY

(In Art, Literature, Music, Crafts and Life generally)

The inner dynamism of creative activity, its true motive force, is a mystery. What creativity is, what is its source and sustaining power, its different levels and qualities, and allied questions, stand unanswered. And, therefore, true and original writing is generally regarded as inexplicable, a gift of the gods to man; and, if so, a science of the creative process is not possible.

Modern Depth Psychology, however, has discovered what it calls the subconscious mind, and has ventured to enquire into the nature and character of inspiration and the faculty of creative work and has attempted some explanations of these secrets of human nature. The sum of its answers is that inspiration and creative work are determined by the deep dynamisms of the individual's subconscious, whether sexual or otherwise in character. This is the most that modern psychology is able to offer. It does not provide a basis for distinguishing between the different qualities and levels of inspiration and creativity, nor does it give a plan of practical and educational discipline for the cultivation and development of these great faculties. If these higher activities of the human mind and spirit are really incapable of educational handling, and if they are to remain wholly mysterious facts and rare phenomena, then the prospects for the progress of human culture are rather depressing.

This, however, cannot be true. Our consciousness and awareness, by their very nature, admit of indefinite growth and, therefore, it should be perfectly possible to know the creative process, as we do other activities that take place within us. Yoga is claimed to be a discipline to ensure this knowledge, an art of the growth of self-awareness which lights up the secret corners of one's personality and its different planes and dimensions, revealing the true nature of creative activity.

Our normal personality, which consists of our reactions and adjustments to the external world, physical and social, is essentially a thing of convention and habit. Its normal attention is directed outward, it is *Bahirmukha*, and it seeks adjustments and conformity, competitiveness, distinctiveness and novelty. But creativity is not its *Dharma*, its quality and function. It is not capable of self-existence, it is basically dependent in character, it cannot act out of itself and, therefore, it cannot create.

C.G. Jung, a profound psychologist, while discussing the essential quality of personality in his work, *The Integration of the Personality*, says that man commonly lives by tradition. His habitual thought, feeling and action are quite adequate for the usual situations of life and they constitute, as it were, the line of least resistance for the flow of this life's energy. But when an unprecedented situation arises, 'personality' shows its true worth. It may be able to rise above tradition and habit and put forth a creative act. Personality, which is usually determined by externalities, has also a unique 'centre' above and behind our normal consciousness. Jung attributes to this 'centre' the power to integrate the varied thoughts, feelings and volitions of our normal personality.

In yogic philosophy, this centre is the true spiritual selfhood of man, which is a fact to be experienced and the realization of which admits of a systematic cultivation. To discover this centre and exercise its faculties is to live creatively. To view all life and existence from that centre is to experience them creatively. And, if one has the power of expression in words, he will be able to embody his experience in written or spoken speech.

Our usual normal personality is, to this deeper centre of experience, an outer instrument or mask, and the cultivation of this is no more than the improvement of the equipment necessary for the embodiment, conservation and expression of the creative experience. Our training in the use of a language is only an equipment for creative work. The outer personality and the inner conscious centre are parts of our integral personality and even when we are primarily and largely identified with and limited to the outer part, the spiritual centre does continue to influence us more or less, directly or indirectly. Such influence has been recognised by poets and writers as inspiration. But most often it is an indeterminable factor and, therefore, not usually intentionally utilisable. If this truly creative factor could become better known and its working conditions better understood, it would be a great aid to the cultivation of creative writing.

The whole tradition of Yoga bears witness to the possibility of our being able to discover the inner consciousness or self, behind and above the environment-involved and environment-dependent personality. In our own time, this knowledge and the discipline which leads to it have received fresh verification and amplification at the hands of Sri Aurobindo. Sri Aurobindo maps out, in great detail, the varied parts of the integral human personality and gives in his books practical directions for the discovery and identification of these parts. And, since he was a poet and a writer too, he gives also an assessment of these in respect of their creative powers.

Our normal personality has its physical, vital and mental aspects and the quality of a piece of writing may be marked by one or the other, or a combined working of two or more of these. It bears the stamp of the source from which it proceeds. If it proceeds from the inner conscious centre, which Sri Aurobindo calls the Psychic Being, it will possess another quality. There are also the parts and planes where the individual directly experiences his identity with the universal and the general, and such participation would involve a great widening of the ordinary narrow and divided outlook on life. There are also the ranges of consciousness which Sri Aurobindo calls the overhead planes; they open up, successively, fresh perspectives of transcendent harmonies.

This is a bare indication of the possible, varied and wide ranges of experience which our personality carries hidden within itself, while we normally continue to live and exercise its most limited, divided and externally determined part. Evidently, for true and creative writing, these inner, richer and self-conscious planes of personality must be discovered and made dynamic in our lives. Sri Aurobindo has given the testimony of his own experience:

"As the Yoga increased, I read very little – for when all the ideas in the world come crowding from within or from above, there is not much need for gathering mental food from outside sources; at most a utility for keeping oneself informed of what is happening in the world, – but not as material for building up one's vision of the world and Truth and things. One becomes an independent mind in communion with the cosmic Thinker." (*Sri Aurobindo on Himself*, SABCL, Vol. 26, p. 221)

Evidently, it is most important to discover the inner sources of knowledge and learn to see things more deeply and fully. But how is this to be done? The way is indeed long and difficult and, above all, it demands great sincerity of purpose. And yet the general advice of Sri Aurobindo is simple. It is just this: "Allow your consciousness to grow." The consciousness as such, by persistent and sincere aspiration, should grow in width, depth and height; the measure of comprehension and sympathy should become larger and greater. Increasing one's stock of ideas and words is not growth of consciousness. True growth, in due course, automatically brings us into contact with our creative nature. And while the process of growth is difficult, it is in itself a source of deep joy.

II

The Integral Personality

Since man is the leader of the evolutionary march and, in humanity, the individuals have to take the initiative, the individual human personality acquires, as a practical fact, supreme value. And Sri Aurobindo's yogic work really consisted in the exploration of the fullest resources of the individual personality and the discovery of the methods of developing them.

His view of personality is both a systematisation and an elaboration of the past Indian views on the subject and being supported by fresh yogic exploration and experience, it acquires a great significance for the present. To Sri Aurobindo too, the mind is an outer formation, produced by nature and adapted as an instrument of action on nature. The real personality is the spirit within. However, while in the past Indian philosophy has called it an unchanging soul, Sri Aurobindo affirms it as a fact of evolution and calls it the Psychic Consciousness. This Psychic Consciousness is, according to him, slowly growing up as a potentiality and is due for expression as an actuality in life in the normal course of things. This makes a great deal of difference so far as the previous position is concerned. The spirit is not indifferent to and detached from our normal life, but involved in it and seeking to express itself in it. This spiritual principle, which is of itself seeking expression, would naturally admit of an easier realisation or at least would be directly helpful in the transformation of existing life. Soul, as a substance, detached and independent, however, is not denied, but that is affirmed as another fact of personality serving as its static basis. The psychic being is the dynamic counterpart of it. This is one capital point of Sri Aurobindo's view of personality.

Another is the relation of the unconscious, the conscious and the superconscious. Evolution, cosmic and individual, is a hearty principle with Sri Aurobindo. All nature is moving up towards higher and higher levels of consciousness. Out of the unconscious matter has emerged life and out of subconscious and semiconscious life has emerged the mind of man. The unconscious is, therefore, progressively becoming conscious and the conscious arising to higher degrees of consciousness, which are now superconscious to us. The whole process is determined teleologically, by a pull and attraction of the superconscious states. However, the growth of consciousness is a difficult and a slow process since the unconscious offers resistance and seeks to persist in its own action. This is the principle of mechanism in personality, but the fact that a progressive growth of consciousness does take place and that at the higher stages of growth the attraction of the superconscious states tends to become clearer, shows that the chief causal factor of personality is the superconscious. This gives a new orientation and movement and thereby accords to the "teleological determination" and "goal-seekingness" its full validation.

Western psychology normally does not even recognise the fact of the superconscious. A psychologist like Jung too, who has made illuminating studies of yogic practice and affirms progressive integration as almost the law of personality, contends that the "wholeness", of which, he admits, the Yogis are "pastmasters", is reducible to the unconscious. But the unconscious, which is essentially "chaotic" in character, could not in the same breath be credited with the quality of wholeness. Besides, in an evolutionary process, if there is a past and a present, there must also be a future, unless we affirm that the process has entirely run its course. The human consciousness is, in fact, a superconscious state to that of the animal and likewise there must be states of a yet higher order than the present human consciousness. The yogic discipline is able to demonstrate these in individuals. And what is achieved in such cases is surely indicative of racial possibilities.

The superconscious has been the special field of exploration and mastery for Sri Aurobindo and he has identified many successive levels of it reaching up to that of the completest integration, which he has called the Supermind. The significance of this work is really tremendous. It gives a new basic orientation to personality for the science of psychology, releases new forces for the change and growth of human capacity and character with regard to education and creates new prospects for the cultural advancement of the race as a whole.

Sri Aurobindo has also identified a further part of personality and yogically demonstrated its reality as a fact. This is what he has called the subliminal in personality. The normal personality, which plays up in interaction with the environment, is a self sharply set against a non-self. It is a finite particular, in the language of philosophy. Now, if an individual, by a progressive self-dissociation, separates himself from this finite selfhood, he may discover within himself a form of consciousness, which is felt as widely continuous with others. Here we participate in the universal consciousness and then get into direct contact with other minds. This consciousness is not superconscious to our individual mind, but is of the same level and order though universal in character. Suprasensory phenomena of physical research and parapsychology, which are causing so much difficulty, are to Sri Aurobindo primarily the behaviour and action of the subliminal in human personality. This part is, in some personalities, normally more active and, therefore, they are able to display supra-sensory capacity. But it admits of cultivation too as the superconscious states do.

This is a broad outline of the view of human personality which Indian philosophy, in the person of Sri Aurobindo, has contributed to the subject. This view, by virtue of its wide comprehensiveness and due appreciation of the different aspects of personality, can truly be called the integral view of personality. It can easily accommodate, within its broad scope, the Western science of psychology as a most useful body of knowledge of the outer personality, of the environment-dependent mind and of the subconscious. And in doing so, it will give to Western psychology the larger perspective of the integral personality; in particular, the determining orientation of the superconscious. In this, the gain of the integral view too would be great. It will get annexed to it a vast body of detailed knowledge of the inter-relations of the organism to the environment.

Evidently this is a fine possibility, a possibility of a tremendous advance in the knowledge of human personality. A corresponding possibility in the objective life of human culture will also go with it.

And that will mean a reorientation of the whole life through a reorientation of human personality.

III

The Subconscious and the Superconscious

Tapping them for Creative Activity

The subconscious is the whole life of our past experiences carried along in us as our present personality and character. But this vast body of past experiences abides in us at a much diminished consciousness and we are not aware of its contents at our normal waking consciousness. It is, therefore, called 'sub-consciousness'. We might recall the experience of our becoming aware of the stopping of a clock in the room, while being unaware of its going on. Surely, we were somehow aware of its going on, otherwise how could we become aware of its stopping. The fact is that our awareness of its going on was subconscious, but when it stopped, we became conscious of it because of our interest in its going on.

To become aware of the subconscious and its working is an achievement. It is an immense extension in one's self-awareness and then one can turn that vast body of past experiences to good use, as also be on guard against the unhelpful experiences of the past.

The experiences in the subconscious are not only of a lower degree of consciousness, but they are also not in an organised form. The subconscious is actually said to be 'chaotic', since there are all kinds of experiences in it. In fact, the experiences, as they occur at the conscious level, are of all kinds, good, bad and indifferent. They are not harmonious, but much varied and even contradictory. They are just allowed to drop off into the subconscious, without our exercising a careful discrimination and an attempt to co-ordinate and organise them. The result is the persistence of these contradictions and unpleasantnesses in us almost perpetually. And they continue to exert themselves and exercise their influence on our conscious level. We are so often sad without an identifiable cause. The reason possibly is that some unpleasantness of the past acquires, through some favourable circumstances, more than its usual intensity and we become sad without being able to identify it. But one who has an eye on his subconscious might be able to do so and thus soon liberate himself from its influence. To acquire a concrete feeling for one's subconscious, one needs to recall one's dreams of the night on waking up. During sleep, when the normal consciousness lapses, the subconscious activity becomes dominant and the dreams are an expression of the same. The cravings, the hankerings, the gratifications, the disorderliness of the dreams are a representation of the character of the subconscious.

The subconscious is our whole past continuing to live with us and exercising its influence and determination on our present as also the future. To live under its determination is to continue to live as we have lived in the past more or less. This is the psychological foundation for the general opinion that the nature of man does not change.

The superconscious, on the other hand, is the range of consciousness not yet realised at a particular level of evolution. The human consciousness is superconscious to the animal and a unified and an integrated consciousness is superconscious to the ordinary human consciousness, which is so subject to conflicts, divisions, vacillations and regrets. A unified and an integrated consciousness, capable of wholeness in its quality and character and its action in thought, feeling and will, is evidently a clear possibility indicated by the growth of consciousness at the animal and the human ranges of consciousness already covered by evolution.

The yogic pursuit, which intensively cultivates self-awareness, slowly brings the subconscious and the superconscious into a direct relationship with the waking consciousness and makes them clearly observable. It is a great thing when that happens and it brings with it a wonderful feeling of self-knowledge, self-direction and self-mastery.

As the subconscious is a thing of the past, so is the superconscious a thing of the future. And as the subconscious means a perpetuation of the conflicts, contradictions, divisions and imperfections of the past, so the superconscious means wholeness, integration, unity, effectivity and perfection in the varied activities of our normal life.

Ordinarily, man is unaware of his subconscious as well as his superconscious. He lives too much centred in the waking moment of the present, unconsciously controlled by the subconscious and occasionally and vaguely guided by his superconscious. But a conscious aspiration can change this scheme of ordinary life. If we generally become aware of these two other vast dimensions of personality and recognise their true qualities and then make up our minds to live for and by the superconscious and take a hearty leap towards it, a most marvellous new dynamism of life can begin to function and radically change life.

Tapping the subconscious is a very powerful device for creative work. Instead of struggling with a problem with the conscious mind and its immediate resources, we turn towards our entire body of past experiences by intentionally contemplating the same and, as it were, entrust our problem to it and give it time to work over it. After some time, maybe we entrusted the matter to our subconscious while going to bed, and as we get up in the morning, the problem seems to be joyously pushing up into consciousness with its solution. If it was a matter of writing an essay or a poem, we feel we are ready for it. Sometimes, the subconscious takes a longer time. We have to wait and give it the time it needs. It can be useful to remind the subconscious of the task by dwelling on it and letting the subject get deeper down into us. It is extremely interesting; sometimes we can feel that some working is going on within us on the problem, that the thing is being prepared and so on. And the moment when it tends to push itself up is really delightful. It is irresistible. We have just to obey the impulse and we are quite surprised at what is done. We feel large and wide, we feel that unexpected resources have collaborated in the work.

Tapping the superconscious is immensely more thrilling. We turn towards not our own past experience, but the infinite possibilities of the future, the all-knowing unknown above and entrust our problem to the same and wait. Hopefully and trustfully waiting is essential to the process of tapping, whether of the subconscious or the superconscious. And in this case, when the matter is entrusted to the superconscious, the answers may be more surprising. We feel they are beyond our capacities, altogether unexpected, so harmonious, so beautiful and with such simplicity and spontaneity they take shape.

The resources of integral personality are most wonderful. Under the stress of egoity, we limit ourselves badly and persistently suffer from the feeling, 'oh, this is difficult, this cannot be done' and so

332   INTEGRAL PSYCHOLOGY

on. If we could, through sustained self-awareness and self-exploration, become aware of our past experiences and the possibilities of future experiences, we would feel ourselves much larger, much deeper and immensely more resourceful. What a wonderful prospect for creative activity!

Section VII

One man's perfection still can save the world.
SRI AUROBINDO

INTEGRAL PERSONALITY AND THE FUTURE

The present-day world is marked by a keen turning towards the future. Scientists and thinkers are talking of the future course of evolution and of the shape of things to come. Popular mind too is showing a loss of faith in the past, traditional values and looking for the new. Students' movements the world over want to know about the future.

In fact, it is a matter of fundamental interest to seek to know how past, present and future stand related to human life. It is evident all the three have their due places. But what are they?

The world is an evolutionary process. The *Jagat* is in motion. It is *Saṁsār*, a thing of change. But its main thrust is towards more consciousness, more integration, more harmoniousness, more creativity. Repetitiveness and mechanical movement is a secondary phase and it belongs to the unconscious in existence. The conscious surging into greater consciousness of the Superconscious is creative. This is all turned towards the future. The past covers the course of evolution or growth already covered or which is yet unconscious. The present represents the actual situation now faced. Thus life constantly moves into the future though under the pull and pressure of the unconscious, which slows down progress and even causes a reversionary movement.

It can also be observed that the more progressive men are more concentrated on the future and less progressive ones are more under the influence of the past and the unconscious. They are more conventional and repetitive.

If we consider integral personality in detail we will find that our body, life and mind, the more unconscious parts, are more repetitive and mechanical. Even the mind, the most conscious among them, is nine-tenths unconscious and is governed by the past instinctual urges in spite of its purposiveness. The spirit in man, the self-existent conscious principle, is alone wholly turned to the future and is normally creative.

It is extremely interesting how some thinkers are now discovering these truths, each in his own way. Julian Huxley is a biologist and Teilhard de Chardin a palaeontologist; both are keenly looking into the future and trying to find out what the future course of evolution possibly would be. Bergson, a philosopher but proceeding on biological basis, has a similar interest and says something similar.

Julian Huxley conceives individual growth as the line of evolutionary progress for the future. And Bergson and Teilhard de Chardin think of a higher race of men. How interesting are the following words from Julian Huxley, Teilhard de Chardin and Bergson:

Huxley in his Introduction to Teilhard's 'The Phenomenon of Man' says:

"With his genius for fruitful analogy, he (Teilhard) points out that the process of evolution on earth is itself now in the process of becoming cephalised. Before the appearance of man, life consisted of a vast array of separate branches, linked only by an unorganised pattern of ecological interaction. The incipient development of mankind into a single psycho-social unit, with a single noosystem or common pool of thought, is providing the evolutionary process with the rudiments of a head. It remains for our descendants to organise this global noosystem more adequately, so as to enable mankind to understand the process of evolution on earth more fully and to direct it more adequately.

"I had independently expressed something of the same sort, by saying that in modern scientific man, evolution was at last becoming conscious of itself – a phrase which I found delighted Père Teilhard. His formulation, however, is more profound and more seminal: it implies what we should consider inter-thinking humanity as a new type of organism, whose destiny it is to realise new possibilities for evolving life on this planet.

"The conditions of advance are these: global unity of mankind's noetic organisation or system of awareness, but a high degree of variety within that unity; love, with goodwill and full co-operation; personal integration and internal harmony; and increasing knowledge.

"We, mankind, contain the possibilities of the earth's immense future, and can realise more and more of them on condition that we increase our knowledge and our love. That, it seems to me, is the distillation of the *Phenomenon of Man*."

This represents well enough both Huxley and Teilhard.

And Bergson's concluding sentences of his 'Two Sources of Morality and Religion' are:

"Mankind lies groaning, half crushed beneath the weight of its own progress. Men do not sufficiently realise that their future is in their own hands. Theirs is the task of determining first of all whether they want to go on living or not. Theirs the responsibility, then, for deciding if they want merely to live or intend to make just the extra effort required for fulfilling, even on their refractory planet, the essential function of the universe, which is a machine for the making of gods."

These are fine ventures, very well supported, in the realm of thought. For the Integral Yoga of Sri Aurobindo and the Mother, the future becomes a practical proposition, even though most adventurous and extremely difficult. In Sri Aurobindo, we find the higher planes observed and characterised in great detail; their cognitions, conations and affections well stated and duly organised and inter-related, the new worlds which they create also cogently shown. All this makes a most illuminating study. We clearly see and feel that this disjointed world of facts, this vast plurality, this struggle of egos, is not the end of the matter, that a vivid unity rules over all this, which transforms this apparent purposelessness into a coherent and well-directed movement. This is a fact of experience of high yogic pursuit.

In the context of Integral Personality, it is simpler to say that the psychic and spiritual parts are normal potentialities of man and that they must get their chance of development. And if that happens, things would change in man as well as in his world. These possibilities are the clearest indications of the future shape of things. These possibilities of man, which are ascertainable, can show the new trends of evolution, of human development. And these are also cultivable. Thus man can, in a clear-minded way, look forward to his future and prepare himself for it.

APPENDICES

1. The Crust and the Core in Personality: Sri Aurobindo and Bergson

2. Authentic Words – Pertaining to the Psychic Being, Past and Present

3. How to Test the Presence and State of Activity of the Psychic Being in a Child (or an Adult)

4. Charts

5. A Substitute for Glossary

(1)

THE CRUST AND THE CORE IN PERSONALITY: SRI AUROBINDO AND BERGSON

Sri Aurobindo

As the crust of the outer nature cracks, as the walls of inner separation break down, the inner light gets through, the inner fire burns in the heart, the substance of the nature and the stuff of consciousness refine to a greater subtlety and purity, and the deeper psychic experiences, those which are not solely of an inner mental or inner vital character, become possible in this subtler, purer, finer substance; the soul begins to unveil itself, the psychic personality reaches its full stature. The soul, the psychic entity, then manifests itself as the central being which upholds mind and life and body and supports all the other powers and functions of the Spirit; it takes up its greater function as the guide and ruler of the nature. A guidance, a governance begins from within which exposes every movement to the light of Truth, repels what is false, obscure, opposed to the divine realisation: every region of the being, every nook and corner of it, every movement, formation, direction, inclination of thought, will, emotion, sensation, action, reaction, motive, disposition, propensity, desire, habit of the conscious or subconscious physical, even the most concealed, camouflaged, mute, recondite, is lighted up with the unerring psychic light, their confusions dissipated, their tangles disentangled, their obscurities, deceptions, self-deceptions precisely indicated and removed; all is purified, set right, the whole nature harmonised, modulated in the psychic key, put in spiritual order. This process may be rapid or tardy according to the amount of obscurity and resistance still left in the nature, but it goes on unfalteringly so long as it is not complete. As a final result the whole conscious being is made perfectly apt for spiritual experience of every kind, turned towards spiritual truth of thought, feeling, sense, action, tuned to the right responses, delivered from the darkness and stubbornness of the tamasic inertia, the turbidities and turbulences and impurities of the rajasic passion and restless unharmonised kinetism, the enlightened rigidities and sattwic limitations or poised balancements of constructed equilibrium which are the character of the Ignorance.

This is the first result, but the second is a free inflow of all kinds of spiritual experience, experience of the Self, experience of the Ishwara and the Divine Shakti, experience of cosmic consciousness, a direct touch with cosmic forces and with the occult movements of universal Nature, a psychic sympathy and unity and inner communication and interchanges of all kinds with other beings and with Nature, illuminations of the mind by knowledge, illuminations of the heart by love and devotion and spiritual joy and ecstasy, illuminations of the sense and the body by higher experience, illuminations of dynamic action in the truth and largeness of a purified mind and heart and soul, the certitudes of the divine light and guidance, the joy and power of the divine force working in the will and the conduct. These experiences are the result of an opening outward of the inner and inmost being and nature; for then there comes into play the soul's power of unerring inherent consciousness, its vision, its touch on things which is superior to any mental cognition; there is there, native to the psychic consciousness in its pure working, an immediate sense of the world and its beings, a direct inner contact with them and a direct contact with the Self and with the Divine, – a direct knowledge, a direct sight of truth and of all truths, a direct penetrating spiritual emotion and feeling, a direct intuition of right will and right action, a power to rule and to create an order of the being not by the gropings of the superficial self, but from within, from the inner truth of self and things and the occult realities of Nature. (SABCL, Vol. 19, pp. 907-9)

Bergson

There is at least one reality which we all seize from within, by intuition and not by simple analysis. It is our own person in its flowing through time, the self which endures. With no other thing can we sympathize intellectually, or if you like, spiritually. But one thing is sure: we sympathize with ourselves.

When, with the inner regard of my consciousness, I examine my person in its passivity, like some superficial encrustment, first, I perceive all the perceptions which come to it from the material world. These perceptions are clear-cut, distinct, juxtaposed or mutually juxtaposable; they seek to group themselves into objects.

Next, I perceive memories more or less adherent to these perceptions and which serve to interpret them; these memories are, so to speak, as if detached from the depth of my person and drawn to the periphery by perceptions resembling them, they are fastened on me without being absolutely myself. And finally, I become aware of tendencies, motor habits, a crowd of virtual actions more or less solidly bound to those perceptions and these memories. All these elements with their well-defined forms appear to me to be all the more distinct from myself the more they are distinct from one another. Turned outwards from within, together they constitute the surface of a sphere which tends to expand and lose itself in the external world. But if I pull myself in from the periphery towards the centre, if I seek deep down within me what is the most uniformly, the most constantly and durably myself, I find something altogether different. (*Introduction to Metaphysics*, Wisdom Library, 1961, pp. 9-10)

*

We penetrate it, nevertheless, and the only way possible is by an intuition. In this sense, an absolute internal knowledge of the duration of the self by the self is possible. But if metaphysics demands and can obtain here an intuition, science has no less need of an analysis. And it is because of a confusion between the roles of analysis and intuition that the dissensions between schools of thought and the conflicts between systems will arise.

Psychology, in fact, like the other sciences, proceeds by analysis. It resolves the self, first given to it in the form of a simple intuition, into sensations, feelings, images, etc. which it studies separately. It therefore substitutes for the self a series of elements which are the psychological facts. But these elements, are they parts? That is the whole question, and it is because we have evaded it that we have often stated in insoluble terms the problem of the human personality.

It is undeniable that any psychological state, by the sole fact that it belongs to a person, reflects the whole of a personality. There is no feeling, no matter how simple, which does not virtually contain the past and present of the being which experiences it, which can be separated from it and constitute a "state", other than by an effort of abstraction or analysis. But it is no less undeniable that without this effort of abstraction or analysis there would be no possible development of psychological science. Now, of what does the operation consist by which the psychologist detaches a psychological state in order to set it up as a more or less independent entity? He begins by disregarding the person's special coloration, which can be expressed only in common and known terms. He then strives to isolate, in the person thus already simplified, this or that aspect which lends itself to an interesting study. If, for example, it is a question of inclination, he will leave out of account the inexpressible shading which colors it and which brings it about that my inclination is not yours; he will then fix his attention on the movement by which our personality tends towards a certain object; he will isolate this attitude, and it is this special aspect of the person, this point of view on the mobility of the inner life, this "schema" of the concrete inclination which he will set up as an independent fact. (Ibid., pp. 22-24)

*

That the personality has unity is certain; but such an affirmation does not teach me anything about the extraordinary nature of this unity which is the person. That our self is multiple I further agree, but there is in it a multiplicity which, it must be recognised, has nothing in common with any other. What really matters to philosophy is to know what unity, what multiplicity, what reality superior to the abstract one and the abstract multiple is the multiple unity of the person. And it will know this only if it once again grasps the simple intuition of the self by the self. Then, according to the slope it chooses to come down from the summit, it will arrive at unity or multiplicity or any one of the concepts by which we try to define the moving life by the person. But no mixing of these concepts among themselves, I repeat, would give anything resembling the person which endures. (Ibid., p. 35)

(2)

AUTHENTIC WORDS PERTAINING TO THE PSYCHIC BEING, PAST AND PRESENT

अङ्गुष्ठमात्रः पुरुषो मध्य आत्मनि तिष्ठति ।
ईशानो भूतभव्यस्य न ततो विजुगुप्सते । एतद्वै तत् ॥

(1) The Upanishads (Katha Upanishad): "The Purusha who is seated in the midst of our self is no larger than the finger of a man; He is the Lord of what was and what shall be. Him having seen one shrinks not from aught, nor abhors any. This is That thou seekest." (Sri Aurobindo Birth Centenary Library, Vol. 12, p. 256)

अङ्गुष्ठमात्रः पुरुषो ज्योतिरिवाधूमकः ।
ईशानो भूतभव्यस्य स एवाद्य स उ श्वः । एतद्वै तत् ॥

"The Purusha that is within us is no larger than the finger of a man: He is like a blazing fire that is without smoke, He is Lord of His past and His future. He alone is today and He alone shall be tomorrow. This is That thou seekest." (Ibid., p. 256)

The heart is seat of the individual soul as well as the universal Self. The mention "no larger than the finger of man" pertains to the individual soul. Both kinds of references are present in the Upanishads. The five koshas of the Upanishads represent, beyond body, life and mind, the above-head spiritual dimension of integral knowledge (विज्ञान) and of Bliss (आनंद). The heart consciousness is not included.

यदा सर्वे प्रमुच्यन्ते कामा येऽस्य हृदि श्रिताः ।
अथ मर्त्योऽमृतो भवत्यत्र ब्रह्म समश्नुते ॥

"When every desire that finds lodging in the heart of man, has been loosened from its moorings, then this mortal puts on immortality: even here he tastes God, in this human body." (Ibid., p. 264)

अङ्गुष्ठमात्रः पुरुषोऽन्तरात्मा सदा जनानां हृदये सन्निविष्टः ।
तं स्वाच्छरीरात्प्रवृहेन्मुञ्जादिवेषीकां धैर्येण ।
तं विद्याच्छुक्रममृतं तं विद्याच्छुक्रममृतमिति ॥

"The Purusha, the Spirit within, who is no larger than the finger of a man is seated for ever in the heart of creatures: one must separate Him with patience from one's own body as one separates from a blade of grass its main fibre. Thou shalt know Him for the Bright Immortal, yea, for the Bright Immortal." (Ibid., p. 265)

(2) Meera (so also many other Bhaktas of the Medieval period)

प्रभुजी, हरो मेरे हिय की जड़ताई

This is a keen aspiration to awaken the heart centre. Kabir is a Jnāna-margi with Bhakti.

(3) Anahata-Nad of the Nad Sampradaya is the sound equivalent of the heart illumination.

(4) The Sufi literature too is strong in its appeal to the heart. This dimension of spiritual life is their main seeking.

Sri Aurobindo

(5) "The psychic being is quite different from the mind or vital; it stands behind them where they meet in the heart. Its central place is there, but behind the heart rather than in the heart; for what men call usually the heart is the seat of emotion, and human emotions are mental-vital impulses, not ordinarily psychic in their nature."

*

"The psychic being may be described in Indian language as the Purusha in the heart or the *Chaitya Purusha*; but the inner or secret heart must be understood, *hṛdaye guhāyām*, not the outer vital-emotional centre."

*

"The being of man is composed of these elements – the psychic behind supporting all, the inner mental, vital and physical, and the outer, quite external nature of mind, life and body which is their instrument of expression."

*

"The psychic being is always there, but is not felt because it is covered up by the mind and vital; when it is no longer covered up, it is then said to be awake."

*

"When the psychic being awakens, you grow conscious of your own soul; you know your self."

*

"...when the psychic being is awakened, it throws out all the dross from the emotional being and makes it free from sentimentalism or the lower play of emotionalism."

*

"...when the psychic being comes forward all is happiness, the right attitude, the right vision of things."

(*SABCL*, Vols. 22 & 24, 'Planes and Parts of Being', 'Triple Transformation')

A few words of poetry

"O Bliss who ever dwellst deep hid within
While men seek thee outside and never find..."
(SABCL, Vol. 28, p. 345)

*

"But once the hidden doors are flung apart
Then the veiled king steps out in Nature's front..."
(Ibid, Vol. 29, p. 530)

*

"Out of the mystic cavern in man's heart
The heavenly Psyche must put off her veil..."

(Ibid., p. 486)

*

"Our souls can visit in great lonely hours
Still regions of imperishable Light,
All-seeing eagle-peaks of silent Power
And moon-flame oceans of swift fathomless Bliss
And calm immensities of spirit Space."

(Ibid., Vol. 28, p. 47)

THE MOTHER

(6) "We give the name "psychic" to the psychological centre of our being..."

*

"It is therefore of capital importance for us to become conscious of its presence within us, to concentrate on this presence and make it a living force for us and identify ourselves with it."

*

"Whatever you do, whatever your occupation and activity, the will to find the truth of your being and to unite with it must always be living, always present behind all that you do, all that you experience, all that you think."

*

"It is like a light that shines at the centre of the being radiating through the thick coverings of the external consciousness. Some have a vague perception of its presence; a good many children are under its influence which shows itself very distinctly at times in their spontaneous reactions and even in their words."

*

"To become conscious of the psychic being you must will for it, silence your mind as far as possible, and enter deep into the core of your heart beyond all sensations and thoughts."

(*On Education*, Collected Works of the Mother, Vol. 12, 'The Science of Living' and 'Psychic Education and Spiritual Education')

(3)
HOW TO TEST THE PRESENCE AND STATE OF ACTIVITY OF THE PSYCHIC BEING IN A CHILD (OR AN ADULT)

1. The first thing is, we must be ourselves in our best psychic state – psychic identification, aspiration for the psychic, inwardness, depth, contented joyous self-poise, remembrance of the Divine, of the most revered personality.

The psychic vibration of the child can express itself directly in spontaneity, in joy of the heart, simplicity, but we must learn to recognise the quality of this vibration. The vibration of the vital being, its force, its vivacity is distinctive, so is that of the mind, intelligence, thinking, etc. And the vibration of the physical has a dullness of consciousness about it, expressing itself in obstinacy, laziness, slowness of reaction, etc.

Appreciation of the psychic vibration is the real thing, but it requires long pursuit and self-training. It is a thing of peace, joy, quietude, depth, inwardness, spontaneity and a thrilling contact. And it requires a vivid experience of one's own psychic being.

2. One's best psychic state secured, one should proceed to seek the Higher Presence and in this setting, get into touch with the child concerned. Feel his inner being and ask ordinary questions, what is your name, your age, what play you like, etc., and watch his reactions, his feelings, his self-confidence, simplicity, ease, joy, etc. The psychic vibration can come into play and be recognised more easily. His eyes may be looked into particularly during this time and seen if one can go deep into them and how one feels there. The child's recent photograph may also be examined to see whether the eyes reflect some depth in them. That will be additional evidence. He may also be shown the pictures selected for this purpose and asked, 'which face you like most.' His reactions will reveal the quality of his inner sensibility.

A Few Words of the Mother

1. "I have known children who were much more conscious of their psychic being at the age of five than at fourteen, and more at

fourteen than at twenty-five; particularly from the moment they start going to school and undergo the kind of intensive mental culture which draws their attention to the intellectual part of their being, they lose almost always contact with their psychic being." (*Bulletin*, 1964, Feb.)

"If you were an experienced observer, if you could take note of what happens in a being, simply by looking at his eyes!... It is said the eye is the mirror of the soul; it is a popular way of saying, but if the eyes do not express the psychic, the reason is that it is very much behind, veiled by very many things; look at the eyes of children with care and you will see a kind of light – people say candid – but so true, so true that looks at the world with wonder. Well, this wonder, it is the wonder of the Psychic that sees the truth but does not understand much of the world, for it is too far from there. Children have that, but as they learn, become more intelligent, more educated, that thing fades away and you see in their eyes all kinds of things; thoughts, desires, passions, wickedness, but that kind of a small very pure flame is no more there. And you may be sure that it is the mind that has entered there and the psychic has gone very much behind." (Ibid.)

2. "...what most often men call 'soul', unless they are initiates, is only vital activity. When someone has a strong, active wilful vital dominating the bodily activities, has a very living or intense contact with persons and things and happenings, when someone has a pronounced taste for art, for all expression of beauty, you are generally tempted to say and to believe that he has a living soul; but it is not his soul, it is his vital being that is living and dominates the bodily activity. That is the first difference between one who is beginning to be developed and those who are still in the inertia and tamas of a purely material life. That gives at first to the appearance and also to the activity a kind of vibration, an intensity of vibration which often leaves the impression that the person has a living soul, but it is not that, it is his vital being which is developed, has a special capacity, is stronger than the physical inertia and gives an intensity of vibration and life and action that is missing in those whose vital being is not developed. This confusion between vital activity and soul is very common. The vital vibration is indeed much more easily perceptible to the human consciousness than the vibration of the soul." (*Questions and Answers*, 1958)

"Generally to perceive the soul in anyone, one must have a very quiet mind, very quiet, because when the mind is active, it is the mind's vibrations that one sees, not the soul's vibrations." (Ibid.)

"And when you look at someone who is conscious of his soul and who lives in his soul, you have the impression that you are going down, entering deep, deep into the person, far, far, very far within." (Ibid.)

3. "To find out the soul, you must draw back from the surface, withdraw into the deep and enter, enter, enter, go down and down and down and down into a pit deep, silent, immobile; there is something warm, quiet, rich with content and very immobile, and very full, something like a sweetness – that is the soul." (Ibid.)

(4)

CHARTS

INTEGRAL PERSONALITY

Principal Planes and Parts

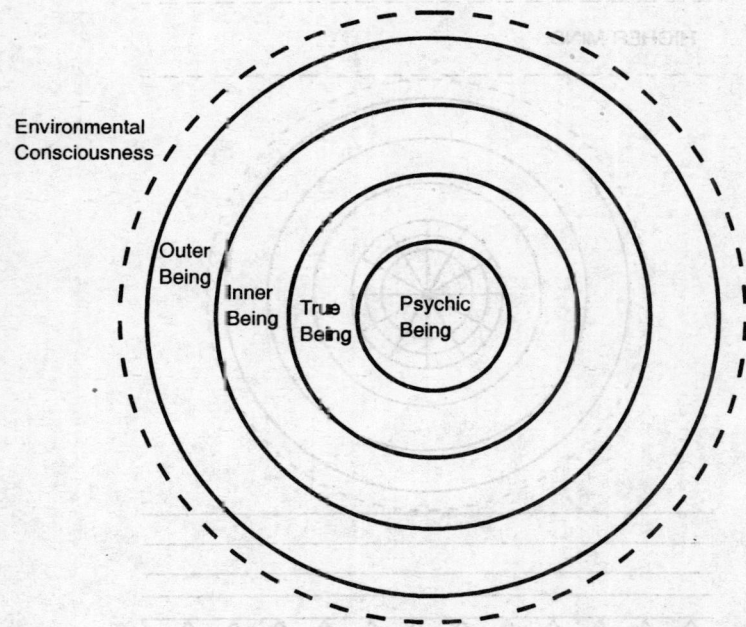

OUTER BEING = Outer Body, Life and Mind
INNER BEING = Inner (Subtle) Body, Life and Mind (Subliminal) in contact with the universal body, life and mind
TRUE BEING   = True Body, Life and Mind (parts most under the influence of the Psychic)

Environmental Consciousness - the protective envelope around the individual

INTEGRAL PERSONALITY
(3) The Conscient, Subconscient, Inconscient and Superconscient

SUPERCONSCIENT
- SUPERMIND
- OVERMIND
- INTUITIVE MIND
- ILLUMINED MIND
- HIGHER MIND

CONSCIENT

SUBCONSCIENT

INCONSCIENT

Psychic Being, True Being and Inner Being are veiled. Mind, Life, Body and Environmental Consciousness are conscious in varying degrees.

PERSONALITY AND EXISTENCE

(1) The outer Personality and its world

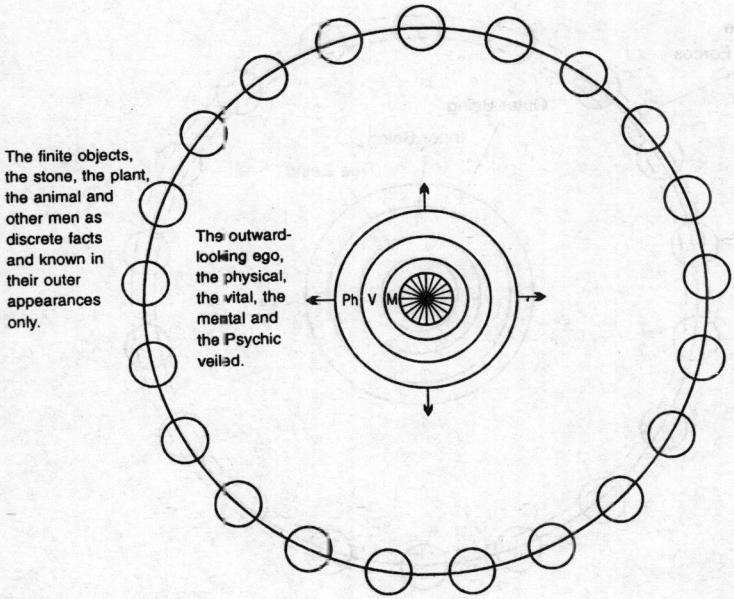

1. The self of the ego is a superficial formation, which seeks and is adapted to deal with the surface qualities (the appearances, Rupa Rasa Gandha etc.) of the external world, which to it, consist of material bodies, animate bodies and mental animate bodies like himself.
2. The self as well as the world are marked by dualities i.e. a play of opposite impulses, qualities, ideals, principles, forces.
3. The self consists of a plurality of impulses of dual character and the world too consists of a plurality of objects and forces of dual nature. Division, conflict and struggle is the normal course of things in the self and the world.

PERSONALITY AND EXISTENCE

(2) The inner Personality (the personality of the inner being) and its world

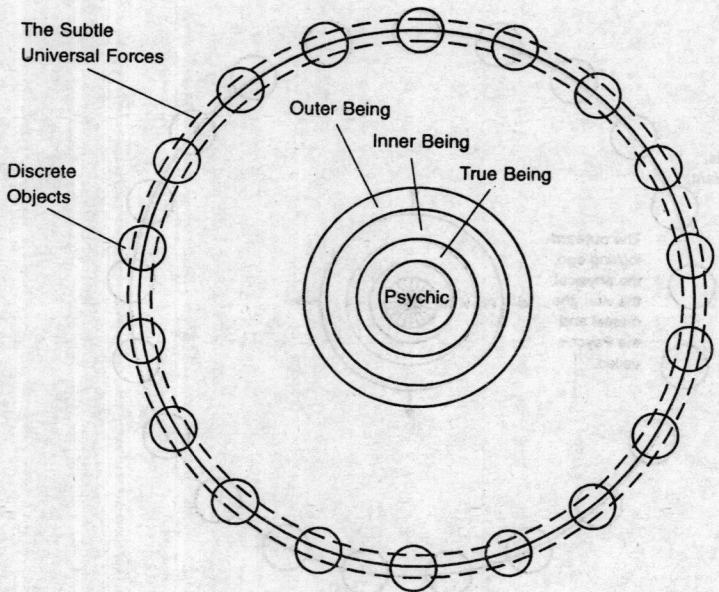

1. As the individual draws back or detaches himself a little from his outer surface personality, he emerges into a larger inner self of a wider mind and a wider vital and a wider physical. And then he feels himself to be in the realm of the universal mind, universal vital and universal physical. There new awarenesses, feelings and volitions become possible to it. To know objects at a distance in space and time, to feel about them and to act on them becomes a possibility.

PERSONALITY AND EXISTENCE

(3) The inmost Personality and its world

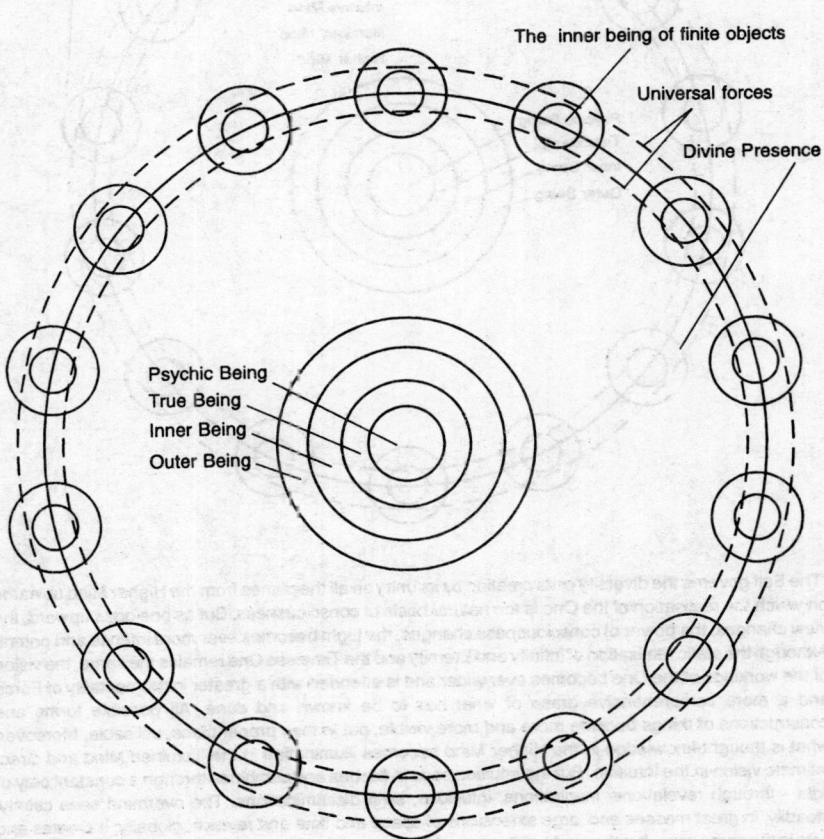

PERSONALITY AND EXISTENCE

(4) The Higher Personalities and their Worlds

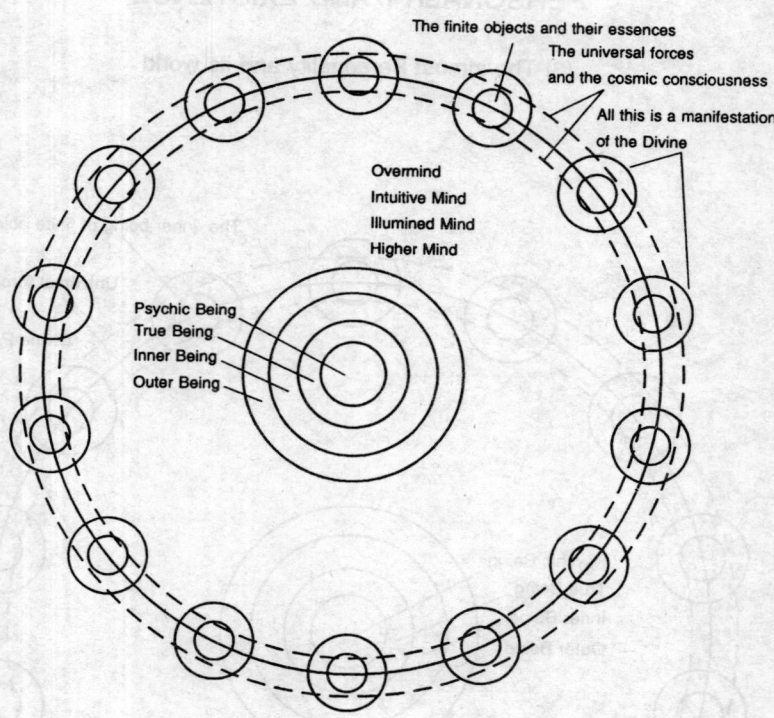

"The Self governs the diversity of its creation by its unity on all the planes from the Higher Mind upwards on which the realisation of the One is the natural basis of consciousness. But as one goes upward, the view changes, the power of consciousness changes, the Light becomes ever more intense and potent. Although the static realisation of Infinity and Eternity and the Timeless One remains the same, the vision of the workings of the One becomes ever wider and is attended with a greater instrumentality of Force and a more comprehensive grasp of what has to be known and done. All possible forms and constructions of things become more and more visible, put in their proper place, utilisable. Moreover, what is thought-knowledge in the Higher Mind becomes illumination in the Illumined Mind and direct intimate vision in the Intuition. But the Intuition sees in flashes and combines through a constant play of light - through revelations, inspirations, intuitions, swift discriminations. The overmind sees calmly, steadily, in great masses and large extensions of space and time and relation, globally; it creates and acts in the same way - it is the world of the great Gods, the divine Creators. Only, each creates in his own way; he sees all but sees all from his own viewpoint. There is not the absolute supramental harmony and certitude." (On Yoga, Tome Two, pp. 262-63)

PERSONALITY AND EXISTENCE

(5) The Integral Personality and its Worlds
The Unlimited Beyond Sachchidananda

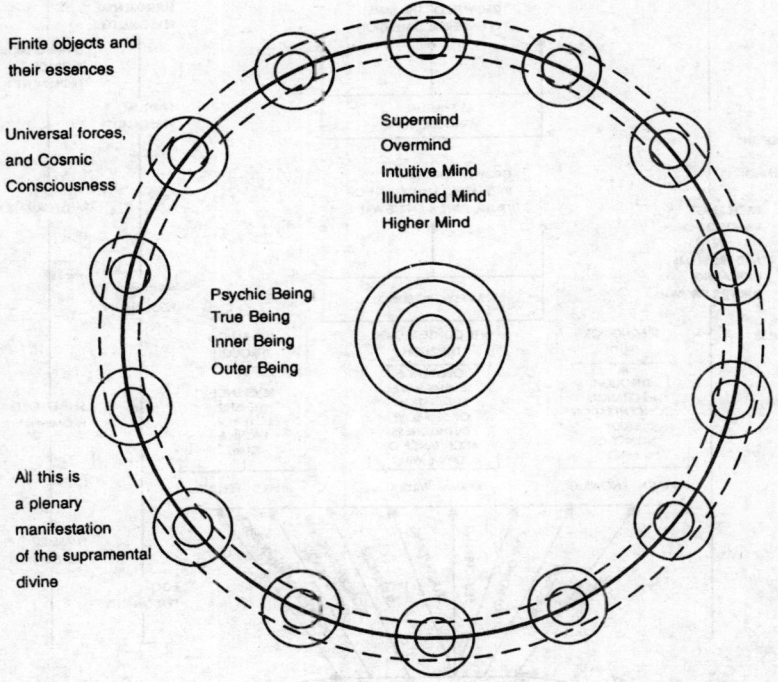

The principal domains of Integral Personality are:
1. The outer personality which is the instrument of action on the external world.
2. The inner personality which consists of the inner mental, vital and physical. They constitute the cosmic consciousness and deal with universal forces.
3. The Inmost personality which consists of the psychic being.
4. The Higher personalities which consist of the ranges from the Higher mind to Overmind.
5. The Integral personality, which involves ascent to supermind and its descent up to matter, achieves complete transformation and integralisation of all the parts of personality.

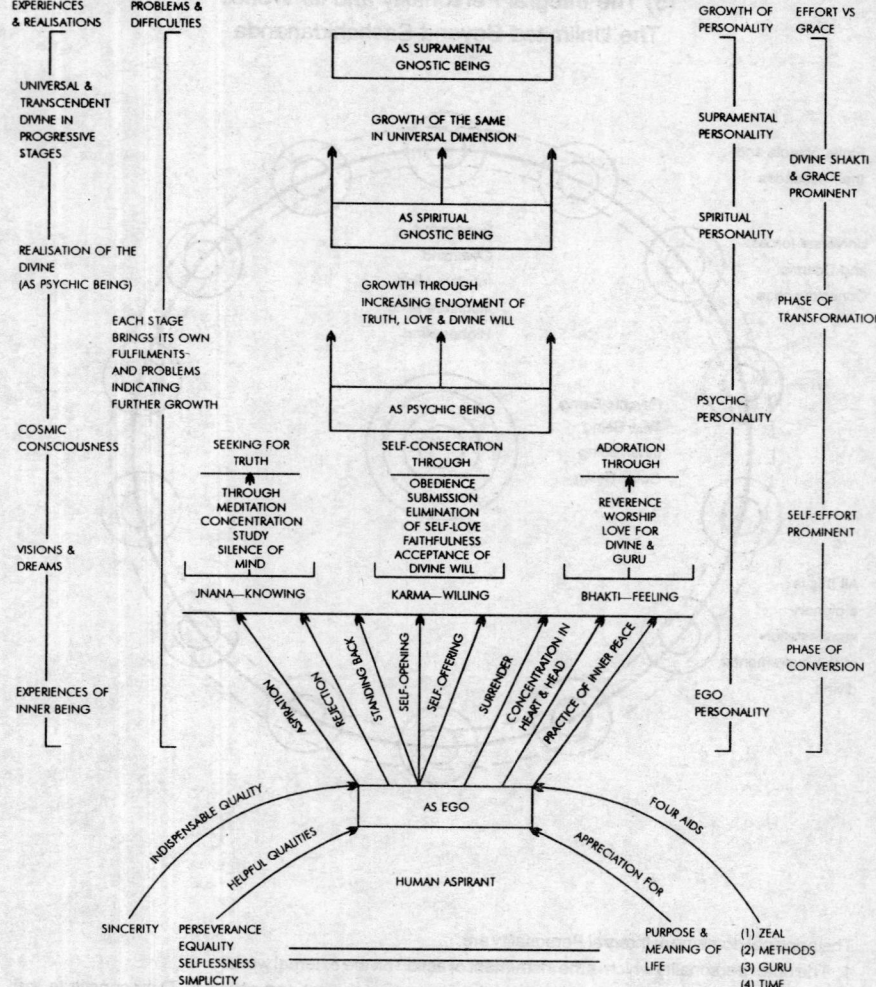

(5)
A SUBSTITUTE FOR GLOSSARY
SRI AUROBINDO'S VIEW OF MAN AND EXISTENCE

(1) Its Special Terms

Each original creative personality has its own way of viewing man and existence. A seer's seeing and a thinker's thinking have an originality. That is, in fact, its contribution to the sum of human knowledge. That necessitates the creation of new terms and they need to be specially attended to and their original sense duly comprehended. Then it becomes easy enough to appreciate and enjoy the force and the power of the personality concerned.

Man and existence are, in Sri Aurobindo, closely interconnected. Man in his constitution and make-up represents the world existence. The *Pinda* is a miniature *Brahmanda*; the microcosm and macrocosm are significant terms. The cosmos has a micro-form and a macro-form. This perspective is a great help in understanding and enjoying Sri Aurobindo. Besides this, one needs to get the feeling for Sri Aurobindo's Yoga, his system of Sadhana. The Appendix of this book gives a few diagrams, graphic representations of Man, Existence and Yoga. They represent Sri Aurobindo's insights regarding these in visual forms. If one dwells on these and tries to get into the spirit of the basic insights involved there, it will help a great deal in feeling clear about the variant new terms created and used by Sri Aurobindo. The notes appended to the diagrams will be found helpful.

The more important terms are given here in some elaboration:

The Physical, the Vital and the Mental as distinct parts and various combinations like *Physical*-Vital, *Vital*-physical, *Physical*-mental, *Mental*-physical, *Mental*-vital and *Vital*-mental. The first term is dominant and the second subordinate and the third yet less influential. When the vital is combined with the mind, it becomes higher vital and when it is combined with the physical it becomes lower vital. Thus the three principal factors acquire a higher and a lower quality too. The Psychic too can enter into these combinations and lend its own quality more or less when it becomes active and dynamic at the surface. Ordinarily, it is a silent influence from behind the surface consciousness.

The important thing is that we get the essential characteristics of the three main factors, the physical, the vital and the mental, and not get mixed up with their endless combinations. All the three have a reference to the external situation. They are all outward oriented. The Psychic alone is an inner self-existent fact, not dependent on the external. Now, the physical is the bodily, basically unconscious fact. The vital is energy and force for external activity and mind is thinking, an ideational operation: on this basis one can proceed and build up one's own self-knowledge slowly and wait for finer discriminations to emerge.

The following words of Sri Aurobindo are a clear guidance on the subject: —

(i) "It must be remembered that while this classification is indispensable for psychological self-knowledge and discipline and practice, it can be used best when it is not made too rigid and cutting a formula. For things run very much into each other and a synthetical sense of these powers is as necessary as the analysis."

(ii) "In the outer surface nature mind, psychic, vital, physical are jumbled together and it needs a strong power of introspection, self-analysis, close observation and disentanglement of the threads of thought, feeling and impulse to find out the composition of our nature and the relation and interaction of these parts upon each other. But when we go inside, we find the sources of all this surface action and there the parts of our being are quite clearly distinct from each other; it is as if we were a group-being, each member of the group with its separate place and function, and all directed by a central being who is sometimes in front above the others, sometimes behind the scenes."

(iii) "It is a little difficult to equate this old nomenclature (*manas, buddhi, chitta* and *ahaṅkāra*) with that of this yoga, for the former takes the mixed action of the surface and tries to analyse it while in this yoga what is mixed together on the surface gets separated and seen in the light of the deeper working behind which is hidden from the surface awareness."

All the three are present in every human individual and in every state, but their proportions or the degrees of prominence vary and that gives rise to the individual quality of a personality or a state.

(2) The Psychic Being

The Psychic Being is the evolving self-existent conscious joyous principle in man, which supports the body, life and mind. It is the inmost central fact of personality accessible through a persistent inward penetration. It is the essential integrating and harmonising fact of life.

The individual soul is the substantive reality commanding the individual's life. The Psychic Being may be regarded as its representative in evolution.

(3) The Conscient, the Subconscient, the Inconscient and the Superconscient

The 'Unconscious' is really not the denial of consciousness. It is only less conscious. Further, it is a dynamic fact, not just a storehouse of old memories and experiences. To stress these two features, Sri Aurobindo prefers the term inconscient. The other terms are allied to it and need to represent the dynamic quality. The 'Superconscient' covers the consciousnesses of the Psychic Being and of the Higher Planes mentioned above.

(4) The Higher Mind, The Illumined Mind, The Intuitive Mind, The Overmind, The Supermind

Instincts and habits in man are much less conscious than thinking and man is so much divided within himself. Higher integrations involve progressive unifications and higher luminosities. Sri Aurobindo identifies the above-named stages in this process. Here are Sri Aurobindo's own words in this connection:

"The Self governs the diversity of its creation by its unity on all the planes from the Higher Mind upwards in which the realisation of the One is the natural basis of consciousness. But as one goes upward, the view changes, the power of consciousness changes, the Light becomes ever more intense and potent. Although the static realisation of Infinity and Eternity and the Timeless One remains the same, the vision of the workings of the One becomes ever wider and is attended with a greater instrumentality of Force and a more comprehensive grasp of what has to be known and done. All possible forms and constructions of things become more and more visible, put in their proper place, utilisable. Moreover, what is thought-knowledge in the Higher Mind becomes illumination in the Illumined Mind and direct intimate vision of the Intuition. But the Intuition sees in flashes and combines through a constant play of light – through revelations, inspirations, intuitions, swift discriminations. The Overmind sees calmly, steadily, in great masses and large extensions of space and time and relation, globally; it creates and acts in the same way, it is the world of the great Gods, the divine Creators. Only, each creates in his own way; he sees all but sees all from his own viewpoint. There is not the absolute supramental harmony and certitude."

(5) The Environmental Consciousness

The individual acts in the environment and receives the impacts of the same on himself through a sort of a sheath around his body, which needs to be cultivated to become well conscious. Then one can become aware of an attack of a disease when it is trying to get in and more easily remain free from it.

(6) The Chakras

The chakras are the subtle centres of consciousness commanding the larger capacities of integral personality, which need to be consciously cultivated. But they can become active on their own as integral personality grows up.

(7) Transformation

Sublimation is recanalisation of an energy into new forms of expression, sex energy finding expression in art, literature, religion, social service, etc., as affirmed by Freud.

Transformation is not recanalisation, but a change of the energy itself into one of a higher quality, sex energy itself becoming qualitatively different and the individual enjoying basically the freedom of the higher spiritual energy.

(8) The 'Out-look', the 'In-look' and the 'Up-look', Bahir-mukha, Antar-mukha, Urdhwa-mukha

These three terms are not much used by sri Aurobindo in his writings, but in thought they are much employed and they are helpful in understanding him. Our ordinary attitude is of looking outward (of 'out-look'), in looking within ('in-look') we turn towards the Psychic Being and in 'up-look', we turn towards the Higher planes.

(9) Man, a Transitional Being

Man in his present constitutional make-up clearly indicates or refers to higher integrations of progressive unifications. He is evidently not a finished formation. He is, therefore, transitional.

(10) Sri Aurobindo's Philosophy of Life and Existence

All existence is a progression from unconsciousness to consciousness. The stone, the plant, the animal and the man are a vivid demonstration of it. With man, it becomes a conscious process through education and culture. Through intensive spiritual pursuits, it can rise to higher integrations and realisations of life. And the experience of growth, which involves search and discovery, is a joyful pursuit. When it gets obstructed or thwarted, then sorrow and suffering arise.

To grow in consciousness more and more would be then the essential task of life. And all limitations of life, lack of knowledge, dullness of feeling and incapacity of action are really forms of unconsciousness. With the growth of consciousness, we progressively overcome them.

The cosmic evolution is such growth and individuals through intensified effort can achieve it more quickly. The goal of all evolution, cosmic and individual, seems to be integral consciousness or divine perfection of life and existence.

If this basic thought of Sri Aurobindo's is duly appreciated it can help enormously to understand his special terms in philosophy as also his perceptions as to social progress, political life, national and international, and literary creation.

The self-existent, all-conscious all-joyous spirit is the true Truth.

The world is Its evolving manifestation from unconsciousness to increasing consciousness. All falsehood, all evil, all mechanism is the work of unconsciousness, which is being progressively overcome.

Psychic consciousness, the individual spiritual principle of life, when realised affords assured self-existence, freedom from environmental dependence and essential joyfulness. That is a demonstrative proof of this philosophy of life and existence.

Now the more significant terms of this philosophy and its expression in various fields of knowledge may be considered.

(1) Brahman, Sachchidananda, Omnipresent Reality, and the Divine, the Absolute and the Unknowable represent the ultimate reality. The Unknowable is the last and the highest range of it.

Sachchidananda is directly accessible to man. Omnipresent Reality is with reference to manifestation. Brahman and Absolute are the same.

Evolution

(2) Darwin's discovery of the origin of species made this word and this concept the most dynamic fact of life and existence. But he studied the change in the forms of life, the apparent species. But these represent different levels and degrees of consciousness and they all involve a process of growth of consciousness. Thus evolution is really a growth of consciousness from Amoeba to man. And life and non-life cannot be sharply divided and so consciousness may be extending further down into the plant and even the stone. And man surely points to higher integration. Thus all existence seems to present a picture of growth of consciousness from the infinitesimal to the Integral Infinite consciousness.

Planes of Progressive Manifestation in Evolution

(3) This long evolutionary process displays and involves many planes of being. They are these:

1. Existence
2. Consciousness-Force
3. Bliss
4. Supermind
5. Matter
6. Life
7. Psychic
8. Mind

Involution and Evolution (Descent and Ascent)

(4) "The Divine descends from pure existence through the play of Consciousness-Force and Bliss and the creative medium of Supermind into cosmic being; we ascend from Matter through a developing life, soul and mind and the illuminating medium of supermind towards the divine being."

Sri Aurobindo

Death, Suffering, Evil and Limitation

(5) "If all is in truth Sachchidananda, death, suffering, evil, limitation can only be the creations, positive in practical effect, negative in essence, of a distorting consciousness which has fallen from the total and unifying knowledge of itself into some error of division and partial experience."

Sri Aurobindo

"...if we could grasp the essential nature and the essential cause of error, suffering and death, we might hope to arrive at a mastery over them which should be not relative but entire. We might hope even to eliminate them altogether and justify the dominant instinct of our nature by the conquest of that absolute good, bliss, knowledge and immortality which our intuitions perceive as the true and ultimate condition of the human being."

Sri Aurobindo

Knowledge and ignorance (Unity and Multiplicity)

(6) "Through Avidya, the Multiplicity, lies our path out of the transitional egoistic self-expression in which death and suffering predominate; through Vidya consenting with Avidya by the perfect sense of oneness even in that multiplicity, we enjoy integrally the immortality and the beatitude."

Sri Aurobindo

"The creation depends on and moves between the biune principle of unity and multiplicity; it is a manifoldness of idea and force and form which is the expression of an original unity, and it is an eternal oneness which is the foundation and reality of the multiple worlds and makes their play possible."

Sri Aurobindo

The Transcendent, the Universal and the Individual

(7) These three are the key words for the understanding of Sri Aurobindo's weltanschauung (world view) as a whole, his view of existence, of social progress and creativity in life.

Says Sri Aurobindo:

"The progressive revelation of a great, a transcendent, a luminous Reality with the multitudinous relativities of this world that we see and those other worlds that we do not see as means and material, condition and field, this would seem then to be the meaning of the universe, – since meaning and aim it has and is neither a purposeless illusion nor a fortuitous accident."

*

"The universe and the individual are necessary to each other in their ascent. Always indeed they exist for each other and profit by each other. Universe is a diffusion of the divine All in infinite Space and Time, the individual its concentration within limits of Space and Time."

Matter and Spirit

(8) Matter and Spirit have been handled very often in mutual exclusiveness. Either Matter is real or the Spirit is real. But Sri Aurobindo holds both real, and a reconciliation of the two is the issue of his philosophy. It is the same as the reconciliation of the world with God. Sri Aurobindo takes pains to demonstrate this. The discovery of the supramental consciousness, where plurality is seen coming out of unity, explains what was inexplicable. But otherwise the truth of the cosmic consciousness – comprehending the mental, vital and physical – also shows itself to be the meeting of Matter and Spirit.

Here are a few words of Sri Aurobindo himself in this connection.

"Attaining to the cosmic consciousness Mind, illuminated by a knowledge that perceives at once the truth of Unity and the truth of Multiplicity and seizes on the formulae of their interaction, finds its own discords at once explained and reconciled by the divine Harmony; satisfied, it consents to become the agent of that supreme union between God and Life towards which we tend.

Matter reveals itself to the realising thought and to the subtilised senses as the figure and body of Spirit, – Spirit in its self-formative extension."

The Life Divine

(9) "A Divine Life in the manifestation is then not only possible as the high result and ransom of our present life in the Ignorance but, if these things are as we have seen them, it is the inevitable outcome and consummation of Nature's evolutionary endeavour."

Knowledge by Identity and Knowledge by External Contacts

(10) Our ordinary knowledge is through the sense-organs by the Manas and as elaborated by reason. But our best knowledge, most certain knowledge is of self-awareness, "I am, I exist." This is knowledge by identity, of being one with the object of knowledge. Through a similar identity with other things and persons, we can know them intuitively which would be qualitatively a different knowledge. Psychic Being can afford us this knowledge. By the same, we can seek to know ultimate reality.

Here are a few words from Sri Aurobindo on the subject:

"The one means we have left in our mentality is an extension of that form of knowledge by identity which gives us the awareness of our own existence. It is really upon a self-awareness more or less conscient, more or less present to our conception that the knowledge of the contents of our self is based. Or to put it in a more general formula, the knowledge of the contents is contained in the knowledge of the continent. If then we can extend our faculty of mental self-awareness to awareness of the self beyond and outside us, Atman or Brahman of the Upanishads, we may become possessors in experience of the truths which form the contents of the Atman or Brahman in the universe. It is on this possibility that Indian Vedanta has based itself."

The foregoing exposition of Sri Aurobindo's weltanschauung (world view) is extremely concise, but it can give an idea of his seeing and his thinking, which can help much in understanding him as a whole. This statement includes practically all his important terms.

＃ BIBLIOGRAPHY, REFERENCES, INDEX

BIBLIOGRAPHY

A. Source Books

1. Sri Aurobindo, *The Synthesis of Yoga*, Sri Aurobindo Ashram, Pondicherry.

    This propounds, in a systematic form, the contemporary creation of Integral Yoga and constitutes the contemporary Indian contribution to the knowledge of man and his personality.

2. Sri Aurobindo, *The Life Divine*, Sri Aurobindo Ashram, Pondicherry.

    This is primarily a work of philosophy but contains a great deal of psychological exposition.

3. Sri Aurobindo, *Letters on Yoga*, 3 volumes, Sri Aurobindo Ashram, Pondicherry.

    As letters written to yogic seekers, they expound the subject with a practical reference and provide an encyclopaedic guidance on problems of human nature.

4. Sri Aurobindo, *Savitri*, Sri Aurobindo, Sri Aurobindo Ashram, Pondicherry.

    Deals with existence, evolution, man, his destiny, etc., in vivid poetic expression. It affords fine insights into the anomalies of human nature and their resolution. Above all, it gives a vision of human perfectibility.

5. *Collected Works of the Mother*, Sri Aurobindo Ashram, Pondicherry. In particular, volume 12, *On Education*.

    Here, Integral Psychology and Integral Personality find their own expression in the context of personal development and education.

The above-mentioned five works constitute the Source Books of our subject.

B. Further Indian Sources

1. Sinha, J.N., *Indian Psychology*, 2 volumes, Calcutta.

    An exposition and interpretation of Indian Psychology based on traditional sources.

2. Books on *Hathayoga, Rajayoga, Bhakti Yoga, Jnana Yoga, Karma Yoga, the Gita*, all abound in insights regarding man and his personality.

C. Imporant Western Literature

1. Jung, C.G., *The Integration of the Personality*, Bollingen Series.

2. Jung, C.G., *Collected Works*, in particular volumes 8, 11 & 16, Bollingen Series.

3. Jung, C.G., *Psychological Types*, Bollingen Series.

4. Jung, C.G., *Memories, Dreams, Reflections*, Vintage Books.

5. Stein, Murray (Editor), *Jungian Analysis*, Shambhala, 1984.

6. Fordham, Freida, *Introduction to Jung's Psychology*, Pelican.

7. Moustakas, Clark E., *The Self*, Harper and Brothers, New York.

8. Wilber, Ken, *A Sociable God*, New Science Library, Shambhala, Boulder and London, 1984.

9. Murphy, Gardner, *Personality*, City College, New York, 1947.

10. Murphy, Gardner, *Historical Introduction to Modern Psychology*, Kegan Paul, 1932.

11. Freud, S., *Introductory Lectures on Psycho-analysis*.

12. Freud, S., *New Introductory Lectures on Psycho-analysis*.

13. Rickman, *Selection from Freud*.

14. Marcuse, Herbert, *Eros and Civilisation*, Vintage Books, 1961.

15. Bergson, H., *Introduction to Metaphysics*, Wisdom Library, 1961.

16. Mueller, P.L., *La Psychologie Contemporaine*, Petite Bibliotheque Payot, Paris, 1963.

17. Henning, Hans, *Psychologie der Gegenwart*. In Mauritius Verlag, Berlin, 1925.

D. **Recent Indian Studies**

1. Kuppuswamy, B., *Yoga and Self-actualisation*, Psychology Department, Mysore University.

2. Ganguli, H. C., *Monograph on Meditation*, Psychology Department, Delhi University.

E. **Recent Textbooks of Psychology at Graduate (Pass) Level**

1. James, W., *Text-Book of Psychology*.

2. Stout, G. F., *A Manual of Psychology*.

3. Woodsworth, R.S., *Psychology*.

REFERENCES

(For the excerpts in part one only; other references are given along with the text itself)

The excerpts from Sri Aurobindo are all from the following books:

1. *The Synthesis of Yoga* (Sri Aurobindo Birth Centenary Library, Vols. 20 & 21)
2. *The Life Divine* (SABCL, Vols. 18 & 19)
3. *Letters on Yoga* (SABCL, Vols. 22, 23 & 24)
4. *The Hour of God* (SABCL, Vol. 17)
5. *Social and Political Thought* (SABCL, Vol. 15)

The page references here are all to the SABCL Vols. The excerpts have been numbered for convenience of reference. The first figure is the Volume number, the second the page.

1: **17**, 21-22
2: **19**, 561
3: **22**, 233-34
4: **22**, 235
5: **22**, 236
6: **22**, 237
7: **20**, 3
8: **20**, 39-40
9: **20**, 508
10: **20**, 496
11: **21**, 597-98
12: **20**, 68-70
13: **20**, 170-72
14: **18**, 555-62
15: **19**, 898-900
16: **24**, 1108
17: **19**, 907-08
18: **19**, 901
19: **22**, 115-116
20: **20**, 514-16
21: **20**, 520
22: **22**, 365
23: **22**, 365
24: **23**, 1011-20
25: **15**, 29
26: **15**, 231-32

27: **15**, 27-8
28: **22**, 408-501
29: **24**, 1563-64
30: **24**, 1565
31: **24**, 1566
32: **24**, 1568
33: **24**, 1568
34: **24**, 1722
35: **21**, 843
36: **21**, 843
37: **21**, 844-45
38: **21**, 547
39: **22**, 485-86
40: **21**, 620
41: **22**, 289
42: **24**, 1606-07
43: **24**, 1607-08
44: **24**, 1608-09
45: **21**, 833
46: **21**, 623-24
47: **21**, 839-41
48: **21**, 620-21
49: **21**, 621-22
50: **21**, 632-35
51: **21**, 822-23
52: **21**, 629-30

53: **21**, 631-32
54: **20**, 203
55: **20**, 205
56: **20**, 205
57: **20**, 206
58: **20**, 193
59: **21**, 630-31
60: **21**, 640-41
61: **21**, 641-42
62: **22**, 216
63: **22**, 216-17
64: **22**, 218-19
65: **22**, 169
66: **22**, 169-70
67: **24**, 1688-89
68: **24**, 1697
69: **24**, 1708
70: **21**, 694-95
71: **21**, 696
72: **24**, 1393-94
73: **24**, 1660
74: **19**, 906
75: **19**, 906-07
76: **19**, 907-09
77: **19**, 910
78: **19**, 917-18

INDEX

Ādhāra, 301
Adhikārabheda, 208
Adler, 155, 175
Ahaṅkāra, 46
Allport, 130
Anna, 196, 200, 212
Antaḥkaraṇa, 48
Antarmukha, 262
Āsanas, 297-98, 303-04, 307
Associationism, 175
Ātmajñāna, 117, 121
Ātman, 118, 207, 276, 301
Auroville, 322

B

Bacon, 290
Bahirmukha, 93, 323
Behaviourism, 47, 86-87, 130, 175
Bergson, H., 182, 335, 340-42
Bhatia, C.M., 114, 121-22
Bhoga, 303
Body:
  approach of Integral Yoga, 297
  body consciousness, 293, 297, 300
  divine body, 296
  its unconscious organisation, 292, 299
  spiritual quality in, 295
Bose, G., 113, 120, 124, 173, 209
Bose, S.K., 121
Buddha, 224
Buddhi, 46
Buddhism, 288, 301

C

Caitya Puruṣa, 187, 344
Cakras:
  Integral Yoga and, 34, 35
  subtle centres of consciousness, 30-33
Chardin, Teilhard de, 334-35
Citta, 46, 48, 57
Christianity, 242
Christian mystics, 301
Circumconscient, 7

Cittavṛttis, 301
Condillac, 175
Consciousness:
  levels of in our being, 6-7
  movement of, 9
  nature of, 7-9, 13
  spiritual consciousness, 284

D

Darwin, C., 176-77
Dayananda Saraswati, 274
Delight:
  will to delight, 62
Depth Psychology, 323
Desire-soul, 48, 59-60

E

Ebbinghaus, 119, 175
Education:
  problem of, in India and in the West, 313-15
Educational Psychology:
  a learning situation, 321-22
  its integral form, 318
Ego:
  as formation of Nature, 63-64
Einstein, 291
European Culture (modern), 283
Evil Persona, 72
Experimental Psychology, 89, 110
Existentialist Philosophy, 272
Extraversion, 195

F

Fechner, G.T., 252
Ferenczi, 155
Freud, S., 87-88, 95, 110, 116, 125, 144, 152-63, 172, 175-76, 192, 201-02, 243-53
Freudian Revisionists and Deviants:
  Abraham, 250
  Adler, 245
  Ferenczi, 246-49
  Freud, Anna, 249

Fromm, Erich, 250
Horney, Karen, 250
Jones, Earnst, 250
Jung, C.G., 245
  Marks, R.W., 246
Rank, 246-49
Sullivan, H.S., 250

G

Gandhian Emphasis, 280
Ganguli, H.C., 114, 124, 185-91
Gestaltism, 48, 87, 130, 165, 175
Gita:
  psychology of personality, 204, 12
  self-poised consciousness of, 90
Goldstein, K., 111
Gopalaswami, 124
Greek Culture, 283
Guṇas, 204

H

Healing:
  how illnesses come, 39-41
  their cure, 40-41
Hegel, 275
Hinduism, 242, 274
Hormism, 87
Huxley, J., 334-35

I

Imagination, 61
Inconscient:
  nature of, 6-7
Indian Culture:
  foundations of, 274, 283
  problem of, 313-15
  yogic pursuit and, 302
Indian Philosophy:
  issue before it, 275, 280
Indian Psychology:
  basis of, 92-95
  contribution of, 119, 207-10
  difficulty of, 122-24
  history of, 211-15
  its urge for wholeness, 171-74

nature of human personality in, 283
  old Indian system, 48-49
Indian Psychologists, 119-20, 124, 211
Indra Sen, 185-91
Integral Education:
  the revolution it seeks, 316-17
Integral Personality:
  concept of, 27, 259
  diagrammatical presentation of, 261-63
  domains of, 15-22, 34, 46-47, 93-95, 103-06, 277, 324-25
  growth of consciousness, 325-26
  its future thrust, 333-35
  psycho-analysis and, 308-12
  the individual, 273-74, 277
  the transcendent, 273-74, 277
  the universal, 273-74, 277
  view of personality, 326-29
Integral Psychology:
  Cultural Science Psychology and, 170
  domain of, 34-35
  Integral Psychologist, 310
  its contribution to Freudian Psychology, 162-63
  its essential features, 76-79, 177
  its method, 178-79
  Jungian Collective Unconscious in relation to levels of experience, 203
  Jungian Psychology and, 143
  levels of consciousness, 180-84
  levels of experience, the physical, the vital, the mental, 195-205
  Natural Science Psychology and, 170
  parallelism between psychic being and Jungian 'centre' of personality, 183-84, 217-19, 267
  principle of evolution in, 177-78, 259-60
Psychic Being, 163
Supermind, 260, 327
  the subconscious in, 329-32
  the subliminal in, 181, 260-61, 328
  the Superconscious in, 180-81, 193, 260, 327-28, 330-32

the unconscious in, 179-80, 192-93
Western Psychology and, 327-28
Integral Psycho-therapy:
   Psycho-analysis and, 308-12
   Integral Psycho-therapists, 311
Integral Yoga:
   a contemporary creation, 302
   aim of, 11
   domains of personality, 93-95
   it is practical psychology, 69
   integral Psycho-therapy and, 312
   Jungian psychology and, 145-47, 223-24
   other systems of yoga and, 117-18
   physical education in, 298
   psychic quality in children, 231-32
   structure of personality in, 221-22, 224-25
   Superconscious in, 224
   therapeutic effects of psychic experience, 232-37
   what is psychic experience? 226-31
Introspection:
   method of, 107-09, 118, 121, 124, 178-79
Introspectionism, 86-87
Introversion, 195
Islam, 242
   sufis, 301

J

Jainism, 301
James, William, 86, 125, 128
Jean, James, 267
Jīva, 207
Jung, C.G., 5, 96, 111, 113-14, 116-18, 125, 126-27, 129-31, 132-45, 173, 175-76, 180, 183, 192, 206, 240, 271, 324, 327
Jungian Psychology, 260
   Archetypes in, 244
   conscious and unconscious in, 132-43, 180-81, 192
   individuation in, 240
   Integral Psychology and, 143
   Jungian Analysis, 144, 232-33, 250-51

Jungian analysts, 147-51, 223-24
personality in, 240
'self'— see 'Self'

K

Kant, 177, 276
Kantor, 130
Koṣas, 46, 128, 212, 276
Kretschmer, 195, 204
Krishnamurthy, J., 186
Kriyās, 304
Kulpe, 118-19, 175
Kuṇḍalinī Śakti, 31
Kuppuswamy, B., 113, 124, 129

L

Lecky, P., 112
Leibnitz, 177
Logical Positivism, 276

M

Manas, 46, 55, 196, 200, 212, 276, 301
Maslow, A.H., 113, 130
Mcdougall, W., 54, 87, 96 108, 171, 173, 194
Meera, 344
Memory, 60-61
Mental:
   mental man, 23-24
Mill, J.S., 175
Mind:
   as instrument of organisation and action, 182
   emotional mind, 58-59
   mind as sixth sense, its action thereof, 55-56
   Silent Mind, 185-91
   universal mind, 7
Mitra, S.C., 173
Mokṣa, 278-79
Mother, 34, 288, 312, 315, 316, 335, 346-47
Murphy, Gardner, 5, 95, 111, 117, 128-30, 206, 217

N

Nāḍī, 30
Natural Science Psychology, 167-170
Nature:
 movement of, 10-11
Nietzsche, 252

O

Organismic School, 130
Oversoul, 7, 21

P

Personality:
 integration of, 28-29
 normal personality, 53-55
Physical:
 physical man, 22
Plato, 275
Prāṇa:
 Prāṇa as life principle, 48, 196, 200, 212, 276, 301
 range of pranic experience, 57
Prāṇāyuma, 303-04, 307
Pratyāhāra, 185-86
Psychic:
 psychical consciousness, range of, 42-44
 psychic change, its action, 73-75, 339-340
 psychic entity, 25-26, 37, 163, 343-47
 quality of psychic consciousness, 172, 348-50
Psycho-analysis:
 conflicts in, 153
 dangers inherent in, 49-51
 defence reactions, 152, 162
 ego, 111, 127, 156-159, 163, 201-02, 244, 309
 Free Association method in, 198, 243-45, 309
 hypnosis in, 155
 id, 111, 127, 156-59, 163, 202, 244, 309
 Integral Psycho-therapy and, 308-12

interpretation of dreams, 88-89, 153-54
method of, 86-89
Oedipus or Electra complex, 247-48
repression and suppression, 47, 88, 153, 243
sex instinct, 88, 156, 162, 243
subconscious in, 96
suggestionism, 154-55
superego, 111, 127, 156-159, 163, 244, 309
unconscious in, 152, 192
Psychology:
 history of, 85-91
 Indian — see Indian Psychology
 Integral — see Integral Psychology
 its scope, 5-6
 of animals and plants, 37-38
 of education, 37
 of social development, 35-36
 Yogic Psychology, 53, 90, 95-99
Purposivism, 175
Puruṣa, 207
 the witness, 72-73, 108-09

R

Radhakrishnan, S., 121
Rajas, 53, 204, 221
Religion, 287-89
Rig Veda, 211-12
Rogers, Carl R., 112, 130
Roy, Ram Mohan, 274

S

Saccidānanda, 21
Sattva, 53, 204, 221
Saupe, 167
Schopenhauer, 252
Science:
 re-definition needed, 290-91
Self (in Jungian Psychology):
 parallels with Chinese and Indian traditions, 145, 324
 parallels with Integral Psychology, 145-47

'Self' or 'Centre' according to Jung, 5, 29, 96, 111, 118, 126-27, 130, 143, 145, 173, 187, 244, 262, 324
Social Thought:
  in India and in the West, 279-81
Spinoza, 177
Spiritism, 44-45
Spranger, 86, 118-19, 166, 168-69, 195
Sri Aurobindo, 5, 13, 28-29, 34-35, 46, 93, 100, 108, 117, 172, 176-84, 189, 192, 195, 259-64, 266, 277, 284-85, 288-89, 312, 316, 325-28, 335, 339-40, 344-46
  yoga of, 5, 134-35
  yoga-force, 66-68
  yogic psychology of, 90-91, 93-95
Sri Aurobindo Ashram, 220-21, 223, 225, 238-42
Sthūla śarīra, 48
Stout, 194
Subconscient:
  province of, 18-20
Subliminal:
  subliminal self, 17-18, 20-22, 49-50
Suggestology, 116
Sūkṣma deha, 32
Superconscient:
  range of being, 7, 21-22

T

Tamas, 53, 204, 221
Telekinesis, 94
Telepathy, 94, 116
Titchner, 86, 128, 164-65
Transformation:
  meaning of, 26, 29
Transpersonal Psychology, 131
Typology, 195

U

Upanishadic Seers, 282-83
Upanishad, Katha, 343-44

V

Varṇas, 92, 208
Vital:
  vital man, 23
Vivekananda, Swami, 188-89
Von Ehrenfels, 165

W

Ward, J., 166, 194
Watson, 86
Wholeness:
  in Jungian thought, 244-45, 260, 271
  of spiritual consciousness, 286
  quality of, 237-38
  yoga aims at, 245, 248-49
Wilber, K., 128
Windleband, 164
Wittgenstein, 276
Wolff, 177
Wundt, 175

Y

Yoga:
  as education, 301-02
  as science and art, 264-65
  integral — see 'Integral Yoga'
  principles of practice, 11, 302-07
  psycho-physical science of, 30-32
  various systems of, 117, 212
  yoga and psychology, 10-12, 92-93
  yoga and Western psychology, 117-19
  yogic methods, 10, 264
  yogic psychology, 53, 90, 92-99, 109, 117-19